Piers the Plowman

A CRITICAL EDITION OF THE A-VERSION

Piers the Plowman

A CRITICAL EDITION OF THE A-VERSION

Edited

with Introduction, Notes, and Glossary by

THOMAS A. KNOTT AND DAVID C. FOWLER

1952

THE JOHNS HOPKINS PRESS · BALTIMORE

Baltimore: The Johns Hopkins Press
London: Geoffrey Cumberlege
Oxford University Press
Printed in the United States of America
by the J. H. Furst Company, Baltimore
Copyright 1952, The Johns Hopkins Press

To

Myra P. Knott

and

Mary Gene Fowler

PREFACE

Work on this edition actually started in the summer of 1907, when the late Thomas A. Knott began collating the fourteen MSS of the A-version then known to students of *Piers the Plowman.* In January, 1915, Knott published the results of his study of these MSS (*Modern Philology* XII, 389-421), and expressed the hope that he would soon be able to publish the text of A_1 (as far as 8. 126) in the form of a reading edition. He was, however, drawn off to other activities, and the text, together with the introductory material and glossary which he had prepared, remained unpublished.

A major portion of my own contribution to the present edition originally took the form of an unpublished dissertation submitted to the faculty of the Division of the Humanities, the University of Chicago, in candidacy for the Ph. D. degree in English. This dissertation, " A Critical Text of Piers Plowman A_2 " (Chicago, 1949), continued the text from 8. 126, the point at which Knott stopped, to the end of the poem. During the past three years, as opportunity afforded, I have been engaged in preparing for publication the text and apparatus of the complete A-version.

It has been my purpose to utilize as fully as possible the materials which Knott had collected for his edition. His text of A_1 appears virtually as he left it, except that I have restored four lines (7. 70-73) which he considered, I think rightly, to be a scribal insertion. It seemed best, however, to leave these lines in the text, and allow the reader to judge for himself. Sections I, II, and VI of the INTRODUCTION are, for the most part, Knott's work, though I have made occasional changes and additions wherever these were required by the findings of more recent scholarship, and have expanded the material in section VI. In preparing the TEXTUAL NOTES I have used his collations as a guide for purposes of selection, but the actual variants

[vii]

listed are in most cases taken directly from reproductions of the MSS, including three MSS which were unknown at the time Knott did his original work. His GLOSSARY, of course, had to be enlarged to include words or special meanings of words found only in A₂. For the remainder of the apparatus, and for the critical text of A₂, I alone must be held responsible.

The form of the edition as a whole represents a compromise between a critical and a reading edition. It is hoped that the *Piers Plowman* scholar will find the section on the critical text (INTRODUCTION, Section V) and the TEXTUAL NOTES adequate for his purposes, and that the undergraduate student of Middle English will profit by reading the INTRODUCTION and consulting the EXPLANATORY NOTES and GLOSSARY.

The monumental edition of *Piers the Plowman* produced by W. W. Skeat for the Early English Text Society will always have value for students of the poem. I wish to thank the Oxford University Press for permission to quote from this work, as well as from the parallel text edition of 1886.

In preparing the EXPLANATORY NOTES I have relied heavily on the work of modern scholars, to such an extent, indeed, that it is impossible to acknowledge my debt here in detail. I do, however, especially want to express my gratitude to the Reverend Thomas P. Dunning, C. M., and to the Talbot Press, Dublin, Ireland, publishers of Father Dunning's *Piers Plowman: An Interpretation of the A-Text*, for granting me permission to quote freely from that excellent study.

The preparation of an edition such as this, carried on over a long period of time, would have been impossible without the help of other scholars, many of whom are no longer living. The senior editor would most certainly have wished to acknowledge the assistance of F. J. Furnivall, W. W. Skeat, G. L. Kittredge, and, of course, his teacher and friend, John M. Manly. He would likewise have expressed his gratitude to the authorities and the librarians of the British Museum, the Bodleian,

Trinity College, Dublin, Trinity College, Cambridge, and Lincoln's Inn, for their courtesy and cordiality, and to the Duke of Westminster, the late Sir Henry Ingilby, and Sir William Ingilby, for the courteous and liberal spirit with which they made their MSS accessible.

I am pleased to add my own thanks to those listed above, as well as to the officers of these additional libraries, all of whom very generously authorized the microfilming of their MSS: the Librarian of the University of Liverpool, the Master and Fellows of University College, Oxford, the Society of Antiquaries of London, the Trustees of the Pierpont Morgan Library, New York, and the National Library of Wales, Aberystwyth. The microfilms which I used were obtained through University Microfilms, Ann Arbor, Michigan, and are now on file in the Library of the University of Chicago.

I wish, further, to thank Professors Donald F. Bond and Theodore Silverstein of the University of Chicago for their advice relating to my work on the critical text of A_2 and Professor Edwin E. Aubrey of the University of Pennsylvania for his valuable criticism of the introductory material. I am greatly indebted, also, to Professor Kemp Malone of Johns Hopkins University for his advice and encouragement in the preparation of this edition.

My greatest debt, however, is to Professor James R. Hulbert, who first interested me in the task of completing Knott's work, and who has been a constant source of inspiration both as teacher and friend. His extensive knowledge, and his skeptical attitude, combined with sympathetic guidance, have helped me become aware of and, I hope, avoid many of the pitfalls that beset the path of the textual critic.

I am much obliged to Mrs. Myra P. Knott for placing at my disposal all of her late husband's collations and other material relating to the text of *Piers the Plowman*, and for her continued interest in the job of preparing the complete A-version for publication.

The drawing of the monastery at Montecassino is from *A Brief Commentary on Early Mediaeval Church Architecture*, by Kenneth John Conant, and the excellent woodcuts of the Seven Deadly Sins, by Denis Tegetmeier, appeared originally in *A Version By Donald Attwater of The Vision of William concerning Piers the Plowman*, published by Cassell and Co., London.

Finally, in the unspectacular but very important work of proofing the MS I had the devoted assistance of my wife, whose share in my work, both tangible and intangible, merits formal recognition.

DAVID C. FOWLER

Drexel Hill, Pennsylvania
July 1, 1952

CONTENTS

LIST OF ILLUSTRATIONS

Piers the Plowman

A CRITICAL EDITION OF THE A-VERSION

INTRODUCTION

I. THE THREE TEXTS OF THE POEM

PIERS THE PLOWMAN exists in three distinct versions. The one usually regarded as earliest, called the A-text, contains (in round numbers) 2,500 lines. The second, called the B-text, is 7,200 lines long; it expands the 2,500 lines of the A-text into 3,200 by inserting numerous lines and passages, and then adds 4,000 lines. The third, called the C-text, is practically the same length as B (about 100 lines longer), but omits, transfers, and inserts lines and passages, and, like B, frequently changes the wording. The A-text is divided into a prologue and eleven passus or cantos, the B-text into a prologue and twenty passus, and the C-text, according to Skeat, into twenty-two passus. In the case of the A-version, at least, it is true that the evidence of the MSS indicates that the A-text is in reality two poems: (1) a prologue and eight passus of the *Vision concerning Piers the Plowman,* and (2) a prologue and two passus of the *Life of Do-well, Do-better, and Do-best.* But since the continuous numbering of the passus is well established in editorial tradition, and also very convenient for reference purposes, it is retained in this edition, though the correct numbering is given at the beginning of each passus as it occurs in the MSS. The so-called " John But " passus does not belong organically with the A-text. It is found, wholly or in part, in only three MSS after passus 11, and is probably spurious. Certainly, the latter portion of it was written by one John But, who tells us that he " made this end."

Each of the three versions exists in seventeen or more MSS (there are twenty-eight C manuscripts, nine of which are partly A or B).

Until recently the A-text was thought to have been composed

[3]

about 1362. The poem mentions Edward III's Norman wars and the Treaty of Bretigny of 1360 (3. 174–193). The southwest wind on a Saturday at eve (5. 14) refers to a storm which occurred Saturday, January 15, 1362. A later view—that the A-text was being composed in 1369–70—seems to account more satisfactorily for some of the references to the Norman wars.

The belief that the B-text could be dated approximately 1377 was based mainly on the evidence afforded by the famous passage about the rat-parliament inserted in the prologue, concerning the kitten-heir to the throne. Here the author, as Skeat saw it, had in mind the period between the death of the Black Prince (June, 1376) and the death of Edward III a year later, when the boy Richard was heir to the throne. This date for B as a whole has been questioned, but present scholarly opinion is divided. Possible dates for various sections of B range from 1370 to 1379 or later.

The C-text cannot be definitely dated. There is an allusion to contemporary events in 4. 210, where the land is said not to love its king. Skeat takes this to refer to the disorders of 1393, Jusserand to those of 1397–99, while Manly pointed out that as early as 1386 Parliament presented to the king a threat to depose him. More recently, Sister Mary Aquinas Devlin has made a strong case for an earlier date, even suggesting a time prior to 1381, citing C's failure to mention the peasants' revolt (1381) and other events of this and succeeding years. It is possible that C refers to the fire at St. Albans in 1377 (C 4.94–107). At any rate, the date is most likely somewhere between 1377 and 1387.

The Printed Editions

The first printed edition of *Piers the Plowman* was one of the B-text, issued by Robert Crowley in 1550, and reprinted twice in the same year. In 1561 Owen Rogers issued a reprint of Crowley's second edition. These were the only printed editions till that of the C-text by T. D. Whitaker in 1813. The B-text was printed in 1842 by Thomas Wright. A second and revised edition of this was issued in 1856.

The A-text was first printed in 1867 by W. W. Skeat for the Early English Text Society. In 1869 appeared the B-text, in 1873 the C-text, in 1877 the Notes, and in 1884 the Glossary. The first school text appeared in 1874. It contained the prologue and seven passus of the B-text. Skeat was the editor. The three texts were printed together by Skeat in two volumes in 1886.

Recognition of the Three Texts

We have no evidence that for four hundred years any reader or critic recognized the existence of more than one version of the poem. Though students knew many MSS, Crowley's edition was regarded as furnishing the *textus receptus*. Finally, however, in 1802, Ritson did distinguish between B and C. Whitaker, who edited C in 1813, saw the difference between C and B, but thought that C was the earlier of the two, and that B was the revised text. Price, the editor of the 1824 edition of Warton's *History of English Poetry*, first noticed the existence of A, and held that it preceded B and C; he also suggested the order A, B, C. Wright, in 1842, failed to follow Price in distinguishing three versions, but argued for the priority of B to C.

Finally, in 1867, Skeat, who during his studies preliminary to publication of his pioneer EETS edition located and examined most of the MSS of all the versions, grouped the MSS into three separate versions and established the familiar arrangement A, B, and C.

A_1 and A_2

As explained above, the A-text falls into two distinct parts: the first, consisting of prologue and passus 1 through 8, is the *Vision concerning Piers the Plowman*; the second, passus 9–11,

[5]

is the *Life of Do-well, Do-better, and Do-best.* The two parts
are separated in some MSS by a colophon reading, " Here ends
the vision concerning Piers the Plowman, and here commences
the life of Do-well, Do-better, and Do-best, after Wit and Reason." These two parts may be called A_1 and A_2. There is no
evidence that the two parts ever circulated separately, but there
is in A_1 no sign that A_2 is to follow, though within A_1 there is
preliminary motivation and preparation for every important
event, and considerable skillful use of suspense. No such co-ordi-
nation exists between A_1 and A_2. On the other hand, the problems dealt with in A_2 follow logically from the ruminations of
the dreamer concerning Do-well toward the end of passus 8
(8. 127–181).

Contents of A_1

A_1 falls into three main divisions: (1) an Introduction (prologue and passus 1), (2) the Vision of Lady Meed (passus 2–4),
and (3) the Vision of the Confession of Sins and the Search for
Truth (passus 5–8). The action may be summarized as follows:

(1) The dreamer sees a tower on a hill, a dungeon in a dale,
and between them a field full of folk—the world—whose vicious
activities are satirically described. (Prologue.) A woman de-
scends from the tower, tells him that it is the abode of God, or
Truth, and that she is Holy Church: she expounds Truth and
Love. (Passus 1.)

(2) The dreamer inquires about Falsehood, who, she has
told him, dwells in the dungeon, and turning to look, he sees
Meed (as Bribery, or Graft) about to marry Falsehood. The
wedding is stopped by Theology, and the king's writ of arrest
disperses the evil crew about Falsehood. Meed is taken before
the king, who attempts to get Conscience to marry her, but on
Conscience's denunciation of her, the king agrees to ask the
advice of Reason. Reason comes, catches Meed red-handed in

the exercise of her vice before the king, and the wedding to Conscience is abandoned. (Passus 2–4.)

(3) The dreamer returns to the field full of folk, where Conscience and Repentance preach to sinners, and convert, one by one, the personified Deadly Sins. (Passus 5.) The repentant sinners resolve to start on a pilgrimage to the shrine of Truth, and are directed by Piers the Plowman, who advises them to go by way of the ten commandments and the seven virtues. The pilgrims ask Piers to accompany them, but he replies that first he must finish his work. They begin to assist him, but some of the wasters and idlers soon grow tired. Piers calls in Hunger, who helps keep them at work. (Passus 6–7.) Truth sends Piers a pardon, which applies to all who do well. (Passus 8.) The poem closes with an epilogue in which the dreamer ponders the significance of his dream, and concludes that doing well is superior to indulgence.

Contents of A_2

The divisions of A_2 are not so clear-cut as those of A_1, and the allegorical action, so prominent a feature of A_1, is conspicuously absent in A_2. The dreamer wanders in search of Do-well. He questions two friars about Do-well, but is not satisfied with their reply and leaves them. He stops by a woodside to hear the birds sing, and once again he falls asleep. In his dream a character named Thought appears, calls him by name, and, in answer to the dreamer's question, defines Do-well, Do-better, and Do-best. (Prologue.) Thought then leads the dreamer to Wit, who discourses at length on Do-well, Do-better, and Do-best. (Passus 1.) The discussion is taken up in turn by Dame Study, Clergy, and Scripture, with intermittent questions and objections by the dreamer. (Passus 2.) Finally, the dreamer summarizes and reflects on what he has learned (11. 250–303), in a passage similar in function to the one given at the conclusion of A_1.

[7]

The B-addition

The long addition by B (4000 lines) cannot be summarized coherently. Except where, here and there, the poet has borrowed some bit of material—like The Good Samaritan, The Crucifixion, The Four Daughters of God, The Harrowing of Hell, or The Struggle with Anti-Christ—the poem becomes simply a series of discourses on moral, theological, and religious topics, often incomplete in themselves, and usually suggested by the mere occurrence of a word or an idea connected with some other topic which the author happens to be discussing. In recent years scholars have looked for unified structure in the B text (and in C as well), without notable success. But even if a coherent plan of organization for B is discovered, it is already apparent that it will be something quite different from what we find in the A-text. " Indeed " (as Dunning says), " it is to B only that the charge commonly made against the author of *Piers Plowman* of lacking the art of construction must be held to refer; it is the B text M. Legouis has in mind when he says that Langland ' loses himself, and us with him, in his labyrinthine allegories and pictures.' " Or, as an earlier authority, Jusserand, remarked, " He was the victim and not the master of his thought."

II. AUTHORSHIP

Most of the numerous studies of *Piers the Plowman* published in the last fifty years have dealt in one way or another with the vastly complicated problem of the authorship of the three versions. At various times it has been argued that there were different authors for A_1, A_2, B, and C; for A, B, and C; for AB, and C; and so forth.

Of course, as long as it was not recognized that the *Piers the Plowman* poems existed in more than one version, it was

[8]

quite natural that a single authorship should be assumed. But from the earliest times there has been diversity of opinion as to what was the name of the author. William (or Robert) Langland (or Langley), Willelmus W., John Malverne, and others are all mentioned in one or another of the early catalogues and MSS of the poem.

In taking up the problem of the name of the author, we may first consider the internal evidence of the poems themselves. The passages in A that have been regarded as evidence of the poet's name are these:

> Thanne ran Repentaunce and reherside his teme,
> And made Wil to wepe watir with his eighen.
>
> (5. 43–44)

> Thanne were marchauntis merye and wepe for joye,
> And yaven Wille for his writyng wollene clothis;
> For he copiede thus here clause, thei couden hym gret mede.
>
> (8. 42–44)

> Thanne Thought in that tyme seide this wordis:
> "Where that Do-wel and Do-bet and Do-best beth in londe,
> Here is Wil wolde wyte, yif Wit couthe hym teche."
>
> (9. 116–118)

Between A₁ and A₂ occurs the colophon:

> *Explicit hic Visio Willelmi de Petro de Ploughman.*
> *Eciam incipit Vita de Do-wel, Do-bet, & Do-best*
> *secundum wyt & resoun.*

Against this evidence it has been urged that the author may not have identified himself with the "Wille" in the dream; that each of the above quotations refers to "Wille" in the third person, whereas when the dreamer represents himself as taking part in the action, he speaks in the first person; e. g., the dreamer is obliged to look over the shoulder of Piers and the priest in order to discover what is in the document:

[9]

And I, behynde hem bothe, beheld al the bulle.
In two lynes it lay, and nought a lettre more,
And was writen right thus, in witnesse of Treuthe:

(8. 92–94)

In the B-text occurs this passage:

" What is Charite? " quod I tho. " A childissh thinge," he seide;
" *Nisi efficiamini sicut paruuli, non intrabitis in regnum celorum;*
With-outen fauntelte or foly, a fre liberal wille."
" Where shulde men fynde such a frende, with so fre an herte?
I have lyved in londe," quod I, " my name is Longe Wille,
And fonde I nevere ful charite before ne bihynde."

(B 15. 145–149)

Here the dreamer is speaking in the first person, but what
does line 148 mean? Is it the name of the author, inverted
and fitted into the line? Or does it mean " I have lived in the
world, my very name is Long Wille [i. e., I have had long
experience], and nevertheless I have never found full charity? "
If we could be sure that the testimony of the early ascriptions
of *Piers the Plowman* were independently derived, and not
simply acrostic interpretations of line 148, we might regard
this passage as substantiating evidence. Without such assur-
ance, however, neither interpretation can be regarded as con-
clusive, and we therefore cannot accept the line as independent
evidence of the name of the author.

The C-text has no definite evidence in the text about the
author's name. C, however, changes completely B 15. 148 to:

Ich have lyved in London meny longe yeres.

and changes A 9. 118 to:

Her is on wolde wite yf Wit couthe teche.

Allusions to the dreamer's size or height are found in all three
versions (if we consider " Long Wille " such an allusion). In
A the dreamer encounters Thought, whom he describes as " A

[10]

muchel man . . . lik to my selve " (9. 61) ; in B, the dreamer seems to call himself " Long Wille " ; in C, the dreamer, in answer to Reason, who has asked him what he can do, says :

> " Ich am to waik to worche with sykel other with sythe,
> And to long, leyf me, lowe for to stoupe,
> To worchen as a workeman, eny whyle to dure."
>
> (C 6. 23–25)

As mentioned above, three MSS of A have in whole or in part a twelfth passus which finds no counterpart in B or C. In the one MS which has the entire passus, the last twelve lines at least are stated in the text to be the composition of John But :

> And so bad Johan But, busily wel ofte.   (12. 106)

In this twelfth passus the dreamer is again called Wille (12. 51, 89, 99, 103). There are strong arguments for believing that John But wrote the whole of passus twelve. If so, or even if he wrote only the latter part, we have no means of deciding whether he actually knew the name of the author of A, or whether he based the name on the references to Wille in the text or the Colophon between A_1 and A_2.

We may now deal with the external evidence.

In 1580 Stow attributed the poem to John Malverne. He was followed by several later commentators. In 1550 Crowley, in the preface to his edition, says that he consulted learned antiquarians and found that the author was named Roberte Langlande.

In 1557 Bale published his *Scriptorum illustrium Brytannie . . . Catalogus.* Here he attributed the poem to Robertus Langlande. Bale's *Index* (the note book in which he collected the materials for his *Catalogus*) contains four entries, scattered through it, in all of which the poem is ascribed to Robertus Langlande; two entries were obtained from Nicholas Brigham, one from William Sparke, and one from John Wysdome. Sparke, Brigham, and Crowley have practically the same statement, and Sparke's seems to have been based on Crowley's. We cannot determine what the source of Brigham's and Crowley's information was, nor of Wysdome's.

In the Huntington Library manuscript HM 128 (formerly Ashburnham 130) is an entry in a fifteenth-century hand (according to Skeat, the hand of Bale) which says: "Robert or William Langland made Pers Ploughman." This note would seem to be a composite of two different ascriptions of authorship. Further, on grounds of probability, the name Robert seems more likely to be correct than William. William might easily be drawn from A₁, A₂, B, or the colophon, and considered the name of the author. There is little reason for supposing that the name Robert could have been similarly derived, though, as Skeat pointed out, the opening line of A₂:

> Thus yrobid in rosset I romide aboute,

may have been misread as:

> Thus I, Robert, in rosset romide aboute,

and as a matter of fact one A manuscript (M) does have the reading:

> Thus Roberd in Russet I Romyd abowtyn.

If, as Skeat suggested, a tradition containing the name Robert did develop in this way, one can easily see how much stronger the temptation must have been to seize on the name William, for which clues are much more abundant.

In a C-text MS in Trinity College, Dublin, is an entry ascribing the authorship to William de Langlond, the son of Stacy de Rokayle. This is perhaps the most important bit of external evidence we have—first, because of the detailed nature of its testimony, and second, because the name Stacy de Rokayle seems independent of the text. There are, naturally, two views on this subject. One is that we have genuine testimony of Langland's authorship; that William was probably the illegitimate

[12]

son of de Rokayle—thus accounting for the difference in name. The other view is that the note is composite, one tradition attributing the poem to a son of Stacy de Rokayle, and another to William de Langlond.

Modern Theories

We have seen that Wright was the first modern scholar to arrange B and C in the order generally accepted. Wright believed that these two versions were by different authors. In 1860–61 the American scholar George Marsh also suggested that more than one author might be involved. Skeat, however—though he deserves the greatest credit for distinguishing three versions of the poem and arranging them A, B, C,—did not attempt to deal with the statements of Wright and Marsh that two authors may very well have been concerned in the composition. Yet Skeat did explicitly argue this problem. He believed that all three versions were by one man, for two reasons: the similarity of style, and the improbability that two or more authors of such great power could have lived contemporaneously.

Subsequent studies of the *Piers the Plowman* poems, based on the assumption that they were all by one author, naturally paid primary attention to the B- and C-texts, and especially to B, which was regarded as an exhibition of the full and mature powers of the poet. Not until 1906 was this view questioned, or even the possibility of a different view suggested. In that year Manly printed the announcement of his belief that at least five authors (including John But) were concerned in the composition of the poems.

In considering the possibility that A_1, A_2, B, and C are by different authors, as Manly thought, we must keep in mind medieval methods of composition and transmission of literature. Before the invention of printing, an author's control over his work ceased as soon as he released one copy from his possession. Any scribe-editor, or any other poet, was thereafter absolutely

[13]

free to introduce into the text such changes as he saw fit, to rewrite the whole work, or to add an extension. We have plenty of instances in point. Perhaps the most notable is the *Roman de la Rose*. The first 4,000 lines of this famous poem were composed by Guillaume de Lorris, the last 18,000 lines forty years later by Jean de Meun. " Robert of Gloucester's *Riming Chronicle* " is by three different persons, one of whom merely worked over some portions. The English *Guy of Warwick* exists in at least two versions by different authors. Into twenty-five MSS of Chaucer's *Canterbury Tales* was inserted the spurious tale of Gamelyn, which passed as authentic till the eighteenth century. The Old French *Floris and Blauncheflur* exists in two very different versions, one based on the other, but containing many additions, insertions, and modifications. Many Middle English poems, such as *Floris and Blauncheflur, Awntyrs of Arthure, Debate between the Body and the Soul*, and Lagamon's *Brut*, exist in MSS which exhibit such variations of form and content that it is generally agreed that the differences are due to different persons. Furthermore, the attitude of medieval authors toward property rights in their work was very different from the modern attitude. Apparently few authors cared to attach their names to their work. The amount of anonymous poetry and prose is therefore very great.

In view of the effect of Manly's theory on subsequent studies of the different versions, it will be well to give here a very brief summary of his argument in favor of multiple authorship.

There are important differences between A_1 and A_2, between A and B, and between B and C. Some of these differences may be found in the diction, meter, sentence structure, dialect, figures of speech, views on the same social and theological questions, and the power of visualizing objects and scenes. Further, B has copied textual imperfections in A_1 which he would have corrected had he been A_1. Finally, the merits of the A-text have been greatly underestimated. Instead of being a rough,

[14]

crude, preliminary sketch for B, A₁ has remarkable unity and coherence of structure, directness of movement, and freedom from digression.

This introduction is obviously not the place to review and weigh the extensive literature of the controversy aroused by Manly's article. The serious student should study the arguments pro and con, and decide for himself. Of course the best test, as Manly suggested, is to read carefully A₁, A₂, and the long addition by B separately, with an open mind for similarities and differences. It is upon this test, together with careful studies of the differences, that the ultimate general decision must eventually be made.

III. METER AND ALLITERATION

Piers the Plowman, along with the Alexander romances, *William of Palerne, Wynnere and Wastoure, Sir Gawain and the Green Knight,* and many others, is associated with that movement of the second half of the fourteenth century known as the alliterative revival. A great number of poets of this period employed the alliterative long line which had, as a rule, four main stresses or accents, held together by alliteration, that is, repetition of the initial sound of accented syllables. According to this system, the first four lines of our poem would be scanned as follows:

> In a sómer sésoun, whanne sófte was the sónne,
> I shóp me in-to a shróud, as I a shép wére;
> In ábite as an érmyte, unhóly of wérkis,
> I wente wýde in this wórld, wóndris to hére.

In the most common type line, the first three accented syllables alliterate, and the fourth does not (aa/ax):

> Me be*f*el a *f*erly, of *f*airie me thoughte.   (pr. 6.)

About 60 per cent of the lines in the A-text are of this type.

[15]

However, many variations on this basic pattern are to be found, notably the following:

aa/xa:
And seide, " *M*ercy, *m*a dame, what is this to *m*ene?"

(1. 11)

aa/aa:
And alle the *d*enis and su*d*enis as *d*estreris hem *d*ighte,

(2. 137)

aaa/ax:
With *d*epe *d*ikes and *d*erke, and *d*redful of sight.   (pr. 16)

ax/ax:
There that *m*eschief is gret, *M*ede may helpe;   (3. 162)

xa/ax:
Thanne gan I *m*ete a *m*erveillous swevene,   (pr. 11)

aa/bb:
Thorugh *y*eftis han *y*onge men to *r*enne and to *r*ide.

(3. 199)

aa/xx:
Tok *M*ede be the *m*yddel, and broughte hire to chaumbre.

(3. 10)

Very few lines in A fail to alliterate.   One example is:

And yet he betith me ther-to, and lith be my maiden;

(4. 46)

A special feature, found in Old as well as Middle English poetry, is the alliteration of certain consonant groups, notably *sp*, *st*, and *sc*.   In the A-text we find all of these represented, including both *sh* and *sk*:

*S*piceris *sp*eke with hym, to a*sp*ie here ware,   (2. 187)
And be *st*eward of youre *st*ede til ye be *st*owid betere. (5. 39)
Be*ss*hette hym in here *sh*oppis to *sh*ewen here ware,   (2. 175)
" I nile not *sc*orne," quath *S*cripture; " but *sc*ryveyns lighe,

(11. 221)

On the other hand, these consonant groups are not always treated

[16]

(as they were in Old English) as separate consonant sounds for purposes of alliteration. For example we find:

> *S*ymonye and *C*yvyle *st*ondith forth bothe, (2. 54)
> And *s*eide ful softely, in *sh*rifte as it were, (3. 36)
> How that *s*cabbide *sh*ep *sh*ul here wolle save, (8. 17)

Vowels alliterate, as in Old English, but they may also, contrary to Old English practice, alliterate with *h*. Examples are:

> *A*dam and *E*ve he *e*ggide to *i*lle. (1. 63)
> As *a*ncris and *e*rmytes that *h*olden hem in here sellis
>   (pr. 28)

One further characteristic deserves attention. Especially noticeable in our poem is the alliteration of voiced and voiceless stops and fricatives (b:p, g:c, v:f). For example:

> *B*rochide hem with a *p*akke-nedle, and *p*leitide hem togidere,
>   (5. 125)
> And become a *g*ood man for any *c*oveitise, I rede. (2. 32)
> And *f*etten oure *v*itailes of *f*ornicatouris; (2. 142)

IV. DIALECT

The dialect of a piece of Middle English verse may sometimes be fixed with a fair degree of certainty, if we do not have the author's original MS, from rhymes and alliteration. Rhymes have been regarded as making fairly sure those forms which occur in rhyme. In the same way, alliteration may be used to ascertain those forms which are regarded as dialect criteria. *Ben* occurs in rhyme in Chaucer's authentic verse, but in the *Romaunce of the Rose, arn,* which never occurs in Chaucer's genuine poetry, is also found. This is one of the arguments that have been used to prove that Chaucer did not write Fragment B of the *Romaunce.*

If, on the other hand, it becomes apparent that the author is

[17]

familiar with more than one dialect, the problem is not so simple; for like many modern poets, he may use different dialect forms to satisfy the varying needs of his rhyme or alliteration.

Among the usually reliable dialect criteria are the present indicative plural forms of the verb " to be." Generally speaking, we find *are* in the North, *ben* and *arn* in Midland, and *beth* in the South of England in the latter half of the fourteenth century. In the A-text there are several instances where *ben* alliterates. For example:

How *b*esy thei *b*en a*b*oute the mase   (1. 6)

Further, we find one or two instances where *arn* is evidently the author's choice:

*A*ungelis and *a*lle thing *a*rn at his wille,   (10. 31)
Oure *e*nemys and *a*lle men that *a*rn nedy and pore: (11. 238)

It should be noted that such examples cannot be used to decide between *are* and *arn*, or *ben* and *beth*. For example, in the line

Beggeris and bidderis ben not in the bulle,   (8. 67)

four MSS of our poem (TUH₃Di) have the form *ben,* four others (H₂DWN) have *be*, and no less than six (ChRMLVH) have *beth* (T₂A are defective at this point, and I has *weryn*).

Another test is the form used for the third singular feminine, and third plural pronouns. By the time of our poem, *she* and *thei* were common in London (cf. Chaucer) and in Midland generally, while *heo* and *hy* were in use in the South and West. In the A-text both forms, *heo* and *hy,* are authenticated by the alliteration:

But *h*oly chirche and *h*y *h*olden bet togidere,   (pr. 63)
*H*endely thanne *h*eo be*h*ighte hem the same,   (3. 28)

It is worth mentioning that thè forms *heo* and *hy* are frequently obscured in the MSS of the A-text. In pr. 63, where the critical

[18]

reading is *hy*, no MS has *hy*, while five MSS (H₂DUMI) have
he, five others (TChRT₂L) have *thei*, and four (WDiVH)
change the line in an obvious effort to " improve " the alliteration. In 3. 28, five manuscripts (TH₂LVH) have *heo*, and
eight MSS (ChDURIWNDi) have *she*. These two instances,
especially the former, illustrate the importance of utilizing
alliteration in dialect tests wherever possible.

There seems to be one instance in A₂ where *she* may be
intended to alliterate:

> I say it be tho," quath she, " that shewen be here werkis
>
> (11. 13)

It seems fairly safe to say, however, that the A-text—certainly
A₁—attests the use of the provincial forms *heo* and *hy* as against
she and *thei*.

It appears very likely, therefore, that the author (or authors)
of the A-text knew more than one dialect, or perhaps even used
varying dialect forms in his own speech. In support of this
supposition, it is possible to deduce the Northern form, *kirke*,
in the A-text, in several instances where the alliteration is
obviously on *k*, e. g.,

> The *k*ing and his *k*nightes to the *ch*irche [i. e. *k*irke] wente,
>
> (5. 1)

while on the other hand we find the same word in alliteration
where initial *ch* is clearly the voiceless affricate:

> And ek as *ch*ast as a *ch*ild that in *ch*irche wepith,　(1. 154)

The alliteration of *f* and *v* is sometimes cited as evidence of
dialect. As already mentioned (see above, under METER AND
ALLITERATION), this phenomenon is to be found in the A-text,
but it is doubtful that we can be sure that it represents anything
more than the exercise of poetic license on the part of the writer.

It must be emphasized that the dialect of the base MS—in

[19]

the case of the A-text, Trinity College, Cambridge R 3. 14—
cannot be assumed to be that of the author, since this will vary
with the choice of MS used as the basis of the text.

V. THE CRITICAL TEXT

Scholars have recognized the need for an edition of *Piers the
Plowman* based on modern methods of textual criticism ever
since the appearance of Manly's articles on the authorship of
the three versions. Manly himself, though he never abandoned
his theory of multiple authorship, declined to publish further
on the subject pending the construction of adequate critical
texts. Work on a new edition by the Early English Text Society
has been in progress for over forty years, but during this time
students of the poem have had to rely solely on Skeat's text.

Any textual study of *Piers the Plowman* must begin with a
consideration of the A-text, since it in all probability represents
the poem in its earliest form, and is the base from which the
later versions diverge. It is of course true that the B- and
C-texts are of value in reconstructing the A-text where the A
manuscripts are divided and where, at the same time, revisions
of the later texts do not obscure the original reading. Any
critical text of A issued at this time, therefore, may be subject
to some minor revisions once those of B and C have appeared.
The value of having a critical text of A, however, even with
this limitation, will certainly be obvious to any scholar who has
tried to study the poem with only Skeat's text to guide him.

Skeat's A-text, in spite of its shortcomings, was of great value
for many years. No previous editor had recognized the existence of A, as distinct from B and C, and the publication of
the Vernon text with variants from a number of other A manuscripts represented a tremendous advance in our knowledge of
the texts of *Piers the Plowman*. Nevertheless, Skeat himself
eventually recognized that it was inevitable that his work should

be superseded. In the first place it is now apparent that the Vernon MS, though it is early, and an important member of the A family, represents a decidedly inferior tradition in the transmission of the A-text. Furthermore, in using this MS as his text, Skeat inserted lines from other MSS (notably Harleian 875) as he saw fit, and emended the text with the aid of these other MSS " where it seemed to need it." This practice resulted in the adoption of erroneous readings peculiar to the Vernon tradition, and the inclusion of spurious lines and passages often supported by a single MS.

A little over a year after the appearance of Manly's article on the lost leaf, Thomas A. Knott, in the summer of 1907, began work on the text of the first part of the A-version, or A₁, ending with 8. 126, the point at which Manly believed the work of the original author may have terminated. Shortly thereafter a similar study was undertaken independently by R. W. Chambers and J. H. G. Grattan. The latter were the first to appear in print on the subject, and the results of their research were summarized as follows:

1. That a nearer approximation to the original A-text can be drawn from the MSS of the TU group than from the Vernon MS.

2. That any text which is to reproduce closely the original poem, must be founded both upon the TU group and also, although to a less degree, upon the VH group; the MSS which belong to neither tradition must be used to turn the scale in doubtful cases; whilst the danger of introducing readings which may themselves be the result of correction from a B- or C-text, must be borne in mind.

3. That a text so formed will be found to approximate much more closely to the received B-text than the received A-text does.

4. That only when we know what is the " diction, metre and sentence structure " of the original A-text, can we argue with certainty whether these are, or are not, materially different from those of the B-additions, or decide whether B's treatment of the A-text is really inconsistent with unity of authorship.

[21]

Some six years later Knott published his findings, concluding that the A manuscripts fall into two main groups—the first consisting of Vernon and Harleian 875, called x, and the second of all other extant A manuscripts, called y. He pointed out that the B-text can be used to settle doubtful questions, since it is derived from a MS of A not belonging to either x or y. The archetype of B he called z.

In many ways these two studies confirmed each other in their classification of the MSS. In other instances there were serious differences. For example, before Knott published in 1915, Chambers and Grattan had concluded that aside from the two main groups of MSS (the so-called VH and TU groups), the MSS A, H_3, L, and possibly I, were all independent witnesses. In subsequent articles on the A-text, however, they locate all the MSS in two groups—one, VH, the other, all other A manuscripts—in accordance with Knott's x and y classification.

This edition of the A-text is based on Knott's study of A_1, together with the present editor's study of the text of A_2, completed at the University of Chicago in 1949. The student interested in the detailed results of these studies should consult Knott's article in *Modern Philology*, January, 1915, and the present editor's unpublished dissertation, *A Critical Text of Piers Plowman A_2*, Chicago, 1949.

MSS of the A-text

Knott's work was based on the readings of fourteen A manuscripts. Since that time three previously unknown MSS of the A-text have been discovered. They are 733 B in the National Library of Wales, the MS now in the Library of the Society of Antiquaries of London, and a recent and most important discovery, the Chaderton MS in the Library of the University of Liverpool.

For the benefit of students of the A-text, a revised list of A manuscripts is given below, including those newly discovered,

[22]

the new locations of MSS that have changed hands in recent
years, and peculiar characteristics of other MSS which may be
of value in studying the variants given in the textual notes. The
sigla appear to the left, with those used by Chambers and Grattan given in parentheses where they differ from Knott's.

T—Trinity College, Cambridge R 3. 14. End of fourteenth
   century. Used as the basis of the critical text. (See
   p. 27 f.)

H_2—Harleian 6041. Mid-fifteenth century. Parts of folios 23,
   24, 26, and 27 are torn out, thus causing the loss of
   7. 59–78, 86–109, 119–140, 148–192, 202–222, 232–251,
   and 262–284; and the loss of parts of 7. 53–58, 81–85,
   112–118, 143–147, 193–201, 223–231, 252–261, 285–
   293. A folio between folios 33 and 34 has been lost
   (though the numbering is consecutive) causing the
   omission of 10. 104–162; and part of folio 35 is torn
   away, resulting in the loss of parts of 11. 34–41 and
   64–71.

Ch—Chaderton. University of Liverpool. Early fifteenth century. Like T, H_2, W, and Di, this MS is C-text after
   A 11, beginning with C 12. 297 (W begins with C 13. 1).

D—Douce 323. Second half of fifteenth century. Has 3. 135–
   159 before 3. 77; then omits 3. 120–134. Wrongly placed
   after 11. 203 are 11. 127–163.

U—University College, Oxford, 45. Early fifteenth century.
   Omits 1. 33–99 (folio torn out). Omits 8. 170–181. The
   first, seventh, and eighth folios of the fifth quire have
   been lost, causing the omission of 10. 205–11. 47 and
   all after 12. 19. This MS, along with R and T_2, trans-
   poses 7. 70–213 to a position immediately preceding
   1. 180. In U, however, the line preceding the shifted
   matter is not 1. 179, but 2. 23. Thus 1. 180–2. 23 is
   given twice. Readings from this second occurrence of
   the passage are indicated in the variants by *U*.

R—Rawlinson Poet. 137. First half of fifteenth century. All

[23]

practically complete save for a few sporadic omissions
of single lines. Contains the whole of passus 12 (see
APPENDIX I). Has the dislocation of part of passus 7
already described (see U above).

T₂ (E)—Trinity College, Dublin, D 4. 12. End of fifteenth
century. Omits 7. 45–69 and 7. 214 to the end. 7. 44 is
actually the final line in the MS, but 7. 70–213 had been
transposed in an archetype (as described above—see
under U) to a position before 1. 180, and therefore were
preserved.

A—Ashmole 1468. About the end of the fifteenth century (?).
Begins at 1. 142, because the preceding leaves have been
cut out; then omits 2. 18–145, 3. 112–226, 7. 33–85,
8. 32–80, because leaves have been cut out. One folio
(numbered pp. 339–40—the numbering is consecutive)
has been wrongly pasted in on a new inserted stub,
causing lines 7. 237–286 to appear before 7. 86.

M—MS in the Library of the Society of Antiquaries of London
(formerly the Bright MS). End of fifteenth century
(?). Has a few insertions from the B-text, mainly in
passus 5.

H₃—Harleian 3954. About 1420. Is B-text to (B) 5. 128, then
A-text beginning with (A) 5. 106. Omits 8. 112–9. 96
(no break in the text).

I (J)—M 818 in the Pierpont Morgan Library (formerly the
Ingilby MS). Early fifteenth century (?). Last line
in the MS is 12. 88.

L—Lincoln's Inn 150. About 1450. The last page of the MS,
beginning with 8. 102, is dim, faded, and rubbed, and
at times completely illegible. The last line is 8. 152.

W—Duke of Westminster's MS, Eaton Hall. Mid fifteenth
century (?). Inserts a large number of lines and pas-
sages from the B- and C-texts: B1. 32–33 after A1. 31;
B1. 113-116 after A1. 111; C3. 28–29 after A2. 20;
C3. 84–87, 89, 92, 98–100, 102-104 after A2. 65;
C3. 185–188 after A2. 130; C3. 243-248 after A2. 194;

C4. 32–33 after A3. 33; B4. 17-18 after A4. 17; B4. 62 after A4. 48; B4. 119-122 after A4. 105; then follows A 108, then B4. 123–125; B4. 152–156 after A4. 143; B4. 165–170 after A4. 145; B5. 36–41 after A5. 33; B5. 49–56 after A5. 39; B5. 60 after A5. 42; B5. 87–93 after A5. 68; B5. 120–121 after A5. 98.

N—733 B, National Library of Wales. Early fifteenth century. Numerous passages are inserted, mostly from the C-text: C2. 112–122 after A1. 111; C2. 140 after A1. 129; C2. 147–161 (omitting 149) after A1. 139; C3. 28–41 after A2. 20; C3. 60–66 after A2. 45; C3. 84–87, 89, 92, 98–100, 102–104 after A2. 65; C3. 121–136 (omitting 126) after A2. 83; C3. 185–188 after A2. 130; C3. 243–248 after A2. 194; C4. 32–33 after A3. 33; B3. 51–62 in place of A3. 50–51; C4. 86–114 after A3. 74; C4. 134–136, 138, 140–145 after A3. 96. The MS is imperfect at the beginning. The first line is 1. 76, but the text is not legible before 1. 104. Is C-text after 9. 13, beginning with C11. 14.

Di (K)—Digby 145. End of the fifteenth century. No extended omissions. Has several contaminations from the C-text, especially in the prologue, which is chiefly C-text, with a few readings from A. The other insertions are B3. 52–54, 56–58 after A3. 45; C7. 423–8. 55 after A5. 220; then A5. 215–220 is repeated (Digby changes 214 so that it reads " this glotoun " for " sleuthe "); C8. 70–154 after A5. 251; C8. 189–306 substituted for A6. 31–123.

V—Vernon (Eng. Poet. A–1). About 1385. This was the MS printed by Skeat. Omits 1. 176–183 and 2. 106–121. Last line of *Piers the Plowman* is 11. 180 (a leaf has been cut out).

H—Harleian 875. About 1400. Omits 6. 49–7. 2 because a leaf has been lost. Last line is 8. 139 (leaf lost).

[25]

Classification of the MSS

It is not possible to include in this brief introduction the large body of evidence supporting the classification of MSS of the A-text. It seems well, however, to indicate briefly the genealogical relationships which have been deduced from the errors, deviations, omissions, and so on which the various MSS have in common. This can best be done by means of a diagram, or genealogical " tree." Of course no single diagram can account for all of the complexities that we inevitably find in a study of this kind, where the text exists in seventeen MSS, copied over a period of more than a hundred years. For example, the UR manuscripts reveal that in different portions of the text they (or rather an ancestor) were copied from different exemplars, or " parent " MSS. No attempt is made to indicate such aberrations in the diagram given below.

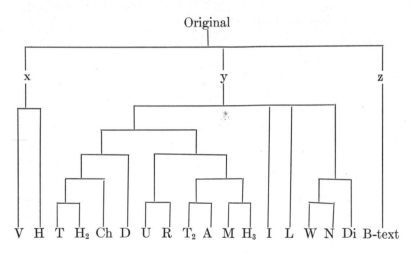

A glance at the list of MSS of the A-text will reveal the fact that for the second part of the A-text only thirteen MSS are available for classification. The four delinquent MSS are: T_2, which is defective after 7. 213; L, defective after 8. 152; H, defective after 8. 139; and N, which becomes C-text after 9.13.

The loss of H, companion MS to V in the x group, is a serious one, since it is no longer possible in A_2 to distinguish the peculiar deviations and errors of V from those of x. But it is assumed in the classification that V continues to represent an independent line of descent in A_2, since it fails to share the common errors of the y group. For the most part the y manuscripts in A_2 maintain the same relationships which they had in A_1. An exception to this is W, which joins the minor group AMH_3. The B-text remains as a third independent line of transmission in A_2, though it is frequently not available for comparison because of its revisions, which are much more extensive than the revisions of A_1. A separate tree for A_2 will help clarify these differences.

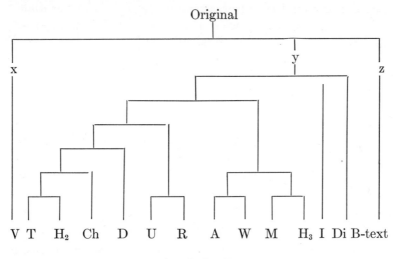

Basis of the Text

The basis of the text is manuscript R 3. 14 in the library of Trinity College, Cambridge (represented by the symbol " T "). This does not mean that the MS is simply printed as it stands, with occasional readings from other MSS. On the contrary, the readings adopted into the critical text are always the critical readings, as attested in every case by the weight of evidence, genealogical and other. No matter how plausible the reading of T may seem, it must not be retained if not supported. By " basis " is meant, therefore, little more than the basis for spelling and dialect, for whenever the reading of T is replaced by the critical reading, it seems better to make the latter conform in spelling and dialect to T. Otherwise we should have a critical text containing too many inconsistent forms and spellings.

Manuscript T was chosen as the basis of the critical text because it is early (about 1400), because it is well spelled, and because it contains comparatively few individual deviations and errors, and therefore probably requires less changing to make a critical text than any other MS. It should be said that the critical text would have been exactly what it is, save for dialect and spelling, no matter what particular MS had been chosen for a basis.

VI.   HISTORICAL BACKGROUND

The student whose only acquaintance with medieval literature is derived from reading Chaucer will no doubt find the world of *Piers the Plowman* different in many ways from that of the Canterbury pilgrims. He will recognize, of course, that while Chaucer is primarily an observer of life, our author is a zealous reformer. One of the main reasons, however, for differences in their work, aside from any speculation about the personalities or aims of the authors, is that Chaucer's outlook is essentially that of a layman, while the interests of our author are clearly identified with the church, whether he was ever a member of the clergy or not. Hence some knowledge of the organization and influence of the Church—that great institution

[28]

overshadowing all others during the Middle Ages—is essential for an understanding of *Piers the Plowman.*

The Church and Ecclesiastics

Ecclesiastics in the medieval church fell into two divisions— the " secular " and the " regular." At the head of both were the Pope and the college of cardinals. In England the secular establishment—which derived its name from the fact that it administered the religious affairs of the people—was divided into the two archbishoprics of Canterbury and York. Under each of these were the bishoprics, and these, if large, were divided into smaller territories under archdeacons. The local unit was the parish. In England there were twenty-one bishoprics, each with from one hundred to seventeen hundred parishes. There were about nine thousand parishes. The regular clergy were those who lived in communities under a rule. The monks and friars were regulars. There were several hundred monasteries in England, and about two hundred brotherhoods of friars. At the head of each monastery, unless it was dependent on another, was an abbot. The monastery was nominally under the control of the bishop, who had the technical right to visit and inspect it every three years.

The term " clerk " was loosely used to mean every person who adopted the religious life as a profession, who became a priest, monk, or friar, or who, having been educated in ecclesiastical schools—and there were no others—entered some other profession, such as the law, medicine, teaching, architecture, or clerical work in the service of the king. The clergy formed a very important class in society, socially, economically, and numerically. In 1377 a poll tax was levied on the whole body of clergy over fourteen years of age in England and Wales, exclusive of the friars. The tax showed nearly thirty thousand clerks—that is, probably over one in fifty of the population above fourteen years of age. Moreover, the ecclesiastical

[29]

communities, especially monasteries, had come to own about one-third of the land in England, so large a proportion that in 1279 the Statute of Mortmain was passed, forbidding the further acquisition of land by the church, unless by the permission of the king.

Education

Practically the only avenue to an education—that is, a "schooling" in the modern sense of the term—was through the schools and universities, which were almost exclusively conducted and taught by priest, monk, or friar, and maintained by some church or monastic subsidy. Through the training here gained, a "career" lay open to the poorest boy that he could not hope for otherwise. Bishop Grosseteste was the son of a serf. The clerks came chiefly, however, from the middle classes and the younger sons of the landed gentry.

Entering a parish or monastic school at the age of seven, the boy began the study of "grammar," that is, of the Latin language, with Donatus, Priscian, and Terence as textbooks. "Donet" became a synonym for primer, as in *Piers the Plowman* A 5. 122, where Covetousness, telling of his apprenticeship, says, "Thanne drough I me among drapers, my *donet* to lerne." After seven years, during which the pupil might, and usually did, take minor orders—advancing from door-keeper to lector and exorcist—he was admitted at the age of fourteen to the University of Oxford or Cambridge. Here he studied grammar, rhetoric, and logic for four years before taking the degree of Bachelor of Arts. Meanwhile, he had been admitted as an acolyte.

At eighteen, if he were nominated to a benefice or guaranteed a living by a monastery, or a patrimony by his family, he would become a subdeacon. After pursuing the study of the seven arts—grammar, dialectic, rhetoric, music, arithmetic, geometry, and astronomy—and the three philosophies—physics, metaphysics, and ethics—for three or four years, he would be-

[30]

come Master of Arts. Meanwhile, at the age of twenty, he would be ordained a deacon. Four more years of study followed, especially of the *Quattuor Libri Sententiarum*, a twelfth-century compilation by Peter Lombard of the opinions of the older teachers, especially St. Augustine and Gregory the Great, and the newer teachers, welded together into a body of doctrine. This book, which furnished a rich store of matter, treated with sobriety and moderation, had become the standard manual of theology. Upon showing ability to lecture on this book, the candidate became a Bachelor of Divinity, and at the age of twenty-five, if physically perfect and of good life, and if possessed of a patrimony, a membership in a brotherhood, or a benefice, he was ordained priest. He might then go into parish work; or, if educated by a monastery, he might return to his community; or, unlike Chaucer's clerk, who was not so worldly as to have office, but rather like those in the prologue of *Piers the Plowman*, he might become a clerk " of acountis, the king for to serve," or a clerk " of the kinges bench, the cuntre to shende." Or he might prefer, if he had means, to remain at the University, and, eighteen or twenty years after matriculation, upon showing ability to lecture on one of the canonical books of the Bible, he would take the degree of Doctor of Theology. Or he might go to Italy to study canon law, or civil law, which was largely based on the ancient Roman code, and which was widely employed on the continent.

The scholastic career here sketched is a composite one, and not, of course, what every student went through. Many, probably the majority, after entering sacred orders, became attached to cathedrals, colleges, and parish churches, and never went any further with their schooling.

The Bishopric

The two archbishoprics, Canterbury and York, were divided into twenty-one bishoprics. These larger bishoprics were again

[31]

divided, for administrative purposes, into from two to eight archdeaconates. At the head of the diocese was the bishop, with his cathedral and his cathedral chapter, and under him the archdeacons. The bishop had general charge of all ecclesiastical affairs in his jurisdiction, with powers of visitation and inspection, and the presiding power over the annual synod. All the clergy of the diocese were required to attend this synod or to send representatives, and the synodsmen were questioned regarding the affairs of their parishes. Periodically the bishop held a court, called a consistory, to settle ecclesiastical questions. Each archdeacon had charge of minor matters of general or parish administration in his district. He installed the priests, held a court for the adjudication of cases in his jurisdiction, and visited and inspected in his territory.

The Cathedral Chapters

The bishop and the clergy were originally one family. Some were always at headquarters, where the choir and the cathedral school were conducted, and some were preaching in the field. The development of the parochial system led to the establishment of the permanent local residence of the parish clergy, and to their separation from the staff of the bishop. The duties of this staff were the conduct of divine service at the cathedral, and the handling of the general diocesan work. Several officers developed special powers and duties. The dean had general command in the absence of the bishop. The chancellor had charge of the school. The precentor was responsible for the services, especially the music. The treasurer was in charge of the bishop's common fund.

The body of cathedral canons developed an independent corporate life. The common property of the cathedral was divided up: one part was assigned to the bishop; one to the endowment of the chapter; separate and distinct endowments, called prebends, were assigned to each member of the chapter, and there was also a common fund divisible among the canons, or some of them. When a parson obtained leave of his bishop to "sette his benefice to hyre," and went to London to St. Paul's, he frequently assumed one of these prebends. This is referred to in *Piers the Plowman* A 3. 137, where Meed, it is said, "provendrours parsones."

The chapter came to elect their own dean, and became a separate corporation. They frequently elected the bishop, subject, of course, to the king's approval, and actually in practice, at the nomination of the king. Some chapters adopted the Benedictine rule, and became monasteries. There were seven of these, notably that at Canterbury. In this case, the bishop was nominally the abbot, but the prior was actually the ruler of the chapter.

The Parish

The parish over which the priest exercised spiritual rule did not necessarily coincide with any other geographical boundaries, though in the country it often did include a manor. In the towns, there were often several parishes.

In charge of the parish church was the rector or parson, who was appointed by the patron of the living, who might be the lord of the manor or the abbot of a monastery, with the approval of the bishop. It was the duty of the archdeacon to put the priest in charge of the parish, and the fee for the ceremony was usually two shillings to forty pence.

The rector, if his parish was poor, and if he had sufficient influence with the bishop, might obtain leave to run off to London to seek a chantry, " To synge there for symonye, for silver is swete " (pr. 83). Or perhaps he might be one of those who held pluralitics (cf. 11. 197), that is, more than one benefice. Or the parish might be one which had had its revenues " impropriated " by a monastery. In such cases, the deputy of the rector, or the appointee of the monastery, was called a vicar. In addition to the rector or the vicar, if the work of the parish was heavy, or if its revenues permitted, there might be a curate or two, receiving their salary from the rector; or perhaps there might be a chantry priest, who, in addition to singing in a chantry attached to the church, served as an assistant priest of the parish. Also there were two kinds of chaplains, one employed by a nobleman or a person of distinction to say mass in his private chapel, the other attached to a "chapel of ease," founded in some outlying but thickly settled portion of a large, scattered parish. Deacons and subdeacons were frequently employed to assist the priest when the means of the parish afforded their services.

The house of the rector was very simple. It usually consisted of one hall—which was, of course, the living room, dining room, and office—a kitchen, and a chamber. In rural parishes the house was generally located on a main road, so that there was much travel, and consequently hospitality was constantly in demand. There was therefore often a special room or building for guests, and a stable for their horses. Part of the revenues were usually set aside for hospitality.

Chantries were a form of religious foundation much in fashion in the fourteenth and fifteenth centuries. They met with much opposition and were often attacked by the satirists. A chantry was a foundation for the maintenance of one or more priests, to offer up prayers for the soul of the founder, his family and ancestors, and usually of all Christian souls. Other motives than the mere perpetuation of the name of the founder might govern the establishment. The benefactor often aimed to render it possible for the outlying population of a large and scattered parish to worship in a chapel under a so-called chantry priest. Or he chose this means of adding to the working clerical staff of the town. Or he thus furnished extra teaching for a grammar school. The greatest numbers of chantries were created between 1450 and 1500, but there were many before 1400. A majority were established at an already existing altar of a cathedral, or a

[34]

monastic or parish church, although many chapels were specially provided. In cathedrals, many small chapels were screened off. Not all chantries were perpetual. Often they were for only a year or two, or perhaps ten or twenty years. The pay was not large, even for the time; it usually amounted to about five pounds a year.

Preaching

Preaching was frequently enjoined on the parish clergy, and many manuals and helps were provided. The canons of Edgar required preaching every Sunday. Ælfric (1030) directed the clergy to preach the ten commandments and the eight capital vices. Alexander, Bishop of Coventry (1224–40), required his clergy to preach every Sunday on the seven deadly sins. Grosseteste (1235–54) instructed his clergy to preach every Sunday, and furnished them with topics. Archbishop Peckham in his constitutions of 1281 commanded preaching at least four times a year. The sermons had to cover the fourteen articles of faith, the ten commandments, the two evangelical precepts of charity, the seven deadly sins, the seven principal virtues, the seven works of mercy, and the seven sacraments of grace. In 1357 Thoresby, Archbishop of York, wrote in English an exposition of the fourteen points of the creed, the ten commandments, the seven sacraments, etc., and sent it to all his parish priests, bidding them to preach often to the people, and to urge them to teach them to the children. A synod at Ely in 1364 enjoined the priests to preach frequently, and to expound the commandments, and so forth.

Monasteries

A monastery was the abode of a society of men or women who lived together in common, were supposed to eat together, sleep in one common dormitory, attend services together in the church, transact business and pursue their employment in the sight and hearing of each other in a common cloister, and who were buried

[35]

in a common graveyard. The "convent" was the association
or corporation of persons; the "monastery" was the dwelling
place.

The first requisite of the group was of course the church,
the heart of the place. It was built in the form of a cross,
with the nave running east and west, with the chancel east, and
the transepts north and south. The arrangement of the other
buildings varied, but they were regularly built so as to form

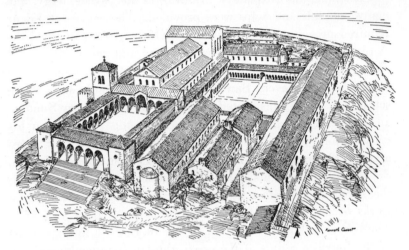

MONTECASSINO

within the group a rectangular open space, surrounded by
covered and screened walks, which constituted the "cloister."
The buildings included the chapter-house, the meeting place for
business and corporate purposes of the whole chapter; the dormitory and the refectory; the cellar and the kitchen; and the rooms
for dispensing alms and for the housing of guests—for this was
an important function of the medieval monastery. One room,
or one part of the cloister, was assigned as the *scriptorium*, or
writing room, which was one of the busiest departments of the
institution. Here was transacted the business of the agents and

the clerks, here were drawn up the deeds and other documents, the conveyances, leases, enfeoffments, here were written the school books, service books, the annals or chonicle, and probably much secular literature.

Administration of the Monasteries

At the head of the monastery was the abbot, with a prior under him, and perhaps, if the corporation was a large one, with many interests, one or two subpriors. If there were large possessions at some distance, there might be a subordinate group of monks nearby, with a building, to care for the business. Such an outpost was called a cell. Chaucer's monk was the head, or keeper, of such a cell. In the main monastery were a kitchener, whose care was the meals and the dispensation of hospitality; a precentor, who had charge of the choir boys, the organ, the music, and the processions; an infirmarer, who took care of the hospital; and a cellarer, who brewed and baked.

The Three Kinds of Monastic Rule

There were three chief kinds of monastic rule in England: Benedictine, Cluniac, and Cistercian. The first followed the rule of St. Benedict (d. 542), which had been the principal instrument in giving a permanent and effective organization to monasticism. This rule was designed to meet the need of cenobitic or community monasticism, as distinguished from eremitical or solitary asceticism. It defined the duties and responsibilities of the abbot and the subordinate officers, and prescribed and defined the daily labor and worship of the monks. It detailed the kind and amount of food and clothing to be given each monk. Four hours of work a day were required of each inmate. The monks were assembled at intervals of three or four hours through the day for divine worship. The name given these frequent services, aside from the mass, was the " Hours."

[37]

Benedict had prescribed seven of these services daily, probably basing the number on the 164th verse of the 119th psalm, " Seven times a day do I praise thee. . . ." The hours were: Matins, which came at midnight and at certain seasons just before sunrise; Lauds, immediately following sunrise; Prime, at six A. M.; Tierce, at 9 A. M.; Sext, at 12 M.; Nones, at 3 P. M.; Vespers, at sunset; and a supplementary service, at first at 9 P. M., called Compline, which in practice was conjoined to Vespers.

The Cluniac Benedictine rule was a reformed Benedictine rule. The establishers of this order gave up field work and manual labor, and lengthened, multiplied, and elaborated the church services so that they filled nearly the whole day. As distinguished from the Benedictines, with whom each monastery formed an independent corporation, with full autonomy, the monasteries belonging to Cluny (the main abbey, situated in a village in France) formed a real order. Every house, no matter in what country it was situated, was completely subject to Cluny and its abbot, who was the absolute ruler of the whole system. He appointed all the heads of subordinate monasteries (priors) and personally admitted all candidates to the order. Every member was obliged to spend his first years at Cluny.

The Cistercians, of whom there were about one hundred houses in England, attempted to restore strictly the original rule of Benedict. They eliminated all the elaborations of the Cluniacs, and restored the manual labor, especially field work. They were great farmers and cattle and horse breeders. Originally they refused as sources of income all benefices, tools, tithes, and rents, and depended for sustenance entirely on the profits of their fields. Because of the immense amount of labor their system required, and its interference with church services, they introduced the system of lay brothers. These lay brothers, who became very numerous, were drawn from the peasantry, and were employed in the fields and at trades. They had a separate order of prayer and religious exercises in order to make their daily life more convenient. They had little voice in the government, and were rarely ordained or inducted into the higher offices. In this kind of monastery, each abbey was fully independent so far as internal matters were concerned, but all were subject to an annual meeting of all the abbots at Cîteaux. The abbey at Cîteaux was in some respects the model for each independent abbey.

A monastery aimed to be an entirely self-supporting community; it produced its own food and drink, clothing, shoes, wood, iron work, and so far as possible every material thing used by its members. Of the production and use of all these things, as of all financial transactions, the most minute accounts were kept.

Although the primary idea in monastic life was complete withdrawal from every temporal activity of the world, and consequent freedom to live a purely spiritual life, the very nature of the institution made this ideal difficult to attain. Merely the material wants of a community of men withdrew considerable attention from the religious life. But the monastic ideal continued to hold an appeal for devout men everywhere.

Friars

As has been seen, the parish clergy were concerned with local administration and preaching, the cathedral chapters with diocesan administration, and the monks—theoretically at least—with a life of religious contemplation and worship. The spirit of the friars was originally something different from any of these. The monastic system had never been designed to meet the needs of anyone outside the organization. The parochial system, ideal for rural districts and for small villages, broke down almost completely in the rapidly growing towns and cities that resulted from the increased trade and manufacture

[39]

of the twelfth and thirteenth centuries. The slums were scarcely touched even superficially by any form of religious work. It was originally to reach these wretched and bitterly poor outcasts that St. Francis of Assisi grouped around himself the preachers whom he termed the *Fratres Minores*.

Giovanni Bernardone, born at Assisi in 1182, son of a merchant, and intended for that career, engaged in trade till his twenty-fourth year. At that time he fell seriously, almost mortally ill, and upon his recovery changed his whole view of life. He saw the inefficiency of the parish organization, the corruption of the Italian monasteries, because of wealth, luxury, and greed, and heard the call from God, as he said, to " build my church again." At first, without any special aim, he worked among the poor in his own town. Then he preached the misery of these poor so eloquently among his associates that soon he had twelve disciples from the better classes, all of whom, under the inspiration of his preaching, gave up their property, took vows of poverty, humility, and service, and went forth to help the wretched and despairing. St. Francis was not a theologian or a clerk—a learned man. He proposed no dogma. He preached only simplicity and self-surrender, and the return to the primitive and unorganized work among the poor that he found recounted in the life of Christ.

With amazing rapidity the brotherhood expanded in Italy and spread into other countries. In 1210 the founder obtained formal recognition from the Pope. In 1215 the first chapter was held, at which were appointed provincial ministers for France, Germany, and Spain.

At about this same time another brotherhood was being established, for a different purpose, by Dominic, a Spanish Augustinian canon. He was twelve years older than Francis, an educated theologian, and, in a subordinate capacity, had been for ten years concerned in the prosecution of the Albigensian heretics. He was deeply concerned by the ignorance and error that seemed to him to be corrupting the kingdom of God, rather than by the ungodliness and wretchedness of the city poor, which had appealed so vividly to St. Francis. In 1217 Dominic went to Rome, and there received high favor from the Pope, and attracted the cultivated classes, the scholars and ecclesiastics. His main purpose was to preach to the heretic and the infidel.

In 1221 the Dominicans reached England, a small group of poor and humble, but attractive and effective preachers. They met with immense success everywhere, especially, as one might expect from their scholastic origin, at Oxford. A little band of Franciscans came to England in 1224. They first reached Oxford in 1225. There they were entertained by monks, by the Dominicans, and by ecclesiastics of other sorts. The first property that they acquired, at Canterbury and London, was made over to groups of townspeople or merchants as trustees, in order to conform with the regulations of their order, which specifically denied them the right to possess property. Within five years the Dominicans and Franciscans, side by side, were in almost every important town in England. Their earliest buildings were of the very poorest sort, sheds or huts of mud or twigs, situated in those quarters of the towns inhabited by the most wretched of the people. At Norwich they lived in a barn with mud walls, in a filthy swamp. At London they located in the shambles, in a street fittingly called " Stinking Lane."

The rapidity of their growth and the consequent need for organization quickly caused modifications of the more primitive ideas of Francis about simplicity of life and action among the *Fratres Minores.* He seems to have been impatient of the necessity for machinery and ordered work. His emphasis was always on poverty, and fervent preaching and self-sacrifice. His Rule forbade the possession of property of any kind, not only by the friars as individuals (as among the monks) but also by the organization. The brothers were forbidden to touch money, or to own rents or revenues. They were not allowed to own

books or parchment or ink. They were required to toil daily
at hard labor. His original idea seems to have been that they
were to receive from those for whom they labored enough to
sustain them, and were to live by begging their food only when
the results of their work did not suffice. They soon, however,
practiced begging as the regular means of livelihood.

From the general favor in which the friars were quite evidently held by the better and middle classes for almost a century, it is difficult to believe anything except that in the main
their observance of their rule was faithful. Yet by the fourteenth century, at any rate, we find that not only satirists, but
also other people seriously interested in the welfare of common
folk, especially, for instance, Wyclif and Fitz-Ralph, Archbishop of Armagh, in their sermons against the friars, point to
very wide-spread and serious abuses.

In fact, nearly every provision of the Testament of St. Francis
seems to have been violated or evaded. The prohibition against
owning property was evaded by putting land and buildings in
the name of the Pope, or of trustees. The friars did not touch
money because they wore gloves or received it in bowls. They
not only owned books, but when they came to dominate, as
they did, the universities, there were bitter complaints that they
had a monopoly on the books prepared for students, so that
students had to join their orders or go bookless. They became
the most learned body in England. They developed their begging into an exact science. They divided the whole country
into districts, which they called "limits," and assigned these
districts to pairs of friars, called "limitors"; and there is some
evidence that they even exacted an agreed rent from the limitor.
One of the most widely satirized abuses was their power of
hearing confession. Of course, when the orders were young
and uncorrupted, this power had been a great help to them in
their work. But as time went on, they encroached more and
more on the province of the parish priest, even where the secular

clergy was honest and conscientious. A priest had to obtain leave of his bishop to absolve parishioners who had committed serious sins. But the friar had no superior in the matter, and consequently could immediately absolve even those who had committed the gravest crimes. From the comments of the satirists they seem to have been rather liberal in giving penance, especially, like Chaucer's friar, where they knew they would have a " good pitaunce."

Another serious abuse arose in connection with the " Tertiaries." These were originally men and women of devout lives who wished to aid the work of the friars more intimately without actually entering the orders and taking the full vows. For the sake of the money, friars ultimately sold letters of fraternity, admitting rich and well-to-do persons to this degree, and guaranteeing the full benefits of membership in the order after death. This is referred to in *Piers the Plowman* where Meed says that if she were certain that the friar confessor were telling the truth about the benefits, she would donate generously to the making or mending of windows (3. 50 ff.), and again at the end of A₁ where the dreamer deems membership in a fraternity worthless without Do-well (8. 172 ff.).

The internal organizations of the different orders of friars were similar. Each order had a general in Rome, who was under the special protection and correction of a cardinal. In each country there was a head called a " provincial." Under him the houses were grouped into districts called " visitations " by the Dominicans and " custodies " by the Franciscans. By the late fourteenth century, the English province of the Franciscans contained seven custodies, each embracing eight or nine convents. The Dominicans had fifty-eight convents, the Franciscans seventy-five. The order of Carmelites originated in the East, and had been introduced into England in the thirteenth century. There were five houses in England. The Austin friars had been founded in the middle of the thirteenth cen-

[43]

tury. There were forty-five houses in England. These are the " four orders " we hear about, though there were other small bodies, such as the Crutched Friars, referred to in *Piers the Plowman* under the name of " Paulines people " and of Piers the pardoner, " Paulines doctor." In 1370 the smaller orders were suppressed, and their members and houses were united with the Austins.

Hermits

St. Benedict, in Chapter I of his Rule, distinguishes between the cenobitic monks, who live in communities, and the anchorites, or hermits, who, " not in the first fervor of conversion, but after long trial in the monastery, and already taught by the example of others, have learned to fight against the devil, are well prepared to go forth from the ranks of the brothers to the single combat of the desert. They can now, by God's help, safely fight against the vices of their flesh and against evil thoughts singly, with their own hand and arm, and without the encouragement of a companion." That there were still in the fourteenth century anchorites and hermits who observed the ascetic rule of life our author himself testifies in the prologue, and in the account of Piers, who says that he will support anchors and hermits who hold themselves in their cells. That there were many false hermits, however, all three versions of our poem attest. In the prologue we are told that these great tall lubbers, who were loth to work, make themselves hermits to have their ease. In England at our period not all these hermits, good or bad, lived in the waste places. They lived by the roadside, or at the end of a bridge which it was supposed to be their duty to keep in repair, or even sometimes, curiously enough, in the midst of cities.

The most notable of the good hermits was Richard Rolle of Hampole, who died in 1349. At the age of nineteen he left Oxford, where he had become more interested in sacred literature than in secular and scientific studies. Returning home, he improvised garments for himself from some of his sister's clothing, and retired into uninhabited places to meditate and pray. Coming out in order to attend church, he was regarded as mad by his friends, but finally convinced them of his sanity and the genuineness of his inspiration. They furnished him with robes suitable for a hermit, and he devoted himself to the contemplative life, a life full of fasts and vigils, mortifications, raptures, ecstasies and visions. He was constantly filled with the most rapturous divine love. He was tempted by the devil, but repulsed the attack. He wrote voluminously in Latin and English, he wrought miracles, and he preached with such fervor that he won many men to God. Finally he settled at Hampole, where he reached absolute perfection of life, and soon afterward died. After his death the nearby nunnery was the object of numerous pilgrimages from those who came to worship at the shrine of the hermit.

Clerks in Worldly Office

We hear in the prologue and elsewhere of clerics of low and high rank who held worldly office. They were, indeed, the only men with sufficient education to fill these jobs. Chaucer's clerk of Oxford, it will be remembered, was not so worldly as to have office. But ecclesiastics, both ordained and unordained, beneficed and in high position, bishops, and even archbishops and cardinals, held administrative positions in the service of the king and of lords. Thomas Becket, Archbishop of Canterbury, had been chancellor of Henry II, and later Cardinal Wolsey held the same office under Henry VIII.

Pardoners

Throughout the Middle Ages, not only in Chaucer and *Piers the Plowman*, but in the edicts of bishops and popes, we hear

[45]

of these curious traveling evangelists and their bulls of popes and bishops, their relics, their preaching, their collections, sometimes in collusion with the parish priest and sometimes with the bishop. The reason for their origin goes back to the infliction of penance for sin—at first penance consisting of fasting and prayer and singing psalms, but later, at times, commuted to money payments which, inflicted judiciously and exacted properly, in themselves involved no abuses. In order to justify freedom from the punishment of sin without due penance—a freedom which could not be attributed to the merit of the sinner —the doctrine of the " treasury " was developed. This, briefly, was that the merits of Christ and the Virgin and the apostles were so much greater than required for themselves that they constituted an accumulation of merit, which was at the disposition of the pope, with his power, handed down from St. Peter, of remitting sin and absolving from its consequences. This treasury was available for sinners who had little or no merit of their own, and whose sin otherwise doomed them to long punishment in purgatory. The Holy See sent out *quaestores*, or pardoners, as they were called in the vernacular, to dispense grants from this treasury under proper authority. But the success of the authorized pardoners caused the appearance of numbers of imposters, among whom we may count some of those mentioned in our poem.

The Pestilence

The " Black Death "—or, as it was called in its own time, the " pestilence," or simply " the death "—first appeared in Europe in the autumn of 1347, coming apparently from Asia by an overland trade route which had its western terminus at Caffa, a Genoese commercial port in the Crimea. The first ship from Caffa carried the infection to Genoa, leaving in its trail new foci at other points, from which, as well as from Genoa, all Italy was soon overspread. The disease immediately

[46]

scattered to France, Spain, and Germany, reached the south-western part of England in August, 1348, and within a year swept the whole island. The plague recurred periodically in England till the seventeenth century. During the latter half of the fourteenth century we hear of especially violent epidemics in the years 1361–62, 1368–69, 1375, and 1390–91. The attack of 1361–62 is referred to by two separate chroniclers as the *pestis puerorum*, because it was especially fatal to the young. This perhaps gives force to the reference in *Piers the Plowman* (A 5. 32–33), where Repentance " chargide chapmen to chasten here children—' Let no wynnyng forwanye hem whiles thei ben yonge.' "

The Black Death was some form of the Eastern or bubonic plague, as we know from the descriptions by contemporary writers. It manifested itself either in dark, hard, dry, tense swellings, as large as an egg, in the neck, the groins, and the armpits, or in smaller swellings or boils over the whole body, either variety being often accompanied by inflammation of the throat and lungs, violent pains in the chest, and spitting and vomiting of blood. The patient was afflicted with fever, delirium, and sometimes frenzy. The disease was almost invariably fatal in from twelve hours to three days, though in the later epidemics recovery sometimes followed the lancing of the swellings.

From recent investigations of the bubonic plague in India, we know that it is communicable not only between human beings, but also between rats, and between rats and human beings. The fact has been established that the disease is carried among these animals by the rat flea—*pulex cheopis*—and almost certainly from rat to man by the same means. Sanitation, personal cleanliness, and the prompt destruction of garbage and offal have apparently given the inhabitants of modern civilized countries a very high degree of protection against the disease.

The mortality of the epidemic of 1348–49 was undoubtedly

[47]

very high. Our sources of information are various: (1) contemporary statements from various sources; (2) the chronicles; (3) the records of the appointments of parish priests to vacancies which we find in the institution books of the bishops; (4) and the registries of the deaths of tenants in the rolls of the manor courts. The last two are the most definite and reliable. The contemporary estimates of the death rate place it at from one-fifth to nine-tenths of the population, but these statistics are not dependable. Some of them, especially some for London and Norwich, are absurdly high, though the figures for London may well have reached 20,000 or 30,000, amounting to about half the population; and in Norwich the population may have been reduced from about 25,000 to about 7,000. The records for certain monasteries give us more reliable figures. In the Yorkshire abbey of Meaux, only 10 inmates survived out of 50. At Ely 28 survived out of 43; at Hickling in Norfolk, 9 out of 10 died. At Heveringham, in the same county, all died. At Canterbury, however, only 4 out of 80 died. The statistics of the parish clergy point to the death of about two-thirds. The records of the manor courts indicate that from one-third to two-thirds of the rural population died everywhere. For example, the Roll for the manor of Cornard Parva in Suffolk shows that in six months, in about fifty holdings, there were deaths of 51 tenants, and 29 families were obliterated. In the small parish of Hunstanton in Norfolk, 172 tenants died in six months, 74 leaving no male heirs, 19 no heirs at all.

Because of the way that Boccaccio uses the plague as a background for his *Decameron*, and Chaucer for his *Pardoner's Tale*, it has been customary to write as if the pestilence was influential in coloring the life of the whole second half of the fourteenth century in two ways, making part of the people deliriously intoxicated with despair, others somber with grief and dread. There can of course be little doubt that for a short time after the first attack, and perhaps from time to time afterwards, the stricken families and friends were so numerous that practically the whole country was plunged into mourning. But all the evidence is against accepting the theory that this condition prevailed for fifty years, or anything like so long a time. All the ordinary activities, the amusements, diversions, and life generally, must within a very few years at the most have resumed their customary courses.

The most direct effects of the plague were upon economic, social, and ecclesiastical institutions.

Perhaps the most profound effect was upon the agricultural laborers, the artisans, and all other classes of society depending upon the labor of these two classes, especially the wealthier, land-holding classes. For centuries the agricultural unit—the manor—had been farmed by serfs and freeholders, both paying rent in the form of shares of their produce or by "week-work"— that is, by working certain hours or days of the week or in the season, not on their own plots or holdings, but upon the sections of the manor which were farmed under the direction of the bailiff for the lord. But for a long time the custom had been growing of farming this part of the manor by hired labor, paid by wages. The very decided inconvenience to the tenants of plowing, sowing, and harvesting on their lord's land at the very seasons of the year when the same sorts of labor were absolutely necessary on their own holdings, led to a commutation of labor rents into money rents. This was better for them, because it left them free to do their own work when the need was most pressing, and it was far more convenient for the bailiff, the agent of the lord, because it made it possible for him to hire steady labor to do the work under his supervision. By 1325 money payments had practically superseded labor rents. As the bailiff farmed about as much land as all the tenants together, the number of hired labors must have been rather large.

Suddenly, in one year, both laborers and tenants were reduced by the plague by from one-third to two-thirds in number.

The resultant scarcity of labor immediately operated to raise wages, and for many years we find Parliament, largely composed of land-holders, legislating repeatedly to enforce the wage scale which had prevailed before the plague. It should not be thought, however, that the chief factors in the raising of wages were the laborers themselves. We hear that one reason for the passage of the statutes was to prevent landlords from bidding against one another in order to steal away the workmen of others. One result of the rise in wages was to detach from the land the villeins, who would go from one manor to another at the call of higher pay. As a result of this detachment, many were idle during the lighter seasons, and it was undoubtedly from this frequent unemployment that so many laborers joined the roving gangs of " sturdy beggars " of whom we hear so many complaints.

The diminution in income from the manors is reflected in the prologue to *Piers the Plowman,* where we hear that parsons and parish priests complained to their bishops because of the reduction in their income. Not only were wages high, but much land had to lie idle, and the decrease in production had its effect on prices. This, with the reduction in the income of the landlords, caused great economic distress.

The effect of the pestilence on the clergy was fully as great, and far more unfortunate, than on any other class of the population. Five thousand of the beneficed clergy died in a year, and several times that number of monks and friars. The demand from the parishes resulted in the institution of young, ignorant, and inexperienced clerks. Many were instituted who were not yet in sacred orders. Some parishes were left utterly without priests. The number of candidates for orders was reduced by from one-fifth to one-half, because of the pressure due to decreased population. The friars, who for the most part had their abodes in the most insanitary parts of the towns, were undoubtedly among the hardest hit. The monastic institutions were hopelessly crippled. They never fully recovered from the breach of their traditional practice and the loosening of their discipline, nor from the reduction in their numbers and in their incomes. It must be believed that the ravages and results of the pestilence were at least partially responsible for the ecclesiastical abuses which led the satirists to their frequent attacks on the clergy.

England in the Fourteenth Century

The fourteenth century in England was a period of extensive changes in political, economic, and religious institutions. The long struggle against the absolute authority of the king had borne fruit during the reigns of Edward I and II, so that by the time Edward III came to the throne in 1327 the commons had gained the right to be present at all sessions of parliament. Economically the lower classes were still under the yoke of feudalism, but the rapid rise of a new commercial class heralded the overthrow of the old order, and an awareness of the inadequacy of wages and working conditions on the part of laborers was heightened by the effect of the plague on the labor market. Successive re-enactments of the Statute of Laborers in the fifties and sixties produced a state of unrest which reached its climax in the Peasants' Revolt of 1381. The program of religious reform launched by the friars had largely spent itself, and French domination of the pope in Avignon during most of the fourteenth century led to a marked decline in papal prestige. A rising opposition in England to ecclesiastical policy and practices found expression in the heresies of John Wyclif (c. 1328–84), and the attack by William of Ockham (1280–1347) on the political authority of the Church.

While medieval institutions were on the decline in England, there began to spring up at the same time a new spirit of national unity, which grew in strength and intensity during the long reign of Edward III (1327–77), and was reflected in the

[51]

literature of the period, including *Wynnere and Wastoure, Piers the Plowman,* and other popular works. Although the rise of nationalism in England had its parallels on the continent, it can nevertheless be fully understood only in the light of earlier English history, with special reference to Anglo-French relations following the Norman Conquest.

As soon as William the Conqueror (1066–87) had secured the English throne, he began to reward his Norman followers with the rich lands of the shattered English nobility, and, more gradually, to replace native churchmen by drawing from the ranks of the Norman clergy. As a result of this policy there arose an aristocracy, both lay and ecclesiastic, sharply distinguished in both language and culture from the great mass of the English-speaking population. Moreover, a number of the Norman barons held land on both sides of the channel, and their economic interests thus served to strengthen the ties between the two countries. The reign of Henry II (1154–89) saw the expansion of continental holdings by the English king, and produced that vast conglomeration of feudal states known to historians as the Angevin Empire. After Henry's death, however, the Empire began to disintegrate, and, in 1204, King John lost Normandy to the French king, Philip Augustus. After this complete reversal of fortunes there developed an antagonism between English and French interests which culminated in the Hundred Years' War (1337–1453).

Perhaps the most striking development in fourteenth-century England, for the student of literature, is the dramatic resurgence of the English language in a land where, for nearly three hundred years, the tongue of the ruling classes had been French. The slogan " England for the English," which the baronial forces had utilized so effectively against the monarchy in the thirteenth century, took on new significance with the opening of hostilities against France in 1337, and the movement toward the revival of the English language gained strength as a symbol of defiance of the French-speaking enemy. The author of *Piers the Plowman* seems to have known some French, but his choice of English as the vehicle of his poetry speaks for itself, and his anti-French sentiment is quite obvious when, for example, he identifies the devil allegorically as "a proud prikere of Fraunce" (10. 8).

The Literary Revival

The return of English to a dominant position led, in the second half of the century, to a literary revival which produced many works of enduring value. For virtually the first time since the end of the Old English period there appeared a number of English authors who asserted considerable independence of continental literary models. Although the French influence was still at work in English poetry, the slavish imitation of French originals became less and less popular, and romances like *Sir Gawain and the Green Knight* bore an unmistakable stamp of English authorship. Pious works of religious instruction continued to appear, but a new critical spirit was evident in some of the best literature of the period, including the prose of Wyclif and the poetry of Chaucer.

Unquestionably the high point of the revival is represented by the poetry of Geoffrey Chaucer (c. 1340–1400), whose *Canterbury Tales* remains one of the greatest poems of the English language. Chaucer's insight into the inner workings of human personality enabled him to produce the widely admired portraits of the pilgrims in the General Prologue, and his critical spirit led him to record the evils of his age, even though he was primarily a court poet, writing for the entertainment of an aristocratic London society.

The universal admiration of Chaucer, justified as it is, has had one unfortunate effect in connection with the study of Middle English literature. It has meant that other works, composed during the same period, have often been neglected. Yet without this other literature our knowledge of English life and manners in the fourteenth century would of necessity be somewhat limited, since Chaucer's outlook, in spite of his broad human sympathies, is fundamentally aristocratic.

Piers the Plowman

Piers the Plowman has provided social historians with a wealth of material illustrating the life and manners of the common people in fourteenth-century England. Intimate glimpses of daily living, such as the tavern scene accompanying the confession of Glotoun (5. 145–213), offer us evidence in some ways more revealing than conventional historical records, and the critical spirit of the time is nowhere more evident than in the satirical portrait of Lady Meed (passus 2–4). It will be well, by way of conclusion, to consider briefly the nature of the social and religious criticism found in the poem, and to determine, if possible, the place which the author occupies in the revolt against existing conditions which culminated in the Reformation of the sixteenth century.

Nearly every branch of the secular government comes in for criticism at one point or another in *Piers the Plowman.* Lady Meed, for example, representing bribery, succeeds in corrupting officials at Westminster (3. 12) before the proceedings of the king in council. The court is described as being full of influence-peddlers. Mayors and magistrates are included among those who, for the sake of a bribe, agree to act contrary to the dictates of conscience. They give free rein to profiteering merchants, who own homes and property of far greater value than their legitimate incomes could possibly justify (3. 73–4).

Although Piers himself, the simple plowman, represents the potential good in ordinary people, he is an ideal rather than a reality. The author has no rose-colored conception of the common man. Some of the laborers helping Piers in the plowing

[54]

of the half-acre are " wasters," who refuse to put in an honest day's work until hunger compels them to do so (7. 286 ff.). Many supposed beggars are miraculously " cured," and aid Piers in his labor, only after being goaded by hunger (7. 177 ff.). Traders and craftsmen, operating at fairs such as the one at Winchester, teach their apprentices tricks of the trade in order to swindle the purchaser (5. 114 ff.).

Professional men, especially lawyers, are often bitterly attacked. Most lawyers refuse to make use of their God-given abilities on behalf of poor men without first demanding unreasonable payments. You might as well try to measure the mist on Malvern Hills, says the author, as get a free word out of them (pr. 88–89). Many physicians are simply liars, and their medicines more often than not hasten the patient's death (7. 257-8). The list of such abuses could be extended almost indefinitely.

In spite of the poet's reverence for the Church, he is most unsparing in his denunciation of ecclesiastical corruption and the various abuses of both the secular and regular clergy. He sees the great wealth of the medieval church as a primary cause of its weaknesses. The greed of parsons and parish priests draws them from their impoverished flocks in the country to the rich preferments in London (pr. 80–84). Pardoner and bishop collaborate to profit by the unjust sale of indulgences (pr. 65 ff.). In criticizing priests who accept money for singing masses, the author has Conscience quote the words of Christ: *Verily I say unto you, They have their reward* (3. 230). The regular clergy, instead of living in accordance with the rule of St. Gregory, roam freely over the country-side dressed in worldly clothing, totally unmindful of their calling (11. 208–213). Even Rome itself does not escape censure. Lady Meed, as bribery, is described as having free access to the pope's palace in the exercise of her vice.

In view of the severity of these attacks on contemporary

[55]

society and on the Church, the author of *Piers the Plowman* has at times in the past been depicted as a sort of revolutionary, guiding his contemporaries on a pilgrimage out of feudal darkness into the coming dawn of modern society. His satire of clerical abuses has been especially emphasized as a revolt against the Church, or at least an inspired prophecy of the coming Reformation. A close reading of the poem will, I think, reveal that there is little justification for either of these views. The poet's ideas on the proper place of king, lords, and commons in the society of his day are thoroughly orthodox. It is the duty of the king and lords to enforce obedience to God's law, and our author only asks that the king govern the country in accordance with reason. In spite of the flagrant abuses of the clergy, both secular and regular, the poet is unswerving in his devotion to the Church and its doctrine. He is extremely critical of the system of indulgences, for example, yet he hastens to add that he believes firmly in the pope's power to grant pardon (8. 150–161).

While the satire of contemporary conditions looms large in the text of the poem, we must not lose sight of the fact that the author has a positive message for his generation. In the humble figure of the plowman, follower of St. Truth, he expresses his faith in the possibility of ultimate good in the common man, uncorrupted by the evils of wealth and high position; and from the legalistic tangle of ordinances governing good conduct, so wide-spread in his day, he extracts the simple rule of doing well, and offers the promise of eternal life. The utter simplicity and directness of this message reveal the author's own simple yet intense Christian faith. In spite of the evils in the world around him, which he boldly condemns, he presents to us his vision of an ideal Christian society, governed only by the law of Love, and nourished by Holy Church, the lovely lady who first called to him in his dream beside the brook in Malvern Hills.

[56]

BIBLIOGRAPHY

A͟L͟T͟H͟O͟U͟G͟H͟ this bibliography is necessarily select, some attempt has been made to include most of the recent studies of *Piers the Plowman* not to be found in the *Cambridge Bibliography of English Literature* (1941).

ABBREVIATIONS

EETS: Early English Text Society
ELH: Journal of English Literary History
JEGP: Journal of English and Germanic Philology
MLN: Modern Language Notes
MLQ: Modern Language Quarterly
MLR: Modern Language Review
MP: Modern Philology
N&Q: Notes and Queries
PMLA: Publications of the Modern Language Association
RES: Review of English Studies
SP: Studies in Philology
TLS: London *Times* Literary Supplement

I. MANUSCRIPTS

Bennett, J. A. W. A New Collation of a PP Manuscript [HM 137]. *Medium Aevum* XVII (1948), 21.

Chambers, R. W. The Manuscripts of PP in the Huntington Library, *Huntington Library Bulletin* No. 8 (Oct., 1935).

——. A PP Manuscript [NLW 733B]. *National Library of Wales Journal* II (1941–42), 42.

Grattan, J. H. G. A Newly Discovered Manuscript and its Affinities [Chaderton]. *MLR* XLII (1947), 1.

Haselden, R. B. The Fragment of PP in Ashburnham No. CXXX. *MP* XXIX (1931–32), 391.

Mitchell, A. G. A newly Discovered MS. of the C-text of PP. *MLR* XXXVI (1941), 243.

II. Editions

Crowley, Robert. London, 1550. [B-text]

Rogers, Owen. London, 1561. [B-text]

Whitaker, T. D. London, 1813. [C-text]

Wright, Thomas. London, 1842 (2nd ed. 1856; re-ed., 1895).
[B-text]

Skeat, Walter W. London, 1867–84. (*EETS* O. S. nos. 28, 38, 54,
67, 81). [A, B, & C-texts]

——. Oxford, 1886. [Parallel text edition in 2 vols.]

III. Modern Renderings

Attwater, Donald. London, 1930. [B-text]

Burrell, Arthur. London, New York, etc., 1912 (reprinted, 1931;
Everyman no. 571). [B-text]

Coghill, Nevill. Visions from PP. London, 1949.

Skeat, Walter W. London, 1905. [B-text]

Warren, K. M. London, 1895. (2nd ed., 1899; 1913). [B-text, pr.
and passus I-VII]

Webster, K. T. G. and W. A. Neilson. Two Middle English Poems.
Boston, New York, etc., 1917. [Sir Gawain and the Green
Knight, and PP A-text, pr. and passus I-VIII]

Wells, H. W. New York, 1935 (2nd ed., 1945). [a conflation]

Weston, J. L. Romance, Vision and Satire. Boston, 1912. [A-text,
pr. and passus I-VIII; also prologue to B-text]

IV. Text

Blackman, Elsie. Notes on the B-text MSS. of PP. *JEGP* XVII
(1918), 489.

Carnegy, F. A. R. An Attempt to Approach the C-text of PP.
London, 1934.

Chambers, R. W. and J. H. G. Grattan, The Text of PP. *MLR* IV
(1909), 357.

——. The Text of PP: Critical Methods. *MLR* XI (1916), 257.

——. The Text of PP. *MLR* XXVI (1931), 1.

Fowler, D. C. Contamination in Manuscripts of the A-text of PP.
PMLA LXVI (1951), 495.

[58]

Grattan, J. H. G. The Text of PP: Critical Lucubrations with Special Reference to the Independent Substitution of Similars. *SP* XLIV (1947), 593.

Kane, G. J. Problems and Methods of Editing the B-text. *MLR* XLIII (1948), 1.

Knott, Thomas A. An Essay toward the Critical Text of the A-version of PP. *MP* XII (1915), 389.

V. VERSE

Day, Mabel. Alliteration of the Versions of PP in its Bearing on their Authorship. *MLR* XVII (1922), 403.

Fischer, J. and F. Mennicken. Zur Mittelenglischen Stabzeile. *Bonner Beitrage zur Anglistik* XI (1901), 139.

Luick, K. Die Englische Stabreimzeile. II. William Langley und seine Schule. *Anglia* XI (1888–89), 429.

——. in Paul's *Grundriss der germanischen Philologie*, 2nd ed., vol. II², Strasburg, 1905 (p. 141).

Oakden, J. P. Alliterative Verse in Middle English. Manchester, 1930–35 (2 vols.).

Schipper, J. Englische Metrik. Bonn, 1881–88 (esp. # 95).

Schneider, A. Die Mittelenglische Stabzeile im 15. und 16. Jahrhundert. *Bonner Beitrage zur Anglistik* XII (1902), 103.

Schuhmacher, Karl. Studien über den Stabreim in der Me. Alliterationsdichtung. Bonn diss., 1913.

Stewart, G. R. Jr. The Meter of PP. *PMLA* XLII (1927), 113.

Teichman, E. Zur Stabreimzeile in William Langland's Buch von PP. *Anglia* XIII (1890–91), 140.

VI. GENERAL STUDIES

Donaldson, E. T. PP: the C-text and its Poet. New Haven, 1949.

Dunning, T. P. PP: an Interpretation of the A-text. London, New York, etc., 1937.

Jusserand, J. A. A. J. Les Anglais au Moyen Âge. L'Épopée Mystique de William Langland. Paris, 1893. [trans. New York, London, 1894]

Robertson, D. W. Jr. and B. F. Huppé. PP and Scriptural Tradition. Princeton, 1951.

Stone, G. W. An Interpretation of the A-text of PP. *PMLA* LIII (1938), 656.

VII. Dating

Bennett, J. A. W. The Date of the A-text of PP. *PMLA* LVIII (1943), 566.

——. The Date of the B-text of PP. *Medium Aevum* XII (1943), 55.

Cargill, Oscar. The Date of the A-text of PP. *PMLA* XLVII (1932), 354.

Coghill, N. K. The Abbot of Abington and the Date of the C-text. *Medium Aevum* IV (1935), 83.

Devlin, M. A. Date of the C-version of PP. Univ. of Chicago diss., 1928.

Gwynn, A., S. J. The Date of the B-text of PP. *RES* XIX (1943), 1.

Huppé, B. F. The A-text of PP and the Norman Wars. *PMLA* LIV (1939), 37.

——. The Date of the B-text of PP. *SP* XXXVIII (1941), 34.

——. PP: the Date of the B-text Reconsidered. *SP* XLVI (1949), 6.

VIII. Miscellaneous Studies

Adams, M. R. The Use of the Vulgate in PP. *SP* XXIV (1927), 556.

Ashton, J. R. Rymes of . . . Randolf, Erl of Chestre. *ELH* V (1938), 195.

Baum, P. F. The Fable of Belling the Cat. *MLN* XXXIV (1919), 462.

Bennett, J. A. W. Lombards' Letters. *MLR* XL (1945), 309.

Bloomfield, M. W. Present State of PP Studies. *Speculum* XIV (1939), 215.

von Bonsdorff, Ingrid. Hankyn or Haukyn? *MP* XXVI (1928–29), 57.

Brett, Cyril. Notes on Old and Middle English. *MLR* XXII (1927), 260.

Burdach, Konrad. Der Dichter des Ackermann aus Böhmen und

seine Zeit (*Vom Mittelalter zur Reformation*, [Berlin, 1926–32], III^2, p. 140).

Carnegy, F. A. R. The Relations between the Social and Divine Order in . . . PP. Breslau, 1934.

Chambers, R. W. Man's Unconquerable Mind. London, 1939.

——. Poets and their Critics: Langland and Milton. London, 1942.

Coghill, N. K. The Sexcentenary of William Langland. *London Mercury* XXVI (1932), 40.

——. Langland, the "Naket," the "Nauȝty," and the Dole. *RES* VIII (1932), 303. [A 7. 209]

——. Two Notes on PP. *Medium Aevum* IV (1935), 83.

——. The Pardon of PP. (Sir Israel Gollancz Memorial Lecture) *British Academy Proceedings* XXXI, 1945.

Dawson, C. H. Medieval Religion . . . and Other Essays. London, 1934. [pt. III: The Vision of PP]

Day, Mabel. "Mele Tyme of Seintes" (B 5. 500). *MLR* XXVII (1932), 317.

——. PP and Poor Relief. *RES* VIII (1932), 445.

Devlin, (Sister) Mary A. The Chronology of Bishop Brunton's Sermons. *PMLA* LI (1936), 300.

——. Bishop Thomas Brunton and his Sermons. *Speculum* XIV (1939), 324 (esp. p. 344).

Döring, G. Personennamen in Langland. Leipzig, 1922.

Dunning, T. P. Langland and the Salvation of the Heathen. *Medium Aevum* XII (1943), 45.

Fairchild, H. N. "Leyde here legges aliri" (A 7. 114). *MLN* XLI (1926), 378.

Frank, Robert W. The Conclusion of PP. *JEGP* XLIX (1950), 309.

——. The Number of Visions in PP. *MLN* LXVI (1951), 309.

——. The Pardon Scene in PP. *Speculum* XXVI (1951), 317.

Glunz, H. H. Die Literarästhetik der poetischen Rhetoric des Mittelalters. Bochum-Langendreer, 1937, p. 520.

Gwynn, A., S. J. Archbishop FitzRalph and the Friars. *Studies* XXVI (1937), 50.

[61]

Hanford, J. H. Dame Nature and Lady Life. [A 10. 27–34] *MP*
XV (1917–18), 313.

Hench, A. L. Dunmow Bacon, 1949. *College English* XI (1950),
350.

Hittmair, R. Der Begriff der Arbeit bei Langland. *Neusprachliche
Studien* Festgabe, Karl Luick (*Die Neueren Sprachen*, 6
Beiheft [1925]).

Hulbert, J. R. PP after Forty Years. *MP* XLV (1948), 215.

Huppé, B. F. "Petrus Id Est Christus": Word Play in PP, the
B-text. *ELH* XVII (1950), 163.

James, Stanley B. Back to Langland. London & Edinburgh, 1935.

Jones, H. S. V. Imaginatif in PP. *JEGP* XIII (1914), 583.

Kaske, R. E. The Use of Simple Figures of Speech in PP B . . .
SP XLVIII (1951), 571–600 (*Studies in Medieval Culture
Dedicated to George Raleigh Coffman*).

Kellogg, A. L. Satan, Langland, and the North. *Speculum* XXIV
(1949), 413.

Kellogg, E. H. Bishop Brunton and the Fable of the Rats. *PMLA*
L (1935), 57.

Kirk, Rudolph. References to the Law in PP. *PMLA* XLVIII
(1933), 322.

Kittner, Heinz. Studien zum Wortschatz William Langlands.
Würzburg, 1937.

Lawlor, John. PP: the Pardon Reconsidered. *MLR* XLV (1950),
449.

Maguire, Stella. The Significance of Haukyn, *Activa Vita*, in PP.
RES XXV (1949), 97.

Marcett, M. E. Uhtred de Boldon, Friar William Jordan, and PP.
New York, 1938.

Marx, Kitty. Das Nachleben von PP bis zu Bunyan's: The Pilgrim's Progress . . . Quakenbrück, 1931.

Meroney, Howard. The Life and Death of Long Wille. *ELH*
XVII (1950), 1.

Mitchell, A. G. The Text of PP. C prologue 1. 215. *Medium
Aevum* VIII (1939), 118.

Owst, G. R. The "Angel" and the "Goliardeys" of Langland's
Prologue. *MLR* XX (1925), 270.

Shute, H. W. [note on A 1. 38] *Archiv* C (1898), 155.

Sledd, J. H. [note on C 6. 65–9] *MLN* LV (1940), 379.

Spencer, H. "Worth both his Ears" [A pr. 75] *MLN* LVIII (1943), 48.

Stillwell, G. Chaucer's Plowman and the Contemporary English Peasant. *ELH* VI (1939), 285.

Sullivan, (Sister) Carmeline. . . . the Latin Insertions and the Macaronic Verse in PP. Washington, D. C., 1932.

Wells, H. W. The Construction of PP. *PMLA* XLIV (1929), 123.

IX. Comparisons

Chambers, R. W. Long Will, Dante and the Righteous Heathen. (in *Essays and Studies by members of the English Association*. Oxford, 1924. vol. 9, pp. 50–69).

Cornelius, R. D. PP and the Roman de Fauvel. *PMLA* XLVII (1932), 363.

Day, Mabel. Duns Scotus and PP. *RES* III (1927), 333.

Donna, (Sister) Rose B. Despair and Hope: A Study in Langland and Augustine. Washington, D. C., 1948 (Catholic University of America diss.).

Gaffney, Wilbur. The Allegory of the Christ Knight in PP. *PMLA* XLVI (1931), 155.

Iijima, Ikuzo. Langland and Chaucer . . . Boston, 1925.

Krog, Fritz. Studien zu Chaucer und Langland. Heidelberg, 1928.

Le May, (Sister) Marie d. L. The Allegory of the Christ Knight in English Literature. Washington, D. C., 1932.

Owen, D. L. PP. A Comparison with French Allegories. London, 1912; 1915.

Powell, C. L. The Castle of the Body. *SP* XVI (1919), 197.

Traver, H. The Four Daughters of God. Philadelphia, 1907.

X. Life, Education, Character, Views, the Times

Bloomfield, M. W. Was William Langland a Benedictine Monk? *MLQ* IV (1943), 57.

Bright, A. H. New Light on PP. London, 1928.

Chadwick, Dorothy. Social Life in the Days of PP. Cambridge, 1922.

Coghill, N. K. The Character of PP considered from the B-text. *Medium Aevum* II (1933), 108.

Durkin, J. T. Kingship in the Vision of PP. *Thought* XIV (1939), 413.

Eberhard, Oscar. Der Bauernaufstand vom Jahre 1381 in der englische Poesie. *Anglistische Forschungen*, LI, 1917.

Eliason, Mary H. Study of some Cultural Relations between Literature and History in the Third Estate of the 14th Century. University of North Carolina diss., 1938.

Gebhard, H. Langlands und Gowers Kritik der Kirchlichen Verhältnisse. Strasburg diss.; Homberg, 1911.

Gerould, G. H. The Structural Integrity of PP B. *SP* XLV (1948), 60.

Görnemann, Gertrud. . . . Zur Verfasserschaft und Entstehungsgeschichte von PP. Heidelberg, 1915.

Hort, Greta. PP and Contemporary Religious Thought. London, New York, 1938.

Jack, A. S. The Autobiographical Elements in PP. *JEGP* III (1900), 393.

Keiller, M. M. The Influence of PP on the Macro Play of *Mankind*. *PMLA* XXVI (1911), 339.

Macauley, G. C. The Name of the Author of PP. *MLR* V (1910), 195.

Owst, G. R. Preaching in Medieval England. Cambridge, 1926.

——. Literature and the Pulpit in Medieval England. Cambridge, 1933.

Sanderling, G. The Character " Liberum Arbitrium " in the C-text of PP. *MLN* LVI (1941), 449.

Wells, H. W. The Philosophy of PP. *PMLA* LIII (1938), 339.

Wiehe, H. PP und die sozialen Fragen seiner Zeit. Münster diss., 1935.

XI. Authorship Controversy

Bradley, H. The Misplaced Leaf of PP. *Athenaeum* 21 Apr., 1906, p. 481. Cf. also *Nation* (NY) 29 Apr., 1909, p. 436.

——. The Word " moillere " in PP. *MLR* II (1907), 163.

——. The Authorship of PP. *MLR* V (1910), 202.

——. Some Cruces in PP. *MLR* V (1910), 340.

——. Who Was John But? *MLR* VIII (1913), 88.

Brown, C. F. The "Lost Leaf" of PP. *Nation* (NY) 25 Mar., 1909, p. 298.

Cargill, Oscar. The Langland Myth. *PMLA* L (1935), 36.

Chambers, R. W. The Authorship of PP. *MLR* V (1910), 1.

——. The Original Form of the A-text of PP. *MLR* VI (1911), 302.

——. The Three Texts of PP and their Grammatical Forms. *MLR* XIV (1919), 129.

——. Incoherencies in the A– and B–texts of PP and their Bearing on the Authorship. *London Medieval Studies*, London, 1937, p. 27.

Coulton, G. C. PP, One or Five. *MLR* VII (1912), 102, 372.

Day, Mabel. The Revisions of PP. *MLR* XXIII (1928), 1.

Hall, T. D. Was Langland the Author of the C-text . . . ? *MLR* IV (1909), 1.

——. The Misplaced Lines, PP, (A) V, 236–41 [5. 228–33]. *MP* VII (1909–10), 327.

Hopkins, E. M. Who Wrote PP? (reprinted from *Kansas Univ. Quarterly*, April, 1898).

Huppé, B. F. The Authorship of the A and B Texts of PP. *Speculum* XXII (1947), 578.

Jusserand, J. J. PP. The Work of One or Five. *MP* VI (1908), 271.

——. PP. The Work of One or Five. A Reply. *MP* VII (1909–10), 289.

——. The PP Controversy. London and New York, 1910. (contains articles by Jusserand, Manly, Chambers, and Bradley. *EETS* O. S. 139b-f).

Knott, Thomas A. The "Lost Leaf" of PP. *Nation* (NY) 13 May, 1909, p. 482.

——. Observations on the Authorship of PP. A Reply to R. W. Chambers. *MP* XIV (1916–17), 531; XV (1917–18), 23.

Krog, F. Autobiographische oder Typische Zahlen in PP? *Anglia* LVIII (1934), 318.

Manly J. M. The Lost Leaf of PP. *MP* III (1906). 359.

——. PP and its Sequence. (in *Cambridge History of English Literature*, Cambridge, 1908, vol. II).

——. The Authorship of PP. *MP* VII (1909–10), 83.

——. The Authorship of PP. *MP* XIV (1916–17), 315.

Mensendieck, Otto. Die Verfasserschaft der drei Texte des PP. *Zeitschrift für Vergleichende Literatur* XVIII (1910), p. 10.

——. The Authorship of PP. *JEGP* IX (1911), 404.

Moore, Samuel. Studies in PP. *MP* XI (1913), 177; XII (1914), 19.

Rickert, E. John But, Messenger and Maker. *MP* XI (1913), 107.

Skeat, W. W. "John of Malvern" and PP. *Academy* vol. 43 (1893), 242.

Stroud, T. A. Manly's Marginal Notes on the PP Controversy. *MLN* LXIV (1949), 9.

Troyer, H. W. Who is PP? *PMLA* XLVII (1932), 368.

PIERS THE PLOWMAN

[*Prologus.*]

In a somer sesoun, whanne softe was the sonne,
I shop me in-to a shroud, as I a shep were;
In abite as an ermyte, unholy of werkis,
I wente wyde in this world, wondris to here.
But on a May morwenyng on Malverne hilles   5
Me befel a ferly, of fairie me thoughte.
I was wery for-wandrit and wente me to reste
Undir a brood bank be a bourne side;
And as I lay and lenide and lokide on the watris,
I slomeride in a slepyng, it swighede so merye.   10

  Thanne gan I mete a merveillous swevene,
That I was in a wildernesse, wiste I nevere where;
Ac as I beheld in-to the est, on heigh to the sonne,
I saigh a tour on a toft, trighely i-makid;   *Holy chirch*   *excellently*
A depe dale benethe, a dungeoun there inne,   15
With depe dikes and derke, and dredful of sight.
A fair feld ful of folk fand I there betwene,
Of alle maner of men, the mene and the riche,
Worching and wandringe, as the world askith.

  Summe putte hem to the plough, and pleighede ful selde,   20
In settyng and sowyng swonke ful harde
That many of thise wastores with glotonye destroigheth.
And summe putte hem to pride, aparailide hem there aftir,
In cuntenaunce of clothing comen disgisid.   *attire*
In preyores and penaunce putten hem manye,   25
Al for love of oure Lord lyvede ful streite,
In hope for to have hevene-riche blisse,
As ancris and ermytes that holden hem in here sellis,
Coveite not in cuntre to cairen aboute,
For no likerous liflode here likam to plese.   30

means of living líflāde

[67]

And somme chosen chaffare, thei cheven the betere,
As it semith to oure sight that suche men thriven.
And somme merthis to make, as mynstrales conne,
And gete gold with here gle, synneles, I trowe.   35
Ac japeris and jangleris, Judas children,
Founden hem fantasies and foolis hem make,
And have wyt at wille to wirche yif hem liste.
That Poule prechith of hem I dar not preve it here:
Qui loquitur turpiloquium is Luciferis hyne.   40
    Bidderis and beggeris faste aboute yede,
Til here belyes and here bagges were bretful ycrammid;
Fayteden for here foode, foughten at the ale;
In glotonye, God wot, go thei to bedde,
And risen up with ribaudie, tho roberdis knaves;
Slepe and sleuthe sewith hem evere.   45
    Pilgrimes and palmeris plighten hem togidere
For to seke Seint Jame and seintes at Rome;
Wenten forth in here wey with many wise talis,
And hadde leve to leighe al here lif aftir.
    Ermytes on an hep with hokide staves   50
Wenten to Walsyngham, and here wenchis aftir.
Grete lobies and longe, that loth were to swynke,
Clothide hem in copis to be knowen from othere;
Shopen hem ermytes, here ese to have.
    I fond there freris, alle the foure ordris,   55
Prechinge the peple for profit of here wombe,
Gloside the gospel as hem good likide,
For coveitise of copis construide it as thei wolde.
Manye of thise maistris mowe clothe hem at lyking,
For here mony and here marchaundise meten togidere.   60
Sith charite hath ben chapman, and chief to shryve lordis,
Manye ferlis han fallen in a few yeris;
But holy chirche and hy holden bet togidere,
The moste meschief on molde is mountyng up faste.

[68]

There prechide a pardoner, as he a prest were,   65
Broughte forth a bulle with bisshopis selis,
And seide that hym self mighte assoile hem alle
Of falsnesse of fastyng and of vowes broken.
Lewide men levide hym wel, and likide his speche,
Comen up knelynge to kissen his bulle;   70
He bunchide hem with his brevet, and bleride here eighe,
And raughte with his rageman ryngis and brochis.
Thus ye yeven youre gold glotonis to helpe,
And levith it loselis that leccherie haunten!
But were the bisshop yblissid and worth bothe hise eris,   75
His sel shulde not be sent to disseyve the peple.
It is not al be the bisshop that the boy prechith;
But the parissh prest and the pardoner parte the silver
That the pore peple of the parissh shulde have yif thei ne were.

Parsonis and parissh prestis pleynide hem to here bisshop,   80
That here parissh were pore siththe the pestilence tyme,
To have a licence and leve at Lundoun to dwelle,
To synge there for symonye, for silver is swete.

There hovide an hundrit in houvis of silk,
Serjauntis, it semide, that servide at the barre;   85
Pleden for penis and poundis the lawe,
And nought for love of oure Lord unlose here lippes ones.
Thou mightest betere mete the myst on Malverne hilles
Thanne gete a mom of here mouth til mony were shewid.

I saugh bisshopis bolde and bacheleris of devyn   90
Become clerkis of acountis, the king for to serve;
Archideknes and denis, that dignite haven
To preche the peple and pore men to fede,
Ben lopen to Lundoun, be leve of hire bisshopis,
And ben clerkis of the kinges bench, the cuntre to shende.   95

Barouns and burgeis, and bondemen also,
I saugh in that semble, as ye shuln here aftir,
Baxteris and bocheris, and breusteris manye,

Wollene websteris, and weveris of lynen,
Taillores and tokkeris, and tolleris bothe,   100
Masonis and mynours, and manye othere craftis,
As dikeris and delveris, that doth here dedis ille,
And driveth forth the longe day with *" Dieu save, dame Emme."*
Cookis and here knaves crieth, " Hote pyes, hote!
Goode gees and gris, gowe dyne, gowe! "   105
Taverners to hem tolde the same,
With white wyn of Osay, and wyn of Gascoyne,
Of the Ryn and of the Rochel, the rost to defie.
Al this I saugh slepyng, and sevene sithes more.

Primus passus de visione.

What this mounteyne bymenith, and ek the derke dale,
And ek the feld ful of folk, I shal yow faire shewe.
A lovely lady of lere, in lynene yclothid,
Com doun fro that clyf, and callide me faire,
And seide, " Sone, slepist thou? sest thou this peple   5
How besy thei ben aboute the mase?
The moste partie of this peple that passith on this erthe,
Have thei worsshipe in this world, kepe thei no betere;
Of other hevene thanne here holde thei no tale."
I was a-ferd of hire face, theigh heo fair were,   10
And seide, " Mercy, ma dame, what is this to mene? "
" The tour on the toft," quath heo, " Treuthe is there inne,
And wolde that ye wroughten as his word techith,
For he is fadir of feith, and fourmide yow alle
Bothe with fel and with face, and yaf yow fyve wyttes   15
For to worsshipe hym there with, whiles ye ben here;
And therfore he highte the erthe to helpe yow ichone
Of wollene, of lynene, to liflode at nede,
In mesurable maner, to make yow at ese,
And comaundite of his curteisie in comoun thre thinges;   20

[70]

Arn none nedful but tho, and nempne hem I thenke,
And rekne hem be resoun; reherse thou hem aftir:
  "That on is vesture, fro chele the to save;
That other is mete at meel, for myseise of thi selve;
And drink whanne thou drighest—ac do it nought out of resoun, 25
That thou worthe the wers whanne thou werche shuldist;
For Loth in his lyf dayes, for lykyng of drink,
Dede be his doughteris that the devil lykide,
Delyted him in drynke, as the devel wolde,
And leccherie hym laughte, and lay be hem bothe; 30
And al he wytide it wyn, that wykkide dede.
Dred delitable drynk, and thou shalt do the betere;
Mesure is medicine, theigh thou muche yerne;
Al is not good to the gost that the gut askith,
Ne liflode to the lykam, that lef is to the soule. 35
Leve not thi lycam, for a lighere hym techith,
That is the wrecchide world, the to betraye.
For the fend and thi flessh folewith togidere,
And that shent thi soule; set it in thin herte.
And for thou shuldist be war, I wisse the the beste." 40
  "A, ma dame, mercy," quath I, "me likith wel youre wordis;
Ac the money on this molde, that men so faste holdith,
Tel me to whom that tresour apendith."
  "Go to the gospel," quath heo, "that God seide him selven,
Tho the peple hym aposide with a peny in the temple, 45
Yif thei shulde worsshipe ther with Cesar the king.
And God askide of hem of whom spak the lettre,
And the ymage like, that there inne standis.
'Cesar,' thei seide, 'we se wel ichone.'
'*Reddite Cesari*,' quath God, 'that *Cesari* befallith, 50
Et que sunt dei deo, or ellis ye don ille.'
For rightfulliche resoun shulde rewele yow alle,
And kynde wyt be wardeyn, youre welthe to kepe,
And tutour of your tresour to take it yow at nede;

[71]

For husbondrie and he holden togideris."   55

    Thanne I fraynide hire faire, for him that hire made:
" The dungeon in the dale, that dredful is of sight,
What may it mene, ma dame, I the biseche? "

    " That is the castel of Care; who so comith there inne
May banne that he born was to body or to soule.   60
There inne wonith a wight that Wrong is yhoten,
Fadir of falshed—he foundede it hym selve.
Adam and Eve he eggide to ille;   *incite*
Counseilid Kaym to kiln his brother;
Judas he japide with Jewene silver,   65
And sithen on an ellir hongide him aftir.   *elder-tree*
He is lettere of love, leigheth hem alle;
That trusten on his tresour betraid arn sounest."

    Thanne hadde I wondir in my wyt what womman it were
That suche wise wordis of holy writ shewide;   70
And halside hire on the heighe name, er heo thennis yede,
What heo were witterly that wisside me so faire.   *assuredly*

    " Holy Chirche I am," quath heo, " thou aughtest me to knowe;
I undirfang the ferst, and thi feith taughte.
Thou broughtest me borewis, my biddyng to werche,   *pledge* 75
And to love me lelly, whiles thi lif durith."

    Thanne I knelide on my knes and crighide hire of grace,   *crien of crie*
Preighede hire pitously to preighe for my sennes,
And ek kenne me kyndely on Crist to beleve,
That I mighte werchen his wil that wroughte me to man.   80
" Teche me to no tresour, but tel me this ilke:
How I may saven my soule, that seint art yholden."

Lady:
on truth   " Whanne alle tresours arn trighed, treuthe is the beste;   *trien of trier*
I do it on *Deus caritas* to deme the sothe;
It is as derworth a dreury as dere God hym selven.   85
For who so is trewe of his tunge, tellith non other,
Doth the werkis ther with, wilneth no man ille—
He is a god be the gospel, on ground and on lofte,

[72]

And ek lyk to oure Lord, be Seint Lukis wordis.
The clerkis that knowe it shulde kenne it aboute,   90
For cristene and uncristene cleymeth it ichone.
Kinges and knightes shulde kepe it be resoun,
And riden and rappe doun in reaumes aboute,   *hasten*
And taken trespassours, and teighen hem faste,
Til treuthe hadde ytermined here trespas to the ende.   95
For David in hise dayes dubbide knightes,
Did hem swere on here swerd to serve treuthe evere;
That is the professioun apertly that apendith to knightes,
And nought to fasten a Friday in fyve score wynter;
But holde with hym and with hire that aske the treuthe,   100
And nevere leve hem for love ne lacching of yeftis;   *seizing of gifts*
And who so passith that poynt is *apostata* in his ordre.   *who does it*
And Crist, kingene king, knightide tene,   *? them*
Cherubyn and seraphyn, and such sevene other;
Yaf hem might in his mageste, the meryere hem thoughte,   105
And over his meyne made hem archaungelis;
Taughte hem thorugh the trinite the treuthe to knowe;
To be buxum at his bidding, he bad hem nought ellis.   *obedient*
Lucifer with legionis leride it in hevene,
And was the lovelokest of sight, aftir oure Lord,   110
Til he brak buxumnesse thorugh bost of hym selven;   *boast*
Thanne fil he with his felawis, and fendis bicome.   *fiend*
Out of hevene in-to helle hobelide thei faste,   *hobble, limp*
Summe in eir, summe in erthe, summe in helle depe;
Ac Lucifer lowest lith of hem alle;   115
For pride that he put out, his peyne hath non ende.
And alle that werchen with Wrong, wenden thei shuln,
Aftir here deth day, and dwelle with that shrewe.
Ac tho that werchen the word that holy writ techith,
And enden, as I er seide, in perfite werkis,   120
Mowe be sikur that here soule shal wende to hevene,
There Treuthe is in trinite, and tronen hem alle.

[73]

For-thi I seye, as I seide er, be sighte of thise textis,
Whanne alle tresours arn trighed, Treuthe is the beste.
Lerith it this lewide men, for lettrid it knowith,   125
That Treuthe is tresour, trighest on erthe."
      " Yet have I no kynde knowyng," quath I, " ye mote kenne me
Be what craft in my cors it compsith, and where."   [betere,
      " Thou dotide daffe," quath heo, " dulle arn thi wittes !
It is a kynde knowyng that kenneth in thin herte   130
For to love thi Lord levere thanne thi selve ;
No dedly synne to do, dighe theigh thou shuldist.
This, I trowe, be Treuthe ; who can teche the betere,
Loke thou suffre hym to seyn, and siththe lere it aftir.
For thus witnesseth his woord (werche thou ther aftir) :   135
That love is the levest thing that oure Lord askith,
And ek the plante of pes—preche it in thin harpe
Ther thou art mery at mete, yif men bidde the yedde.
For in kynde knowyng in herte ther comsith a might,
And that fallith to the fadir that fourmide us alle,   140
Lokide on us with love, and let his sone deighe
Mekliche for oure misdedis, to amende us alle ;
And yet wolde he hem no woo that wroughte him that pyne,
But mekly with mouthe mercy he besoughte,
To have pite on that peple that pynede hym to dethe.   145
Here might thou sen ensaumplis, in hym self one,
That he was mightful and mek, and mercy gan graunte
To hem that hongide him hyghe, and his herte thirlide.
For-thi I rede the riche, have reuthe on the pore ;
Theigh ye ben mighty to mote, beth mek of your werkis.   150
For the same mesour that ye mete, amys other ellis,
Ye shuln be weighe ther with, whanne ye wende hennes.
For theigh ye be trewe of youre tunge, and treweliche wynne,
And ek as chast as a child that in chirche wepith,
But yif ye love lelly and lene the pore,   155
Of such good as God sent goodlyche parten,

Ye ne have no more meryt in masse ne in oures
Thanne Malkyn of hire maidenhod, that no man desirith.
For James the jentil juggide in his bokis,
That feith withoute fait is feblere than nought,   160
And ded as a dorenail, but yif the dede folewe.
Chastite withoute charite worth cheynide in helle;
It is as lewid as a laumpe that no light is inne.
Manye chapellenis arn chast, ac charite is aweye;
Arn none hardere than heo whanne heo ben avauncid,   165
Unkynde to here kyn and to alle cristene,
Chewen here charite and chiden aftir more;
Such chastite withoute charite worth cheynid in helle.
Ye curatours that kepe yow clene of your bodies,
Ye ben acumbrid with coveitise, ye conne not out crepe,   170
So harde hath avarice haspide yow togideris!
That is no treuthe of trinite, but treccherie of helle,
And a lerning to lewide men the lattere to dele.
For thise ben the wordis writen in the Evaungelie:
' *Date et dabitur vobis,* for I dele yow alle;   175
That is the lok of love that letith out my grace
To counforte the carful acumbrid with synne.'
Love is the leveste thing that oure Lord askith,
And ek the graith gate that goth in-to hevene.
For-thi I seighe as I seide er, be sighte of the tixtes,   180
Whan alle tresouris arn trighede, Treuthe is the beste.
Now have I told the what Treuthe is, that no tresour is betere,
I may no lengere lenge; now loke the oure Lord."

Passus secundus de visione.

Yet knelide I on my knes, and crighede hire of grace,
And seide, " Mercy, ma dame, for Marie love of hevene,
That bar that blisful barn, that boughte us on the rode,
Kenne me be sum craft to knowe the False."

[75]

PRIDE

Lady: "Loke on thi left half, and lo, where he standis,   5
Bothe Fals and Favel, and hise feris manye!"
I lokide on my left half, as the lady me taughte,
And was war of a womman wondirliche clothide,
Ipurfilid with pelure, the pureste upon erthe,
Icorounid with a coroune, the king hath non betere.   10
Alle here fyve fyngris were frettid with rynges
Of the pureste perreighe that prince werde evere;
In red scarlet robid, and ribande with gold;
There is no quen queyntere that quyk is o lyve.
    "What is this womman," quath I, "so worthily atirid?"   15
    "That is Mede, the maide," quath she, "hath noighede me ful
And lakkide my lore to lordis aboute.   [ofte,
In the popis paleis heo is prevy as my selve,
And so shulde heo not be, for Wrong was hire sire;
Out of Wrong heo wox, to wrotherhele manye.   20
I aughte ben highere thanne heo; I com of a betere.
To-morewe worth the mariage mad of Mede and of Fals;
Favel, with fair speche, hath forgid hem togidere,
Gile hath begon hire so, heo grauntith alle his wille,
And al is Ligheris ledyng that hy lighen togideris.   25
To-morewe worth the mariage ymad, as I the telle;
There mighte thou wyte, yif thou wilt, whiche thei ben alle
That longith to that lordsshipe, the lasse and the more.
Knowe hem there yif thou canst, and kep the from hem alle,
Yif thou wilnest to wone with Treuthe in his blisse;   30
I may no lengere lette—oure Lord I the bekenne,
And become a good man for any coveitise, I rede."
    Alle the riche retenaunce that regnith with False
Were boden to the bridale on bothe two sides.
Sire Symonye is of-sent to assele the chartres   35
That Fals and Favel be any fyn halden,
And feffe Mede ther with, in mariage for evere.
Ther nas halle ne hous to herberwe the peple

[77]

That iche feld nas ful of folk al aboute.

In myddis a mounteyne, at mydmorewe tide,   40
Was pight up a pavyloun, proud for the nones;
And ten thousand of tentis teldit beside,
Of knightes of cuntré, of comeres aboute,
For sisours, for somenours, for selleris, for byggeris,
For lerid, for lewid, for laboureris of thropis,   45
Alle to wytnesse wel what the writ wolde,
In what maner that Mede in mariage was feffid;
To be fastnid with Fals the fyn is arerid.

Thanne Favel fettith hire forth, and to Fals takith,
In foreward that Falshed shal fynde hire for evere,   50
And heo be bounde at his bode his bidding to fulfille,
At bedde and at boord, buxum and hende,
And as Sire Symonye wile segge, to sewen his wille.
Symonye and Cyvyle stondith forth bothe,
And unfolde the feffement that Fals hath ymakid,   55
And thus begynne thise gomes and gredde wel heighe:

    "Wyten and wytnessen, that wonen upon erthe,
That I, Favel, feffe Falsnesse to Mede,
To be present in pride, for pore or for riche,
With the erldom of Envye for evere to laste,   60
With alle the lordsshipe of Leccherie, in lengthe and in brede,
With the kingdom of Coveitise I croune hem togidere,
And al the ile of Usurie and Avarice the faste,
Glotonye and grete othes I gyve hem togidere,
With alle the delites of lust the devil for to serve,   65
In al the seignourie of Slouthe I sese hem togidere,
Thei to have and to holde, and here eires aftir,
With alle the purtenaunce of purgatorie, in-to the pyne of helle:
Yeldinge for this thing, at o yeris ende,
Here soulis to Sathanas, to synken in pyne,   70
There to wone with Wrong, while God is in hevene."

    In witnesse of whiche thing Wrong was the furste,

[78]

And Piers the pardoner, Poulynes doctor,
Bette the bedel, of Bokyngham shire, *oE bydel = crier, herald*
Randolf the reve, of Rutelondis sokne, *O E sōcn = soke,* 75 *jurisdiction, territory*
Munde the mylnere, and manye mo othere.
In the date of the devil the dede was asselid, *sealed*
Be sighte of Sire Symonye and signes of notories. *signatures > oF signe*

    Thanne tenide hym Theologie, whan he this tale herde, *tenen = vex, make angry*
And seide to Cyvyle, " Now sorewe on thi bokes   80 *> OE teona, tynan*
Such weddyng to werche to wraththe with Treuthe;
And er this weddyng be wrought, wo the betide!
For Mede is moylere of Mendes engendrit; *legitimately born*
God grauntith to gyve Mede to Treuthe,
And thou hast gyven hire to a gilour—now God yive the sorewe! 85 *> oF guileor*
The texte tellith not so, Treuthe wot the sothe:
    Dignus est operarius mercede sua.
'Worthi is the werkman his huyre to have.' *hire = O E hȳr*
And thou hast fastnid hire with Fals—fy on thi lawe!
For al be lesinges thou lyvest, and leccherous werkis;
Symonye and thi self shenden holy chirche;   90
Ye and the notories noye the peple.
Ye shuln abigge it bothe, be God that me made!
Wel ye wyte, wernardis, but yif youre wyt faile,
That Fals is a faitour, and feithles of werkis,
And as a bastard yborn of Belsaboubis kynne.   95
And Mede is a moylere, a maydene of goode;
She mighte kisse the king for cosyn, yif she wolde.
Werchith be wysdom, and be wyt aftir:
Ledith hire to Lundoun, there lawe is yhandlit,
Yif any leaute wile loke thei ligge togidere.   100
And yif the justice jugge hire to be joyned with Fals,
Yet be war of the weddyng, for witty is Treuthe;
For Consience is of his counseil, and knowith yow ichone;
And yif he fynde yow in defaute, and with the Fals holden,
It shal besette youre soulis wel sore at the laste."   105

Here-to assentith Cyvyle, ac Symonye ne wolde
Til he hadde silver for his selis and signes.
Thanne fette Favel forth floreynes ynowe,
And bad Gile go gyve gold al aboute,
And nameliche to the notories, that hem non failide;   110
And feffe False-wytnesse with floreynes ynowe—
" For he may Mede amaistrien, and maken at my wille."
    Tho this gold was gyve, gret was the thonking
To False and to Favel for here faire yeftis;
And comen to counforte fro care the False,   115
And seide, " Certis, cese shuln we nevere
Til Mede be thi weddit wyf, thorugh wyt of us alle;
For we have Mede amaistried with oure mery speche
That she grauntith to gon with a good wille
To Lundoun to loke yif that the lawe wolde   120
Juggen yow joyntly in joye for evere."

judge

    Thanne was Fals fayn, and Favel als blithe,
And let somoune alle the segges in shires abouten,

>ON béíinn
ready

And alle be boun, beggeris and othere,
To wende with hem to Westmynstre, to wytnesse this dede.   125
Thanne caride hy for capelis to carien hem thider;
Thanne Favel fette forth folis of the beste,
And sette Mede on a shirreve, shod al newe,   *OE scir gerēfa = sheriff*
And Fals sat on a sisour that softeliche trottide,   *reeve*
And Favel on a fair speche, fetisliche atirid.   130
Tho hadde notories none, anoyed thei were,
That Symonye and Cyvyle shulde on here fet gange.
Thanne swor Cyvyle, and seide be the rode,
That somenours shulde be sadelit and serve hem ichone—
" And let apparaille thise provisours in palfreis wise;   135
Sire Symonye hym self shal sitte on here bakkis,
And alle the denis and sudenis as destreris hem dighte,
For thei shuln bere thise bisshopis and bringe hem to reste.
Paulynes peple, for pleyntes in constorie,

Shuln serve my self, that Cyvyle hatte;   140
And let cartesadil the comissarie—oure carte shal he drawe,
And fetten oure vitailes of fornicatouris;
And makith of Lyere a lang carte, to leden al this othere,
As folis and faitours that on here feet rennen."

    Fals and Favel farith forth togidere,   145
And Mede in the myddis, and al the meyne aftir.
I have no tom to telle the tail that hem folewith,
Of many maner of men that on this molde libbeth;
Ac Gile was forgoere and gyede hem alle.   *guide*
Sothnesse seigh hem wel and seide but litel,   150
But prikede on his palfray, and passide hem alle,
And come to the kinges court, and Consience tolde,
And Consience to the king carpide it aftir.

    "Be Crist," quath the king, "and I mighte cacche
Fals other Favel, other any of his feris,   155
I wolde be wroken of tho wrecchis that werchen so ille, *O E wrecan*
And do hem hange be the hals, and alle that hem mayntenith;
Shal nevere man on this molde meynprise the leste, *go bail*
But right as the lawe lokis, let falle on hem alle!" *> main · prendre*
And comaundite a cunstable, that com at the ferste,   160
To "atache thise tirauntis, for any tresour, I hote;
Feterith Falsnesse faste, for any kynnes yeftis,
And gurdith of Giles hed, let hym go no ferthere;   *stroke off*
And bringeth Mede to me, maugre hem alle.
Symonye and Cyvyle, I sende hem to warne   165
That holy chirche for hem worth harmid for evere.
And yif ye lacche Leighere, let him not askape,
Er he be put on the pillorie, for any preyour, I hote."

    Dreed at the dore stood and that doom herde,
And wightliche wente to warne the False,   170
And bad hym fle for fer, and hise feris alle.
Thanne Falsnesse for feer fleigh to the freris,
And Gile doth him to go, agast forto deighe;

[81]

Ac marchauntis mette with hym, and made him abide,
Besshette hym in here shoppis to shewen here ware,   175
Aparailide hym as a prentice the peple to serve.
Lightliche Lighere lep awey thennes,
Lurkyng thorugh lanes, to-luggid of manye.
He was nowhere welcome, for his many talis,
Overal yhuntid and yhote trusse;   180
Til pardoners hadde pite, and pulden him to house,
Wosshen hym and wypide him and wounde hym in cloutis,
And senten hym on Sundais with selis to chirchis,
And yaf pardoun for panis, poundmel aboute.
Thanne louride lechis, and lettris hy sente,   185
For to wone with hem, watris to loke.
Spiceris speke with hym, to aspie here ware,
For he coude on here craft, and kneugh manye gommes.
Mynstrales and messangeris mette with him ones,
And withheld him half a yer and ellevene dayes.   190
Freris, with fair speche, fetten hym thennes,
For knowing of comeris, copide hym as a frere;
Ac he hath leve to lepen out, as ofte as him likith,
And is welcome whanne he wile, and wonith with hem ofte.
Alle fledden for fer and flowen into hernis;   195
Save Mede the maide, no mo durste abide.
Ac trewely to telle, heo tremblide for fere,
And ek wep and wrang, whan heo was atachid.

Passus tercius de visione.

Now is Mede the maide, and no mo of hem alle,
With bedelis and baillifs ybrought to the king.
The king callide a clerk—I can not his name—
To take Mede the maide, and make hire at ese:
" I wile assaie hire my self, and sothly apose   5
What man of this world that hire were levist;

LECHERY

And yif heo werche be my wyt, and my wil folewe,
I wile forgyve hire this gilt, so me God helpe."
  Curteisliche the clerk thanne, as the king highte,
Tok Mede be the myddel, and broughte hire to chaumbre.   10
Ac there was merthe and mynstralcie Mede to plese;
Thei that wonith at Westmenstre worsshipeth hire alle.
Jentily with joye, the justices somme
Buskide hem to the bour, there the byrde dwellide;
Counfortide hire kyndely, be clergies leve,   15
And seide, " Mourne nought, Mede, ne make thou no sorewe;
For we wile wisse the king and thi wey shapen,
For al Consience caste a craft, as I trowe."
  Mildeliche Mede thanne merciede hem alle
Of here grete goodnesse, and yaf hem ichone   20
Coupis of clene gold, and pecis of silver,
Rynges with rubies, and ricchesses manye;
The leste man of here mayne a motoun of gold.
Thanne laughte hy leve, thise lordis at Mede.
  With that come clerkis to conforten hire the same,   25
And beden hire be blythe—" for we ben thin owene
For to werche thi wil, while oure lif lastith."
Hendely thanne heo behighte hem the same,
To love hem lelly and lordis hem make,
And in constory at court callen here names: 30
" Shal no lewidnesse hym lette, the lede that I love,
That he ne worth ferst avauncid; for I am beknowe
There cunnyng clerkis shuln clokke behynde."
  Thanne com there a confessour, ycopid as a frere;
To Mede the maiden mekeliche he loutide,   35
And seide ful softely, in shrifte as it were,
" Theigh lerid and lewide hadde leighe be the ichone,
And theigh Falshed hadde folewid the this fiftene wynter,
I shal assoile the my self, for a sem of whete,
And ek be thi baudekyn, and bere wel thin erande   40

[84]

Among clerkis and knightes, Consience to felle."
Thanne Mede, for hire mysdedis, to that man knelide,
And shrof hire of hire shrewidnesse, shameles, I trowe;
Tolde hym a tale, and tok hym a noble,
For to be hire bedeman, and hire baude aftir.   45
Thanne he assoilide hire sone, and sithen he seide,
" We have a wyndowe in werching, wile stonde us ful heighe;
Woldist thou glase the gable, and grave therin thin name,
Sikir shulde thi soule be hevene to have."
" Wiste I that," quath the womman, " there nis wyndowe ne auter 50
That I ne shulde make or mende, and myn name writen,
That iche segge shal se I am sistir of your hous."
    Ac God to alle good folk such gravyng defendith,
And seith, *Nesciat sinistra quid faciat dextera*:
" Let not thi left hond, late ne rathe,
Be war what thi right hond werchith or delith."   55
Ac so prevyliche parte it that pride be not seighe
Neither in sight ne in soule; for God hym self knowith
Who is curteis or kynde, coveitous or ellis.
For-thi I lere yow lordis, levith such wrytyng,
To writen in wyndowis of youre wel dedis,   60
Or to grede aftir Godis men whan ye yive dolis;
An aunter ye have youre hire therof here.
For oure saviour it seide, and hym self prechide:
    Amen, amen dico vobis, receperunt mercedem suam.
    Meiris and maistris, hij that ben mene
Betwyn the king and the comunes, to kepe the lawis,   65
As to punisshen on pillories, and on pynyng-stolis,
Breowesters and bakeris, bocheris and cokes—
For thise arn men on thise molde that most harm werchith
To the pore peple that parcel-mel biggen.
For thei poisone the peple prevyly and ofte,   70
And richen thorugh regraterie, and rentis hem biggen
With that the pore peple shulde putte in here wombe.

For tok thei on trewely, thei tymbride not so heighe,
Ne boughte no burgages, be ye wel certayn!
 Ac Mede the maide the mair heo besoughte   75
Of alle suche selleris silver to take,
Or presauntis withoute panis, as pecis of silver,
Rynges or other richesse, the regratouris to meynteyne.
" For my love," quath that lady, " love hem ichone,
And suffre hem to selle sum-del ayens resoun."   80
 Salamon the sage, a sarmon he made,
For to amende meiris and men that kepith lawis,
And tolde hem this teeme that I telle thinke:
 Ignis devorabit tabernacula eorum qui libenter accipiunt munera.
Among thise lettride lordis this Latyn amountith
That fuyr shal falle and forbrenne at the laste   85
The houses and the homes of hem that desiren
To have yeftis for here service in youthe or in elde.
 The king fro counseil com, and callide aftir Mede,
And of-sente hire as swithe; serjauntis hire fecche,
And broughte hire to boure with blisse and with joye. 90
Curteysly the king compsith to telle,
To Mede the maide melis thise wordis:
" Unwittily, womman, wrought hast thou ofte;
Ac wers wroughtest thou nevere than whanne thou Fals toke.
Ac I forgyve the that gilt, and graunte the my grace; 95
Henis to thi deth day do thou so nomore.
I have a knight hatte Consience, com late fro beyonde;
Yif he wilneth the to wyve, wilt thou hym have?"
 " Ya, lord," quath that lady, " Lord forbede ellis;
But I be holy at youre heste, let hange me sone."   100
Thanne was Consience callid to comen and aperen
Before the kyng and his counseil, clerkis and othere.
Knelynge, Consience to the kyng loutide,
To wite what his wille were, and what he do shulde.
 " Wilt thou wedde this womman, yif I wile assente? 105

For heo is fayn of thi felasshipe, for to be thi make."
   Quath Consience to the kyng, " Crist it me forbede!
Er I wedde such a wif, wo me betide!
She is freel of hire feith, fikel of hire speche;
She makith men mysdo manye score tymes;   110
In trust of hire tresour she tenith ful manye.
Wyves and wydewis wantonnesse she techith;
Lerith hem leccherie that lovith hire yeftis;
Youre fadir she fellide thorugh false behestis;
Apoisonide popis, apeiride holy chirche.   115
Is not a betere baude, be hym that me made,
Betwyn hevene and helle and erthe theigh men soughte.
She is tykil of hire tail, talewys of hire tunge,
As comoun as the cartewey to knaves and to alle;
To monkis, to mynstrelis, to myselis in heggis.   120
Sisours and sompnours—suche men hire preisith;
Shirreves of shires were shent yif heo ne were.
She doth men lese here land, and here lif bothe,
And letith passe prisoners, and paieth for hem ofte,
And yiveth the gaileris gold, and grotis togidere,   125
To unfetere the fals, fle where hym lykith.
She takith the trewe be the top, and teigheth hym faste,
And hangith hym for hattrede that harmide nevere.
To be cursid in constorie heo countith not a risshe,
For heo copith the comissarie, and cotith hise clerkis;   130
Heo is assoilid as sone as hire self likith.
She may neigh as muche do in a moneth ones
As youre secret sel in seve score dayes.
She is prevy with the pope, provisours it knowith;
Sire Symonye and hire self selith the bullis.   135
She blissith thise bisshopis, theigh thei be lewid;
Provendrours parsones, and prestis she mayntenith
To holde lemmanis and lotebies alle here lif dayes,
And bringen forth barnes ayens forboden lawis.

There she is wel with the king, wo is the reaume; 140
For she is favourable to Fals, and foulith Treuthe ofte.
Barouns and burgeis she bringeth in sorewe;
Be Jesu, with hire juelx youre justices she shendith,
And leith ayen the lawe, and lettith the treuthe,
That feith may not have his forth, hire floreynes go so thikke. 145
She ledith the lawe as hire list, and lovedaies makith,
The mase for a mene man, theigh he mote evere.
Lawe is so lordlich, and loth to maken ende,
Withoute presentis or panis heo plesith wel fewe.
Clergie and coveitise heo couplith togidere. 150
This is the lif of that lady, now Lord yif hire sorewe!
And alle that meyntenith hire men, meschaunce hem betide!
For povere men mowe have no power to pleyne, theigh hem smerte,
Such a maister is Mede among men of goode."

Thanne mournide Mede, and menide hire to the king, 155
To have space to speke, spede yif she mighte.
The king grauntide hire grace with a good wille:
"Excuse the, yif thou canst—I can no more seighe;
For Consience acusith the, to cunge the for evere."

"Nay, lord," quod that lady, "leve him the werse 160
Whanne ye wyte wytterly where the wrong liggeth.
There that meschief is gret, Mede may helpe;
And thou knowist, Consience, I cam nought for to chide,
Ne to deprave thi persone with a proud herte.
Wel thou wost, Consience, but yif thou wilt leighe, 165
Thou hast hongid on myn half ellevene tymes,
And ek gripen my gold, and gyve it where the likide.
Why thou wraththest the now, wondir me thinkith;
Yet I may, as I mighte, menske the with yeftis,
And maynteyne thi manhod more than thou knowist. 170
And thou hast famide me foule before the king here,
For kilde I nevere no king, ne counseilide ther aftir;
Ne dide as thou demist, I do it on the king.

" In Normandie was he nought anoyed for my sake;
Ac thou thi self, sothly, asshamidest hym ofte,   175
Crope in-to a caban, for cold of thi nailes,
Wendist that wynter wolde han last evere,
And dreddist to be ded for a dym cloude,
And hastidest the homward for hunger of thi wombe.
Withoute pite, thou pilour, pore men thou robbidest,   180
And bar here bras on thi bak to Caleis to selle.
There I lefte with my lord, his lif for to save,
And made hym merthe, mournyng to lete,
And bateride hym on the bak, boldite his herte,
Dede hym hoppe for hope to have me at wille.   185
Hadde I be marchal of his men, be Marie of hevene,
I durste han leid my lif, and no lesse wed,
He shulde have be lord of that lond, in lengthe and in brede,
And ek king of that kith, his kyn for to helpe;
The leste brol of his blood a barouns pere.   190
Cowardly, thou Consience, consayldist him thennes,
To leven his lordsshipe for a litel silver,
That is the riccheste reaume that reyn over-hovith!
  " It becomith to a king that kepith a reaume
To yiven meede to men that mekly hym serven;   195
To alienes, to alle men, to honoure hem with yeftis.
Mede makith hym be lovid and for a man holde.
Emperours and erlis, and alle maner lordis,
Thorough yeftis han yonge men to renne and to ride.
The pope and his prelatis presentis undirfongith,   200
And medith men hem selven to mayntene here lawis.
Servauntis for here servyse—we se wel the sothe—
Takith mede of here maistris as thei mowe accorde.
Beggeris for here bidding biddith men mede;
Mynstrales for here merthe, mede thei asken.   205
The king hath mede of his men to make pes in londis;
Men that ben clerkis craven of hym mede.

Prestis that preche the peple to goode
Asken mede and messe penis and here mete alse.
Alle kyn crafty men crave mede for here prentis;   210
Mede and marchaundise mote nede go togidere.
No wight, as I wene, withoute mede mighte libbe."
   Quath the king to Consience, " Be Crist, as me thinkith,
Mede is worthi the maistrie to have ! " succes in the lansuit [erthe,
   " Nay," quath Consience to the king, and knelide to the   215
" There beth two maner of medis, my lord, be your leve.
That on God of his grace gyveth, in his blisse,
To hem that wel werchen whiles thei ben here.
The prophet prechide it, and put it in the Sauter :
   Qui pecuniam suam non dedit ad usuram, &c.
Tak no mede, my lord, of men that ben trewe ;   220
Love hem and lene hem, for oure Lordis love of hevene.
Godis mede and his mercy ther with mighte thou wynne.
There is a mede mesurles that maistris desirith ;
To mayntene mysdoeris mede thei taken.
And ther of seith the Sauter in a salmis ende :   225
   In quorum manibus iniquitates sunt ; dextera eorum repleta
      est muneribus.
And he that gripith here giftes, so me God helpe,
Shal abighe it bitterly, or the bok ligheth.
Prestis and personis that plesing desirith,
That take mede and money for massis that thei synge,
Shal have mede on this molde that Mattheu hath grauntid : 230
   Amen, amen, receperunt mercedem suam.
That laboureris and lough folk taken of here maistris,
It is no maner mede, but a mesurable hire.
In marchaundise is no mede, I may it wel avowe ;
It is a permutacioun, apertly, a peny-worth for a-nother.
Ac reddist thou nevere *Regum,* thou recreighede Mede,   235
Why the vengeaunce fel on Saul and on his children ?
God sente hym to segge, be Samuels mouthe,

That Agag of Amalek, and al his peple aftir,
Shulde dighe for a dede that don hadde his eldren
Ayens Israel, and Aaron, and Moyses his brother.   240
Samuel seide to Saul, 'God sendith the and hotith
To be buxum and boun his bidding to fulfille:
Wende thidir with thin ost wommen to kille;
Children and cherles, choppe hem to dethe;
Loke thou kille the king, coveite nought hise godis   245
For any mylionis of money; murdre hem ichone,
Barnes and bestis, brenne hem to dethe.'
And for he kilde not the king, as Crist him bode sente,
Coveitide here catel, kilde nought hire bestis,
But broughte with hym the bestis, as the bible tellith,   250
God seide to Samuel that Saul shulde deighe,
And al his sed for that synne shendfully ende.
Such a meschef Mede made the kyng to have,
That God hatide hym for evere, and alle hise heires aftir.
The *culorum* of this kepe I not to shewe;   255
An aunter it noighide me, an ende wile I make.
I, Consience, knowe this, for kynde wit me taughte,
That resoun shal regne, and reaumes governe;
And right as Agag hadde, happen shal somme;
Samuel shal slen hym, and Saul shal be blamid,   260
And David shal be dyademid and daunten hem alle,
And on cristene king kepe us ichone.
Shal no more Mede be maister on erthe,
But love and loughnesse and leaute togideris.
And who so trespassith to trewthe, or takith ayens his wille,   265
Leaute shal do hym lawe, or lese his lif ellis.
Shal no serjaunt for that servyse were a silk houve, *Haube*
Ne no ray robe with riche pelure.
Mede of mysdoeris makith hem so riche
That lawe is lord waxen, and leaute is pore.   270
Unkyndenesse is comaundour, and kyndenesse is banisshit.

[91]

Ac kynde wyt shal come yet, and consience togidere,
And make of lawe a labourer, such love shal arise."

Passus quartus de visione.

"Sessith," seide the king, "I suffre yow no lengere.
Ye shuln saughten, for sothe, and serve me bothe.
Kisse hire," quath the king, "Consience, I hote."
  "Nay, be Crist," quath Consience, "cunge me rathere;
But Resoun rede me ther to, arst wole I deighe." 5
  "And I comaunde the," quath the king to Consience thanne,
"Rape the to riden, and Resoun that thou fecche;
Comaunde hym that he come, my counseil to here.
For he shal rewele my reaume, and rede me the beste
Of Mede and of othere mo, what man shal hire wedde; 10
And acounte with the, Consience—so me Crist helpe—
How thou lerist the peple, the lerid and the lewid."
  "I am fayn of that foreward," seith the freke thanne,
And rit right to Resoun, and rounith in his ere,
Seide as the king sente, and siththe tok his leve. 15
  "I shal araye me to ride," quath Resoun; "reste the a while,"
And calde Catoun his knave, curteis of speche:
"Sette my sadil upon Suffre-til-I-se-my-tyme,
And let warroke hym wel with witful gerthis;
Hange on hym the hevy bridel to holde his hed lowe; 20
Yet wile he make many 'wehe,' er we come there."
  Thanne Consience on his capil carieth forth faste,
And Resoun with hym rit, and rapith hym swythe;
Ac one Waryn Wisdom, and Witty his fere,
Folewide hem faste, for hy hadden to done 25
In cheker and in chauncerie, to be dischargid of thinges;
And riden faste, for Resoun shulde rede hem the beste
For to save hem self from shame and from harmes.
Ac Consience com arst to court be a myle wey,

[92]

ENVY

And romide forth with Resoun right to the king.   30
Curteisliche the king thanne com in to Resoun,
And betwyn hym self and his sone sette hym on benche,
And wordiden a gret while wel wisly togidere.
    Thanne com Pes in to parlement, and putte up a bille,
How Wrong ayen his wil hadde his wyf take;   35
And how he ravisshide Rose, Reynaldis love,
And Margerete of hire maydenhod, maugre hire chekis.
" Bothe my gees and my gris hise gadelynges fecchen;
I dar not for fer of hym fighte ne chide.
He borewide of me Bayard, and broughte him nevere ayen,   40
Ne no ferthing therfore, for nought I couthe plede.
He mayntenith his men to murthre myne hynen,
Forstallith my feiris, fighteth in my chepyng,
Brekith up my berne doris, and berith awey my whete,
And takith me but a taile for ten quarteris otis.   45
And yet he betith me ther-to, and lith be my maiden;
I am not so hardy for hym unnethe to loke."
    The king kneugh he seide soth, for Consience hym tolde.
Wrong was aferd tho, and Wisdom he soughte
To make his pes with his panis, and profride hym manye;   50
And seide, " Hadde I love of my lord the king, litel wolde I recche,
Theigh Pees and his power pleynide hem evere."
    Wysdom wan tho, and so dede Wyt also,
For that Wrong hadde wrought so wykkide a dede,
And warnide Wrong tho, with suche a wys tale: 55
" Who so werchith be wil wraththe makith ofte;
I sey it be thi self, thou shalt it sone fynde.
But yif Mede it make, thi meschief is uppe;
For bothe thi lyf and thi lond lith in his grace."
Wrong thanne on Wysdom wepide hym to helpe,   60
For of hise penys he proffride hise handy-dandy to paye.
Thanne Wisdom and Wyt wente togidere,
And nomen Mede with hem mercy to wynne.

[94]

Pees putte forth his hed and his panne blody:
"Withoute gilt, God wot, gat I this skathe."   65
Consience and the king knewen wel the sothe,
And wisten wel that Wrong was a shrewe evere.
Ac Wisdom and Wyt were aboute faste
To overcome the king with catel yif thei mighte.
The king swor be Crist, and be his croune bothe,   70
That Wrong for his werkes shulde wo thole,
And comaundide a constable to casten hym in irens:
"He shal not this seven yer se hise feet ones!"

   "God wot," quath Wysdom, "that were not the beste;
And he amendis mowe make, let maynprise hym have,   75
And be borugh for his bale, and biggen hym bote,
And amende that mysdede, and evere more the betere."
Wyt accordide there with and seide the same:
"Betere is that boote bale adoun bringe,
Thanne bale be bet, and bote nevere the betere."   80
Thanne gan Mede to meke hire, and mercy besoughte,
And profride Pees a presaunt al of purid gold:
"Have this of me, man," quath heo, "to amende thi skathe,
For I wile wage for Wrong, he wile do so nomore."

   Pees thanne pitousliche preyede to the king   85
To have mercy on that man, that mysdede hym ofte:
"For he hath wagid me wel, as Wysdom hym taughte,
I forgyve hym that gilt with a good wille;
So that ye assente, I can sey nomore,
For Mede hath mad me amendis, I may no more axen."   90

   "Nay," quath the king tho, "so God yive me blisse!
Wrong wendith not so awey, er I wyte more;
Leep he so lightly awey, laughen he wolde,
And eft the baldere be to beten myn hynen;
But Resoun have reuthe on hym, he shal reste in the stokkis   95
As longe as I lyve, but more love it make."

   Thanne summe redde Resoun to have reuthe on that shrewe,

[95]

And to counseile the king and Consience bothe;
That Mede muste be meynpernour Resoun thei besoughte.
" Rede me not," quath Resoun, " no reuthe to have,   100
Til lordis and ladies loven alle treuthe,
And Pernelis purfile be put in hire hucche;
Til childris cherisshing be chastid with yerdis,
And harlotis holynesse be holden for an hyne;
Til clerkis and knightes be curteis of here mouthes,   105
And haten to here harlotrie or mouthe it;
Til prestis here prechyng preve it hem selve,
And do it in dede to drawe us to goode;
Til Seint Jame be sought there I shal assigne,
That no man go to Galis but yif he go for evere;   110
And alle Rome renneris for robberis of beyonde
Bere no silver over se that signe of king shewith,
Neither grotis ne gold ygrave with kynges coroune,
Upon forfaiture of that fe, who so fynt hym at Dovere,
But it be marchaunt or his man, or messanger with lettres,   115
Or provisour or prest that the pope avauncith.

   " And yet," quath Resoun, " be the rode, I shal no reuthe have,
Whil Mede hath the maistrie to mote in this halle;
Ac I may shewe ensaumplis, as I se other;
I seighe it for my self, and it so were   120
That I were king with croune, to kepe a reaume,
Shulde nevere wrong in this world, that I wyte mighte,
Be unpunisshit be my power, for peril of my soule;
Ne gete my grace thorugh giftes, so me God helpe;
Ne for no mede have mercy, but meknesse it made.   125
For *nullum malum* the man, mette with *impunitum*,
And bad *nullum bonum* be *irremuneratum*.
Let thi confessour, sire king, construe the this in Englissh.
And yif thou werche it in werk, I wedde myne eris
That lawe shal ben a labourer and lede a-feld donge,   130
And love shal lede thi land, as the lef liketh."

[96]

Clerkis that wern confessours couplide hem to-gideris,
For to construe this clause declynede faste.
Ac whanne Resoun among thise renkis hadde reherside thise wordis,
There nas man in the mothalle, more ne lesse,   135
That ne held Resoun a maister, and Mede a muehe wrecche.
Love let of hire light, and lough hire to scorne,
And seide it so loude that sothnesse it herde:
" Who so wilneth hire to wyve, for welthe of hire godis,
But he be cokewald ycald, kitte of my nose! "   140
Waryn Wisdom tho, ne Witty his fere,
Couthe nought warpen a word to with-sigge Resoun;
But stareden for stodyenge and stoden as bestis.

    The king acordite be Crist to Resonis sawis,
And reherside that Resoun hadde rightfulliche shewide: 145
" Ac it is wel hard be myn hed, herto it to bringe,
And alle my lige ledis to leden thus evene."

    " Be hym that raughte on the rode," quath Resoun to the king,
" But yif I reule thus thi reaum, rend out my ribbes,
Yif it be so that buxumnesse be at myn assent."   150

    " And I assente," quath the king, " be Seinte Marie my lady,
Be my counseil ycome of clerkes and of erlis.
Ac redily, Resoun, thou shalt not riden henne;
For as longe as I lyve, lete the I nille."

    " I am redy," quath Resoun, " to reste with yow evere;   155
So Consience be of oure counseil, kepe I no betere."

    " I graunte," quath the king, " Godis forbode he faille;
As longe as I lyve, libbe we togideris."

Passus quintus de visione.

The king and his knightes to the chirche wente
To here matynes and masse, and to the mete aftir.
Thanne wakide I of my wynkyng, and wo was with alle
That I ne hadde yslepe saddere and yseyn more.

[97]

WRATH

Er I hadde faren a furlong feyntise me hente,   5
That I ne mighte ferthere a fote, for defaute of slepyng.
I sat softely a-doun, and seide my beleve,
And so I babelide on my bedis thei broughte me a-slepe.
        Thanne saugh I muche more than I before tolde,
For I saugh the feld ful of folk that I before of tolde,   10
And Consience with a cros com for to preche.
He preyede the peple have pite on hem selve,
And previde that the pestilence was for pur synne,
And the southwest wynd on Satirday at eve
Was apertly for pride, and for no poynt ellis;   15
Piries and plumtrees wern puffed to the erthe,
In ensaumple, segges, that ye shulde do the betere!
Bechis and broode okis wern blowen to the grounde,
And turnide upward here tail in toknyng of drede
That dedly synne er domisday shal fordon hem alle.   20
        Of this mater I mighte mamele ful longe,
Ac I shal seighe as I saigh—so me God helpe—
How Consience with a cros cumside to preche.
He bad wastour go werche what he best couthe,
And wynne that he wastide with sum maner craft;   25
And preyede Pernel hire purfil to leve,
And kepen it in hire coffre for catel at nede;
Thomas he taughte to take two staves,
And fecche hom Felis fro wyvene pyne;
He warnide Watte his wyf was to blame,   30
That hire hed was worth a mark and his hod not worth a grote;
He chargide chapmen to chasten here children—
" Let no wynnyng forwanye hem whiles thei ben yonge."
He preyide prelatis and prestis togidere,
That thei preche the peple and preve it hem selve—   35
" And libbe as ye lere us, we wile love yow the betere."
And siththe he redde religioun here rewele to holde—
" Lest the king and his counseil your comunes apeire,

[99]

And be steward of youre stede til ye be stowid betere.
And ye that seke Seint Jame, and seintes at Rome,   40
Sekith Seint Treuthe, for he may save you alle :
Qui cum patre et filio, faire mote yow befalle."
   Thanne ran Repentaunce and reherside his teme,
And made Wil to wepe watir with his eighen.
   Pernel proud herte plat hire to the erthe,   45
And lay longe er heo lokide, and " Lord mercy " criede,
And behighte to hym that us alle makede
Heo shulde unsewe hire serke and sette there an heire
For to affaiten hire flessh, that fers was to synne :
" Shal nevere heigh herte me hente, but holde me lowe,   50
And suffre to be misseid, and so dide I nevere ;
But now wile I meke me, and mercy beseke
Of alle that I have had envye in myn herte."
   Lecchour seide " Allas," and on oure lady criede
To make mercy for his mysdede betwyn God and his soule,   55
With that he shulde the Satirday, seve yer ther aftir,
Drinke but with the doke and dyne but ones.
   Envye, with hevy herte, askide aftir shrift,
And carfulliche his gilt begynneth to shewe.
He was as pale as a pelet, in the palesie he semide,   60
Clothid in a caury-maury, I couthe it nought descryve ;
A kertil and a courtepy, a knyf be his side,
Of a freris frokke were the fore-slevys.
As a lek that hadde leyn longe in the sonne,
So lokide he with lene chekis, louryng foule.   65
His body was bolnid for wraththe that he bot his lippes,
And wrothliche he wrong his fest, to wreke hym he thoughte
With werkis or with wordis, whanne he saigh his tyme.
" Venym or verjous or vynegre, I trowe,
Walewith in my wombe, and waxith, as I wene.   70
I mighte not many day do as a man oughte,
Such wynd in my wombe wexith er I dyne.

[100]

I have a neighebour neigh me, I have noighed hym ofte,
And blamide hym behynde his bak to bringe hym in fame;
To apeire hym be my power I have pursuide ful ofte,   75
And belowen hym to lordis, to don hym lese silver,
And don hise frendis ben hise fon, thorugh my false tunge;
His grace and hise gode happis grevide me ful sore.
Betwyn hym and his meyne I have mad wraththe;
Bothe his lyme and his lif was lost thorugh my tunge.   80
Whanne I mette hym in market that I most hatide,
I halside hym as hendely as I his frend were.
He is doughtiere thanne I; I dar non harm don hym.
Ac hadde I maistrie and might, I wolde murdre hym for evere!
Whanne I come to the chirche, and knele to the rode,   85
To preye for the peple, as the prest techith,
Thanne I crighe on my knes that Crist gyve hem sorewe
That bar awey my bolle and my broken shete.
Fro the auter myn eighe I turne and beholde
How Heyne hath a newe cote, and his wyf another;   90
Thanne I wysshe it were myn, and al the web after.
And of his lesing I laughe—it liketh myn herte;
Ac for his wynnyng I wepe, and weile the tyme.
I deme men that thei don ille, and yet I do werse;
I wolde that iche wight were my knave;   95
And who so hath more thanne I, that angrith myn herte.
Thus I lyve loveles, lyk a lyther dogge,
That al my brest bolnith for bittir of my galle;
May no sugre ne swet thing aswage it unnethe,
Ne no dyapendyon dryve it fro myn herte;   100
Yif that shrift shulde, it shop a gret wondir."
   " Yis, redily," quath Repentaunce, and reddc hym to goode,
" Sorewe for synne savith wel manye."
   " I am sory," quath Envye, " I am but selden othere;
And that makith me so mad, for I ne may me venge."   105
   Thanne com Coveitise—I can hym nought descryve—

[101]

So hungri and holewe, Sire Hervy hym lokide.
He was bitel-browid and babirlippid, with two bleride eighen;
And as a letherene purs lollide his chekis;
In a torn tabbard of twelve wynter age—   110
But yif a lous couthe lepe, I may it nought leve
He shulde wandre on that walsshe, so was it thred-bare.
"I have ben coveitous," quath this caityf, "I beknowe it here.
For sum tyme I servide Symme at the noke,
And was his prentis yplight, his profit to loke.   115
Ferst I lernide to leighe a lef other tweighe;
Wykkidly to weighe was my ferste lessoun.
To Wynchestre and to Wy I wente to the feire,
With many maner marchaundise, as my maister me highte;
Ne hadde the grace of gile gon among my ware,   120
It hadde be unsold this seven yer, so me God helpe!
Thanne drough I me among drapers my donet to lerne,
To drawe the list along, the lengere it semide.
Among the riche rayes I rendrit a lessoun,
Brochide hem with a pakke-nedle, and pleitide hem togidere,   125
Putte hem in a pressour, and pynnede hem there inne
Til ten yardis other twelve tollide out thrittene.
My wyf was a wynstere, and wollene cloth made,
And spak to the spynsteres to spynnen it softe.
The pound that heo payed by peiside a quarter more   130
Thanne myn aunsel dede, whanne I weighede trewethe.
I boughte hire barly—heo breugh it to selle;
Penyale and pile-whey heo pouride togidere
For laboureris and lough folk that lay be hem selve.
The beste in my bed chaumbre lay be the wough,   135
And who so bummide therof boughte it there aftir,
A galoun for a grote, God wot, no lasse,
Whanne it com in cuppe-mel—that craft my wyf uside.
Rose the regratour was hire righte name;
Heo hath holde huxterie ellevene wynter.   140

Ac I swere now sothly, that synne shal I lete,
And nevere wykkidly weighe, ne wykkide chaffare usen;
But wende to Walsyngham, and my wyf alse,
And bidde the rode of Bromholm bringe me out of dette."
   Now begynneth Glotoun for to go to shrift,   145
And carieth hym to chircheward, his synne for to shewe;
And Betoun the breustere bad him good morewe,
And heo askide of hym whidirward he wolde.
" To holy chirche," quath he, " for to here masse;
And sithen I wile be shriven, and synne no more."   150
" I have good ale, gossib," quath heo; " Glotoun, wilt thou assaie? "
" Hast thou ought in thi pors," quath he, " any hote spices? "
" Ya, Glotoun, gossib," quath heo, " God wot, wel hote;
I have pepir and pyanye, and a pound of garlek,
And a ferthing worth of fenel seed, for fastyng dayes."   155
Thanne goth Glotoun in, and grete othis aftir;
Cisse the sewstere sat on the benche,
Watte the warinar, and his wyf bothe,
Tom the tynkere, and tweyne of his knaves,
Hikke the hakeneyman, and Hogge the nedelere,   160
Claris of Cokkislane, and the clerk of the chirche,
Sire Pers of Pridye, and Pernel of Flaundres,
Dawe the dykere, and a doseyn othere;
A ribibour, a ratoner, and a rakiere of Chepe,
A ropere, a redyng-king, and Rose the disshere,   165
Godfrei of Garlekithe, and Griffin the Walsche;
And upholderis an hep, erliche be the morewe,
Yeve Glotoun with gladchiere good ale to hansele.
Clement the cobeler cast of his cloke,
And at the newe feire he nempnide it to selle.   170
Hikke the hostiler hitte his hood aftir,
And bad Bette the bocher be on his side.
There were chapmen chosen, that chaffare to preise;
Who so hadde the hood shulde have amendis of the cloke.

Thei risen up in rape, and rouneden togideris,   175
And preisiden the peneworthis aperte be hem selven;
There were othes an hep, who so it herde.
Thei couthe not be here consience acorden togidere,
Til Robyn the ropere was red to risen,
And nempnide for a noumpere, that no debate were.   180
Hikke the hostiller hadde the cloke,
In covenant that Clement shulde the cuppe fille,
And have Hikkes hood the hostiller, and holde hym yservid;
And who so repentith rathest shulde arise aftir,
And grete Sire Glotoun with a galoun ale.   185
There was laughing and louryng and "lete go the cuppe!"
Bargaynes and beverechis begonne to rise,
And seten so til evensong, and songe sum while,
Til Glotoun hadde ygluppid a galoun and a gille.
He pisside a potel, in a *pater noster* while,   190
And bleugh the rounde rewet at the rigge-bones ende,
That alle that herden that horn held here nose aftir,
And wisshide it hadde be wexid with a wysp of firsen.
He hadde no strengthe to stonde, er he his staf hadde,
And thanne gan he to go lyk a glemans bicche,   195
Sum tyme asid, and sum tyme arere,
As who so leith lynes to lacche with foules.
Whanne he drough to the dore, thanne dymmede hise eighen;
He stumblide on the thresshewold and threw to the erthe,
That with al the wo of this world, his wyf and his wenche   200
Bere hym hom to his bed, and broughte hym ther inne.
And aftir al this surfet, an axesse he hadde,
That he slepte Satirday and Sonneday, til sonne yede to reste.
Thanne wakide he of his wynkyng, and wypide his eighen;
The ferste woord that he spak was, "Where is the bolle?"   205
His wyf blamide hym thanne, of wykkidnesse and synne.
Thanne was the shrewe asshamide, and shrapide hise eris,
And gan grete grymly, and gret doel to make

[104]

For his lither lif, that he lyved hadde,

And avowide to faste, for hungir or for thrist : 210

" Shal nevere fissh on the Friday defie in my mawe,

Er Abstinence myn aunte have ygyve me leve ;

And yet have I hatid hire al my lif tyme."

    Sleuthe for sorewe fel doun aswowen,

Til *Vigilate*, the veil, fette watir at his eighen, 215

And flatte on his face, and faste on him criede,

And seide, " War the, for wanhope wile the betraye.

' I am sory for my synnes,' sey to thi selven,

And beet thi self on the brest, and bidde hym of grace ;

For is no gilt here so gret that his goodnesse nis more." 220

Thanne sat Sleuthe up, and seynide hym faste,

And made avowe tofore God, for his foule slouthe :

" Shal no Sonneday be this seven yer, but seknesse it make,

That I ne shal do me er day to the dere chirche,

And here masse and matynes, as I a monk were ; 225

Shal non ale aftir mete holde me thennis,

Til I have evensong herd, I behote to the rode.

And yet wile I yelde ayen, yif I so muchel have,

Al that I wykkidly wan, sithen I wyt hadde ;

And theigh my liflode lakke, leten I nille 230

That iche man shal have his, er I hennis wende ;

And with the residue and the remenaunt—be the roode of Chestre—

I wile seke Treuthe, er I se Rome."

Roberd the robbour on *Reddite* lokide,

Ac for there was nought where with, he wepte swithe sore ; 235

Ac yet the synful shrewe seide to hym selve :

" Crist, that on Calvarie upon the cros dighedist,

Tho Dismas my brother besoughte the of grace—

And thou haddist mercy on that man for *memento* sake—

Thi wil worth upon me, as I have wel deservid, 240

To have helle for evere yif that hope nere.

So rewe on this roberd, that no red have,

[105]

Ne nevere wene to wynne with craft that I knowe;
But for thi muchel mercy, mytygacioun I beseche:
Dampne me nought at domisday, for I dede so ille." 245
Ac what befel of this feloun, I can not faire shewe;
Wel I woot he wepte faste watire with his eighen,
And knowelechide his gilt to Crist yet eft-sones,
That *Penitencia* his pik shulde pulisshe newe,
And lepe with hym over lond, al his lif tyme; 250
For he hadde leighe be *Latro,* Luciferis aunte.

A thousand of men tho throngen togideris,
Wepynge and weylyng for here wykkide dedis,
Criede upward to Crist, and to his clene modir,
To have grace to seke Treuthe, so God leve that hy moten. 255

Passus sextus de visione.

Ac there were fewe men so wys that the wey thider couthe,
But blustride forth as bestis over valeis and hilles,
Til late and longe that hy a lede mette,
Aparailid as a paynym, in pilgrimes wyse.
He bar a burdoun ybounde with a brood list 5
In a withwindes wyse ywounden aboute.
A bagge and a bolle he bar be his side;
An hundred of ampollis on his hat seten,
Signes of Synay, and shilles of Galis,
And many a crouch on his cloke, and keighes of Rome, 10
And the vernicle beforn, for men shulde knowe
And sen be his signes whom he sought hadde.
This folk fraynide hym faire fro whenis that he come.

"Fro Synay," he seide, "and fro the sepulcre;
At Bedlem, at Babiloyne, I have ben in bothe; 15
In Ermonye, in Alisaundre, in manye othere places.
Ye mowe se be my signes, that sitten on myn hat,
That I have walkid ful wide, in wet and in drighe,

[106]

COVETOUSNESS

And sought goode seintes for my soule hele."   [callen Treuthe?

" Knowist thou ought a corseint," quod thei, "that men   20
Canst thou wisse us the wey where that wy dwellith?"

" Nay, so me God helpe," seide the gome thanne,
" I saugh nevere palmere, with pik ne with scrippe,
Axen aftir hym, er now in this place."

" Petir!" quath a plough-man, and putte forth his hed,   25
" I knowe hym as kyndely as clerk doth his bokis;
Clene consience and wyt kende me to his place,
And dede me suren hym sithen to serve hym for evere,
Bothe to sowen and to setten while I swynke mighte.
I have ben his folewere al this fourty wynter;   30
Bothe sowen his seed, and sewide hise bestis,
And kepide his corn, and cariede it to house;
Dyked and dolven, and do what he highte,
Withinne and withoute, waytide his profit;
There is no labourer in his lordsshipe that he lovith betere,   35
For theigh I sey it my self, I serve hym to paye.
I have myn hire of hym wel, and other-while more;
He is the presteste payere that pore men knowen.
He with-halt non hyne his hire that he ne hath it at eve;
He is as lough as a lomb and loveliche of speche;   40
And yif ye willeth wite where that wy dwellith,
I shal wisse yow wel the right way to his place."

" Ya, leve Piers," quath the pilgrimes, and profride hym hire.

" Nay, be the peril of my soule," quath Piers, and gan to swere,
" I nolde fonge a ferthing, for Seint Thomas shryne;   45
Treuthe wolde love me the wers a long tyme aftir.
Ac ye that wilneth to wende—this is the weye thider:
Ye mote go thorugh Meknesse, bothe men and wyves,
Til ye come in to Consience, that Crist wyte the sothe,
That ye love hym levere thanne the lif in youre hertis,   50
And thanne youre neighebours next in none wise apeire
Other wise thanne thou woldist men wroughte to thi selve.

[108]

And so bougheth forth be a brok, Be-buxum-of-speche,
For to ye fynden a forde, Youre-fadris-honourith;
Wadith in that watir, and wasshith yow wel there,   55
And ye shuln lepe the lightloker al youre lif tyme.
So shalt thou se Swere-nought-but-yif-it-be-for-nede-
And-nameliche-on-ydel-the-name-God-almighty.
Thanne shul ye come be a croft, ac come ye nought there inne;
The croft hattith Coveite-nought-menis-catel-ne-here-wyves-   60
Ne-none-of-here-servauntis-that-noighe-hem-mighte;
Loke thou breke no bow there, but yif it be thin owene.
Two stokkis there stonde, but stynte thou not there;
Thei hote Stele-nought, Ne-sle-nought; strik forth be bothe.
Leve hem on thi left half, and loke nought there aftir,   65
And holde wel thin haliday, heighe til even.
Thanne shalt thou blenche at a bergh, Bere-no-fals-wytnesse;
He is frithid in with floreynes, and othere fees manye;
Loke thou plukke no plante there, for peril of thi soule.
Thanne shalt thou se Sey-soth-so-it-be-to-done-   70
And-loke-that-thou-leighe-nought-for-no-manis-biddyng.
Thanne shalt thou come to a court, as cler as the sonne;
The mote is of Mercy, the maner al aboute,
And alle the wallis ben of Wyt, to holde Wil theroute;
The kirnclis ben of Cristendom, that kynde to save,   75
Boterasid with Beleve-so-or-thou-best-not-savid.
Alle the housis ben helid, hallis and chaumbris,
With no led but Love and Loughnesse, as bretheren of o wombe.
The tour there Treuthe is hym self is up to the sonne;
He may do with the day-sterre what hym dere likith;   80
Deth dar not do thing that he defendith.
Grace hattith the gateward, a good man forsothe;
His man hattith Amende-yow, for many men he knowith;
Tel hym this tokne: 'Treuthe wot the sothe;
I perfourmide the penaunce that the prest me enjoynide,   85
And am sory for my synnes, and so shal I evere,

Whanne I thenke there-on, theigh I were a pope.'
Biddith Amende-yow meke hym to his maister ones,
To wayve up the wyket that the wy shette,
Tho Adam and Eve eten here bane;   90
For he hath the keighe and the cliket, theigh the king slepe.
And yif Grace graunte the to gon in in this wise,
Thou shalt se Treuthe him self sitten in thin herte;
And lere the for to love hym, and hise lawes holden.
Ac be war thanne of Wraththe-nought, that wykkide shrewe, 95
For he hath envye to hym that in thin herte sitteth,
And pokith forth pride to preise thi selve.
The boldnesse of thi bien faites makith the blynd thanne,
And so worst thou dryven out as dew, and the dore closid,
Ikeighid and ycliketed to kepe the theroute   100
Happily an hundrit wynter, er thou eft entre.
Thus might thou lese his love to lete wel be thi selve,
And geten it ayen thorugh grace and thorugh no yift ellis.
Ac there ben sevene sistris that serven Treuthe evere,
And ben porteris of the posternis that to the place longith. 105
That on hattith Abstinence, and Humilite a-nother,
Charite and Chastite beth hire chief maidenes;
Pacience and Pees, mekil peple thei helpen;
Largesse the lady let in ful manye.
Ac who so is sib to this sistris—so me God helpe—   110
He is wondirliche welcome and faire undirfonge.
But ye be sibbe to summe of this sevene,
It is ful hard, be myn hed, any of yow alle
To gete ingang at any gate, but grace be the more."
    " Be Crist," quath a cuttepurs, " I have no kyn there ! " 115
" Ne I," quath an apeward, " be aught that I knowe ! "
" Wyte God," quath a waffrer, " wiste I this forsothe,
Shulde I nevere ferthere a foote, for no freris preching."
    " Yis," quath Piers the ploughman, and pokide hym to goode,
" Mercy is a maiden ther hath might over hem alle;   120

And she is sib to alle synful, and hire sone alse;
And thorugh the helpe of hem two—hope thou non other—
Thou might gete grace ther, so thou go be tyme."

Passus septimus de visione.

" This were a wikkide weye, but who so hadde a gide
That mighte folewe us iche fote, til we were there."
Quath Perkyn the ploughman, " Be Seint Peter the apostel,
I have an half akir to eren, be the heighe weye;
Hadde y ered that half akir—so me God helpe—   5
I wolde wende with yow til ye were there."
" This were a long lettyng," quath a lady in a scleire;
" What shulde we wommen werche the while ? "
" Summe shal sewe the sak, for shedyng of the whete;
And ye wyves that han wolle, werchith it faste,   10
Spynneth it spedily, sparith not youre fyngris,
But yif it be holy day, or elles holy even.
Lokith forth youre lynen, and laboureth theron faste;
The nedy and the nakid, nymeth yeme how thei liggen,
Casteth hem clothis for cold, for so wile Treuthe;   15
For I shal lene hem lyflode, but yif the lond faile,
As longe as I lyve for the Lordis love of hevene.
And ye loveliche ladies, with youre longe fyngris,
That han silk and sendel, sewith whanne tyme is
Chesiblis for chapeleyns chirches to honoure;   20
And alle maner of men, that be the mete libbith,
Helpith hem werche wightly that wynne youre foode."
" Be Crist," quath a knight tho, " thou kennest us the beste,
Ac on the tem trewely taught was I nevere;
Ac kenne me," quath the knight, " and I wile conne eren." 25
" Be Seint Poule," quath Perkyn, " for thou profrist the so lowe,
I shal swynken and sweten, and sowe for us bothe,
And ek laboure for thi love al my lif tyme,

[111]

GLUTTONY

In covenaunt that thou kepe holychirche and my selven
Fro wastours and wikkide men that wolde us destroye; 30
And go hunte hardily to hares and to foxes,
To boris and to bukkes, that breken myn heggis,
And fecche the hom fauconis the foulis to kille,
For thise comith to my croft and croppith my whete."

   Curteisliche the knight conseived thise wordis; 35
" Be my power, Piers, I plighte the my treuthe,
To fulfille this foreward, whiles I may stande."

   " Ya, and yet a poynt," quath Perkyn, " I preye the more:
Loke thou tene no tenaunt, but Treuthe wile assente;
And thei pore men profre the presauntis or yeftis, 40
Nyme hem nought, an aunter thou mowe hem nought deserve;
For thou shalt yelde it ayen at one yeris ende,
In a wel perilous place that purgatorie hattith.
And mysbede nought thi bonde-men—the beter shalt thou spede;
And that thou be trewe of thi tunge, and talis thou hate, 45
But it be of wysdom or of wyt thi werkmen to chaste.
Holde with none harlotis, ne here nought here talis,
And nameliche atte mete suche men eschewen;
For it ben the develis disours, I do the to undirstonde."

   " I assente, be Seint Jame," seide the knight thanne, 50
" For to werche be thi woord, while my lif durith."

   " And I shal apperaille me," quath Perkyn, " in pilgrymis wyse,
And wende with yow the wey, til we fynde Treuthe."

   He caste on his clothis, ycloutid and hole,
Hise cokeris and his cuffis, for cold of his nailes, 55
And heng his hoper at his hals, in stede of a scrippe—
" A busshel of breed corn bryng me there inne,
For I wile sowe it my self, and siththe wile I wende;
And who so helpith me to eren, or any thing to swynke,
Shal have, be oure Lord, the more hire in hervist, 60
And make hym mery with the corn, who so it begrucchith.
And alle kyne crafty men that conne lyve in treuthe,

[113]

I shal fynde hem foode, that feithfulliche libbeth,
Save Jakke the jugelour, and Jonete of the stewis,
And Robyn the ribaudour for hise rusty woordis.   65
Treuthe tolde me ones, and bad me telle it forther,
Deleantur de libro, I shulde not dele with hem;
For holy chirche is holden of hem no tithe to asken:
   Et cum iustis non scribantur.
Thei ben askapid good auntir—now God hem amende."
   Dame Werche-whanne-tyme-is Piers wyf hatte;   70
His doughter hattith Do-right-so-or-thi-dame-shal-the-bete;
His sone hattith Suffre-thi-sovereynes-to-haven-here-wille-
And-deme-hem-nought-for-yif-thou-dost-thou-shalt-it-dere-abiggen.
   "Let God worthe with al, for so his woord techith;
For now I am old and hor, and have of myn owene,   75
To penaunce and to pilgrimage I wile passe with this othere.
For-thi I wile, er I wende, do wryte my bequest.
   "*In dei nomine, amen*: I make it my selven.
He shal have my soule that best hath deservid,
And defende it fro the fend, for so I beleve,   80
Til I come to his acountes, as my crede me techith,
To have reles and remissioun on that rental I leve.
The chirche shal have my careyn, and kepe my bones;
For of my corn and my catel he cravide the tithe.
I payede hym prestly, for peril of my soule;   85
He is holden, I hope, to have me in mynde,
And menge me in his memorie among alle Cristene.
My wyf shal have of that I wan with treuthe, and namore,
And dele among my frendis and my dere children;
For theigh I deighe today my dettis ben quytte;   90
I bar hom that I borewide er I to bedde yede.
And with the residue and the remenaunt—be the rode of Chestre—
I wile worsshipe there with Treuthe in my lyve,
And ben his pilgrym at the plough, for pore menis sake.
My plough-pote shal be my pyk-staf, and pyche at the rotis,   95

And helpe my cultir to kerve and close the forewis."
    Now is Peris and the pilgrimes to the plough faren;
To eren this half akir helpen hym manye.
Dikeris and delveres dyken up the balkis;
There with was Perkyn payed, and preisid hem yerne.   100
Othere werkmen there were that wroughte ful faste;
Eche man in his maner made hym to done;
And summe, to plese Perkyn, pykide up the wedis.
At heigh prime Peris let the plough stande,
To oversen hem hym self who so best wroughte;   105
He shulde ben hirid there aftir, whan hervist tyme come.
Thanne seten somme, and sungen at the ale,
And holpen eren the half akir with "Hey, trolly-lolly!"
    "Now, be the prince of paradis," quath Piers tho in wraththe,
"But ye rise the rathere and rape yow to werche,   110
Shal no greyn that here growith glade yow at nede,
And theigh ye deighe for doel, the devil have that recche!"
    Thanne were faitours aferd, and feynide hem blynde;
Somme leide here leggis a-lery, as suche losellis cunne,
And pleynide hem to Peris with suche pitous wordis: 115
"We have no lymes to laboure with, Lord ygracid be ye!
Ac we preye for yow, Peris, and for youre plough bothe,
That God of his grace your greyn multiplie,
And yelde yow of your almesse that ye yiven us here.
For we mowe nouther swynke ne swete, such seknesse us eileth." 120
    "Yef it be soth," quath Peris, "that ye seyn, I shal it sone aspie.
Ye ben wastours, I wot wel, and Treuthe wot the sothe;
And I am his holde hyne, and aughte hym to warne
Whiche wastours in this world his werk-men distroyeth.
Ye eten that thei shulde ete that eren for us alle;   125
Ac Treuthe shal teche yow his tem for to dryve,
Bothe to setten and to sowen, and saven his tilthe,
Cacche gees from his corn, kepen hise bestis,
Or ye shuln ete barly bred, and of the brok drynke.

[115]

But he be blynd or brokesshankid, or beddrede ligge,   130
Thei shuln ete as good as I, so me God helpe,
Til God of his grace gar hem to arise.
Ankeris and heremytes that holde hem in here sellis
Shuln have of myn almesse, al the while I libbe,
Inough iche day at non, ac nomore er morewe,   135
Lest his flessh and the fend foulide his soule;
Ones at noon is ynough that no werk usith;
He abideth wel the betere that bummith nought to ofte."
   Thanne gan Wastour arise, and wolde have yfoughte;
To Peris the ploughman he profride his glove;   140
A Bretoner, a braggere, a-bostide hym also,
And bad hym go pisse with his plough—pilide shrewe!
" Wilt thou, nilt thou, we wile have oure wille
Of thi flour and of thi flessh, fecche whanne us liketh,
And make us merye ther with, maugre thi chekis!"   145
   Thanne Peris the ploughman pleynede hym to the knight,
To kepen hym, as covenaunt was, fro curside shrewis,
Fro wastours that waite wynneres to shende.
Curteisliche the knight thanne, as his kynde wolde,
Warnide Wastour, and wisside hym betere—   150
" Or thou shalt abigge be the lawe, be the ordre that I bere."
   " I was not wont to werche," quath Wastour, " now wile I not
And let light of the lawe, and lesse of the knight,   [begynne."
And countide Peris at a pese, and his plough bothe,
And manacide hym and his men, whanne thei next metten. 155
   " Now, be the peril of my soule," quath Peris, " I shal appeire
And houpide aftir Hungir, that herde hym at the ferste: [yow alle!"
" Awreke me on thise wastours," quath Peris, " that this world
   Hungir in haste thanne hente Wastour be the mawe, [shendith!"
And wrong hym so be the wombe that bothe his eighen watride, 160
And buffetide the Bretoner aboute the chekis,
That he lokide lik a lanterne al his lif aftir.
He beet hem so bothe, he brast ner here mawis;

[116]

Ne hadde Peris with a pese-lof preyede hym beleve,
And with a benen batte yede hem betwene,   165
And hitte Hunger ther with amydde hise lippes—
And bledde in-to the bodyward a bolle ful of growel—
Ne hadde the fisician ferst defendit him watir
To abate the barly bred and the benis ygrounde,
Thei hadde be ded be this day, and dolven al warme.   170
Faitours for fer thanne flowen in-to bernis,
And flappide on with flailes, fro morewe til eve,
That Hunger was not hardy on hem for to loke
For a potel of pesen that Peris hadde imakid.
An hep of heremites henten hem spadis   175
And dolven drit and dung to ditte out Hunger.
Blynde and bedrede were botnid a thousand
That layen for blynde and for brokeleggide by the heighe waye.
Hungir hem helide with an hote cake,
And lame menis lymes wern lithid that tyme,   180
And become knaves to kepe Peris bestis,
And preighede pur charite with Peris for to dwelle,
Al for coveitise of his corn, to cache awey Hungir.
And Pieris was proud therof, and putte hem in office,
And yaf hem mete and monie as thei mighte deserve.   185
    Thanne hadde Piers pite, and preighede Hungir to wende
Hom in-to his owene erd, and holde him there evere—
" And yet I preye the," quath Peris, " er thou passe ferthere,
Of beggeris and bidderis what is best to done?
For I wot wel, be thou went, hy wile werche ful ille;   190
Meschief it makith, hy ben so meke nouthe,
And for defaute of foode thus faste hy werchith;
And it ben my blody bretheren, for God boughte us alle.
Treuthe taughte me ones to love hem ichone,
And helpe hem of alle thing, aftir that hem nedide.   195
Now wolde I wite yif thou wistest what were the beste,
And how I mighte amaistrie hem, and make hem to werche."

[117]

"Here now," quath Hungir, "and holde it for a wisdom:
Bolde beggeris and bigge that mowe here mete beswynken,
With houndis bred and hors bred holde up here hertis,   200
And bane hem with benes, for bollnyng of here wombes;
And yif the gromes grucche, bidde hem gon swynke,
And he shal soupe swettere whanne he it hath deservid.
And yif thou fynde any frek that fortune hath apeirid
With fuyr or with false men, fonde suche to knowen;   205
Counforte hem with thi catel, for Cristis love of hevene;
Love hem and lene hem, and so the lawe of kynde wole.
And alle maner of men, that thou mighte aspien,
That nedy ben or nakid, and nought han to spende,
With mete or with mone let hem be the betere,   210
Or with werk or with word, whiles thou art here.
Make the frendis ther with, and so Matheu us techith:
    Facite vobis amicos de mammona iniquitatis."
    "I wolde not greve God," quath Peris, "for al the gold on
Mighte I synneles do as thou seist?" seide Peris thanne.   [ground;
    "Ye, I behote the," quath Hungir, "or ellis the bible   215
Go to Genesis the geaunt, engendrour of us alle: [leigheth;
'*In sudore* and swynke thou shalt thi mete tilien,
And labouren for thi liflode,' and so oure Lord highte.
And Sapience seith the same—I saigh it in the bible:
'*Piger propter frigus* no feld wolde tilie;   220
He shal go begge and bidde, and no man bete his hungir.'
Matheu with the manis face mouthith thise wordis:
That *servus nequam* had a nam, and for he nolde it usen,
He hadde maugre of his maister evere more aftir;
And benom hym his nam, for he nolde werche,   225
And yaf it hym in haste that hadde ten there before;
And sithen he seide, that his servauntis it herde,
'He that hath shal have, to helpe there nede is,
And he that nought hath shal nought have, ne no man him helpe;
And that he wenith wel to have, I wile it be hym berevid.'   230

[118]

Kynde wyt wolde that iche wight wroughte
Or with teching or tiling, or travaillyng of hondis,
Actif lif or contemplatif; Crist wolde it alse.
The Sauter seith, in the salme of *Beati omnes,*
    Labores manuum tuarum quia manducabis, &c.
He that get his fode here with travaile of his hondis—   235
God yiveth hem his blissing that here liflode here so wynneth."
   " Yet I preye the," quath Peris, " pur charite, yif thou conne
Eny lef of lechecraft, lere it me, my dere.
For summe of my servauntis ben seke other while,
Of alle the wyke hy werkith nought, so here wombe akith."   240
   " I wot wel," quath Hunger, " what seknesse hem eileth:
Thei han mangid over muche, that makith hem grone ofte.
Ac I hote the," quath Hunger, " as thou thin hele wilnest,
That thou drynke no day er thou dyne sum-what;
Ete nought, I hote the, er Hunger the take   245
And sende the of his saus, to savoure thi lippes;
And kep sum til soper tyme, and sit nought to longe;
Aris up er Appetit have eten his fille.
Let nought Sire Surfet sitten at thi bord;
Leve hym nought, for he is a lecchour, and likerous of tunge,   250
And aftir many maner metis his mawe is alongid.
And yif thou dighete the thus, I dar ley myn eres,
That Fisik shal his furrid hood for his foode selle,
And ek his cloke of calabre, and the knoppis of gold,
And be fayn, be my feith, his fisik to leten,   255
And lerne to laboure with lond, lest liflode hym faile.
There ben mo ligheris than lechis—Lord hem amende!
Thei do men dighe thorugh here drynkes, er destenye it wolde."
   " Be Seint Poul," quath Peris, " thise ben profitable wordis;
This is a lovely lessoun; Lord it the foryelde!   260
Wende now whanne thi wille is, that wel be thou evere."
   " I behote the," quath Hunger, " henis nile I wende
Er I have dyned be this day, and ydronke bothe."

[119]

"I have no peny," quath Piers, "pulettis to biggen,
Nother gees ne gris; but two grene chesis,　　　　　265
A fewe cruddis and crem, and an haver cake,
A lof of benis and bren ybake for my children;
And yet I seighe be my soule, I have no salt bacoun,
Ne no cokenay, be Crist, colopis to maken.
Ac I have persile and poret, and many cole plantis,　　270
And ek a cow and a calf, and a carte mare
To drawe a-feld my dong, while the drought lastith.
Be this liflode I mote lyve til Lammasse tyme;
Be that I hope for to have hervest in my croft;
And thanne may I dighte thi dyner as the dere liketh."　275
　　　Alle the pore peple pesecoddis fetten,
Benes and baken applis hy broughte in here lappes,
Chibollis and chirivellis, and ripe chiries manye,
And profride Peris this present, to plese with Hungir.
Hungir eet this in haste, and askide aftir more.　　　280
Thanne thise folk for fer fetten hym manye
Grene porettis and pesen, to poysen hym hy wolde.
Be that it neighide ner hervest, that newe corn com to chepyng;
Thanne was folk fayn, and fedde Hunger with the beste,
With good ale and glotonye, and gart hym to slepe.　　285
　　　And tho wolde Wastour not werche, but wandrite aboute,
Ne no beggere ete bred that benis in come,
But coket or clermatyn, or of clene whete;
Ne non halpeny ale in non wyse drynke,
But of the beste and the brouneste that breusteris sellen.　290
Laboureris that have no land to lyve on but here handis,
Deyneth nought to dyne a-day night-olde wortis.
May no penyale hem paye, ne no pece of bacoun,
But yif it be fressh flessh, other fissh yfried,
And *chaud* and *plus chaud*, for chillyng of here mawe.　295
But yif he be heighliche hirid, ellis wile he chide,

[120]

That he was werkman ywrought warie the tyme,
And thanne curse the king, and alle his counseil aftir,
Suche lawis to loke laboureris to chaste.
Ac while Hunger was here maister wolde there non chide   300
Ne stryve ayen the statute, so sternely he lokide.

I warne yow, werkmen, wynneth while ye mowe;
For Hungir hiderward hastith hym faste.
He shal awake thurh water wastours to chaste;
Er fyve yer be fulfild, such famyn shal arise,   305
Thorugh floodis and thorugh foule wederis, fruytes shuln fayle;
And so seith Satourne, and sente yow to warne.

Passus octavus de visione.

Treuthe herde telle here-of, and to Peris sente
To take his tem, and tilien the erthe;
And purchacede hym a pardoun *a pena et a culpa,*
For hym and for hise heires, evere more aftir.
And bad hym holde hym at hom, and eren his laighes;   5
And al that holpen hym to eren or to sowen,
Or any maner myster that mighte Peris helpen,
Part in that pardoun the pope hath ygrauntid.

Kinges and knightes that kepen holy chirche,
And rightfulliche in reaum rewlith the peple,   10
Han pardoun thorugh purgatorie to passe ful sone,
With patriarkes in paradis to pleighe there aftir.

Bisshopis that blissen, and bothe lawes conne,
Loke on that o lawe and lere men that other,
And bere hem bothe on here bak, as here baner shewith,   15
And prechen here parsonis the peril of synne,
How that scabbide shep shul here wolle save,
Han pardoun with the apostlis whanne thei passe hennis,
And at the day of dom at here deis to sitten.

Marchauntis, in the margyn, hadde manye yeris,   20
But non *a pena et a culpa* the pope nolde hem graunte;

[121]

SLOTH

For thei holde nought here haly dayes, as holy chirche techith,
And for thei swere be here soule, and " so God muste hem helpe,"
Ayens clene consience, here catel to selle.
Ac undir his secre sel Treuthe sente hem a lettre,   25
And bad hem bigge boldely what hem best likide,
And sithen selle it ayen, and save the wynnyng,
And make *meson deu* there with, myseise to helpe,
Wykkide weyes wightly to amende,
And bete brugges aboute that to-broke were,   30
Marie maidenis, or maken hem nonnes;
Pore wydewis that wiln be non wyves aftir—
Fynde suche here foode, for oure Lordis love of hevene;
Sette scoleris to scole, or to summe other craftis;
Releve religioun, and renten hem betere—   35
" And I shal sende yow my self Seynt Michel, myn aungel,
That no devil shal yow dere, dighe whan ye dighe,
That I ne shal sende youre soules sauf in-to hevene,
And before the face of my fadir fourme youre setis.
Usure and avarice and othes I defende,   40
That no gile go with yow, but the graith treuthe."
Thanne were marchauntis merye and wepe for joye,
And yaven Wille for his writyng wollene clothis;
For he copiede thus here clause, thei couden hym gret mede.
   Men of lawe hadde lest, for lettride thei ben alle;   45
And so seith the Sauter and Sapience bothe:
   Super innocentem munera non accipies. A regibus et princi-
      pibus, &c.
Of princes and prelatis here pencioun shulde arise,
And of no pore peple no peny worth to take.
Ac he that spendith his speche, and spekith for the pore,
That is innocent and nedy, and no man apeirith,   50
Counfortith hym in that cas, coveitith nought his goodis,
Ac for oure Lordis love, lawe for hym shewith,—
Shal no devil, at his deth day, derie hym a myte,
That he ne worth sykirly sauf, and so seith the Sautir.

Ac to bigge watir, ne wynd, ne wyt is the thridde,   55
Ne wolde nevere holy writ—God wot the sothe!
Thise thre for thrallis ben throwe among us alle,
To waxen and wanyen, where that God likith.
His pardoun in purgatorie wel litel is, I trowe,
That any mede of mene men for motyng resceyveth.   60
Ye legistris and lawyers, ye wyten yif I leighe!
Sithen ye sen it is so, sewith to the beste.
    Alle libbyng laboureris, that lyven be here hondis,
That trewely taken and trewely wynnen,
And lyven in love and in lawe for here lowe hertis,   65
Hadde the same absolucioun that sent was to Peris.
    Beggeris and bidderis ben not in the bulle,
But yif the suggestioun be soth that shapith hem to begge.
For he that beggith or biddith, but he have nede,
He is fals with the fend, and defraudith the nedy,   70
And ek gilith the gyvere, ageyns his wille.
Thei lyve nought in love, ne no lawe holden;
Thei wedde no womman that hy with delen;
But as wilde bestis with " wehe," worthen up togideris,
And bringen forth barnes that bastardis ben holden.   75
Or his bak or his bon thei breken in his youthe,
And gon and faiten with here fauntis for evere more aftir.
There ben mo mysshapen amonges hem, who so takith hede,
Thanne of alle other maner men that on this molde wandrith.
Tho that lyven thus here lif mowe lothe the tyme   80
That evere he was man wrought, whanne he shal hennis fare.
    Ac olde men and hore, that helpeles ben of strengthe,
And wommen with childe, that werche ne mowe,
Blynde and bedrede, and broken here membris,
That takith meschief mekliche, as myselis and othere,   85
Han as pleyn pardoun as the ploughman hym selve;
For love of here lowe hertis oure Lord hath hem grauntid
Here penaunce and here purgatorie upon this pur erthe.
    " Piers," quath a prest tho, " thi pardon muste I rede;

[124]

For I shal construe iche clause, and kenne it the on Englisshe."   90
And Peris, at his preyour, the pardoun unfoldith,
And I, behynde hem bothe, beheld al the bulle.
In two lynes it lay, and nought a lettre more,
And was writen right thus, in witnesse of Treuthe:
    Et qui bona egerunt, ibunt in vitam eternam;   *prayer fasting meditation*
    Qui vero mala, in ignem eternum.
  " Petir! " quath the prest tho, " I can no pardoun fynde,   95
But ' do wel and have wel, and God shal have thi soule;
And do evele and have evele, and hope thou non other,
That aftir thi deth day to helle shalt thou wende.' "
And Piers, for pure tene, pullide it assondir,
And seide, " *Si ambulavero in medio umbre mortis, non timebo*
    mala, quoniam tu mecum es.
I shal cesse of my sowyng," quath Peris, " and swynke not so   100
Ne aboute my liflode so besy be namore;   [harde,
Of preyours and of penaunce my plough shal ben here aftir,
And beloure that I belough er, theigh liflode me faile.
The prophet his payne eet in penaunce and in wepyng,
Be that the Sauter us seith, and so dede manye othere;   105
That lovith God lelly his liflode is well muche: *well enough*
    Fuerunt michi lacrime mee panes, die ac nocte.
And but yif Luk leighe, he lerith us a-nother,
That we shuln nought be to besy aboute the bely joye:
Ne soliciti sitis, he seith in his gospel,
And shewith it us be ensaumple oure selve to wisse.   110
The foulis in the firmament, who fynt hem in wynter?
Whan the frost fresith, foode hem behovith;
Have thei no garner to go to, but God fynt hem alle."
  " What! " quath the prest to Perkyn, " Peter! as me thinketh,
Thou art lettrid a litel; who lernide the on boke? "   115
  " Abstinence the abbesse myn a. b. c. me taughte,
And Consience com aftir, and kennide me betere." [whan the likide:
  " Were thou a prest, Piers," quath he, " thou mightest preche
Quoniam literaturam non cognovi—that mighte be thi teme."

[125]

"Lewide lorel," quath Peris, "litel lokest thou on the bible; 120
On Salamonis sawis seldom thou beholdist:
Ecce derisores et jurgia cum eis, ne crescant."
The prest and Perkyn aposide either other,
And thorugh here wordis I wok, and waitide aboute,
And saugh the sonne evene south sitte that tyme;
Meteles and moneyles on Malverne hilles, 125
Musyng on this metelis, a myle wey I yede.

Manye tyme this metelis hath mad me to stodie,
And for Peris love the ploughman, ful pensif in herte,
For that I saigh slepyng, yif it so be mighte.
Ac Catoun construith it nay, and canonistris bothe, 130
And seggen be hem selve, *Sompnia ne cures.*
Ac for the bible, berith wytnesse how
Daniel devynide the drem of a king,
That Nabugodonosor nempne thise clerkis;
Daniel seide, "Sire king, thi swevene is to mene 135
That uncouthe knightes shuln come thi kingdom to cleyme;
Among lowere lordis thi londis shuln be departid."
As Daniel devynide, in dede it fel aftir:
The king les his lordsshipe, and lesse men it hadde.
And Josep mette merveillously how the mone and the sonne 140
And the enlevene sterris halsiden hym alle.
"*Beau fitz,*" quath his fadir, "for defaute we shuln,
I my self and my sones, seke the for nede."
It befel as his fadir seide, in Faraos tyme,
That Josep was justice, Egipt to kepe. 145
Al this makith me on metelis to thinke,
Manye tymes at mydnight, whan men shulde slepe;
On Peris the ploughman, whiche a pardoun he hadde,
And how the prest inpugnid it, al be pure resoun;
And demide that Do-wel indulgence passide, 150
Bienalis and trienalis, and bisshopis lettres.

[126]

Do-wel at the day of dome is digneliche undirfongen;
He passith al the pardoun of Seint Petris chirche.
Now hath the pope power pardoun to graunte,
The peple withoute penaunce to passe to joye.   155
This is a lef of oure beleve as lettrid men us techith:
    Quodcumque ligaveris super terram, &c.
And so I leve lelly—Lord forbede ellis—
That pardoun and penaunce and preyours do save   *in dulgence*
Soulis that han ysynned seve sithes dedly.
Ac to triste on this trionalis, trewely, me thinketh,   160
Is not so sikir for the soule, certis, as is Do-wel.

    For-thi I rede yow renkes that riche ben on erthe,
Upon trist of your tresour trienales to have,
Be ye nevere the baldere to breke the ten hestis.

    And nameliche ye maistris, as meiris and juggis,   165
That han the welthe of this world, and wise men ben holden,
To purchase pardoun and the popis bullis,
At the dredful dom day whanne dede shal arisen
And come alle before Crist acountes to yelden—
How thou leddist thi lif here, and his lawe keptest,   170
What thou dedist day be day, the dom wile reherce.
A pokeful of pardoun there, ne provinciales lettres,
Theigh thou be founde in the fraternite among the foure ordris,
And have indulgence double fold, but Do-wel the helpe,
I ne wolde yive for thi patent on pye hele!   175
    For-thi I counseil alle Cristene to crighe God mercy,
And Marie his modir to be mene betwene,
That God yive us grace, er we go hennis,
Suche werkis to werche, whiles we ben here,
That aftir oure deth day, Do-wel rcherse,   180
That at the day of dome, we dede as he highte.

    Explicit hic Visio Willelmi de Petro de Ploughman.
    Eciam incipit Vita de Do-wel, Do-bet, & Do-best
    secundum wyt & resoun.

VITA DE DO-WEL, DO-BET, & DO-BEST.

[*Prologus.*]

Thus yrobid in rosset I romide aboute,
Al a somer sesoun, for to seke Do-wel;
And fraynide ful ofte, of folk that I mette,
Yif any wight wiste where Do-wel was at inne,
And what man he mighte be, of many man I askide.　　5
Was nevere wight as I wente, that me wisse couthe
Where this lede lengide, lesse ne more;
Til it be-fel on a Friday, two freris I mette,
Maistris of the menours, men of gret wyt.　　*minorite (Franciscan)*
I hailside hem hendely, as I hadde ylernid,　　10
And preighede hem pur charite, er thei passide ferthere,
Yif thei knewen any cuntre or costis aboute,
Where that Do-wel dwellith, do me to wisse.
　"Marie," quath the menours, "among us he dwellith;
And evere hath, as I hope, and evere shal here aftir."　　15
　"*Contra*," quath I as a clerk, and comside to dispute:　　*commencer*
　"*Sepcies in die cadit iustus.*
'Seve sithes on the day,' seith the bok, 'synneth the rightful.'
And who so synneth," I seide, "sertis, as me thinkith,
That Do-wel and Do-evele mowe not dwelle togidere;
Ergo, he nis not alwey at hom among yow freris;　　20
He is otherwhile ellis where to wisse the peple."
　"I shal seighe the, my sone," seide the frere thanne,
"How seve sithes the sadde man synneth on the day;
Be a forebisene," quath the frere, "I shal the faire shewen:
Let bringe a man in a bot, amydde a brood watir;　　*OE bāt*　　25
The wynd and the watir and the waggyng of the boot
Maketh the man many tymes to falle and to stande;
For stande he nevere so stif, he stumblith in the waggyng.
And yet is he sauf and sound, and so hym behovith,

[128]

ighte to the stere,   30

overthrowe.

se of hym selve.   *negligence*

'be folk here on erthe:

vanith and waxith;

grete wawes,   35

ute;

tel is of kynde,

nd the false world,

day.   *rightteous*

-wel hym helpith,   40

elpe ayens synne;

terith thi soule,

in the watir,

wilt

aftir,   45

selven;

i self hast the maistrie."

I, " to conseyve thi wordis;   *conceive / understand*

lerne betere.

leighede."   50

ro myschaunce,

good lif to ende."

o seken,

yn one,

55

And undir a lynde upon a launde lenide I a stounde,
To lythen the laies that lovely foulis maden.   *on hlysða listen*
Blisse of the briddis broughte me a-slepe;
The merveilleste metyng mette me thanne,
That evere dremide dright in doute as I wene.   60   *dream*
    A muchel man, me thoughte, lik to my selve,
Com and callide me be my kynde name.
" What art thou," quath I tho, " that my name knowist ? "

[129]

"That thou wost wel," quath he, "and no wight betere." [thanne;
"Wot ich," quath I, "who art thou?" "Thought," seide he   65
"I have sewide the this seven yer—seighe thou me no rathere?"
"Art thou Thought," tho quath I, "thou couthest me telle
Where Do-wel dwellith, and do me to wisse."
    "Do-wel," quath he, "and Do-bet, and Do-best the thridde,
Arn thre faire vertues, and ben not fer to fynde.   70
Who so is mek of his mouth, mylde of his speche,
Trewe of his tunge, and of his two handis,
And thorugh his labour or his lond his liflode wynneth,
Trusty of his tailende, takith but his owene,
And is nought drunkelewe ne deynous, Do-wel hym folewith.   75
    "Do-bet doth thus, ac he doth muche more:
He is as lough as a lomb, lovelich of speche,
Whiles he hath ought of his owene he helpith there nede is,
The bagges and the bygirdles he hath broken hem alle,
That the erl Averous hadde, or his eires;   80
And with Mammones money he hath mad hym frendis,
And is ronne to religioun, and hath rendrit the bible,
And prechith the peple Seint Poulis wordis:
    Libenter sufferte, &c.
'Ye wise, suffrith the unwise with yow for to libbe.'
And with glad wil doth hem good, for so God hym self highte.   85
    "Do-best is above bothe, and berith a bisshopis croce,
Is hokid at that on ende to holde men in good lif;
A pik is in the potent to pungen adoun the wykkide,
That waiten any wikkidnesse Do-wel to tenen.
And as Do-wel and Do-bet dede hem to undirstonde,   90
Thei han crounide o king to kepe hem alle,
That yif Do-wel and Do-bet dede ayens Do-best,
And were unbuxum at his bidding, and bold to don ille,
Thanne shulde the kyng come and casten hem in presoun,
And putten hem there in penaunce withoute pite or grace;   95
But yif Do-best bede for hem abide there for evere.

[130]

" Thus Do-wel and Do-bet and Do-best the thridde
Corounid on to be kyng, and be here counseil werchen,
And rewele the reaum be red of hem alle; *rule*
And othere wise and ellis nought, but as thei thre assentide." 100 *Triumvirat !*
 I thankide Thought tho, that he me so taughte—
" Ac yet savourith me nought thi segging, so me God helpe !
More kynde knowyng I coveyte to lere,
How Do-wel, Do-bet, and Do-best don on this erthe."
 " But Wyt can wisse the," quath Thought, " where tho thre 105
Ellis wot no man that now is o lyve."   [dwellen,
 Thought and I thus thre dayes we yeden,
Disputyng on Do-wel day aftir other;
And er we ywar were, with Wyt gonne we mete. *oE-gunnon*
He was long and lene, lyk to non other,   110
Was no pride in his apparail, ne no povert nother,
Sad of his semblaunt, and of softe speche.
I durste meve no mater to make hym to jangle, *talk freely, argue*
But as I bad Thought tho be mene betwene,
To putte forth sum purpos to proven hise wittes.   115
 Thanne Thought in that tyme seide this wordis:
" Where that Do-wel and Do-bet and Do-best beth in londe,
Here is Wil wolde wyte, yif Wit couthe hym teche."
                                         Wil = the dreaming plowman

Passus primus de Do-wel, &c.

" Sire Do-wel dwellith," quath Wyt, " nought a day hennes,
In a castel that Kynde made of foure kynnes thinges;
Of erthe and eir it is mad, medlit togideris; *human = castel = earth, air*
With wynd and with watir, wittyliche enjoynede. *wind   water*
Kynde hath closid there inne, craftily with alle,   5
A lemman that he lovith lik to hym selve.
Anima heo hatte; to hire hath envye
A proud prikere of Fraunce, *Princeps huius mundi*; *pride*
And wolde wynne hire awey with wyles yif he mighte. *guile*

[131]

Ac Kynde knowith this wel, and kepith hire the betere,   10
And hath don hire to Sire Do-wel, duk of thise marchis.
Do-bet is hire damysele, Sire Do-welis doughter,
And servith this lady lelly bothe late and rathe. *oE hreape late & early*
Thus Do-wel and Do-bet and Do-best the thridde
Beth maistris of this maner this maide to kepe.   15
Ac the cunstable of the castel, that kepith hem alle,
Is a wys knight with alle, Sire Inwyt he hatte; *= conscience*
And hath fyve faire sones be his furste wyf:
Sire Se-wel, and Sey-wel, and Here-wel the hende,
Sire Werche-wel-with-thin-hond, a wight man of strengthe,   20
And Sire Godefrey Go-wel, grete lordis alle.
Thise sixe ben yset to save the castel;
To kepe thise womman thise wise men ben chargid,
Til Kynde come other sende to kepe hire hym selve."
    "What calle ye that castel," quath I, "that Kynde hath 25
And what kynnes thing is Kynde, conne ye me telle?"   [ymakid?
    "Kynde," quath he, "is creatour of alle kenis bestis;
Fadir and fourmour, the ferste of alle thing.
And that is the grete God, that gynnyng had nevere, *- beginning*
The lord of lif and of light, of lisse and of peyne.   30
Aungelis and alle thing arn at his wille,
Ac man is hym most lik of mark and of shape;
For thorugh the woord that he warp wexe forth bestis,
And al thing, at his wil, was wrought with a speche:
    Dixit et facta sunt, &c.
Save man that he made ymage to him selve,   35
Yaf hym gost of his godhed, and grauntide hym blisse,
Lif that ay shal laste, and al his lynage aftir.
    "That is the castel that Kynde made—*Caro* it hatte;
As muche to mene as man with his soule,
That he wroughte with werk, and with word bothe;   40
Thorugh might of the majeste man was ymakid:
    Faciamus hominem ad ymaginem nostram.

[132]

Anima = heart
conscience = head
pouk = devil

PASSUS TEN

Inwit and alle wyttes enclosid ben ther inne,
For love of that lady that Lif is ynempnid;
That is *Anima,* that overal in the body wandrith,
Ac in the herte is hire hom, heighest of alle;   45
Heo is lyf and ledere, a lemman of hevene.
Inwyt is the help that *Anima* desirith;
Aftir the grace of God, the grettest is Inwyt.
Inwyt in the hevid is, and an help to the soule,
For thorugh his connyng is kept *Caro & Anima*   of the conscience   50
In rewele and in resoun, but reccheles it make. neglectful of duty, careless
He eggith eighe sight and heryng to gode; urge on > ON eggia
Of good speche and connyng he is the begynnere;
In manis brayn is he most and mightiest to knowe— x if blood is not the stronger
There is his bour bremest, but yif blod it make. strong   55
For whan blood is bremere thanne brayn, than is Inwit bounde,
And ek wantoun and wilde withoute any resoun.
In yonge fauntes and folis—with hem failith Inwyt;
And ek in sottis thou might se, that sitten at the nale— ale-house
Thei helde ale in here hed til Inwyt be drenchit,   60
And ben braynwood as bestis, so here blood wexith.
Thanne hath the pouk power, Sire *Princeps huius mundi,*
Over suche maner of men, might in here soulis.
Ac in fauntis ne in folis the fend hath no might;
For no werk that thei werche, wykkide other ellis.   65
Ac the faderis and the frendis for fauntis shuln be blamid,
But yif thei witen hem fro wauntounesse, whiles thei ben yonge;
And yif thei ben pore and cateles, to kepe hem fro ille,
Thanne is holichirche owyng to helpe hem and save
Fro folies, and fynde hem, til thei ben wisere.   70
Ac iche wight in this world, that hath wys undirstonding,
Is chief sovereyn over hym self his soule to yeme, OE gyman rule
And chevisshen hym fro any charge, whan he childhod passith, x OF chevir save
Save hym self fro synne, for so hym behovith; > capere
For werche he wel other wrong, the wyt is his owene.   75

[133]

" Thanne is Do-wel a duc that destroyeth vices,
And savith the soule, that synne hath no might
To routen ne to resten ne roten in thin herte.
And that is dred of God, Do-wel it makith;
It is begynnyng of goodnesse God for to douten.   80
Salamon it seide for a soth tale:
   Inicium sapiencie, timor domini.
For doute men doth the bet; dred is suche a maister
That he makith men meke and mylde of here speche,
And alle kynne scoleris in scole to lerne.
   " Thanne is Do-bet to ben ywar for betyng of the yarde,   85
And therof seith the Sauter—thi self might it rede:
   Virga tua et baculus tuus, ipsa me consolata sunt.
Ac yif clene consience acorde that thi self dost wel,
Wilne thou nevere in this world for to do betere;
For, *Intencio indicat hominem, &c.*
Be counseil of consience, accordyng with holy chirche,
Loke thou wisse thi wyt, and thi werkis aftir;   90
For yif thou comist ayen consience thou combrist thi selven;
And so witnessith Godis word and holy writ bothe:
   Qui agit contra conscientiam, &c.
Ac yif thou werchist be Godis word, I warne the for the beste,
What so men worden of the, wraththe the nevere.
Catoun counseillith so—tak kep of his teching: 95
   Cum recte vivas, ne cures verba malorum.
But suffre and sit stille, and sek thou no ferthere,
And be glad of the grace that God hath i-sent the;
For yif thou comsist to clymbe, and coveitest herre, *higher*
Thou mightest lese thi loughnesse for a litel pride. *humility meek*
I have lernide how lewid men han leride here children,   100 *²ᴼᴺ lag*
That selde mosith the marbil that men ofte treden; *become mossy*
And right so be romeris, that rennen aboute
Fro religioun to religioun—reccheles ben thei evere; *neglectful of du*
Ne men that conne manye craftis—clergie it tellith—

[134]

prosperity

Thrift other thedom with tho is selde yseighe: 105

   Qui circuit, &c. *a jack-of-all-trade is master of none*

Poule the apostel in his pistil wrot it,

In ensaumple of suche shulde not renne aboute;

And for wisdom is writen and witnessid in chirches:

   In eadem vocacione qua vocati estis, state.

Yif thou be man maried, monk other chanoun,

Hold the stable and stedefast and strengthe thi selven 110

To be blissid for thi beryng, ye, beggere theigh thou were!

Loke thou grucche nought on God, theigh he gyve the litel;

Be paied with thi porcioun, pore other riche.

Thus in dred lith Do-wel, and Do-bet to suffre;

For thorugh suffraunce se thou might how soveraynes ariseth. 115

And so lerith us Luk, that leighede nevere:

   Qui se humiliat, exaltabitur, &c.

  " And thus of dred and his dede Do-best arisith,

Which is the flour and the fruyt fostrid of bothe.

Right as a rose, that red is and swet,

Out of a raggit rote and a rough brere 120

Springeth and spredith, that spiceris desirith,

Or as whete out of weed waxith of the erthe,

So Do-best out of Do-bet and Do-wel gynneth springe

Among men of this molde that mek ben and kynde;

For love of here loughnesse oure Lord yiveth hem grace 125

Such werkis to werche that he is with paied;

Formest and ferst to folk that ben weddit,

And lyven as here lawe wile, it liketh God almighty;

For thorugh wedlak the world stant, who so wile it knowen.

Thei be the riccheste of reaumes, and the rote of Do-wel; 130

For of here kynde thei comen that confessours ben nempnid:

Bothe maidenis and martires, monkes and ancris,

Kinges and knightes, and alle kyne clerkis,

Barouns and burgeis, and bonde-men of tounes.

  " Ac fals folk and feithles, as thevis and leigheris, 135

[135]

Ben conseyvid in cursid tyme, as Kaym was on Eve,
Aftir that Adam and Eve eten the appil
Ayens the hest of hym that hem of nought made.
An aungel in angir highte hem to wende
In-to this wrecchide world to wonen and to libben   140
In tene and in travaille to here lyves ende;   *vexation*
In that curside constellacioun thei knewe to-gideris
And brought forth a barn that muche bale wroughte.
Caym thei hym callide, in cursid tyme engendrit;
And so seith the Sauter—se it whanne the likith: 145
     Concepit dolore et peperit iniquitatem, &c.
Alle that comen of that Caym Crist hatid aftir,
And manye mylions mo of men and of wommen
That of Seth and his sistir siththe forth come;
For thei mariede hem with curside men of Caymes kyn.
For alle that comen of that Caym, acursid thei were,   150
And alle that couplide hem with that kyn, Crist hatide dedliche.
For-thi he sente to Sem, and seide hym be an aungel,   [to-gideris.
To kepe his kynrede fro Kaymes, that thei couplide nought
And sithen Sem and his suster sed wern spousid to Kaymes;
Ageyns Godis hest girlis hy geten,   155
That God was wroth with here werkis, and suche wordis seide:
     Penitet me fecisse hominem.
And is as muche to mene, among us alle:
'That I man makide, now it me forthinketh.'
And com to Noe anon, and bad hym nought lette
Swithe to shapen a ship of shidis and bordis;   160
Hym self and his sones thre, and sithen here wyves,
Busken hem to that boot, and biden there inne,
Til fourty dayes be fulfild, that flood have ywasshe
Clene awey the cursid blood that Caym hath ymakid—
'Bestis that now ben shuln banne the tyme   165
That evere curside Caym com on this erthe;
Alle shuln deighe for his dedis, be dounes and hilles,

[136]

Bothe fisshis and foulis, forth with othere bestis,
Out-take the eighte soulis, and of iche beste a couple,
That in the shynglid ship shuln ben ysavid;   170
Ellis shal alle dighen and to helle wenden.'
Thus thorugh curside Caym cam care upon alle;
And al for Sem and his sister children spouside either other,
Ayen the lawe of oure Lord leighen togideris,
And were mariede at meschief, as men do now here children.   175
    " For summe, as I se now, soth for to telle,
For coveitise of catel unkyndely be maried.
A carful concepcioun comith of suche weddyng,
As fel of the folk that I before shewide.
It is an uncomely copil, be Crist, as me thinketh,   *couple*   180
To yiven a yong wenche to an old feble,
Or wedde any wydewe for any wele of godis,
That nevere shal barn bere, but it be in armes.
In gelosie joyeles and janglyng on bedde
Manye peire sithen the pestilence han plight hem togidere.   185
The fruyt that thei bringe forth arn manye foule wordis;
Have thei no children but cheste, and choppis hem betwene. *strife, blows*
Theigh thei don hem to Dunmowe, but yif the devil helpe
To folewe aftir the flicche, fecche thei it nevere; *flitch = side of bacon >OE*
But yif thei bothe be forsworn, that bacoun thei tyne. *lose, fail* /190   *flicce*
    " For-thi I counseile alle Cristene, coveite not be weddit   *to harm >ON tyna*
For coveitise of catel or of kynrede riche;
But maidenis and maidenis, macche yow togideres;
Wydeweris and wydewis, werchith right also.
And thanne glade ye God, that al good sendith;   195
For in untyme treweliche, betwyn man and womman,
Shulde no bed-bourd be, but thei were bothe clene   *>OF bourde*
Of lif and of love and of lawe also.
That dede derne do no man shulde,   *secret*
As betwyn sengle and sengle, siththe lawe hath ygrauntid   200
That iche man have a make in mariage of wedlak,

[137]

And werche that werk on his wyf and on no womman ellis.
That othere gatis ben geten, for gadelynges ben holden;
And that ben fals folk and fals eires, alse foundlynges and leigheris,
Ungracious to gete love, or any good ellis,   205
But wandrith and wastith what that thei mowe;
Ayens Do-wel hy don evele, and the devil plesen,
And aftir here deth day shuln dwelle with the same,
But yif God yive hem grace here to amende.

" Thanne is Do-wel to dreden, and Do-bet to suffre,   210
And so comith Do-best aboute, and bringeth doun mody;
And that is wykkide wil, that many werk shendith."

Passus secundus de Do-wel, &c.

Thanne hadde Wyt a wyf, was hoten dame Studie,
That lene was of lich, and of lough chere.
She was wondirliche wroth that Wyt me thus taughte,
And al staringe dame Studie sterneliche seide:
" Wel art thou wys," quath she to Wyt, " any wisdomis to   5
To flatereris or to folis, that frentyk ben of wittis!"   [telle
And blamide hym and bannide hym, and bad hym be stille,
With suche wise wordis to wisse any foolis.
And seide, " *Nolite mittere,* man, margerie-perlis
Among hogges that haven hawen at wille;   10
Thei do but dravele theron; draf were hem levere
Thanne al the precious perrie that in paradis wexith.
I say it be tho," quath she, " that shewen be here werkis
That hem were levere lond and lordsshipe on erthe,
Or ricchesse or rentis, and reste at here wille,   15
Thanne alle the sothe sawis that Salamon seide evere.
Wisdom and wyt now is not worth a risshe,
But it be cardit with coveitise, as clotheris don here wolle.
That can conterfeten deseites and conspire wrongis,
And lede forth a loveday to lette the treuthe—   20

[138]

That suche craftis conne to counseil ben yclepid,
And ben servid as sires that serve the devil.
Job the jentile in his gestis seide it:
   Quare via impiorum prosperatur, bene est omnibus qui prave et
     inique agunt?
And he that hath holy writ ay in his mouth,
And can telle of Tobie and of the twelve apostlis,   25
Or prechen of the penaunce that Pilatus wroughte
To Jesu the gentil that Jewis to-drowe
On crois upon Calvarie as clerkis us techith—
Litel is he lovid or lete by, that suche a lessoun techith,
Or daunselid or drawe forth; thise disours wyte the sothe. 30
For yif harlotrie ne halp hem betere—have God my trouthe—
More thanne musik or makyng of God almighty,
Wolde nevere king ne knight, ne canoun of Seint Poulis,
Yive hem to here yeris-yive the value of a grote!
Ac menstralsie and merthe among men is nouthe;   35
Leccherie and losengerie and loseles talis,
Glotonye and grete othis—thise arn games now adayes.
   " Ac yif thei carpen of Crist, thise clerkis and thise lewid,
At mete in here merthe whanne mynstrales ben stille,
Thanne telle thei of the trinite, how two slowe the thridde, 40
And bringe forth a ballid resoun, tak Bernard to witnesse,
And putte forth presumpcioun to prove the sothe.
Thus thei dryvelen at here deis, the deite to knowe,
And gnawen God in here gorge, whanne here guttis fullen.
Ac the carful may crighen and carpe at the yate,   45
Bothe for hungir and for threst and for chele quake;
Is non to nymen hym in his noye to amende,
But honesshen hym as an hound, and hoten hym go thennes.
Litel lovith he that Lord that lenith hym al that blisse
That thus partith with the poore a parcel whanne hym nedith. 50
Nere mercy in mene men more than in riche,
Manye mendynauntz meteles mighte go to bedde.

God is muche in the gorge of this grete maistris,
Ac among mene men hise mercy and his werkis.
And so seith the Sauter—seke it in *Memento* :   55
   Ecce audivimus eam in Effrata, invenimus eam in campis silve.
Clerkis and kete men carpen of God faste,   *intelligent*
And han hym muchel in here mouth, ac mene men in herte.
Freris and faitours han founden up suche questiouns   *deceiver*
To pleise with proude men sithen the pestilence tyme,
That defoulith oure feith at festis there thei sitten ;   60
For now is iche boy bold, and he be riche,
To tellen of the trinite to be holden a sire,
And fyndith forth fantasies oure feith to apeire,   *o Fempeirer = empirer*
And ek defame the fadir that us alle made,
And carpen ayens clergie crabbide wordis :   65
' Why wolde oure saviour suffre suche a worm in his blisse,
That begilide the womman, and the wy aftir,
Thorugh whiche a werk and wille thei wenten to helle,
And alle here seed for here synne the same wo suffride ? '
Suche motifs thei meven, thise maistris in here glorie,   70
And make men in mysbeleve that musen on here wordis.
Ac Austyn the olde for alle suche prechide,
And for suche tale telleris suche a teme shewide :
   Non plus sapere quam oportet.
That is to seyn, ne wilneth nevere for to wyte why
That God wolde suffre Sathan his sed to begile ;   75
Ac beleve lelly on the lore of holy chirche,
And preye hym of pardoun and penaunce in thi lyve,
And for his muchel mercy to amende us here.
For alle that wilneth to wyte the weyis of God almighty,
I wolde his eighe were in his ars, and his hele aftir !   80
That evere eft wilneth to wyte why that God wolde
Suffren Sathan his sed to begile,
Or Judas the Jew Jesu betraye—
Al was as he wolde : Lord, yworsshipid be thou,

[140]

And al worth as thou wilt, what so we telle!   85
    " And now comith a conyon, and wolde cacche of my wittes
What is Do-wel fro Do-bet—now def mote he worthe!
Sithen he wilneth to wyte which thei ben alle:
But he lyve in the leste degre that longith to Do-wel,
I dar be his bolde borugh Do-bet wile he nevere,   90
Theigh Do-best drawe on hym day aftir other."
    And whanne that Wyt was war how his wif tolde,
He become so confus he couthe nought mele,
And alse doumb as a dore drough hym aside.
Ac for no carping that I couthe, ne knelyng to the ground,   95
I mighte gete no greyn of hise grete wyttes;
But al laughinge he loutide and lokide upon Studie,
In signe that I shulde beseke hire of grace.
And whanne I was war of his wil, to his wif gan I knele,
And seide, " Mercy, ma dame, your man shal I worthe,   100
For to werche your wil the while my lif durith;
Kenne me kyndely to knowe what is Do-wel."
    " For thi meknesse, man," quath she, " and for thi mylde speche,
I shal kenne the to my cosyn, that Clergie is hoten.
He hath weddit a wif withinne thise woukes sixe,   105
Is sib to the sevene ars, that Scripture is nempnid.
Thei two, as I hope, aftir my besekyng,
Shuln wisse the to Do-wel, I dar wel undirtake."
    Thanne was I as fayn as foul of fair morewen,
Gladdere thanne the gleman that gold hath to yifte,   110
And axide hire the heighe wey where Clergie dwellide—
" And tel me sum tokne to hym, for tyme is that I wende."
    " Axe the heighe wey," quath heo, " from henis to Suffre-
Bothe-wele-and-wo yif that thou-wilt-lerne,
And rid forth be Ricchesse, ac reste thou not there inne;   115
For yif thou couplist the with hym, to Clergie comist thou nevere.
And ek the longe launde, that Leccherie hatte,
Leve hym on thi left half a large myle or more,

[141]

Til thou come to a court Kepe-wel-thi-tunge-
Fro-lesinges-and-lither-speche-and-likerous-drinkes.   120
Thanne shalt thou se Sobirte and Simplite-of-speche,
That iche wight be in wille his wyt the to shewen.
So shalt thou come to Clergie, that can many thinges;
Sey hym this signe: I sette hym to scole,
And that I grete wel his wyf, for I wrot hire the bible,   125
And sette hire to Sapience, and to hire Sauter yglosid;
Logik I lerid hire, and al the lawe aftir,
And alle the musons of musik I made hire to knowe.
     " Plato the poete, I putte hym ferst to boke;
Aristotel and othere mo to arguen I taughte;   130
Gramer for girles I garte ferst write,
And bet hem with a baleis but yif thei wolde lerne.
Of alle kynne craftis I contrevide here tolis,
Of carpenteris and kerveris, and kende ferst masons,
And lernide hem lyvel and lyne, theigh I loke dymme.   135
     " Ac theologie hath tenid me ten score tymes;
For the more I muse theron, the mistlokere it semith,
And the deppere I devynide, the derkere me thoughte.
It is no science for sothe for to sotile there inne,
Ne were the love that lith there in, a wel lewid thing it were.   140
Ac for it lat best be love I love it the betere;
For there that love is lord lakkith nevere grace.
Leve lelly theron, yif thou thenke Do-wel;
For Do-bet and Do-best ben drawen of lovis scole.
In other science it seith—I saigh it in Catoun: 145
     Qui simulat verbis, nec corde est fidus amicus.
Ac theologie techith not so, who so takith heed;
He kennith us the contrarie ayens Catonis wordis,
And biddith us ben as bretheren, and blissen oure enemys,
And loven hem that lighen on us, and lenen hem at here nede,
And do good ayens evil; God hym self hotith,   150

[142]

And seide it hym self in ensaumple for the beste:
Necesse est ut veniant scandala.
  " Ac astronomye is hard thing and evil for to knowe;
Geometrie and geomesie is gynful of speche.
That thinketh werche with tho thre thriveth wel late;
For sorcerie is the soverayn bok that to that science longith.   155
Yet arn there febicchis of forellis of many menis wittes,
Experimentis of alkenemye, of Albertis makyng,
Nigromancie and perimansie, the pouke to reisen;
Yif thou thenke Do-wel, deile there with nevere.
Alle thise sciences, sikir, I my self   160
Foundit hem formest folk to desceyve.
I bekenne the Crist," quath she, " I can teche the no betere."
    I seide, " Graunt mercy, ma dame," and mekly hire grette,
And wente wightly my wey withoute more lettyng,
And fond as she fore-tolde, and forth gan I wende,   165
And er I com to Clergie coude I nevere stynte.
I grette the goode man as the gode wyf me taughte,
And aftirward his wyf I worsshipide bothe,
And tolde hire the toknes that me ytaught were;
Was nevere gome upon this ground, siththe God makid hevene, 170
Fairere undirfonge, ne frendliere mad at ese,
Thanne my self sothly, so sone as heo wiste
That I was of Wyttis hous, and with his wyf dame Stodie.
Curteisliche Clergie collide me and kiste,
And axide how Wyt ferde, and his wif Studie.   175
And I seide sothliche, " Thei sente me hider
To lerne at yow Do-wel, and Do-bet there aftir,
And sithen aftirward to se sum what of Do-best."
    " It is a wel lelle lif," quath she, " among the lewide peple;
Actif it is hoten, husbondis it usen;   180
Trewe tilieris on erthe, taillours and souteris,
And alle kyne crafty men that cunne here foode wynne,
With any trewe travaille toille for here foode,

[143]

Diken or delven, Do-wel it hatte.

" To breke beggeris bred and bakken hem with clothis,   185
Counforte the carful that in castel ben fetterid,
And sekert out the seke, and sende hem that hem nedith,
Obedient as bretheren and sustren to othere—
Thus bed the Do-bet; so berith witnesse the Sauter :
Ecce quam bonum et quam iocundum habitare, fratres, in unum.
Sike with the sory, singe with the glade :   190
Gaudere cum gaudentibus, et flere cum flentibus.
God wot, this is Do-bet.

" Sire Do-best hath benefices, so is he best worthi,
Be that God in the gospel grauntith and techith :
Qui facit et docuerit, magnus vocabitur in regno celorum.
For-thi is Do-best a bisshopis pere,
Prince over Godis peple, to prechen or to chaste.   195
Do-bet doth ful wel, and dewid he is also,
And hath possessions and pluralites for pore menis sake.
For mendynauntz at meschief tho men were dewid;
And that is rightful religioun—none renneris aboute,
Ne no leperis over lond ladies to shryve.   200
Gregory the grete clerk, a good pope in his tyme,
Of religioun the rewele he reherside in his morals,
And seide it in ensaumple that thei shulde do the betere :
' Whanne fisshes faile the flood, or the fresshe watir,
Thei dighe for the droughte, whanne thei dreighe liggen;   205
Right so be religioun—it roileth and stervith,
That out of covent and cloistre coveiten to libben.'
Ac now is religioun a ridere, and a romere be stretis,
A ledere of love-daies and a lond biggere,
Poperith on a palfrey fro toune to toune,   210
A bidowe or a baselard he berith be his side;
Godis flessh and his fet and hise fyve woundis
Arn more in his mynde than the memorie of his foundours.
This is the lif of this lordis that lyven shulde with Do-bet,

[144]

And wel-a-wey wers, and I wolde al telle." 215
   " I wende that kinghed and knighthed and caiseris with erlis
Wern Do-wel and Do-bet and Do-best of alle;
For I have seighe it my self, and siththen red it aftir,
How Crist counseillith the comune, and kenneth hem this tale:
   Super cathedram Moisi sederunt principes.
For-thi I wende that tho wyes wern Do-best of alle." 220
   " I nile not scorne," quath Scripture; " but scryveyns lighe,
Kinghod and knighthod, for aught I can aspie,
Helpith nought to hevene ward one heris ende,
Ne ricchesse, ne rentis, ne realte of lordis.
Poul provith it unpossible, riche men in hevene, 225
Ac pore men in pacience and penaunce togidere
Haven eritage in hevene, ac riche men non."
   " *Contra,*" quath I, " be Crist! that can I with-seye,
And proven it be the pistil that Petir is nempnid:
   Qui crediderit et baptizatus fuerit, salvus erit."
   " That is *in extremis,*" quath Scripture, " among Sarisines 230
Thei mowe be savid so, and so is oure beleve, [and Jewis;
That an uncristene in that cas may cristene an hethene,
And for his lele beleve, whanne he his lif tyneth,
Have eritage in hevene as an heigh Cristene.
Ac Cristene men, God wot, comith not so to hevene; 235
For Cristene han a degre and is here comun speche.
   Dilige deum, &c., et proximum tuum sicut teipsum.
Godis word witnessith we shuln yive and dele
Oure enemys and alle men that arn nedy and pore:
   Dum tempus est, operemur bonum ad omnes, maxime autem ad
      domesticos fidei.
Alle kynne creatures, that to Crist ben lyche,
We be holde heighly to herie and honoure, 240
And yiven hem of oure good as good as oure selven,
And sovereynliche to suche that sewen oure beleve;
That is, iche Cristene creature be kynde to other,

[145]

And sithen hethene to helpe in hope hem to amende.
To harme hem ne slen hem, God highte us nevere; 245
For he seith it hym self, in his ten hestis:
Non mecaberis—'ne sle nought' is the kynde Englisshe;
For, *Michi vindictam, et ego retribuam.*
'I shal punisshen in purcatory, or in the put of helle,
Eche man for his misdede, but mercy it make.'"

Yet am I nevere the ner, for nought I have walkid, 250
To wyte what is Do-wel witterly in herte;
For how so I werche in this world, wrong other ellis,
I was markid withoute mercy and myn name entrid
In the legende of lif, longe er I were;
Or ellis unwriten for wykkid, as witnessith the gospel: 255
  Nemo ascendet ad celum nisi qui de celo descendit.
And I leve it be oure Lord, and no lettrure betere;
For Salamon the sage, that Sapience made,
God yaf hym grace and ricchesse to-gidere
For to reule his reaum right at his wille;
Dede he not wel and wisly, as holy writ techith, 260
Bothe in werk and in woord, in world in his tyme?
Aristotle and he, who wroughte betere?
And al holy chirche holden hem in helle!
And was there nevere in this world to wysere of werkis;
For alle cunnyng clerkis, siththe Crist yede on erthe, 265
Taken ensaumple of here sawis in sarmonis that thei maken,
And be here werkis and here wordis wissen us to Do-wel;
And yif I shal werke be here werkis to wynne me hevene,
And for here werkis and for here wyt wende to pyne,
Thanne wroughte I unwisly, with alle the wyt that I lere! 270
  A Goode Friday, I fynde, a feloun was savid
That hadde lyved al his lyf with lesinges and theftis;
And for he kneugh on the crois, and to Crist shref hym,

Sonnere hadde he salvacioun thanne Seint Jon the baptist,
Or Adam or Ysaye, or any of the prophetis,   275
That hadde leyn with Lucifer manye longe yeris;
A robbere hadde remission rathere thanne thei alle,
Withoute penaunce of purcatorie, to have paradis for evere.
Thanne Marie the Maudeleyn, who mighte do wers?
Or who dede wers thanne David, that Urie destroyede?   280
Or Poule the apostil, that no pite ne hadde,
Cristene kynde to kille to dethe?
And arn none, for sothe, so sovereyne in hevene,
As thise that wroughte wykkidly in world whanne thei were.
        And yet am I forget ferthere of fyve wyttis teching,   285
That clergie of Cristis mouth comendite was it evere;
For he seide it hym self to summe of his disciplis:
      Dum steteritis ante presides nolite cogitare.
And is as muche to mene, to men that ben lewid,
" Whanne ye ben aposid of princes or of prestis of the lawe,
For to answere hem have ye no doute;   290
For I shal graunte yow grace, of God that ye serven,
The help of the holy gost to answere hem alle."
The doughtiest doctour or dyvynour of the trinite,
That was Austyn the olde, and higheste of the foure,
Seide thus for a sarmoun, so me God helpe: 295
      Ecce ipsi ydioti rapiunt celum, ubi nos sapientes in infernum
            mergemur.
And is to mene in oure mouth, more ne lesse,
" Arn none rathere yravisshid fro the righte beleve
Thanne arn thise grete clerkis, that conne many bokis;
Ne none sonnere ysavid, ne saddere of consience,
Thanne pore peple as ploughmen, and pastours of bestis."   300
Souteris and seweris, suche lewide jottis,
Percen with a *pater noster* the paleis of hevene,
Withoute penaunce, at here partyng, in-to the heighe blisse.

[147]

APPENDIX I

THE JOHN BUT PASSUS (Passus 12)

As HAS already been stated, the critical text proper of the second half of A consists of a prologue and two passus of the *Vita de Do-wel, Do-bet, & Do-best,* or passus nine, ten, and eleven, according to the consecutive numbering adopted for convenience. The twelfth, or so-called John But passus, cannot be considered a part of the critical text, since its existence is attested by only three members of the *y* family of A-text MSS (U, R, and I), only one (R) of which contains the whole passus—though another (U) probably had it (see the description of U in the INTRODUCTION, under *MSS of the A-text*).

Skeat, assuming that this passus must have been in the Vernon MS (which is defective at this point), concluded that it was an authentic portion of the A-text. It is true that if it were possible to demonstrate that the John But passus was actually in Vernon we would be in a much better position to pass on its authenticity, since Vernon represents an independent branch of the A family. Unfortunately this is impossible. Vernon's missing leaf, containing the latter portion of the eleventh passus, also included the beginning of the alliterative romance, *Joseph of Arimathie,* of which no other copy is known to be extant. Hence there are two obvious possibilities: (1) the missing leaf contained merely the remainder of the eleventh passus of *Piers the Plowman,* plus about two hundred and twenty lines of *Joseph of Arimathie*; or (2) it contained the remainder of the eleventh passus and the John But passus, plus something less than a hundred lines of *Joseph.* Which of the two is correct cannot be determined without more evidence than is now available.

The testimony of the *y* group of A-text MSS (TH₂ChDUR-AWMH₃IDi) is divided, but the evidence suggests that passus 12 was not in the original. As already noted, only manuscripts U, R, and I contain part or all of it. A brief glance at the chart of genealogical relationships (see INTRODUCTION, *Classification of the MSS*) reveals the fact that U and R form a minor subgroup of one branch of *y* MSS. MS I, it is true, represents an independent branch of *y*, but evidence of contamination between U and I (cf. *PMLA*, LXVI [1951], 495 ff.) places it under suspicion. Four MSS (DAMH₃) have nothing after passus 11.

The five remaining MSS of *y* (TH₂ChWDi) are the so-called "conjunct" MSS, that is, they contain the C-addition immediately following passus 11 of A, beginning with C 12. 297 (C 13. 1 in W). In view of the fact that the John But passus describes the death of Will (here identified as both dreamer and author), it is possible that this section might have been suppressed by someone engaged in grafting the C-continuation to the A-text. And the fact that the passus is found in neither the B- or C-text proper might be explained—without begging the question of authorship—in the same way. Against this, however, is the fact that suppression of the entire passus clearly would not have been necessary in order to cut out the account of Will's death. It is worthy of note that although the revisions of A involve many changes in phrasing, and extensive additions, there are very few lines or passages eliminated entirely. Thus the exclusion of passus twelve would have been contrary to the manifest practice of the reviser(s). With due acknowledgment, then, of the complexity of the problem, it seems best to suppose that the absence of the John But passus from most of the A-text MSS, and from the B- and C-revisions is due to the fact that it was not present in the archetype of A.

The following text of passus twelve is based on MS R, with readings from U and I. It should be understood that this is not a critical text. MS U is available for only the first 19 lines,

[149]

MS I for 88 lines; for the remainder of the text only MS R is available. The variant readings admitted in the text can be identified by consulting the variant readings in the TEXTUAL NOTES.

Passus tercius de Do-wel, &c.

" Crist wot," quod Clergie, " knowe hit yif the lyke,
I have do my dever the Do-wel to teche;
And who so coveyteth don betere than the boke telleth,
He passeth the apostolis lyf, and put him to aungelys.
But I se now as I seye, as me soth thinkytz,   5
The were lef to lerne, but loth for to stodie.
Thou woldest konne that I can and carpen hit after,
Presumptuowsly, paraventure, a-pose so manye,
That myghthe turne me to tene, and Theology bothe.
Yif I wiste witterly thou woldest don ther after,   10
Al that thou askest a-soylen I wolde."

  Skornfully tho Scripture set up here browes,
And on Clergie crieth, on Cristes holy name,
That he shewe me hit ne sholde, but yif stryf were
Of the kynde cardinal wit and cristned in a font;   15
And seyde so loude, that shame me thoughthe,
That hit were bothe skathe and sklaundre to holy cherche—
" Sitthe Theologie the trewe to tellen hit defendeth;
David, Godes derling, defendyth hit al-so:
  Vidi prevaricantes et tabescebam.
' I saw synful,' he seyde, ' ther-fore I seyde no thing,   20
Til tho wrecches ben in wil here synne to lete.'
And Poul precheth hit often—prestes hit redyn:
  Audivi archana verba que non licet homini loqui.
' I am not hardy,' quod he, ' that I herde with erys,
Telle hit with tounge to synful wrecches.'
And God graunted hit nevere; the gospel hit witnesseth,   25
In the passioun, whan Pilat a-posed God al-myghthi,
And asked Jesu on hy, that herden hit an hundred:

' *Quid est veritas,*' quod he, ' verilyche, tel us.'
God gaf him non answere, but gan his tounge holde.
Right so I rede," quod she, " red thou no ferther;   30
Of that he wolde wite, wis him no betere.
For he cam not by cause to lerne to Do-wel
But as he seyth, such I am, when he with me carpeth."

   And when Scripture the skolde hadde this wyt y-sheued,
Clergie in-to a caban crepte a-non after,   35
And drow the dore after him, and bad me go Do-wel,
Or wycke, yif I wolde—whether me lyked.

   Than held I up myn handes to Scripture the wise,
To be hure man yif I most, for evere more after,
With that she wolde me wisse wher the toun were   40
That Kynde Wit the confessour, hure cosyn, was inne.
That lady than low, and laughthe me in here armes,
And sayde, " My cosyn Kynde Wit knowen is wel wide,
And his loggyng is with Lyf, that lord is of erthe.
And yif thou desyre with him for to a-byde,   45
I shal the wisse where that he dwelleth."
And thanne I kneled on my knes, and kyste her wel sone,
And thanked hure a thousand sythes with throbbant herte.
   She called me a clerjoun
That hyght *Omnia-probate,* a pore thing with alle.   50
" Thou shalt wende with Wil," quod she, " whiles that him lykyth,
Til ye come to the burgh, *Quod-bonum-est-tenete.*
Ken him to my cosenes hous, that Kinde Wit hyghth;
Sey I sente him this segge, and that he shewe hym Do-wel."

   Thus we laughthe oure leve, lowtyng at onys,   55
And wente forth on my way with *Omnia-probate,*
And ere I cam to the court, *Quod-bonum-est-tenete,*
Many ferlys me by-fel in a fewe yeris.
   The fyrste ferly I fond a-fyngrid me made;
As I yede thurgh youthe a-yen prime dayes,   60
I stode stille in a stodie, and stared a-bowte;

" Al hayl," quod on tho, and I answered, " Welcome, and with
     whom be ye ? "
" I am dwellyng with Deth, and Hunger I hatte;
To Lyf in his lordshepe longyt my weye,
To kyllyn him yif I can, theigh Kynde Wit helpe;   65
I shal felle that freke in a fewe dayes."
" I wolde folwe the fayn," quod I, " but feyntise me henteth;
Me folweth such a feyntise, I may no ferther walke."
" Go we forth," quod the gom; " I have a gret boyste
At my bak of broke bred thi bely for to fylle;   70
A bagge ful, of a beggere I boughthe hit at onys."
Than maunged I with him up to the fulle;
For the myssyng of mete no mesour I coude,
But ete as Hunger me hete, til my belly swellyd.
Ther bad me Hunger have gode day, but I helde me stille;   75
For gronyng of my guttys I durst gon no ferther.
   With that cam a knave with a confessoures face,
Lene and rewlyche, with leggys ful smale.
He halsed me, and I asked him after
Of whennes that he were, and wheder that he wolde.   80
" With Deth I duelle," quod he, " dayes and nyghtes;
Mi name is Fevere-on-the-ferthe-day; I am a-threst evere.
I am masager of Deth—men have I tweyne:
That on is called Cotidian, a courrour of oure hous,
Tercian that other, trewe drinkeres bothe.   85
We han letteres of Lyf, he shal his lyf tyne;
Fro Deth that is oure duk swyche dedis we brynge."
" Myghth I so, God wot, youre gates wolde I holden."
" Nay, Wil," quod that wyghth, " wend thou no ferther,
But lyve as this lyf is ordeyned for the;   90
The tomblest with a trepget, yif thou my tras folwe;
And mannes merthe wroughth no mor than he deservyth here,
Whil his lyf and his lykhame lesten to-gedere.
And ther-fore do after Do-wel whil thi dayes duren,

That thi play be plentevous in paradys with aungelys.   95
Thou shalt be laughth into lyghth, with loking of an eye,
So that thou werke the word that holy wryt techeth,
And be prest to preyeres, and profitable werkes."
   Wille thurgh in-wit, thou wost wel the sothe,
That this speche was spedelich, and sped him wel faste,   100
And wroughthe that here is wryten, and other werkes bothe,
Of Peres the plowman and mechel puple al-so;
And whan this werk was wrought, ere Wille myghte a-spie,
Deth delt him a dent, and drof him to the erthe,
And is closed under clom—Crist have his soule!   105
   And so bad Johan But, busily wel ofte,
When he saw thes sawes busyly a-legged
By James and by Jerom, by Jop and by othere;
And for he medleth of makyng, he made this ende.
Now alle kenne creatures that Cristene were evere,   110
God for his goudnesse gif hem swyche happes,
To lyve as that lord lykyth that lyf in hem putte.
Furst to rekne Richard kyng of this rewme,
And alle lordes that lovyn him lely in herte,
God save hem sound, by se and by land;   115
Marie moder and may for man thou by-seke;
That barn bryng us to blys that bled up-on the rode.

   Amen.

EXPLICIT DO-WEL.

Nomen scriptoris Tilot, plenus amoris.

[153]

EXPLANATORY NOTES

PROLOGUE

3. **unholy of werkis.** That is, a false hermit, one that leaves his cell and wanders about. See INTRODUCTION, *Hermits*, and cf. pr. 50–54.

13 ff. In the east the dreamer sees a tower (heaven), opposite which is a dungeon (hell), and in between a field full of folk (the world). Skeat (*Parallel Texts*, II, 4), Jusserand (*MP*, VI, 310), and others have thought that this passage reflects the author's familiarity with the medieval drama. Jusserand refers to an illustration in the MS of the Valenciennes Passion, which shows, on one side, God's Tower or Palace; on the opposite side, the devil's castle; and between the two, a space where the main action takes place. Skeat calls attention to a sketch of the staging of the *Castle of Perseverance* (a reproduction of which may be conveniently found in J. Q. Adams, *Chief Pre-Shakespearian Dramas*, 264). This sketch shows the castle located in the center of the *platea*, or circular stage, surrounded by a moat or ditch, with the scaffold of God situated to the east of the castle, that of the World to the west, Flesh to the south, Belial to the north, etc. It has also been argued that *Piers the Plowman* itself influenced the later drama (cf. *PMLA*, XXVI, 339 ff.); and of course the *Castle of Perseverance*, though it is one of the earliest moralities, is much later than our poem; it was probably composed about 1425. But references to the so-called *pater noster* plays (first referred to in 1378) indicate that plays something like the *Castle of Perseverance* and *Mankind* were probably being produced prior to our earliest surviving moralities. If this be the case, the striking picture that our author here presents may owe something of its concrete visualization to the medieval stage.

22. As it stands, this line is weak in alliteration; but see the variant readings in the TEXTUAL NOTES. For the words "That many of" Skeat's B- and C-texts have "And wonnen that." Probably "with" is intended to alliterate; cf. 2.30, 5.25, and 7.88; and see *MLR*, XVII, 403 ff.

28. This refers to the good hermits, who stayed in their cells (see note to pr. 3 above, and cf. 7.133). It is of interest to note that the author is not simply satirizing the evils of his day in this picture of the field full of folk, but includes good hermits, as well as hard workers that "pleighede ful selde" and honest minstrels who were rewarded legitimately for their entertainment. Cf. Dunning, *Piers Plowman: An Interpretation of the A-text*, 26 ff.

38. **That Poule prechith of hem.** Perhaps, as Skeat thought, the poet has in mind 2 Thess. 3:10. ". . . if any would not work, neither should he eat."

39. **Qui loquitur turpiloquium.** "He who speaks slander" (cf. Eph. 5:4; Col. 3:8). Our author seems to have been fond of this mixture of Latin and the vernacular, a phenomenon known as macaronic verse. Cf. 1.50–51,

[154]

84, 175, 4. 126–27, 5. 42, etc. See Sullivan, *The Latin Insertions and the Macaronic Verse in Piers Plowman*, especially chapters IV and V.

46 ff. The medieval pilgrimage, initiated for purely devotional purposes, had degenerated till in the fourteenth century we find it unquestionably prompted, for the most part, by worldly motives. In Chaucer's prologue to the *Canterbury Tales*, the pilgrims are actuated by little more than the desire to indulge in the equivalent of our modern summer vacations. **Seint Jame.** Aside from Rome itself, one of the most popular holy places in Christendom was the famous shrine of St. James at Compostella in Spain. Chaucer's well-traveled Wife of Bath had been, among other places, " In Galice at Seint Jame." We are told that " hermits " went to **Walsyngham,** which was an English shrine in Norfolk, second only to that of St. Thomas at Canterbury, where Chaucer's pilgrims were going. It seems clear that the pilgrimages of these false hermits, with " here wenchis aftir," were mere debauches.

55. **friars.** The four orders were: 1) The Franciscans, also called Minorites (cf. 9. 9), or Grey Friars, because of their garb; 2) the Dominicans, also known as the preaching friars, because of their zeal in combatting heresy, or the Black Friars, because of their dress, or the Jacobins, after a Dominican House located in Paris on the Rue St. Jacques; 3) the Carmelites, or White Friars; and 4) the Austins, or Augustine Friars. See INTRODUCTION, *Friars*.

61–64. " Since love has become a merchant (and chiefly to shrive lords), many wonders have occurred in a few years; and unless the Church and they hold better together, the greatest mischief on earth is rapidly approaching." This may be a veiled reference by our poet to some recent event that has impressed him. The " hy " of line 63 seems clearly to refer to the friars; " holy chirche " must, as Skeat noted, refer to the secular clergy. There was, of course, much bitter dissension between these two groups, which can largely be traced to the friars' exaggerated claims about their power of confession. It will be recalled that Chaucer's friar

> . . . hadde power of confessioun,
> As seyde hym self, moore than a curat.   (pr. 218–19)

One critic has suggested (cf. Dunning, 20) that the " Manye ferlies " of line 62 refers to the quarrel between the friars and Richard Fitz-Ralph, Archbishop of Armagh, who delivered a series of sermons against the Mendicants, which were preached in English at St. Paul's Cross in the winter of 1356-7. (cf. *Studies*, XXVI (1937), 50–52).

75. **worth bothe hise eris.** Fit to keep both his ears, i. e., not have them cut off as a form of punishment. Cf. *MLN*, LVIII, 48.

77–79. Collusion between the parish priest and the pardoner seems to have been fairly common. See G. R. Owst, *Preaching in Medieval England*, 103: " The indefatigable Grandisson [Bishop of Exeter in the first half of the fourteenth century] lays bare, in a document glowing with indignation, the system he has detected at work in his diocese, by which a whole army of false questors, many of whom were laymen [cf. " as he a prest were," line 65],

[155]

were being encouraged by the archdeacon's officials, who pocketed the proceeds that came their way" (quoted by Dunning, *Piers Plowman*, 29, note 5).

81. **pestilence tyme.** This is the first mention by our poet of the Black Death. It is later referred to directly in 5.13, 10.185, and 11.59, and perhaps indirectly in 5.32–33. See INTRODUCTION, *The Pestilence*. Although from 1348 to 1370 there were three especially violent epidemics—first in 1348–49, then in 1361–62, and 1368–69—there seems to be no reference to any particular one of these; our author simply says "the pestilence" or "the pestilence tyme."

92. **Archideknes and denis.** The archdeacon was next in rank below a bishop, and acted as the latter's delegate in judicial duties in a certain area of the diocese. The dean exercised a similar function in the rural deanery, which was a subdivision of the archdeacon's sphere of jurisdiction. These offices are still maintained in the Anglican church. On this whole passage see INTRODUCTION, *Clerks in Worldly Office*.

98 f. The OE endings *-estre, -istre, -ystre* were the feminine terminations of nouns. In ME the ending *-stre* or *-ster* originally preserved the OE meaning, but later became confused with words of OF origin ending in *-stre, -ster*, such as *ministre, maistre*; cf. Chaucer's *ydolastre*. It is not clear whether our author had in mind the earlier feminine denotation in such words as baxteris, breusteris, and websteris. Cf. 3.67 f., where of "Breowesters and bakeris, bocheris and cokes" it is said that "thise arn *men* on thise molde that most harm werchith." On the other hand, see 5.128, "my wyf was a wynstere," as opposed to the common form *wynnere* (but see variant readings on 5.128 in TEXTUAL NOTES).

103. **Dieu save, dame Emme.** "God save you, dame Emme." Probably from a popular song of the day. Cf. Skeat's B-text, 13.340.

107 f. These are all wines imported from France—from Alsace, Gascony, Rhine, and Rochelle.

PASSUS ONE

27–31. Compare the biblical account in Gen. 19: 30–38.

36–39. This passage contains an allusion to the three sources of temptation, according to the Church Fathers: the World, the Flesh, and the Devil—a commonplace in medieval literature. Cf. *Castle of Perseverance*, referred to above in note on pr. 13 ff.

44–51. Mark 12: 14–17; Matt. 22: 17–21; Luke 20: 21–25.

59 ff. The account of Wrong (the devil) recalls John 8: 44; especially compare "Father of falsehood" (line 62) with "for he is a liar, and the father of it" (Dunning, *Piers Plowman*, 40).

84. **Deus caritas.** "God is love." 1 John 4: 8.

88 f. The exact reference in Luke is not clear. Skeat thought these lines referred to the parable of the unjust steward, especially Luke 16: 10–13;

he also cited 8: 21. Dunning (p. 44) has plausibly suggested Luke 6: 35: "But love ye your enemies, and do good, and lend, hoping for nothing again; and your reward shall be great, and ye shall be the children of the Highest. . . ." One difficulty here is the phrase "a god" (line 88). Dunning suggests that it may equal "children of the Highest"; or that it is the Middle English form meaning "of God," which would be an even better solution. Though no MS has the reading "of god," there does seem to be some disagreement. For "a god" H₂ has "good," Ch has "on god," I has "in god"; for "a god be the gospel" M has "a good gospel," VH have "a-counted to the gospel."

103 f. **kingene king.** "king of kings." Here may be seen the survival of the OE genitive plural ending *-ena,* a form unfamiliar to most of the scribes of the A-text MSS; see the variant readings in TEXTUAL NOTES. Also compare "Jewene" (1. 65) and "wyvene" (5. 29). **knightide tene.** We might have expected *nine,* since it was commonly thought that there were nine orders of angels, divided into three hierarchies, each of three orders: the first were seraphim, cherubim, and thrones; the second, dominions, virtues, and powers; and the third, principalities, archangels, and angels. The author, however, undoubtedly wrote "tene." A few scribes seem to have been disturbed by this: for "tene" I has "ten that tyme," with "ten" crossed out and "that tyme" added in a different hand; instead of "tene" Di has "in tyme"; H has "somtyme" (T₂V omit line 103; A is defective; H₃ is B-text here). L completely changes lines 103–104 to read:

> For crist creatour cried and kraftely made
> Of Aungles and archangles ordres nyne.

Skeat quotes several passages showing that the order headed by Lucifer was thought of as being the tenth; see his note on this line (*Parallel Texts,* II, 24 f.). Also cf. TEXTUAL NOTES for variant readings on the second half of line 104.

123. **thise textis.** The texts referred to are *Reddite Cesari* (1. 50–51) and *Deus caritas* (1. 84).

150–52. Matt. 7: 2; Luke 6: 38.

157. **in masse ne in oures.** The meaning is that there is no merit in the religious services (Mass and Hours) unless you love your neighbor and give to the poor. For an explanation of the Hours, see INTRODUCTION, *The Three Kinds of Monastic Rule.*

158. **Malkyn.** A conventional name for a country maid; here apparently an unattractive girl, whose virginity is not necessarily the consequence of her virtue. Surely not a wanton, as Skeat thought, or the whole force of the passage is lost. Cf. *MLN,* LXIII (1948), 52–53.

159 f. James 2: 26.

162 f. A reference to the parable of the wise and foolish virgins, Matt. 25: 1–13.

173. Our author points out that the covetousness of the clergy acts as

[157]

an example to laymen to be more grudging in their almsgiving. Compare this sentiment with the words of Simon Islip, Archbishop of Canterbury (from 1349 to 1366):

The unbridled covetousness of men would grow to such a height as to banish charity out of the world, if it were not repressed by justice. The priests that now are, not . . . ashamed that layworkmen make their covetousness an example to themselves, have no regard to the cure of souls though fitting salaries are offered to them, and . . . discharge their intemperance in vice and lust, grow wild and drown themselves in the abyss of vice, to the great scandal of ecclesiastics and the evil example of laymen.

(Quoted by W. W. Capes, *The English Church in the Fourteenth and Fifteenth Centuries*, London (1909), 78; its relevance in this connection was pointed out by Dunning, *Piers Plowman*, 57).

175. **Date et dabitur vobis.** "Give, and it shall be given unto you." Luke 6: 38.

180 f. Cf. lines 123–24 of this passus, and see note on 123.

PASSUS TWO

2. **for Marie love of hevene.** That is, for the love of Mary of heaven. Compare the same construction in " for oure Lordis love of hevene " (3. 221, 7. 17, 8. 33); "Hikkes hood the hostiller" (5. 183); "for Cristis love of hevene" (7. 206); "for Peris love the ploughman" (8. 128).

73. **Poulynes doctor.** See INTRODUCTION, *Friars*. Cf. also 2. 139.

86. **Dignus est operarius mercede sua.** Matt. 10: 10. The author gives his translation of this in line 87.

PASSUS THREE

18. "In spite of any plot that Conscience may devise." Apparently a difficult passage for the scribes. See the TEXTUAL NOTES on this line, and compare the readings in the B- and C-texts.

34 ff. This passage contains a severe indictment of friars. In this connection it is interesting to compare a bill of complaints (cf. A. Gwynn, *Studies*, XXVI [1937], 50–51) submitted to the provincial council of Canterbury, which met at St. Paul's in London on May 16, 1356. "It is drawn up in the name of the clergy of the province of Canterbury, and is addressed to the Archbishop of Canterbury and his suffragans, *contra fratres mendicantes*" (p. 50). Father Gwynn summarizes the bill of complaints as follows: "The friars have given free rein to their questing and begging; they ride round the country on fine palfreys, with splendid equipment, *ultra morem maiorum prelatorum in Anglia*; they have no respect for the canons and censures of the province of Canterbury, but are slanderers of the clergy and flatterers of the nobility (*adulatores magnatum confessores*); they meddle in marriages and secular business under the cloak of religion, and seek to gain the favour of the great; they inflict grave injury on many of the churches of England through their influence with the nobles; they abuse their powers as confessors and dispense freely from the duty of restitution; they soothe the sinner in his sin (*posito pulvillo blandiendi*

[158]

sub capite peccatoris quietant in peccato). The last few lines are corrupt and difficult to translate, but the satire grows more bitter with each clause." (p. 51). With this passage compare that in the prologue (61–64) already noted.

53. **Nesciat sinistra quid faciat dextera.** Matt. 6: 3. Lines 54–55 are the author's translation of this text.

63. **Amen, amen dico vobis, receperunt mercedem suam.** " Verily, verily I say unto you, they have their reward." Matt. 6: 2 (cf. also verses 5, 16).

81–87. The reference is not to Solomon, as the text says, but to Job 15: 34, which is paraphrased by the author in 85–87.

88. **The king fro counseil com.** Under Edward I the " Council " was a large body, comprising the great officers of state—the Chancellor, the Treasurer, etc., the judges of the three courts, the Masters of Chancery, or chief clerks of Chancery, and those prelates and barons whom the king wished to summon.

Its sessions or " parliaments " were engaged in work of a very miscellaneous nature. It was the court of last resort in those cases in which errors of the lower courts were to be corrected. It was a court of the first instance in all cases, civil or criminal, which the king evoked before it. It might hear petitions offered against the king, or complaints against any wrong that could not be redressed in any ordinary court of justice.

In the fourteenth century the " Lords' House of Parliament " was an assembly of prelates and barons whose duty it was to correct mistakes made in the law of the lower courts. There peers of the realm were tried for capital crimes—before a jury of their peers. It set the precedents which developed into the modern " impeachment," a trial on complaint of the House of Commons. Thus the House of Lords appeared as the highest tribunal in the realm, though known as " the king in parliament."

Beside this appeared and developed another tribunal, with claims to indefinitely wider jurisdiction. This was " the king in council." It was not at first or for some time clearly distinguished from " the king in parliament." Before the Lords' House of Parliament might be summoned members of the king's council who were not peers of the realm, especially judges and masters in chancery. When so summoned, they were regarded and treated as mere assistants of the peers, not as equals. On the other hand, there was a wide-spread belief that all peers were by right members of the king's council, and had a right to appear at and to take part in the deliberations at the council board.

The council enforced mostly criminal justice. Trial by jury was clumsy and full of opportunities for bribery and corruption that in practice were beyond redress. For example, many rich and powerful criminals were attacked and punished by the council when, because of their bribes or their influence, no verdict against them could have been obtained in any of the ordinary courts. No one, of course, could be deprived of life or limb without a written judgment rendered by a jury of his equals in a common law court. But the council could and did inflict fines and imprisonment on these influential criminals as well as on rioters, conspirators, bribers, and perjured jurors.

114. Conscience tells the king, who undoubtedly represents Edward III (1327–77), that Lady Meed brought about the death of his father, Edward II (1307–27). It will be recalled that shortly after his deposition Edward II was murdered in Berkeley Castle, September, 1327.

129. Conscience accuses Meed of securing removal of sentences of excommunication by bribing the "comissarie" (see GLOSSARY) and his clerks. The pay comes in the form of clothing, a common means of exchange in the middle ages, when money was not circulating freely. Cf. the B-text, 14. 151. It will be recalled that Chaucer's Sergeant of the Law

> For his science, and for his heigh renoun,
> Of fees and robes hadde he many oon.   (Pro. 316–17)

137 f. Cf. INTRODUCTION, *The Cathedral Chapters.*

172. Meed denies Conscience's accusation made above, line 114 (see note).

174 ff. Here follows the passage alluding to the Norman wars, which has been studied by various critics for the purpose of establishing the date of the A-text. Skeat pointed out the references to the Treaty of Bretigny in 1360 (191–93) and the famous storm which frightened the English at Chartres on "Black Monday" (cf. "a dym cloude" [178]). More recently, B. F. Huppé (*PMLA*, LIV [1939], 37–64) has argued that the references here are to the disastrous winter campaign conducted by John of Gaunt (whom he identifies with Conscience) in 1373. J. A. W. Bennett (*PMLA*, LVIII [1943], 566–72) has shown that this is unlikely, but cites several interesting passages which do suggest a date nearer 1370.

180–81. "The lines are addressed to Conscience, and if we accept the suggestion that Conscience is to be identified with John of Gaunt at this point, we can explain them as referring to the great amount of plunder which John of Gaunt took back with him to Calais in 1369, at the close of his otherwise ineffective and abortive campaign. Alternatively, they may relate more generally to the period 1363–69, during which time a full staple and mint were established at Calais." (Bennett, *PMLA*, LVIII [1943], 570).

182–85. It is possible that in this passage Meed is identified with Alice Perrers, mistress of Edward III. Bennett, no doubt because he was using Skeat's A-text, calls attention to 182–83 only in this connection; but it seems apparent that all four lines go together. The reference to mourning in line 183, according to Bennett, would then indicate that the time is shortly after the death of Queen Philippa in August, 1369.

191–93. As already mentioned, these lines certainly refer to the Treaty of Bretigny, concluded on May 8, 1360, when peace was made between the English and French. Here Edward III waived his claims on the French crown, and apparently Meed is criticizing Conscience for counseling the king to do this. The "litel silver" refers to the sum of 3,000,000 gold crowns to be paid to Edward as ransom for King John of France under the terms of the treaty.

219. Qui pecuniam suam non dedit ad usuram &c. " He that putteth not out his money to usury, nor taketh reward against the innocent." Ps. 15: 5.

225. In quorum manibus iniquitates sunt; dextera eorum repleta est muneribus. " In whose hands is mischief, and their right hand is full of bribes." Ps. 26: 10.

230. Matt. 6: 2, 5, 16. Cf. note to 3. 63 above.

235. Regum. In the Vulgate Samuel and Kings were combined. The story related in this passage is from 1 Sam. 15.

PASSUS FOUR

32. his sone. Presumably a reference to Edward's eldest son, the Black Prince, though it must be recalled that the latter was absent from England during the period 1363–70. It may be, as Bennett suggests (*PMLA*, LVIII [1943], 570, n. 10), that this simply means that Reason was given a place of honor. The line is retained in B and (with minor changes) in C.

34 ff. The complaint of Peace against Wrong recalls the complaints of the people against the King's Purveyors, both real and pretended. Cf. Skeat's note on this line.

109 f. That is, there is no need to seek St. James at the famous shrine in the province of Galicia. See note on Pro. 46 ff.

111. Rome renneris were priests " who can faste renne to rome & bere gold out of the lond & paie it, for deed leed & a litel wrytinge. . . ." (*English Works of Wyclif*, EETS OS 74, 245). Bennett (*Med. Aev.*, XII [1943], 60) cites this reference to Rome-runners as further support for the belief that the A-text was written in the late thirteen-sixties. He points out that the papal court was in Avignon during most of the fourteenth century, but that it was in Rome for a brief period from 1367–70.

126 f. In these two macaronic lines the author adapts a quotation from a treatise by Pope Innocent III, *De Contemptu Mundi*, bk. III, ch. 15: " No evil unpunished, no good unrewarded."

PASSUS FIVE

13. the pestilence. See INTRODUCTION, *The Pestilence*. If we accept the later date (1369–70) for the composition of the A-text, there were three violent epidemics in England which may be alluded to here: 1348–49, 1361–62, and 1368–69. Some A manuscripts have the reading " þise pestilences "; see TEXTUAL NOTES on this line.

14. the southwest wynd refers to a storm which occurred on Saturday, January 15, 1362.

42. Qui cum patre et filio. This is the formula with which sermons were concluded: " Who with the Father and the Holy Spirit lives and reigns

[161]

forever and ever." Here " Son " is substituted for " Holy Spirit," the latter apparently being identified with St. Truth in the preceding line.

45 ff. Here begin the confessions of the Seven Deadly Sins, so frequently referred to in medieval literature. They are: Pride, Lechery, Envy, Wrath, Covetousness, Gluttony, and Sloth. It will be noted that Wrath is omitted from this series.

Manly's much-discussed theory of the lost leaf (*MP*, III [1906], 359–66) is an attempt to account for the omission of Wrath and at the same time explain the rather sudden transition in the confession of Sloth from a vow to attend church regularly, to a promise to restore wicked winnings, made by a person identified as " Roberd the robbour." Briefly, Manly's theory is as follows.

In a MS which was the archetype of all extant A manuscripts, a leaf next to the innermost of a gathering was lost, thus creating two gaps in the text of which subsequent copyists were unaware. The first of these missing folios belonged between lines 5. 105 and 106, and probably contained the conclusion of the confession of Envy as well as the whole of the confession of Wrath. The second belonged between lines 5. 227 and 228, including a conclusion for the confession of Sloth, and a transitional passage introducing " Roberd the Robbour." Between these two gaps in the text there are 122 lines, which would fill a leaf averaging about 30 lines to the page. The bearing of this theory on the problem of the authorship of the three versions of the poem can easily be seen by observing the unsatisfactory alterations and adjustments made by the B and C revisers.

143. **Walsyngham.** See note on pr. 46 ff.

170. **the newe feire** was a game of mock-bargaining designed for the entertainment of the company. Cf. *Sir Gawain and the Green Knight*, 981–89.

215. **Vigilate.** A character by the name of " Watch " exhorts Sloth to repentance. *Vigilate* is apparently thought of as a nun (" þe veil "), though Skeat takes " veil " to mean " watcher " (OF *veile*, LAT *vigilia*). The Latin name, according to Skeat, is taken from Mark 13: 37. In like manner we find in line 234 *Reddite*, " Make restitution " (Rom. 13: 7), and in line 251 *Latro*, " Thief " (Luke 23: 39).

239. **memento.** " remember " (Luke 23: 42).

PASSUS SIX

8–16. This palmer is evidently one of those already satirized in pr. 46 ff. Our author's skepticism about the efficacy of pilgrimages such as those listed here has already been expressed (4. 109–10). By means of his signs, no doubt worn conspicuously for the benefit of provincial admirers, we are led to believe that the palmer has been to Canterbury (ampollis), Sinai (" signes " not specified), St. James in Galicia (shells), the Holy Land (cross), and Rome (cross-keys and vernicle). He tells us specifically that he has also been to Bethlehem, Babylon, Armenia, and Alexandria—that great entry port for pilgrims from the West.

[162]

48 ff. In Piers' directions for finding the abode of St. Truth we find the author's first liberal use of extended allegorical names, indicated in the text by hyphens. Thus Piers tells the pilgrims that they will come to a brook named " Be-buxum-of-speche," etc. The basis of the allegory is of course the Ten Commandments, leading off with the two Great Commandments (Matt. 22: 37–39; Mark 12: 29–31).

89. **wayve up.** Push up, i. e., open (the gate); *up* is regularly used for opening a door or gate: " caste up the yates wyde " (Chaucer, *Troilus*, II, 615). For *wayve*, cf. ON *veifa*; in *Sir Gawain and the Green Knight* the lady " wayveȝ vp a wyndow " (1743); also in *Purity*, " þenne wafte he upon his wyndowe " (453). See the variant readings in the TEXTUAL NOTES.

93 f. Dunning (123 f.) points out the allusion here to John 14: 17, 19, 23, especially the latter: " If a man love me, he will keep my words; and my Father will love him, and we will come unto him, and make our abode with him."

99. **worst.** Consult GLOSSARY, *worthen*. **dryven out as dew.** Cf. Hosea 13: 3.

104. The keepers of the gates of the castle of Truth are the personified Seven Virtues, familiar to students of medieval literature. These virtues are frequently placed in opposition to the corresponding Deadly Sins; thus Abstinence vs. Gluttony, Humility vs. Pride, Charity vs. Envy, Chastity vs. Lechery, Patience vs. Wrath, Peace (or Industry) vs. Sloth, and Largesse vs. Covetousness. See the passage in *Castle of Perseverance* where the Seven Virtues defend Mankind against the assaults of the Seven Deadly Sins (2048 ff.).

PASSUS SEVEN

67–68. **Deleantur de libro [viventium] . . . et cum iustis non scribantur.** " Let them be blotted out of the book of the living, and not be written with the righteous." Ps. 69: 28.

70–73. These four lines, containing the names of the wife and children of Piers were thought by Manly (*CHEL*, II, 37) to be a scribal interpolation, interrupting as they do Piers' remarks about his preparations for the pilgrimage. The fact that the lines are retained intact in the B and C revisions would then provide evidence in favor of the theory of multiple authorship.

212. **Facite vobis amicos de mammona iniquitatis.** " Make to yourselves friends of the mammon of unrighteousness." Luke 16: 9. The author frequently errs on the source of his quotations. Cf. line 220 below.

217–18. Gen. 3: 19.

220–21. **Piger propter frigus,** etc. " The sluggard will not plow by reason of the cold; therefore shall he beg in harvest, and have nothing." Prov. 20: 4. Not the book of Wisdom, as the text says.

222. **Matheu with the manis face.** Skeat, in his note on this line, says: " An allusion to a common representation of the evangelists, which likens

Matthew to a *man*, Mark to a *lion*, Luke to a *bull*, and John to an *eagle*."
Cf. Ezek. 1: 10 and Rev. 4: 7. The reference here is to the parable of the
talents, Matt. 25: 14 ff., and Luke 19: 12 ff.

234. **the salme of Beati omnes,** i. e., the psalm beginning "Blessed is
everyone that feareth the Lord; that walketh in His ways." The quotation
is from the second verse of this psalm (128): "For thou shalt eat the
labour of thine hands."

301. **statute.** References in this passage to high wages and to laws designed
to chasten laborers reflect economic conditions which developed in the
wake of the pestilence. The shortage of farm hands after the epidemic of
1348–49 enabled workers to demand higher wages; a Statute of Labourers
was provided by Edward III, freezing wages at the level prevailing two
years before the beginning of the pestilence. The subsequent re-enactments
of the statute indicate the difficulty encountered in enforcing it.

307. **Satourne.** In medieval astrology the influence of Saturn is always
unfavorable, if not malignant. Compare his role in Chaucer's *Knight's Tale*,
especially 2453 ff.

PASSUS EIGHT

1 ff. With the beginning of this passus the pilgrimage to Truth is discon-
tinued, giving way to discussion of a pardon which applies to all who do
well. Some critics have thought that the author simply forgot about the
pilgrimage, for which elaborate preparation is made in the two preceding
passus. It is true that the expected journey to the abode of St. Truth
is not to be found in the text; but a careful reading of the opening lines
of this passus will reveal that the author has not forgotten it. A key to
the interpretation of this passage is the word "here-of" in the first line.
Most critics have taken it to refer to the plowing of the half-acre (cf.
R. W. Chambers, *Man's Unconquerable Mind*, 117; Dunning, *Piers Plowman*,
141; and Nevill Coghill, *The Pardon of Piers Plowman*, 17). Yet "here-of"
seems clearly to refer to the warning issued by Saturn in the lines immediately preceding. In effect Truth is saying: "Don't start on the
pilgrimage to my shrine; rather take your team and till the earth in order
to store up supplies against the coming famine; I am sending you a pardon
for remission of sins which will apply to all who do well."

3. **a pena et a culpa.** "from punishment and guilt." Most medieval
theologians did not believe that indulgences could remit the guilt of sin.
Nevertheless this idea seems to have been popularized by false pardoners
until the formula came into general use, meaning simply the highest
spiritual favor that the Pope could bestow—without doctrinal significance
(cf. Dunning, *Piers Plowman*, 141–42).

20. **manye yeris.** "i. e. many years' remission of purgatory" (Skeat).

46. **Super innocentem munera non accipies. A regibus et principibus, &c.**
The first part of this quotation comes from Ps. 15: 5, already quoted (cf.
note to 3. 219). The source of the second part is not known, though the
author refers to the book of Wisdom. Skeat points out a resemblance to
Ecclus. 38: 2.

[164]

89 ff. This passage has long puzzled the critics. Piers' tearing of the pardon is evidently intended by the poet as the climax to this section of the poem, for the dreamer awakens shortly thereafter. But why does Piers tear the pardon? Probably the best explanation is that the pardon has a double function in this scene. First, it conveys a message from Truth: do well, and you will be saved; do evil, and you will be damned. Piers accepts this message in good faith. But when the priest " impugns " it and calls it " no pardon," Piers angrily tears up the document. This action does not imply a rejection of the message from Truth; rather, it is Piers' dramatic way of showing the priest that the efficacy of this pardon, unlike papal indulgences, is not dependent on the existence of a piece of paper. For an excellent discussion of this passage, and a convenient summary of earlier views, see R. W. Frank, " The Pardon Scene in *Piers Plowman*," *Speculum*, XXVI (April, 1951), 317–31.

94. **Et qui bona egerunt, ibunt in vitam eternam;**
   Qui vero mala, in ignem eternum.
" And those who did good shall go into eternal life; but those who did evil, into eternal fire." Quoted from the Athanasian Creed, a formulary erroneously attributed to Athanasius, bishop of Alexandria (d. 373).

99. **Si ambulavero in medio umbre mortis, non timebo mala, quoniam tu mecum es.** " Yea, though I walk through the valley of the shadow of death, I will fear no evil, for thou art with me." Ps. 23: 4.

106. **Fuerunt michi lacrime mee panes, die ac nocte.** " My tears have been my meat, day and night." Ps. 42: 3 (cf. Ps. 34: 10).

109. **Ne soliciti sitis** [etc.]. " Take no thought for your life, what ye shall eat, or what ye shall drink. . . ." Matt. 6: 25 (cf. Luke 12: 22).

119. **Quoniam literaturam non cognovi.** " For I have known no learning." Ps. 70: 15 (Vulgate). The King James version (Ps. 71: 15) here reads differently, following the Massoretic text.

121. **Ecce** [for *Eice*, or *Ejice*] **derisores et jurgia cum eis, ne crescant** [etc.]. " Cast out the scorner, and contention shall go out; yea, strife and reproach shall cease." Prov. 22: 10.

131. **Sompnia ne cures.** " Trust not dreams." This quotation is taken from bk. II, distich 32 of *Disticha Catonis de Moribus*, an anonymous fourth-century collection of proverbs composed in the form of couplets and ascribed, during the Middle Ages, to Cato the elder. The complete couplet may be translated: " Trust not dreams; for what the human mind desires, hoping for while it lies awake, that very thing it sees in sleep."

132 ff. Apparently the allusion is to Dan. 2: 39, though it is possible, as Skeat suggests, that the author has confused the interpretation of Nebuchadnezzar's dream with that of Belshazzar's (Dan. 5: 28). In the C-version this passage is altered and reduced in such a way as to suggest that some ambiguity was felt to exist:

> Ac for the bok bible bereth good wyttnesse,
> How Daniel dyuinede and vndude the dremeles

> Of kyng Nabugodonosor that no peer hadde,
> And sitthe after to hus sones, seide hem what thei
> thouhte.   (C 10. 304–307)

In the last line (307), however, we should expect "sone," referring to Belshazzar, who was thought by the author of Daniel to be the son of Nebuchadnezzar.

140 ff. Cf. Gen. 37: 9–10. As Skeat points out, however, Jacob does not make the positive assertion attributed to him in lines 142–43.

150. "And I (that is, the dreamer) concluded that doing well (in accordance with Truth's pardon) surpassed (or was more efficacious than) an indulgence. . . ." Obviously, the priest did not conclude this.

156. **Quodcumque ligaveris super terram, &c.** From Matt. 16: 19. "And whatsoever thou shalt bind on earth shall be bound in heaven."

173. See note to pr. 55.

PASSUS NINE

Title. It is important to note that a new poem begins here: *The Life of Do-well, Do-better, and Do-best*; and that there follows the *prologue* of this poem, in spite of the fact that for editorial convenience the consecutive numbering of the passus continues.

16. **Sepcies in die cadit iustus.** From Prov. 24: 16, translated by the author in the following line.

67 f. The first clause is conditional. Translate: "'If thou art Thought,' said I then, 'thou couldst tell me and have me directed to where Do-well dwelleth.'"

81. A reference to Luke 16: 9.

83. **Libenter sufferte, &c.** Cp. 2 Cor. 11: 19. Translated by the author in the following line.

90–100. A difficult passage; it appears to be a rather clumsy attempt to indicate the relationship in medieval society of Church and State. Surely the "king" referred to here represents the State (as Dunning says) and not God or Christ, as other critics have proposed. Cf. an earlier—and clearer—passage on the moral function of the State: 1. 92–95.

PASSUS TEN

1 ff. In answer to Will's question (formulated by Thought), Wit presents the familiar allegory of the castle representing man's body. This castle, made by "Kynde" (= God) of the four elements (here listed as earth, air, wind, and water), is called *Caro* (flesh), in which dwells *Anima* (soul). In order to protect *Anima* against the malice of *Princeps huius mundi* ("Prince of this world" = the devil), "Kynde" (God) has placed her in the custody of Do-wel, Do-bet, and Do-best, who, together with Inwit (conscience) and his sons (approximating the five senses), will guard her until God comes or sends for her (i. e., until death).

For a comparison of this with other allegories of a like nature cf. C. L.

[166]

Powell, "The Castle of the Body," *SP*, XVI (1919), 197–205; or, for a more detailed study, cf. R. D. Cornelius, *The Figurative Castle*. Dunning (171 f.) sees this first passus of the *Vita* as the "body" of the work: ". . . the line of thought in the *Vita* seems to point quite definitely to Wit's explanation of Dowel, Dobet, and Dobest as that most acceptable to the dreamer."

34. **Dixit et facta sunt, &c.** From Ps. 148: 5. "He commanded, and they were created."

41. **Faciamus hominem ad ymaginem nostram.** From Gen. 1: 26. "And God said, Let us make man in our image."

45. Skeat refers to Prov. 4: 23 for the origin of this notion that the home of the soul is in the heart: "Keep thy heart with all diligence; for out of it are the issues of life."

81. **Inicium sapiencie, timor domini.** "The fear of the Lord is the beginning of wisdom." Ps. 111: 10. Cf. also Prov. 1: 7, 9: 10; Ecclus. 1: 16.

86. **Virga tua et baculus tuus, ipsa me consolata sunt.** ". . . thy rod and thy staff they comfort me." Ps. 23: 4. As Skeat says (A-text, p. 150): "It may be doubted whether David really meant to praise the consolation to be found in a birch-rod!"

88. **Intencio indicat hominem, &c.** "The purpose reveals the man." The source of this quotation is not known.

92. **Qui agit contra conscientiam, &c.** "He who goes against conscience. . . ." The exact source of this quotation is unknown. Cf. Heb. 10: 26–27.

95. **Cum recte vivas, ne cures verba malorum.** "As long as you live uprightly, pay no attention to scandal." Taken from bk. III, distich 3 of *Disticha Catonis de Moribus* (cf. note to 8. 131).

105. **Qui circuit, &c.** Some MSS have a fuller quotation; e. g., U has: "*Qui circuit omne genus nullius est generis,*" which may be freely rendered as "A jack-of-all-trades is master of none." Proverbial. No specific source is known.

108. **In eadem vocacione qua vocati estis, state.** "Let every man abide in the same calling wherein he was called." 1 Cor. 7: 20.

116. **Qui se humiliat, exaltabitur, &c.** From Luke 14: 11. "He that humbleth himself shall be exalted."

145. **Concepit dolore et peperit iniquitatem, &c.** From Ps. 7: 14. "Behold, he travaileth with iniquity, and hath conceived mischief, and brought forth falsehood." Cf. Gen. 3: 16.

156. **Penitet me fecisse hominem.** From Gen. 6: 7, translated in line 158.

188. **Dunmowe.** An allusion to the custom, long followed at the priory of Dunmow in Essex, of rewarding with a side of bacon any couple who could, after a year of marriage, swear that they had never quarreled during this period and had never regretted the marriage. For an account of the history

[167]

of this practice, cf. R. Chambers, *The Book of Days*, I, 748–51. It is of interest to note that as recently as 1949 the custom has been revived. Cf. A. L. Hench, " Dunmow Bacon, 1949," *College English*, XI (March, 1950), 350.

PASSUS ELEVEN

9. **Nolite mittere** [etc.]. From Matt. 7: 6. ". . . neither cast ye your pearls before swine. . . ." Cf. note to pr. 39. *crookedly*

23. **Quare via impiorum prosperatur, bene est omnibus qui prave et inique agunt?** Cf. Job 21: 7. " Wherefore do the wicked live, become old, yea, are mighty in power? " Cf. also Jeremiah 12: 1.

25. **Tobie.** The apocryphal book of Tobit.

55. **Ecce audivimus eam in Effrata, invenimus eam in campis silve.** " Lo, we heard of it at Ephratah: we found it in the fields of the wood." Ps. 132: 6.

73. **Non plus sapere quam oportet.** " Do not desire to know more than is necessary." The exact source of this quotation is not known. Skeat quotes a passage from St. Augustine's *De Baptismo, contra Donatistas*, bk. II, ch. 5, which has some resemblance to this quotation.

145. **Qui simulat verbis, nec corde est fidus amicus.** " Who feigns with words, nor is at heart a true friend. . . ." From bk. I, distich 26 of *Disticha Catonis de Moribus* (cf. note to 8. 131). The second line (quoted in some MSS; cf. variant readings in TEXTUAL NOTES) may be translated: " You in turn deceive [him]; thus art deludes art."

151. **Necesse est ut veniant scandala.** From Matt. 18: 7. " It must needs be that offences come. . . ."

179. **quath she.** " she " is the critical reading (see TEXTUAL NOTES), though we rather expect Clergy to speak first, as he in fact does in the B and C versions. Perhaps Clergy is, after all, intended, as most scholars have assumed (e. g. Dunning, 179), especially if we attach any significance to the John But passus (cf. APPENDIX I), where Clergy says (12. 2): " I have do my dever the Do-wel to teche."

189. **Ecce quam bonum et quam iocundum habitare, fratres, in unum.** " Behold, how good and how pleasant it is for brethren to dwell together in unity! " Ps. 133: 1.

190. **Rom. 12: 15.** The Latin is translated in line 190.

191. Part of this line appears to have been missing in the common ancestor of all the extant MSS. Cf. the variant readings in the TEXTUAL NOTES.

193. **Qui facit et docuerit, magnus vocabitur in regno celorum.** " Whosoever shall do and teach them, the same shall be called great in the kingdom of heaven." Matt. 5: 19.

201 ff. **Gregory.** i. e., pope Gregory I (the Great), ca. 540–604. But the " text " given here (204–207) is probably that attributed in the decretals

to pope Eugenius. It was a commonplace in medieval literature. Cf. Chaucer, *Canterbury Tales*, Pro. 179–82.

219. **Super cathedram Moisi sederunt principes.** Compare Matt. 23: 2. "The scribes and the Pharisees sit in Moses' seat."

225. An allusion to 1 Tim. 6: 9. "But they that will be rich fall into temptation and a snare, and into many foolish and hurtful lusts, which drown men in destruction and perdition."

229. **Qui crediderit et baptizatus fuerit, salvus erit.** "He that believeth and is baptized shall be saved." The quotation is from Mark 16: 16, though the author refers specifically to Peter. Cf. 1 Pet. 3: 21.

236. **Dilige deum, &c., et proximum tuum sicut teipsum.** From Matt. 22: 37, 39. "Thou shalt love the Lord thy God . . . [etc.], and . . . thy neighbour as thyself."

238. **Dum tempus est, operemur bonum ad omnes, maxime autem ad domesticos fidei.** "As we have therefore opportunity, let us do good unto all men, especially unto them who are of the household of faith." Gal. 6: 10.

247. **Non mecaberis.** "Thou shalt not commit adultery." Ex. 20: 14 (Deut. 5: 18). This is the seventh commandment, though the sixth was clearly intended: "Thou shalt not kill," which is rendered "ne sle nought" in this line. Some of the scribes perceived the difficulty; cf. the variant readings in TEXTUAL NOTES. One MS (H_3) substitutes *Non occides* (Vulgate). In view of the variations which are known to have existed in the order of commandments 6, 7, and 8 (cf. Mark 10: 19 [AV], Luke 18: 20, James 2: 11; this order is also found in some of the Fathers), it is possible that the author had before him a copy of the Decalogue in which adultery was number six, and that he looked at the number and carelessly copied *non mecaberis* instead of *non occides*.

Michi vindictam, et ego retribuam. From Deut. 32: 35. "To me belongeth vengeance, and recompence."

250. Although nothing specific is said about an end to the dream (which began at 9. 58), we can assume that the dreamer awakens at this point. In the remainder of this passus he sums up his thinking concerning the search for Do-wel, etc. The whole passage (11. 250–303) may be compared in function with the summing-up of the *Visio* (8. 127–181).

If it has been difficult for critics in the past to perceive the unity of the *Vita*, it is nevertheless true that with the end of this passus the poem comes to an emphatic conclusion. Some of the developments in the B and C versions of the poem seem to have been suggested by questions raised in this passage, but such developments can in no way reflect on the artistic integrity of the A-text. Once it is granted that the A-text is the earliest version of the poem, any attempt to criticize the unity of A on the basis of developments in B and C will involve the critic in a hopeless tangle of anachronistic speculation. For an excellent interpretation of this part of the poem, see Dunning's analysis, *Piers Plowman*, 179–82.

[169]

255. Nemo ascendet ad celum nisi qui de celo descendit. "And no man hath ascended up to heaven, but he that came down from heaven." John 3 : 13.

287. Dum steteritis ante presides nolite cogitare. Mark 13 : 9, 11. Paraphrased in lines 289–92.

295. Ecce ipsi ydioti rapiunt celum, ubi nos sapientes in infernum mergemur. Cf. Augustine, *Confessions*, bk. VIII, ch. 8. Paraphrased in lines 297–300.

PASSUS TWELVE

19. Vidi prevaricantes et tabescebam. "I beheld the transgressors, and was grieved." Ps. 119 : 158. But note the mistranslation in the next line. For *tabescebam* the writer apparently saw *tacebam* "was silent," either inadvertently or because of a corrupt text, though the three MSS have the correct reading.

22. Audivi archana verba que non licet homini loqui. 2 Cor. 12 : 4. Paraphrased in lines 23–24.

28. Quid est veritas. "What is truth?" John 18 : 38.

33. The line seems to mean that Scripture is accusing the dreamer of twisting holy writ to suit his arguments. Perhaps there is an allusion to Luke 22 : 70. ". . . and he said unto them, Ye say that I am."

49. The line is defective. Cf. 11. 191.

50 ff. Omnia probate; quod bonum est tenete. "Prove all things; hold fast that which is good." 1 Thess. 5 : 21.

91. The tomblest. Skeat emends to "Thou tomblest." From line 88 to the end, the only MS available is R.

99. Wille thurgh in-wit, etc. Skeat emends to "Wille *wiste* thurgh in-wit," etc. Another possibility would be: "Wille thurgh in-wit *than wiste* wel the sothe."

117. John But's identity, and the extent of his contribution to this twelfth passus (passus 3 of Do-wel, etc.), together with its significance in relation to the problem of authorship, have been subjects discussed at length by the critics. A good case for the identification of the "maker" in this passus with a certain John But, king's messenger, who died in 1387, was made by Henry Bradley (*MLR*, VIII [1913], 88). The death of this John But occurred in the middle of the reign of Richard II (1377–99), who is mentioned in line 113. It is scarcely possible to locate with certainty the point at which But's work begins. Chambers (*MLR*, VI [1911], 322) believed that he wrote either the whole passus, or only lines 89–117. Manly (*CHEL*, II, 21–22) held that his work begins with line 57. Edith Rickert (*MP*, XI [1913], 107–16) gives cogent reasons for accepting line 83 as the starting point. For a valuable discussion of this problem and the general significance of John But's testimony, consult her article.

TEXTUAL NOTES

THE following textual notes include only a selection of the thousands of variants in the MSS of the A-text. Two considerations have governed the admission of variants in the notes. First, they are admitted wherever the critical reading is not readily apparent. Second, they are admitted whenever the critical text deviates from the reading of manuscript T, the basis of the text. In the latter case, frequently T's reading alone would have been necessary; however, in order to maintain a uniform system throughout, the readings opposite each lemma include all variants, even where the primary purpose is simply to indicate a deviation of T from the critical text. There are a few exceptions to this, usually involving the wanderings of a minor group such as AMH₃.

Most omissions of lines by important MSS have been noted where they occur, but the student may double-check by consulting the list of LINES OMITTED BY MSS OF THE A-TEXT given below.

The spelling of the lemma agrees with that of the text, in which þ is written *th*, and 3 is written *y*, *gh*, or *z*, as appropriate. The tags frequently found at the end of words in manuscript T, which Skeat indicates by an italic *e*, are not represented in the text or in the notes. Certain ambiguities, such as final *n* with a flourish, which may stand for *un* or simply *n*, are normalized to conform to the scribe's general practice (*e. g.*, " pardon " [?] is written " pardoun "). Abbreviations are silently expanded. Capitalization is normalized throughout; for example manuscript T reads " dowel," " do wel," " Dowel," etc., but in the text this is regularly written " Do-wel."

Wherever notes on erasures, the hand and ink of certain MSS, etc., are supplied, these are taken from Knott's collations.

LINES OMITTED BY MSS OF THE A-TEXT

[A is defective to 1.142; H_3 is B-text to 5.106; N is defective to 1.104.
The last line in T_2 is 7.213; the last line in L is 8.152; N is C-text after
9.11; the last line in V is 11.180; the last line in H is 8.139. For further
details about the MSS see INTRODUCTION, *MSS of the A-text.*]

Prologue	Passus 2	Passus 3	Passus 4	Passus 5
19 H	6 Di	46 A	66 U	95 DWN
34 V	11 UUR	48 M	71 TChDUR	96 V
35 Di	18–145 A	70–1 M	72 TCh	110 A
37 I	20 UT$_2$	79 U	78–80 N	115 T$_2$H
50–51 VH	24–5 UR	91–2 L	85–9 R	116 A
54 U	28–9 VH	92 H	89–90 A	118–9 A
58 T$_2$	32 N	100 TH$_2$ChD	90 H	127 UR
79 M	35 U	104 V	93 T$_2$	162 TH$_2$ChD-
82 D	56 V	108 T$_2$	104 N	URILWDi
99 VHDi	63–4 I	112–226 A	106 AWN	164 A
100 VH	71 U	113 Di	107 UW	165 T$_2$A
101–2 Di	78 Di	120–34 D	108 W	166 TH$_2$ChD-
109 VH	83 W	122 U	109–10 H	URILWDi
	84 T$_2$	147 W	113–4 L	172 H$_3$
Passus 1	92 VH	156 T$_2$M	119 VH	176 LDiH
	105 H$_2$	163–4 M	142 U	177–8 LDi
6–7 W	106–21 V	174 T$_2$	155 A	178 A
18 I	120 M	191 Ch		186–7 A
24 Ch	136 V	204 UWN	Passus 5	195 W
29 TChT$_2$	145 R	206 WN		208 M
33–99 U	149 I	211 T$_2$	6 L	217 Ch
40 RT$_2$	150–1 T$_2$	228–30 N	7–8 D	218 U
67 Ch	157 H	240 TH$_2$ChDU	10 TChNH	220 UR
85 M	182 Di	242 N	21–3 WN	228 A
92 M	187 H	245–7 U	25 A	245–6 H
101 M	188 T$_2$	254 WN	32–3 A	251 M
103 T$_2$V	198 T$_2$	256 H	38–9 AL	252–3 A
106 LVH		259 H	40 T$_2$	
110 L	Passus 3		47 I	Passus 6
128 T$_2$		Passus 4	62–3 V	
134 M	6 I		67–8 A	5 I
135 N	15 Ch	12–3 A	71–2 A	6 URAI
145–7 H	22 T$_2$M	23 D	74–5 AM	11 T$_2$
156 M	23 T$_2$MV	32 H	78–80 LH	24 A
168 AWN	27 A	43 A	80 I	28 W
176–83 V	30–2 A	46 A	89 L	31–3 Di
177 U .	33 T$_2$AM	51 H	91 TH$_2$ChD	32 N

[172]

TEXTUAL NOTES

Passus 6	Passus 7	Passus 8	Passus 10	Passus 11
35 Di	*143–7 H$_2$	15 A	7 W	76–8 A
49–123 H	144 T$_2$	27 U	26 TChD	94 M
52 M	145 V	30 UA	40 UR	101 A
54 V	148–92 H$_2$	32–80 A	45 H$_3$	125 U
56 A	148 N	38 MH$_3$	48–9 M	138 A
61 A	177 Di	51–2 R	64 W	140 U
65 Di	178 TChD	60–1 H$_3$	67 RW	141 A
66 U	*193–201 H$_2$	95 M	74 D	147 M
70 AN	197 A	103 AW	77 U	149 A
71 N	198 H$_3$	104 MW	81 V	159 Ch
77 N	202–3 A	106 N	81–2 W	162–3 A
83–4 A	202–22 H$_2$	109 H$_3$	92 TD	168 R
87–8 A	206 T$_2$	111 R	96–7 A	172–3 A
94 A	211 TChDURT$_2$	112–81 H$_3$	104 Ch	174–5 DRW
107 A	216–8 A	118 Di	104–62 H$_2$	181–303 V
108 UR	219 H	162 A	108 U	183 A
113 A	*223–31 H$_2$	164–6 A	114 R	193 U
	224 WDi	167 TH$_2$ChD	116 ChU	200 W
Passus 7	225 W	170–81 U	117 W	217 A
	226 U		119–21 A	222 Di
1–2 H	232–51 H$_2$	**Passus 9**	138 U	231 A
3–6 D	232 U		141 V	244 A
5 W	233 R	1–96 H$_3$	151 UR	247 M
6 UR	241 L	4–5 V	174 M	272 U
11 V	242 A	9 N	176 U	276 AWMH$_3$
19 A	250–1 A	12 W	179 A	285–7 U
21 A	*252–61 H$_2$	26 I	183 R	286 W
25 H	255 UH$_3$N	42–3 A	186 W	287 A
33–85 A	256 A	48–9 A	187 A	
45–69 T$_2$	257 N	54–5 A	195–200 A	
46–7 Di	260 L	56–8 I	203–6 A	
*53–8 H$_2$	262–84 H$_2$	72–7 A	205–12 U	
59–78 H$_2$	273–75 UA	74 U	209 AWMH$_3$	
74 T$_2$V	279–81 W	76–7 U		
*81–5 H$_2$	282 TChD	79 A	**Passus 11**	
86–109 H$_2$	*285–93 H$_2$	88–9 A		
87 A	288 A	93 AV	1–47 U	
95 W	289–90 H	100 A	17 W	
97 H$_3$	296 A	103 A	23 R	
*112–8 H$_2$	297–300 U	108 Ch	29 Ch	
118–9 H		109 H$_3$	*34–41 H$_2$	
119–40 H$_2$	**Passus 8**	111 UR	43 A	
119 A		112 A	52 A	
125 W	5 A	114 A	54 U	
132 UNVH	10 A		*64–71 H$_2$	
			73 Ch	

* Lines partly torn away.

[173]

TEXTUAL NOTES

Title:

T : *No title; top of leaf trimmed.*

H₂: Peorse plowmanne (*in a totally different and much later hand*).

Ch : *no title.*

D : *no title.*

U : *no title.*

R : Hic incipit liber qui vocatur pers plowman. Prologus.

T₂: *no title.*

A : *defective to 1. 142.*

M : Piers Plougmans Vision the author Robert Langland a cheife disciple of John Wickliffs (*in late hand on verso of preceding leaf*).

H₃: *B-text to* (B) *5. 128, then A-text beginning with* (A) *5. 106.*

I : *no title.*

L : Plowman Piers (*late hand*).

W : *no title.*

N : *defective to 1. 104.*

Di : Primus passus de visione Petri ploughmann.

V : *no title.*

H : *no title.*

PROLOGUE

1 whanne softe was the sonne]   as y south wente UT$_2$; whenne I south wente R.

2 in-to a shroud]   in to schrowdes H$_2$L; Into schregges Ch; to schroudes D; in a schrowde UT$_2$M; a schroude R; into ye schropbys I; in to a shrowedes W; into schrubbes Di; vndur a schrowde H.
as I a shep were]   a schep as y were MIV.

3 as]   of ChIDiVH.

4 I wente wyde in]   Wente wyde in TH$_2$ChD; Wente I wyde in M; Went wyde into L; Wende I wydene in V.

5 on (2)]   vpon TH$_2$ChD.

6 of fairie]   of fayre D; of ferrom T$_2$; & fayre I; a ffeyrie V.

7 for-wandrit]   of wandrit TChDi; for wandryng DT$_2$; of wandryng WVH.

8 bourne]   bournis TH$_2$UT$_2$; broke I.

9 watris]   water ChILW.

10 in]   in to TChDI; on H$_2$UT$_2$ML; WDi *om.*
it]   ic T (*over erasure*); hit H$_2$LV; and I; I URT$_2$.
swighede]   swyed H$_2$L; swede Ch; schewed D; sweuenyd UR; swemed T$_2$; semede M; sweuedyn I; swied W; swyyd Di; sownede VH.
so]   me M; ful I.

12 wiste I]   wisty DL; y wyste URT$_2$WDiH.

13 Ac as]   And H$_2$; Bot as ChURT$_2$IDi; Ac L; As WH; And as V; M *om.*
on heigh]   an hei₃ TChWVH; vp URT$_2$; on heght I.

14 on]   in H$_2$URT$_2$MI.
toft]   coste R; coft T$_2$; twist M.
trighely]   tryelyche H$_2$; trewly ChDMIL; triely URT$_2$; trielych WDi; wonderliche VH.
i-makid]   a tired U; ontyrid R; entyred T$_2$; makyd IWH; ytymbred L.

20 the]   TDRW *om.*
and]   TChDUL *om.*

21 settyng]   seed tyme URT$_2$; Eringe VH.
settyng and sowyng]   sowing and harowing I.
harde]   sore H$_2$LWDiH.

22 That many of thise]   Whom þat þise TCh; that many H$_2$; Whanne þat these D; And wonnen þat þese U; þat þes RT$_2$; Wonnyn þat þyse M; þan þer y sygh L; And wonnen þat W; Wann that thes Di; þat monie of þeos VH.
with]   in IVH.

24 cuntenaunce]   quoyntyse H.
comen]   þei comen URM; crafteliche L; comen in W; came in al Di.
comen disgisid]   yai can yaim degyse T$_2$; queinteliche deGyset V; þei conen hem disgyse H.

[175]

26 Al for] and ffor the H₂W; For þe URT₂IH; For V.
   ful] wel TDLWDi; M *om.*
   streite] harde T₂V.

27 for] TChMLDi *om.*

28 here] *indecipherable erasure* T.
   sellis] cellis TRVH; hous L (*faded*).

29 cairen] karien ChDURWDiVH; carry T₂; karyn M; scayre I.

31 chaffare] to chaffare TCh; hem to chaffare DURT₂I.
   thei] to WDiVH.
   cheven] cheuide TChURT₂; preue H.

32 thriven] chewen L; scholden VH.

34 synneles] giltles TCh; synfullyche H₂; gylelas L; gylously W;
   gylefully Di; (V *om. line*).

36 Founden] Fonden TChDDi; Fynden H₂T₂; Gon fynden UR; Foundes
   I; þa feynen H.

37 liste] list TDW; lust H₂; liketh URT₂; like M; wolde LH; luste V.

39 is] his T; Hee is V.

41 belyes] bely TH₂ChDMW.
   bagges] bagge TH₂ChDMW.
   belyes and here bagges] Bagges & heore Balies VH.
   bretful] bratful T; bredful DURT₂; full IW; fully Di; faste VH.

42 Fayteden] Flite þanne TCh; Faytours H₂L; Flytteden & D; þei
   fliten URT₂; Fayted I; they faited W; And flyted fast Di; Feyneden
   hem V.
   at the ale] at nale H₂Di; at þe nale ChUT₂LWH; atte hale M;
   atte alle V.

44 ribaudie] ribaudrie TUI.
   tho] as TChDURT₂WDi; þis V; þese H; I *om.*
   roberdis] robertis TChRM; rowtes of T₂; Rybaldes Di.

45 Slepe and sleuthe] Slep and sorry sleuthe H₂ (sorry *inserted above
   line in late hand*); Slepe & mochull slouthe M; Sleuth & slepe I;
   Sory slep & slouthe L; Slogardie and sleuþ W.

46 plighten] plytyth R; plyten M; pyke I; pight W; pyghten H.

50, 51 VH *om. line.*

52 lobies] lobels T₂; globis M; lobres V; loburs H.

53 from othere] for breþeren VH.

54 Shopen hem] Shapen hem DL; And schopyn hem M; And madyn
   hem I; They shopen hem W; And summe schopen to V; And
   schopen hem to H; (U *om. line*).

56 here] þe TH₂ChLW.
   wombe] wombes URT₂IVH; paunche L.
   here wombe] hem seluen M.

57 Gloside] And glosed H₂; Gloseth D; Glosys T₂; Glosynge VH.
   hem] him TD.

[176]

good] leof L; selfe W (*crossed out*); silf H.
likide] þouȝt Ch; lyketh DT₂LVH.

58 construide] constru I.
construide it as thei wolde] construeth it at wille D; þey construen
hit aȝeyn kynde L; construen it ful yuel H; Construeþ hit ille V.
it] H₂MIW *om.*

59 mowe] may TChDT₂IWDi.

61 Sith] Siþen TDUIDi; Sir T₂; Sen L; Sethe M; Seþþe V.

63 hy] þei TChRT₂L; he H₂DUMI; charite WDi.
and hy holden bet] bi ginne holde bet V; bygynne þe better to
holde H.
bet] URT₂IL *om.*

64 is mountyng] mountith URT₂V; is toward M.

68 vowes] auowes TChURDi; wowes H₂; a wow D.

69 hym] it TChLW; H₂DDi *om.*

71 bunchide] bunchiþ TCh; bonches D; blessid URT₂H; blenchet I.
bleride] bleriþ TCh; blerett T₂.

73 ye yeven youre] þei ȝouen here TCh; þey ȝeuen here DT₂Di; ȝe
ȝeuen oure LV.

74 loselis] to losels DURT₂VH; at losels W; lorelles Di.

77 al] H₂URT₂MILWV *om.*

78 But] Ac TMI; but for RT₂.

79 That the pore peple of the parissh shulde have] That pore peple of
þe parische schulde haue H₂; þat þe pore peple schuld haue U;
That þe pore scholde departyn R; Yat ye poor men schulde depart
T₂; yat ye pore peple suld hauen I; That þe peple shold haue W;
þat haue schulde þe pore parisschens V; þat þe poore of þe
parysche schuld haue H; (M *om. line*).

80 pleynide hem] plenyth H₂RLV; pleynen UT₂M; pleynyd hem
I; pleyned WDi; han playned H.
here] þe ChDMLDi; T₂ *om.*

81 parissh] parisches H₂; paryschenes URDiH; kirkes T₂; cherchys M.
were] was TChW; ben URI; haþ ben V; han ben H.

83 there] TChDURT₂MI *om.*

86 Pleden] Pleten TH₂Ch; Plededen DL; þei pletide UR; Pletand T₂;
to pletyn M; Yat pledeyn I; To pleden W; pladden H; (Di *is
C-text here*).
poundis] poynteþ TCh; poundide UR.

88 Thou] Tho T; ffor þou H.
the] TChDUIL *om.*; a W.

89 were] be TH₂ChDURMILW.

91 clerkis] clerkis clerkis T (*second* clerkis *expuncted*).
acountis] acounte URVH; a comte T₂; countes Ch.

92   denis]   dekenes H$_2$V.
dignite]   dignites TH$_2$ChDML.
dignite haven]   diuine shold preche W.

94   lopen]   ylope TChDM; lepyn I; lope L.
bisshopis]   bisshop TChDURM.

96   and(1)]   TUI *om.*
bondemen]   bondage TH$_2$ChDW; bondages URI.

97   semble]   semele T; symple R.

99   DiVH *om. line.*

100   VH *om. line.*
and (1)]   TChWDi *om.*
tokkeris]   tanneris T; Tauerners ChR; souters D; toucheris UM;
tynkelers T$_2$; Taucheris thackers I (Taucheris *crossed out and*
thackers *written above*); tornors L; tuckyours Di.
tolleris]   tokkeris TD; Tapsters Ch; tynkeres R; tyllyars Di.

101   and(1)]   TChURWV *om.*

102   dedis]   dede TChDW; werk UR.

107   white]   TH$_2$ChDMI *om.*; good VH.

109   VH *om. line.*
sevene]   seue TL.

PASSUS ONE

Title:
TChDT$_2$:   Primus passus de visione.
H$_2$:   Passus primus (*opposite line 109 in margin*).
URW: Passus primus de visione.
MHL: *no title or break.*
I: Primus passus (*opposite line 109 in margin*).
Di: Passus secundus de visione.
V: *no title; one line left blank.*

1   this]   þe TH$_2$ChDMILW.
bymenith]   meniþ TChDM; may mene UR; menys T$_2$.
ek]   URWDiVH *om.*

2   ek]   RT$_2$V *om.*; all W.

3   lere]   lire TCh; lore H$_2$; lyre T$_2$; leer LDi; leor VH.

4   clyf]   kiþ TCh; chyf R; cleffe I; loft VH; (W *om.* fro that clyf).

8   in]   of DURT$_2$MIWH.
kepe thei]   þei kepe TH$_2$RT$_2$L; þey woll M; ne kepe thei WH; ne
willyn thay Di.

12   on]   of TChT$_2$MI; in UR; & V.

14   and]   þat UMIWVH.

16   whiles]   whyl þat R; whil WDiMV; þe whyle þat H.

18   Of wollene of lynene to liflode]   Of lynene of wollene of liflode TCh;
Of wollen and of lynen to lyflode H$_2$W; And wollen & lynen to

[178]

lyflode D; Of wollene and lynnene to lyflode UDi; Of wollene of lynene of lyflode R; Off wollyn of lynnyn to help yow T$_2$; Of wollyn of lynenyn & lyflode MH (to *changed to* &); I *om. line.*

21 Arn] Narn T; Are H$_2$R; Beþ Ch; Ne arn D; Er T$_2$.
Arn none nedful but tho] Eron non so nedful as þo W; Ther ar none so nedefull Di; Heore nomes beþ neodful VH.

22 be] in TChDRT$_2$Di.
thou] ȝow H$_2$; ȝe URT$_2$MWDi; þe L; IVH *om.*
aftir] þer aftir T; here aftere H$_2$DiVH.

23 vesture] cloþing ChDLVH; vesture verrailiche URT$_2$; vesture of cloþe W.
chele] cold DUT$_2$MLW; cheld I.

24 is] DRT$_2$MV *om.;* (Ch *om. line*).

25 thou drighest] þe driȝeþ TH$_2$Ch; ȝow drieth U; you thristes T$_2$; þe thyrstes L; þow drye art W.
ac] at T (*sic*); but H$_2$ChUMIWDiVH; & T$_2$L.
it] H$_2$T$_2$MILW *om.*

26 worthe] worche ChURT$_2$MI; do W; weore V.

28 doughteris] douȝter TUI; douȝtern ChRMV.

29 TChT$_2$ *om. line.*

30 hym] hem TCh.

31 it] H$_2$ChURT$_2$MIDi *om.*
that] þe TL; of yat T$_2$.

34 askith] likiþ TChV.

36 lighere] liþer TCh; leder D; alþer R; lear T$_2$.

37 wrecchide] wikked ChVH.

39 And that shent] For to shende TChM; to schende RT$_2$; And Schendeþ V.
set] seith H$_2$Di; sent L; take W; seo VH.
set it in thin herte] be war with ȝair wyles T$_2$; be war of here wyles M.

42 money] mone TI; monei H$_2$ (i *added to* mone); monoye W.
on] of H$_2$T$_2$MILWDi; in H.

46 shulde] wile T.

47 God] he TChDMVH.

48 And the ymage like] And þe ymagis lik T; And ymage lyke H$_2$DR; And þe Image is like Ch; And qwom to is ye ymage like T$_2$; It an ymage lik M; And to hem ye Image k lykyth I (to hem *and* lykyth *crossed out, with* wat *and* was *respectively added above the line in a later hand;* k *expuncted*); And vnto whom þe ymage is lyke L; And þe ymage y lyke W; And an Image like Di; And whom þe ymage was lyk VH; U *def.*

49 thei] þanne T.

50 *Cesari* befallith] cesari befalle T; sesari befallith H$_2$RIWDiT$_2$;

[179]

sesari befallet Ch; cesar he longeþ D; to cesari fallit M; to cesar falleth LV; to cesar apendiþ H.

51 or] oþer T.

54 to] & TChDMIWDi; ac H₂.

58 mene] by mene RMIDiH.

59 That] þere TH₂Ch.
who so] who þat TH₂H; ho so ChD; hose V.

60 born] bore H₂ChDRMILW.

61 wight] wy TH₂; wey D; wyȝth R; wyth M; wyȝe L.

62 foundede] foundit T; found Di; fonde DRT₂ILW.

63 eggide] eggide hem TChDLDi; heggede hem R; heggyd I.

66 ellir] Eldir TRM; eldren H₂; Eldre Ch; yllern D; eller T₂; elderin I; elrne L; aldre W; helldrun Di; Ellerne treo VH.

67 leigheth] and seyneth R; & gylyd M; he gillith I; laccheth L; & lithers W; and lyyth on Di; & bylyȝeth H; (Ch *om. line*).

68 trusten] tresten TD; truston H₂; trastes T₂; thrustnyn M; treston I; trusteth LVH.
betraid arn sounest] betrayed buþ sounest D; betrayd ar souered R; betrayd is sonest T₂; tyid arn so fast I; betrays he sounest W; þer no truþe is Inne V; þat no trewth is ynne H.

71 halside] hailside TDi; hailised Ch; assched R; askyd M; axed I; quired L.

72 heo] he TH₂; sche ChDRT₂MIWDi.

76 And] TH₂ChDRT₂IWDi *om.*

78 Preighede] And preied ChT₂IDiV; I praied W.
Preighede hire pitously] to haue pytee on þe pepul & H.
to] TH₂Ch *om.*

82 yholden] yhoten TH₂ChI.

85 derworth] derworþi TT₂.

86 tellith] tel hit RW; trow you T₂M; tell he euel of I; & telleth LDiH.

87 wilneth] & wilneþ T; and wyllith H₂Ch; willeþ DRM; at will T₂; & wil I; wilneþ L; wil W; wilneth Di; and doþ VH.

93 And riden and rappe doun] And ryden at randoun D; And ryde rapely to rensake T₂; And biddyn & techyn M; And Rihtfuliche Raymen V; & ryȝtfullyche rule H.

95 ytermined] termined TH₂ChDRLW; determinyd T₂M; turnyd I.

97 Did hem] Made hem to TH₂D; Made hem Ch; And dude hem R; And yaim T₂; Se hem M; & did hem IDi; He dide hem W; & made hem to H.
here] his TH₂ChT₂; a D; he Di.

101 hem] hym TH₂Ch; T₂WVH *om.*
yeftis] siluer URT₂.

[180]

103 kingene king] king of kinges TH₂Ch; kyng of knyȝtes DDiH;
    kyndrede kyng M; knyttene kyng I (*crossed out, with* kyng of
    knyhtys *written above*); knyght & kyng W; L *changes line*; V *om.
    line*; T₂ *om. line.*

104 and such sevene other] such seuene & a noþer TH₂ChWN; suche
    seuene & oþer D; and siche mo oþere U; & seuen moo oþere I;
    & al the foure ordres DiVH; L *changes line.*

106 HVL *om. line.*
    his] al his UIW; al hys mene T₂; his mene M.

107 treuthe] trouþe T.

109 leride] lerned DUMIDi.

110 of sight] to loke on TH₂Ch.

112 his] TH₂D *om.*

115 Ac] And TH₂DRM; But ChT₂LWVH.

116 For pride that he put out] ffor pride that he put out of H₂; ffor
    pride þat he put out was D; ffor þe pride he pute out U; ffor
    pryde at he put out T₂; ffor pride he was yus put owte I; ffor
    his pompe & his pruyde L; ffor pride þat him putte out of W; for
    his pryde he was putte out H (his *cancelled*).

120 perfite] profitable UIWVH; ppletys M (*sic*).

121 to] in to TChRWNDi.

122 tronen] trowe H₂R; crounen ChD; tryeste UI; techys T₂; turnyt
    M; crouneþ WDi; troneþ N; Corouneþ V; crowneþ H.
    hem] hym TH₂; of UI.

125 it this] it þus TH₂ChL; þis D; it UN; þus R; it ȝe T₂; it þe W;
    þys M; to I; it to H.

126 tresour] þe tresour TDILNDi; a tresour WH.
    on] here on T; here in H₂.

127 ye mote kenne me betere] ȝet mote ȝe me bet kenne T; ȝe mote me
    bet kenne H₂; ȝe moȝ me better ken ChU; but ȝe me bet kenne D;
    ȝe mot me betere teche R; me byhofis better to lere T₂; ȝit must
    I lerne betere M; ȝe motyn kennyn me better I; bote kenne me
    bettr L; þe most kenne me bettre W; ȝit mot kenne bettre N;
    ȝet most ȝe kenne me better Di; þou most teche me betere V; þou
    most me teche better H.

129 thi] þine TM.

135 witnesseth] askiþ wytnesse TH₂Ch; wittnes T₂; techeþ us VH.

137 plante] plente RT₂MDi; playnt VH.
    preche it] put it U; prechyd RM; preche you it T₂; priche it I;
    prechet V.
    in thin harpe] in þy herte DUIH (*in* H, harpe *has been changed to*
    harte); ofte T₂; in myn harpe M; þin harpe V.

138 Ther] ȝif TH₂M; When Ch.
    mery] mercy TD (*sic*).
    art mery at mete] sittest at mete W.
    yif] whan URV; & M.

TEXTUAL NOTES

139   ther comsith a might]   þer comeþ a miȝt H₂; conseyue þou myȝte
       D; þer comseth it right U; ther comeþ a merthe R; bygynnys al
       myrth T₂; coueitid alle merthe M; yer comsyt aryht you conseyuys
       a myrth I (yer comsyt aryht *crossed out*); keneth þe þeo sooþ
       L; comseþ a miȝte N; Cumse þer a ffitte V; bygynne such a fytt H.

144   he]   ChURAMIH *om.*

148   hyghe]   by TH₂ChDURIWNDi; eye M; on cros L.
       hongide him hyghe]   hym hangyd T₂; hengyn on hym A.

149   the(1)]   ȝe H₂I; þe þou R; ȝow AMN.

150   of]   in AN.

151   that ye]   ȝe TH₂ChDURDi; þe W; þat þou H (*over erasure of* ȝe).

153   For theigh ye]   For þi TH₂ChDR; ffor yof ȝe T₂; Thow ȝe AM;
       Thow þow WN; ffor þeiȝ þou H (þou *over erasure of* ȝe).

154   ek]   AWNDi *om.*

156   Of]   And VH; Wiþ L.
       parten]   parteþ TH₂ChU; departyn RT₂AH; (M *om. line*).

157   masse]   matynes TH₂ChUI; messes L.
       oures]   masse TH₂ChI (messe *above cancellation of* oures *in* I).
       masse ne in oures]   heuenriche blys T₂AM.

158   maidenhod]   maidenhed TDURAIDi.

159   juggide]   ioynide TH₂Ch; hath wryten D; demys T₂; he iuggith A;
       Iuggit M; iuggeth L; Ivgyth Di; bond V; seyth H.

161   ded]   as ded TH₂ChT₂MLNDi.

162   in helle]   in helle *added in different hand over erasure* T.

165   Arn]   Beþ ChD; Er T₂; Is W; Beo V; þer beoþ H.
       heo(1)]   þei TH₂ChDURT₂AMLWDiVH; hey I; hij N.
       heo(2)]   þei TH₂ChDURT₂ALWNDi; hy I; þe H.
       whanne heo]   þat M.

166   and]   & ek TH₂ChDURMILDi; & als T₂; also W.

169   bodies]   body TH₂DUR; soules H.

170   conne]   mowe T.

171   harde]   faste TH₂ChD.

172   That]   þere TH₂ChI.
       but]   but a TH₂ULDi.

173   T *repeats this line verbatim; the second line is expuncted;* (*for* lering
       second line has leryng).
       lerning]   lering TH₂DI; begynnynge R.
       to(1)]   to þe TChDIW.

174   ben]   arn TH₂URAMILWNDi; ben Ch; beþ DVH; er T₂.
       the(1)]   URILWDiV *om.*

179   graith]   greytheste U; redyeste R; grettest T₂A; geynyist M;
       gracieuse WN; gret Di.
       graith gate]   gate grethed I; redyest waye H; (V *def.*).

180   the]   þise TH₂ChURIDi.

183   lenge]   duellen UW; lette RMN; lende T₂AIH.

[182]

PASSUS TWO

Title:

TH₂ChDURT₂AI: Passus secundus de visione (*DI have title in margin*).

ML:	*no title or break.*
W:	Secundus passus de visione.
N:	Passus secundus de visione vt supra.
Di:	Passus tercius de visione.
V:	*no title; one line left blank.*
H:	Tercius passus de visione.

3 that(2)] þe TH₂ChDUT₂MIWNDiV.
blisful] blisside TUT₂MIWDi; blesful H₂; blessyd DR.

4 knowe] kenne TH₂L; knowene I.

5 lo] se DUƲIDiVH; loke R.
standis] standith H₂ChLNDiV; (þei) stonde U; (þei) standyn AMIH.

7 my] þat TH₂; þe ChV.
the] þat TH₂ChMILWNDi.

9 upon] in TH₂; on ChDUƲRT₂AMWNDi; of I; apon L.

10 with] in TH₂RIW.

14 is(1)] nis TH₂DMWNV.

15 so] þus TH₂ChVH; þat is þus AT₂.
worthily] wortly H₂; worthly Ch; wonderly DUƲRNVH; gentely M.

16 quath she] TH₂ChDUƲRT₂AILWNDi *om.*
ful] wel ChDUDi; T₂AMNVH *om.*

19 heo] it TD; he H₂; sche ChUƲRMIWNDi; sho T₂.

20 wox] wex TChRMIWN; wax H₂DLH; wente U; (UT₂ *om. line*).

21 I] for I TH₂ChDUƲRT₂MWN.

25 lighen] lyuen LVH; (UR *om. line*).

26 as] soth I; soþ as VH.

27 yif] ȝif ȝif T (*sic; second* ȝif *crossed out*).

28 that(2)] þe TH₂DL; (VH *om. lines 28, 29*).

31 oure] TH₂DURIDi *om.*; bot lord T₂L; now lorde N.

34 bridale] bedale T.

35 of-sent] assent TH₂ChDT₂M; after sent IH; sone sent L; I sent W;
sent for Di.
assele] a sele T; ensele H₂Di; sele DRT₂MILWNH.

36 and] oþer URWNVH.

37 with] myde ULNDi.

40 a] an H₂; of a DWDiH; on a V.

41 proud] a prude W; a proude DiVH; was proud D; prow U.

42 teldit] I telded ChT$_2$; teled DI; tight þer UR; telt þere M; teilded
    L; telden Di; I tilled V; I teldyde forþ H.
  beside] by sedes D; by sydes RWNDiVH; by þer sides L.

43 cuntre] cuntres TChIWNDi; þe Contre DT$_2$LH; cortyeres R.

44 byggeris] beggeris TH$_2$ChDT$_2$M; buyers L; Buggers V.

48 is] was VH.

51 heo] he TH$_2$; she DRWT$_2$MNDi; che I; ChULV *om.*
  bounde] buxum URI; boun LWDi; bowen N.
  bounde at his bode] bounde at his bede D; buxum T$_2$M; Boxum and
    Boun VH.

54 Symonye] Now Simonie WNV; þo symonye H.

56 And(1)] TH$_2$ChDURT$_2$MINDi *om.*; (V *om. line*).
  thise] þe TH$_2$ChDUMIH.

59 pore] pouere TH$_2$UMI.
  or for] oþer TH$_2$Ch.

63 And(1)] Wiþ UT$_2$NVH.
  al] VH *om.*
  the faste] þer wyth H$_2$; þe laste Ch; þe false DVH; al hale T$_2$;
    also MLW; (I *om. line*).

66 seignourie] seriure T (*sic*); segoury T$_2$; synnes M; synge I;
    seruyse VH.
  sese] set TD; lese M; seyse ChT$_2$N; ceese H.

68 purgatorie] purcatorie T; penaunce L.

70 synken] dwelle W; sogerne L; senden VH.

73 Poulynes] & paulynes T$_2$H.
  doctor] douctoure D; dottour U; douȝter RNVH; (I *om. half line*).

74 Bokyngham] bukyngham TN.

76 mylnere] myllere TH$_2$ChNDi; Mellere D; melleward ML.

77 was asselid] is asselid TI; is seled D; I assele URMN; yai seyll
    T$_2$; is y seled W; is Insealed Di.

80 Now] ChURT$_2$MWV *om.*
  bokes] chekes W; bokes chekes Di (bokes *crossed out*); lokkes VH.

82 And] TH$_2$ChD *om.*

83 moylere] molere T; medlere H$_2$H; muliere ChDURT$_2$; maydyn M;
    moylere IN; moillour L; mewliere Di; Iuweler V.
  of Mendes engendrit] of frendis engendrit TH$_2$ChDUR; of fendes
    ingendred T$_2$; for monnys engendryng M; of mennis engendrid N;
    A Mayden of goode VH; (W *om. line*).

84 grauntith] grauntide TMWDi; graunt H$_2$Ch; graunte vs VH.

86 texte] textis TH$_2$D; tyxtest Ch (*sic*).
  tellith] telle TH$_2$D.
   sua] TR *om.*; (M *om.* mercede sua; W *om. Latin completely*).

87 huyre] mede TH$_2$ChDURT$_2$ILWNDi.

88 lawe] lawes TH$_2$ChUR.

92 it] TH₂ChDURMILWN *om.*

94 and] TH₂ChD *om.*; a V.
feithles] feyntles TH₂ChDL; fals R; ffalsly T₂; feytles M; defowlys
I; faylere V.

95 And] TH₂D *om.*
Belsaboubis] belsaboukis TChR; belsabouris H₂; bessabukes M.
kynne] kynde TH₂ChT₂MLDi.

96 moylere] mulere T; mened H₂; muliere ChDRT₂; moliere U;
maydyn ML; meylere I; moillere WN; mewlyar Di; Iuweler V;
medelar H.
a maydene of goode] of maides engendrit T; of maidens engendered
Ch; engendryd of goode M; amoiller of goode L; a Mayden ful
gent V; amonge men of goode H.

97 she(2)] he TH₂D; heo DiVH.

101 And yif] And UR; Giff T₂; þey M; And þogh WNDiIL.

102 the] ChINDi *om.*; youre D; þat URL; þis H.

105 sore] sare T₂; soure MILWNDi.

106 assentith] assentid DINH; (V *om. lines* 106-121).

110 failide] ne failiþ T; ne fayle H₂; fayle DT₂MW; lacked H.

112 my] his DLH; our U; hire W; I *om.*

116 cese] cesse TH₂T₂N; ses ChDLDi; cese UW; sece R; secyn I; ceese
H; slepe M.

119 she] he TH₂Ch; heo LH; R *om.*

120 the] TH₂DW *om.*

123 in shires abouten] abouten in shires TH₂ChD; of schyrs aboute M;
in Cuntre a boute V.

124 And alle] þat alle U; And yaim al T₂; & bad hem alle M; þat vche
beorne L; To here bodes WN; þat alle þei myȝten H; (V *changes
line*).

125 this] þe TH₂ChDV.

126 caride] cariede T; karkeden L; caareden H.
hy] he H₂; þei ChDURT₂MIWNDiH; heo LV.
for] forþ T.

127 Favel fette] fette fauel TH₂ChDURIWNDi; fauuell fochis T₂.
forth] TChDRMIWNDi *om.*; fourty H₂.

128 And] TH₂ChDURT₂MLWN *om.*

130 on a] vpon TH₂ChUT₂MILNDi; vp a R; on W.
fetisliche] quentyliche H₂; sotely Ch; fastlyche D; fayntley T₂MVH;
fetelych I; fetosly L.

131 Tho] þere TH₂Ch; Than T₂VH; (WN *C-text here*).

133 swor] seide URWNVH.
seide] swor URNVH.

137 sudenis] southdenis TH₂M; subdenys RT₂; I *om.*; Erchedeknes WN;
officyalles DiH.

[185]

138   to]   at here TH₂ChRI; at DN.

141   comissarie]   Comissare TH₂W; comisarys T₂DiH.

142   of]   fro T; from H₂Ch; at H.

144   rennen]   iotten T; Iotton H₂; trotten Ch; ganges T₂; Rynnen Di.

145   Fals]   Than falsed W; Now ffals VH.

146   the(2)]   þis TH₂DLNDi; þese AM.
meyne]   mene T; mayne DR; men T₂AM.

147   tom]   toom H₂; tong ChUT₂AM; tyme RLN; toome W; while V;
(H *has* tome *with* y *written over the* o *in a later hand*).

148   of(2)]   DRDiV *om.*
men]   man TH₂DDi.

150   litel]   a litelle ChUH; luyte V.

151   on]   forþ on TH₂ChDURALDi.

154   Be]   Now by UNVH.

156   tho]   þise TH₂ChV; yoys T₂; ye I; the Di.

158   on]   of TH₂IL.
leste]   beste TDURMIW.

161   thise tirauntis]   þis tiraunt TH₂; þe tyrauntes RL; yo tratours T₂;
þo terauntes AIDi; tyrauntez M; þis tirauntz W; þe tiraunt N;
þe Traytours VH.

162   kynnes]   skynes TH₂RM; kynne UW.

163   gurdith]   gederiþ TH₂ChUR; gurde DT₂IWH.

165   sende]   sente TH₂ChD.

169   that]   þe UT₂AMV; þis WH; al that Di; grete I.
doom]   dyne I; deone L; dune V.

172   Falsnesse]   falnesse TD (*sic*); falshode Di; ffals VH.

180   yhuntid]   Ihonted DR; huntid AWN; honsched as an hounde H.
yhote]   hote DLV; Ibodyn I; hoted W; hooten H; (T₂AM *change
line*).

182   Wosshen]   Wysshen TD; Whuschen H₂; Weschen Ch; Waschid UR;
yai weshyd T₂; Weschid A; Wyssin M; Wysthyn I; Woschen L;
Washe W; Wisshe N; Wosschen VH; (Di *om. line*).
cloutis]   cloþis TH₂ChDURAL.

183   chirchis]   chirche TH₂DURAMLH.

185   hy sente]   besente T; him sente H₂Di; to him sent Ch; ben sent D;
he sente U; þo sente R; yai send T₂ML; sentyn A; for him sent I;
þei sent WN; him senden VH.

186   watris]   & watris TH₂D.

187   hym]   hem TR; yaim fast T₂; I *om.*

189   Mynstrales]   And mynstrales TH₂DI; Bot mynstrals T₂ML.
messangeris]   messagers H₂DURMWV.

190 half a yer]   half ʒer TURMN; an half ʒere ChH.
      half a yer and ellevene dayes]   wit hem terme of here lyues H₂;
      to þe worldis eynde L.

192 For]   Fro TH₂.

196 maide]   maiden TRT₂MLV.

197 fere]   drede URNH; ferde T₂AM.

198 wrang]   wrong here handis AILVH.

PASSUS THREE

Title:

TH₂ChDURT₂MIWNH: Passus tercius de visione (DI *in margin*; N
                          adds vt prius).
A: Tercius passus de vissone (*sic*).
L: *no title or break.*
Di: Passus quartus de Visione.
V: *no title; one line left blank.*

3 callide]   calliþ TH₂DLWNH; callid in A; clepet V.

6 world]   world molde H₂ (world *crossed out and* molde *added above
      line*); moolde URT₂WDiH.

7 my(1)]   TH₂ChDRT₂AIWDi *om.*

8 this]   þe TH₂ChURV; my T₂AI; here M.

11 Ac]   Bot ChT₂LDi; And RAM; þan WN; VH *om.*

12 Thei that]   þat TH₂ChDUT₂AILNDi; And þo þat R; þo þat M;
      And þai þat W; heo þat V; þei þat H.

13 somme]   sone TH₂ChW; some D; to sowpen U; to sompne R; sone
      come T₂; summe AM; summe icchone I (summe *crossed out*);
      somme LN; soune Di; soone V; wel soone H.

14 Buskide]   Buskiþ TH₂Di.
      byrde]   burde TH₂H; berd ChDAMI; byrde UDi; berthe R; birde
      T₂W; beorde L; bierde N; Buyrde V.
      dwellide]   dwelliþ TH₂DRDi; dwellth U (*sic*); dwellit M; was Inne
      VH.

15 Counfortide]   Counfortiþ TDRT₂Di; Conforteh H₂ (*sic*).
      clergies]   clergie TH₂T₂; (Ch *om. line*).
      be clergies leve]   and made hire good chere V; & made hir at eese H.

17 shapen]   make TH₂ChDURT₂ADi.

18 Consience caste]   consiences cast TH₂URM; konsciens crafte ILV.
      a craft]   or craft UT₂; and craft RMWNDi; is cast I; for casten L;
      and Casten V.

21 and]   TH₂ChI *om.*

22 ricchesses]   ricchesse TChWDi; Riches AL.

23 motoun]   mutoun TH₂; moten L; moton WDiH; (T₂MV *om. line*).

26 beden]   bidden TH₂ChMDi; bedyn D; bad UT₂AW; bode R; bodyn I;
      beden LN; biddeþ VH.

27 oure]   þi TH₂ChD.

[187]

30 callen] telleþ D; to call T₂M; don callen IWNDi; þat calles L; to tellen VH.

31 hym] DMIN *om.*; hem URDiVH; you T₂.
lede] ladde D; clerk M; leod LN; leste Di; lewedeste VH.
love] louye TUR; luffe I (*over original* loue).

36 seide] he seide TH₂.

37 ichone] alle URILV (R *has* walle *with* w *expuncted*); boþe MNH.

40 erande] arnede TH₂; herand Ch; arende U; arnde R; hernde M; erdene I; ernde LV.

47 in] of T; on H₂; a ChD; at RM (at hom M); y(wroght) WN.
ful] wel TH₂ChLNDi; wol U; RAI *om.*

48 therin] þere TDURAWN; I *om.*

52 se] wite U; sen A; seyn M; sayn W; seen N; seye VH.
That iche segge shal se] That I say sall be done T₂; þer to segg y schewe me now L.

53 to] TH₂ChDUR *om.* (to *inserted above line in* H₂; DU *have* & *instead of* to).
sinistra] sinister TH₂DN; senister T₂; synister I.
dextera] dexter TH₂DT₂IN; dextra AMLW.

54 hond] halfe URAIN.

56 Ac] And TH₂ChUR; Bot T₂LDiV; WH *om.*
so prevyliche parte it] parte hit so priueli V; so priuely be it parted H.

57 soule] þi soule TH₂LDi.

58 coveitous] or coueitous TH₂ChIDi; or coueytes RT₂M.

61 Or] Oþer TH₂ChM.
Godis men] gudes T₂; goodes men W; Godus folk VH.
yive dolis] shall oȝt dele T₂; ȝerne A; delyn doles MI; dole deles L; ȝoure good deles W (*over erasure*); ȝiuen or doles V.

62 therof here] þerof hire T; for ȝour gode U; þer of ȝoure gode R; þer fore A; here M; rith here I; resceyued L; þerfore here VHT₂.

63 prechide] prechid TChDRAWNDi; prechys T₂; precheþ V.
Amen amen dico vobis receperunt mercedem suam] Amen Amen recipiebant & cetera TH₂DA; Amen Amen reciperunt mercedem et cetera Ch; Amen dico vobis receperunt mercedem suam MDiVH; Amen amen dico vobis Recipiebant mercedem suam I; Amen dico vobis vobis receperunt mercedem & cetera L (*sic*); Receperunt mercedem suam W; Amen amen receperunt mercedem N.

64 hij] hem Ch; þey DU; ȝe RILN; & thay Di; and ȝe V; T₂AMWH *om.*

66 pynyng] pynnyng TH₂ChRWV (H₂W *actually read* pynnyg); kuckyng M.

67 Breowesters] Breweris TH₂DURWNDi; Bruers I.

68 on] of TH₂ChT₂MIN; in U; vppon V.

70 and] wel TH₂ChDUIILDi; full T₂AWN; (M *om. line*).

71 richen]   risen vp TH₂Ch; rechyn RA; beþ riche W; recheþ V; waxen ryche H.

 regraterie]   regratie T; Regalrye Ch; regratyng R; Regatorie V; regratoures H.

72 With]   Of TH₂DURAMILWNDi.

73 thei(1)]   he TH₂ChRMI.

 thei(2)]   he TH₂ChRI.

74 no]   none TH₂DURMNV.

 Ne boughte no]   shulde bye noo H (*over erasure of* bouȝte no suche).

 wel]   wol U; full T₂; AIVH *om.*

 be ye wel certayn]   so richeliche arayed M.

 certayn]   cterayn T (*sic*); seure W; sure N.

78 Rynges]   Ryng TH₂ChRDi.

 the regratouris]   þat regratour TH₂; þat Regatoures Ch; Regratours DW; þese regratours URH; swych sellerys M; þe Regratour V.

82 meiris and]   TH₂ChD *om.*

 lawis]   þe lawis TH₂ChDURAMH; þe lawe V.

83 tolde]   tok TH₂ChDUR; telyd I; telde N; toulde Di.

 hem]   hym TH₂DU.

 And tolde hem]   Lo þis was H.

 thinke]   þenke TUH.

 that I telle thinke]   þat tellyn ȝow I þynke M; þat I þe telle þinke W; þat I wol telle nouþe V.

84 lettride lordis]   lettride men URMW; leryd lordes T₂; lewede men VH.

85 forbrenne]   bren T₂AMILWVH.

86 houses]   hous TH₂ChDURW.

87 for here service]   for here seruyses D; of here seruises R; wrangwysly T₂; or ȝeriuys A; & ȝerius M; or ȝerisȝeuys IN; or ȝeresȝeftes L; or mede W; or presentes Di; amysse H; V *om.*

89 fecche]   fette ChDURAMILWNDiVH.

90 boure]   borugh T; borugȝ H₂; bourth M; þe boure H.

91 Curteysly]   Certis TD; connyngly Ch.

 the king]   þan þe kyng DT₂W; þe kyng þanne AIDi; þe kyng þo MH; (L *om. line*).

92 melis]   mekely D; moueþ U; mellyt T₂; mevede A; myd M; mengyd I; meled LW; Melioudiouse N; melleth Di; Melodyes V; (H *om. line*).

93 Unwittily womman]   Vnwittily ywys TCh; Ful wyckedely Iwis woman H₂ (woman *added above line*); Vnwittily DUWDi; won wyttyly Ř; Vnwisly T₂A; Vnwyttily þou Mede M; Vnwittily mayde I; Womman vnwittely L; Vnwitly womman N; Qweynteliche quaþ þe kyng V; Certis unwysely H.

94 whanne]   þo TH₂ChDRINDi.

95 that]   þe TH₂W; þy ChD; þat RT₂MILDi; in þi A; þis NVH; U *om.*

 my]   TChDUR *om.*; (H *om. half line*).

[189]

99   Lord(2)]   god ChT$_2$ALWDiVH; goddes I.

100   TH$_2$ChD *om. line.*
> But I be holy at youre heste]   But I be at ȝoure heste MW; Bot
> ȝef y beo holy at ȝor heste L; Bote Ich holde me to oure heste V;
> but I hoolly be at ȝoure heest H.
> let]   URT$_2$DiV *om.*
> sone]   elles URI; hye L; in hast WNDi.
> let hange me sone]   gurd off my nek H.

104   To wite what]   What þat TH$_2$ChDADi; What URN; What at T$_2$;
       To heryn what M; & askyd qwat I.

107   me]   TH$_2$Ch *om.*

109   feith]   fleys R; flesh T$_2$VH; feth A; fait M; flexe I.

111   trust]   trist TCh; trost A; tryste I; treost L.

112   she]   TH$_2$ChDURLWDi *om.*

113   Lerith]   Leride TH$_2$DUR; lerneþ ChMIN; lerys T$_2$; (Di *om. line*).
       lovith]   louiden TH$_2$DUR; louen ChI; loue N; lecching H.

114 . she]   he TH$_2$ (s *inserted before* he *in* H$_2$) ; heo LVH.
       behestis]   behest TIWNV.

115   holy]   al holy TH$_2$UDi.

116   Is not a]   I not a TH$_2$ChD; Is no M; Yer ne his a I; þer is not a
       L; þer nis no VH.

117   and(2)]   in DINVH; or T$_2$.

118   hire(2)]   ChT$_2$ILWN *om.*

119   to knaves and to alle]   to knaue & to monk TChUR; to knaue and to
       alle H$_2$; to knaues & to monkes D; to knaues & al other T$_2$; to
       knaues & othir L.

120   To monkis to mynstrelis]   To mynstrelis to messangeris TH$_2$; To
       mynstrals and messangers Ch; To mynstrales & messagiers U; to
       menstralis and meselys R; To monke & to mynstrell T$_2$; To monkes
       and to mynstrals WNDi; To Preostes to Minstrals V. (D *om. line*).

123   bothe]   after ChULNV; bathe T$_2$; eke H.

125   gaileris]   gailer ChWVH; iauelers T$_2$.

126   fle]   goe H$_2$ (*added above line*); and fle ChWVH; to fle RT$_2$IL.

127   She]   He TH$_2$R; And T$_2$M; Heo LVH.
       and]   TH$_2$ *om.*

130   cotith]   cloþiþ TH$_2$ChUR (D *def.*); cotid T$_2$; cloyth M.

131   as(1)]   so T; als ChT$_2$Di; þus NI.

133   secret]   secre TMWVH.

135   the]   here DRT$_2$ILWNDi.

136   theigh]   ȝif TH$_2$ChIWH.
       theigh thei be]   þo þat ben D; þeigh þat þei ben UV; þey þat he
       be R (he *added above line*); of all yai be T$_2$; þere þat þey ben M.

137   Provendrours]   Prouendours D; Prouendres RH; Prouandrise T$_2$;

Prouendrit M; Prouendreys I; Prouendrers LV; Prouendreþ WNDi.
parsones and prestis] prestis & persones TH₂Ch; persones D;
persones prestes UIV; persons and preuest (*sic*) L; persones &
styfly WN.
mayntenith] maynteniþ to holde TH₂ChDUR.

138 To holde] TH₂ChDUR *om.* (*see preceding line*).

143 Be Jesu with hire juelx] With here riche Iowelles W; Heo Buggeþ
with heore Iuweles VH.
justices] Iustice TH₂ChDUT₂IWNDi.

144 the treuthe] treuthe ofte U; hem ofte RI; hym ye gate T₂M; hem
euere W; him eure N; so faste VH; (DDi *om. half line*; L *changes
line*).

146 ledith] let TH₂; as hase T₂ (as *crossed out*).
the] TH₂ChDURMIL *om.*

148 maken ende] make ende TH₂ChDT₂H; make an eynde LNDi.

149 heo] he TH₂DRDi; sche ChUMIWN; sho T₂.
wel] ful TH₂ChDUT₂V.

150 heo] he TH₂; yai T₂; R *om.*

152 that meyntenith hire men] þat maynten her meny Ch (y *added
to original* men); þat meynteneth here now D; maynteners of hir
T₂; hire meyntenours M; þat here mayntene now W; þat her
mayntene NH; þat Meynteneþ hire V.

153 theigh] ȝif TChIW; if H₂T₂.

159 cunge the] cunge TH₂; congey þe L; hange the Di; Congeye V;
conieye H; I *om.*

160 werse] wers TH₂ChT₂WH.

163 cam] can TT₂; (M *om. line*).
for] URT₂ILWNDiVH *om.*

166 ellevene] enleuene TH₂U; endleue M; mony feole L; Enleue V.

167 gripen] grepe TDM; grepyn R; grypyd T₂WH; gropyn IL; groped
Di; Igripen V.
likide] likiþ TH₂ChDRL; likes T₂; list H.

169 menske] auaunce TH₂ChD; mylde UR; menster T₂; manschippyn I.

171 And] Bot T₂MWNH; Ac I.
famide] famid TH₂ChDURT₂MILNDiVH; defamed W.

178 to be] to haue ben T₂MIWNVH.
cloude] cloud TT₂; knowde R; colde I.

179 hastidest] hastide TH₂DNDi; hastest R; hast T₂.

180 thou] TH₂ChDWV *om.*; yan I.
robbidest] robbest TDM; robbed Di.

183 And made hym merthe] And made hym mery ChH; And made him
mirthes UR; And I made his mery men T₂; And made alle hise
mery men M; And made him mychel myrthe IL; And made him
wiþ myrþe W; And made him with my myrthe N; Maade him
murþe ful muche V.

[191]

mournyng to lete] mournyng to leue TH₂DMLWNDi; mornyng till
leue Ch; fro morwe til eue UR; yair mornyng to leue T₂; his
mornyng to leue I.

184 hym] hem WNT₂IV; men H.
his herte] here hertes MT₂ILWNVH.

185 hym] hem MT₂ILNVH; W *om.*

186 marchal] marchaunt TD.

190 brol] barn RVH; braunche M; brothel I; Baron W.

191 TCh *om. line.*

193 reyn over hovith] regniþ ouer on TChD; regnet vnder heuene over
hangyth H₂ (vnder heuene *crossed out*); reyn ouer houes U; regnes
ouer houes R; is ouer qware T₂; rengnit vnder heuene MWN; reyn
ouer hongeth L; Rayne ouer oveþ erthe Di (oveþ *crossed out*).

194 becomith to] becom TH₂R; becomeþ DUI; be semet to M; bicomeþ
ffor V.

195 meede to men] hise men mede TH₂ChDURT₂MILWNDi.

197 be lovid] y loued R; beo bilouet V; biloued H.

200 and] wiþ TH₂ChDURT₂IDi; of WN.

201 hem selven] hym self TH₂ChURWDi; here self DT₂; hemself MN;
hem seluyn ILV; H *om.*

204 biddith] biddiþ of TH₂ChD; (UWN *om. line*).

205 merthe] merþis TH₂ChDILWNDi.

206 mede] nede TH₂D (*stroke is added to* n *in* H₂).
hath mede of] Meedeþ VH.
londis] land T₂MIDiVH.

207 Men that ben clerkis] Men þat teky techyn childryn M (teky
crossed out); Men yat kennyn clerkys IWN; Men þat clergye
konnen L; Men þat knoweþ Clerkes V; & þese kunnunge clerkis H.
craven of hym mede] crauen after mede ChL; mede of hym crauytʒ
R; crauen here Mede MT₂; crauyn hem of mede I; crauen of hem
mede WNDi (of hem *crossed out in* Di); Meede hem craueþ V;
crauen vpon mede H.

210 Alle] Of alle TH₂; & alle IH.

214 worthi] best worthy T₂M; wel worþy WN.
the maistrie] Muche Maystrie VH.

216 beth] arn TH₂URMIL; er T₂; be N; ar Di.
two] to TH₂ChMI; too DW; ij Di; twey V.
be] with DLN.

218 wel werchen] werchen wel TH₂ChDURT₂ILWNDi; werchyn his welle
M.

219 prechide] prechiþ TH₂RT₂.
non] TH₂DHW *om.*; (W *has only* Qui pecuniam suam &c).
&c] TH₂ChDRMIDi *om.*; & munera super innocentem N.

220 men] hem TH₂ChT₂MI.

[192]

221 lene] lenne T$_2$; leeue V.

225 seith] seide TH$_2$RT$_2$I; spekyt M; witnessiþ H.

226 he that] ho so D; yai yat T$_2$; ȝe þat M; thay that Di; heo þat V.

230 on] of URMIL; in T$_2$V.
  receperunt] recipiebant TH$_2$DUI; recipierunt Ch; reciperunt R;
  (H *om. Latin*; N *om. lines 228-230*).

231 lough] lewd ChT$_2$AMWH; lond UR.
  taken] lacchen N.

232 It is] Is TH$_2$ChT$_2$L; Nis V; hit nys H; (W *om. line here*).
  mede] of mede TH$_2$ChRT$_2$AMILNDi.

233 marchaundise] marchaundie TR; mariaundise H$_2$.

234 peny-worth] peny TH$_2$ChWVH.

237 mouthe] mouþ TADi.

238 Amalek] amaleg T; amalech H$_2$UMDi; amules Ch (*sic; five strokes
  between* a *and* l).
  al] TH$_2$ChD *om.*

239 his] here TH$_2$ChA.
  eldren] eldris H$_2$DUT$_2$AMWDi; eldes Ch; eldere I; aldres L;
  heldres N.

240 TH$_2$ChDU *om. line.*

242 boun] bone Ch; bold UR; bouer T$_2$; bownde Di.

246 money] mone TRI; gold A; (U *om. line*).

247 Barnes] Barnet D (*sic*); Bernes T$_2$AIWVH; Gerdis M; Beornes L;
  Biernes N. (U *om. line*).
  to dethe] to gedere H$_2$; to dede T$_2$AM; to dede dethe I (dede
  expuncted); to þe deþe N; al to askes V; H *om.*

248 him bode sente] bode sente TH$_2$Ch; hym boþe sente D; hym selue
  bad U; hym bad R; him bode sende L; him self hihte V; hym
  self sende H.
  as Crist him bode sente] bot covett hys goodez T$_2$.

249 kilde] and kylde UT$_2$I; slow W; and slouh VH.

250 tellith] hym tolde T; tolde H$_2$ChDR; techith IH.

252 shendfully ende] senfully shulde ende TH$_2$T$_2$; schamfully schuld
  ende Ch; shendfully schuld ende D; schenfullyche ende RMLN;
  synfully endid A; schent ben for euere I; shamfully ende WDi.

253 to] TN *om.*; (N *adds it in margin*).

254 hatide] hatiþ TChDT$_2$.
  hym for evere] þat king TCh; þe kyng H$_2$D; þe kyng for euere UR;
  him euere IV.

255 this] þis clause TH$_2$; þis case ChT$_2$AMN; þis terme D; URILWDiVH
  have simply þis.

256 it noighide me] it me noiȝide TH$_2$Ch; it noyed me DALDi; ȝif it

noiede me URI; yat it noyd me T₂; it greuede M; if I noied me W;
it annuyed me N; hit munged me V; (H *om. line*).

an ende] and ende H₂ (*sic*); now An ende D; ende R; nane end
T₂AMLN; now ende I; amende W (a *is over indecipherable erasure;
abbreviation for* us *is added in lighter ink*); nygh an ende Di.

257 I Consience knowe] In consience knowe I TH₂ChURDi (I *added
above line in* Di); yf Concience knowe D; In consciens knaw T₂;
I conciens schal knowe AM; I consciens knowe ILWN; Concience
knoweþ V; I consciens knew H.

kynde wit] kynde it TH₂ChDDi; resoun it UR; reson has it T₂.

258 reaumes] reumes T; remes H₂Ch; Reames DV; rewmes URLHI;
realmez T₂; realmis ADi; regnys MN; reaumes W.

259 happen shal somme] happe shal somme TChN; happe schal newly
somme H₂; happed ende schul somme D; hap men schul se som tyme
UR (*for* schul R *has* schuld); hape for hisse grett synne T₂; rygth
so schal synne A; happe schal of summe M; happyn schulyn summe
IL; happed shal somme W; happe sum schulden haue Di; hapne
schulle summe V; (H *om. line*).

262 on] o TH₂RW; one UIDi.

on cristene] vncristen T₂.

263 on] vppon T₂AMLVH; in I; of N.

265 to trewthe] trewely TH₂ChUR; treuþe DNDi; aʒeyne trewthe IW.

or] & TH₂ChDURAH.

takith] doth IVH.

takith ayens his wille] aʒeyn him takith L.

ayens his wille] to þe wrong TH₂Ch; ony þyng D; aʒens right UR;
aʒeyne his wille IWNDiV; aʒeyn him L.

266 Leaute] His wykkide leaute TH₂ChUR; His wikydliaunce D.

268 with] of TH₂ChH.

with riche pelure] rechely yforred L.

270 leaute] leute TUV; lewte ChRILNH; lyaunce D; luve T₂AM; lelte
W; lewtie Di.

PASSUS FOUR

Title:

TH₂ChURAMINH: Passus quartus de visione (N *adds* vt prius).

D: Passus quartus (*in margin*).

T₂: Quartus Passus de visione Petri & c.

L: *no title or break.*

W: Quartus passus de visione.

Di: Passus quintus de visione.

V: *no title; one line left blank.*

2 saughten] sauʒte TH₂; sawhte Ch; saghten D; saghtlyn U; sawtlyn
R; saghtyll T₂; a corde AW; sautalyn M; sawtyn I; saghtene L;
saughtle N; sauʒten Di; sauʒtene V; saʒtene acoorde H (acoorde
written above saʒtene).

[194]

4 Crist] god TH₂ChDUR.
  cunge] conge H₂ChMWDi; counge D; hang T₂; coueytid A; con-
  foundyd I; congeye LNV; coiunge H (i *added between* o *and* u
  above line in original hand and ink).

5 arst] erst TH₂IDiV; first U; rather T₂AMWN; leuere H.

7 that thou fecche] þow fecch ChRMN; þou me fecche U; to feche
  T₂WH; fecche to councell A; þou fette V.

10 othere mo] mo oþere TH₂URAWNDi; many oþer Ch; þe maiden L.
   what] & what LNDiVH.

11 acounte] counte TH₂ChDURAWNDi; counpte L.
   the] TH₂DURT₂AIV *om.*; (I *adds* ye *above line*).
   Crist] god DURAVH.

12 lerist] lernest ChIDiH; rewliste UMW; loses T₂; ledest V.
   the(1)] my VH; (A *om. line*).

13 seith] seide ChT₂MV; says D; seytȝ R; quod IH.
   freke] frek TH₂; frayk D; freek U; seytȝ R (*sic*); concience MI;
   ffreike V; (A *om. line*).

14 rit right] riȝt renneþ TChDUR; ryȝt rydyth H₂; rydez right T₂;
   rytte rygth A; wendith M; rod riht IV; ryd riȝt L; rideþ right
   WNH; Rod Di.

15 Seide] Seide hym TH₂ChDRT₂AMILWNDi.
   sente] seide H₂ChI; him sente U; bad WH; sende V.

19 witful gerthis] riȝtful gerþis TH₂ChUR; wytful gartys D; full
   wyght girthes T₂; to goode girþeys M (y *crowded between* e *and* s);
   swiþe feole gurþhes VH.

21 Yet] And ȝet TH₂ChDURLDi; For T₂A; ffor ȝit M.
   wile he] wile we T; we wil DR; schal he U; he will T₂AN.
   make many wehe] makyn we he MW; weheen & wynch L.
   wehe] wey D; a wehe RH; wiche T₂; wey & whehe A; a whi V.
   we] he H₂ChAWDiVH.

22 carieth] cairiþ TH₂L; caried DMWDiH; caryd T₂A; careþ N.

23 rit] riȝt H₂; rideþ ChWNVH; right U; ryȝth RA; to ryde T₂; ryd
   L; Ryte Di.
   rapith hym] rapide hym UT₂AIDi; redeliche L; rouneth W; rapiþ
   N; Rappynge V; hastid hem H; (D *om. line*).
   swythe] ȝerne TH₂Ch; faste UDi; in hast T₂A; nyghe L; in his
   ere W; aftre N.

24 Ac one Waryn Wisdom] Ac vnwary wisdom TH₂; Bot on wary
   wisdom Ch; Ac on warry wysdom D; At on were wysdom UR; Bod
   an warnyd wysdom T₂; And warnyd wisdom A; But on warynd
   wisdam M; And yo waryn wisdum I; At on asent weore wisdam L;
   But one waryn wisdom WNDi; Bote on a wayn wyd V; & in a
   wayn wysdome H.

26 In cheker and in chauncerie] In þe chekir and in þe chancerye UR;
   In cheker in chaunserie A; In chekerie & In chancerye M; In þe
   chauncellery & þe chekere L; In the cheker & chauncery Di; In
   Esscheker and Chauncelrie V; in court & in chauncelrie H.

[195]

28 harmes] harm TH₂ChT₂VH.

29 a myle wey] a myle AMLWNVH; a lang mile T₂; halue a myle I.

30 romide] rombide T; rowned UR; rowmed N.

31 com in to Resoun] come on to resoun Ch; come agayns reson T₂AM;
    welcomyd resoun IH; come vn to reson LDi; to reson he romeþ
    W; come toward resoun N; com to Resoun V.

32 on] a T; on þe ChT₂A.

33 wel] DIWVH *om.*; ful T₂AM; (DT₂AM *rearrange line*).

34 parlement] þe parlement TH₂UAWNH.

37 maydenhod] maydenhed TRAMIDi.

41 plede] plete TH₂ChURT₂AM (U *has* mote plete *with* mote *crossed
    out*).

42 hynen] hinden Ch; hyne U; hynes R; yowes T₂; owis A; hewys M;
    hewyn IDi; owne LV; owen H.
    to murthre myne hynen] to robbe and to slee WN.

43 feiris] faires and T₂ILH; chepyng & W; faier DiV.

44 doris] dore MNV.
    and] TH₂ChDMNDi *om.*

45 quarteris] quartour ChDIWNVH.
    otis] of otis TRLW; of qwete T₂; oten V; ootis H.

47 I] And I TH₂DURW.
    so] TH₂ChDT₂AMILWNDi *om.*
    for hym unnethe] vnneþe on hym TH₂ChD; ones on hym U; onys
    for hym R; for hym ones WN (N *has* hem); for him vp V; for
    hym vneþis H.
    unnethe to loke] to wynke ne to luke T₂AM.
    to loke] for to loke TH₂ChNV; forth to loke W.

48 The king kneugh] þo kneuȝ þe king TH₂ChUR; That knewe þe
    kyng D; þe king seide H.

49 he soughte] by soughte U; he bysoght WDi; souhte V.

50 his(1)] UT₂AILWN *om.*; (T₂L *om.* his pes).
    his(2)] DiVH *om.*

51 my lord] MIWV *om.*; (H *om. line*).

52 hem] him H₂ChDUN; for T₂; on me V; on hym H.

53 wan tho] wan to þo TH₂; went to þo Ch; ran þo D; wrethed yan
    T₂; þan with a wyse tale A; qwan he heryd yoo I; wan out þo
    L (out *added above line*); wept þo N; wente þo VH.
    also] bothe Ch; VH *om.*

57 thi] my TH₂ChDURANDi.

58 thi] TH₂ChD *om.*; þis L.

60 on] vp on AMNVH.
    wepide] wepiþ TH₂DN; wep R; wepit M.

hym to helpe] to hym helpe D; to helpe hym at nede UR; for
  helpe A; to helpyn him for of his I (*sic;* him *added above line;
  see following line*); wel sore L; fast W; & praied N; to helpe hym
  Di; to helpe VH.

61 *The readings are as follows:*
  TH₂: For of hise penys he proffride handy dandy to paye.
  Ch: And of his pans he prroferd handydandy to paie.
  D: For of his handy dandy payd.
  UR: For right þer of is handy dandy payd.
  T₂: And praed hym for of hys & sone had he payed.
  A: And wisdom in handydandy hastely he payed.
  M: Sum what for of his handy dandy paied.
  I: Handy dandy I wisse he payed him yanne (*see preceding line*).
  L: To helpe him for of his handy dandy paied.
  W: And prayed hym for his handydandy help hym at his nede.
  N: To helpe him for of his handy dandy payed.
  Di: For his handy dandy rediliche to be paid.
  VH: Him for his handidandi Rediliche he payede.

63 nomen] tok TH₂ChDURT₂IWH.

64 putte] putte hym TDR (hym *crossed out and expuncted in* T).
  hed] heued TChUT₂.

66 knewen] kneuӡ T; knew H₂ChT₂AMWN; knewe DRDi; knewyn IVH;
    kneow L; (U *om. line*).
  wel] VH *om.*

71 TChDUR *om. line.*
  werkes] wyckidnesse H₂; werk T₂A.
  wo thole] mekyl wa thole T₂; wrong tholyn A; qwoo tholyn I;
    muche wo soffre L.

72 TCh *om. line.*
  And comaundide a constable] DUR *om.;* (*the rest is with following
    line but variant readings are included here*).
  hym] hem RWV.

73 shal] shulde TH₂Ch.
  seven] seue T; vij DUR; viij M (*sic*).

75 mowe] DV *om.;* may T₂AMN; wol H.

76 for] of AIVH.
  biggen] bringen TChR; bemgen H₂ (*sic; three strokes between* e
    and g); beggyn DI; buggen MLDiV; bigge UAWNH; bye T₂.

77 And(1)] TH₂ChDURAMLN *om.;* To Di.
  that] þat he TH₂ChL; þe A; þis W; his VH.

78 accordide] Accordiþ TH₂URAML; acorde DT₂ (*for* Wyt D *has* We).
  -ide there with and sei-] H *om. because of hole in MS.*
  (N *om. lines* 78-80).

80 bet] Ibette ChDI; bote URAW; bute T₂; beten LV; Ilete Di; (H
    om. because of hole).

82 purid] pure ChURWNDi; pewre I; pure Red V; (T₂AM *change
    line*)

[197]

83   of me man]   man of me AWN.
     man]   T₂MIVH *om.*

84   wile(2)]   shal TH₂ChDUR; wolde M; wol LDiVH.

88   that]   þe TH₂ChW; his M; þis H; (R *om. line*).

89   that]   TH₂ChDU *om.*; (RA *om. line*).
     assente]   assente þerto TH₂ChU; assented beo V; assent my lord H.

90   me]   my TH₂DRMLDi; (AH *om. line*); me my Ch.
     amendis]   mendis TH₂ChDRL.

91   tho]   TH₂DURLWDi *om.*; yan T₂.

94   eft]   ofte TH₂ChDDiH; oftere U; after R; eftirward T₂; eke AN;
     oftyn M; Alwey W.
     the baldere be]   þe boldere to be T; the bolder ben H₂IDi; þe bolder
     be ChDW; þe baldere be UR; balder be T₂; þe baldere to be A;
     ben þe baldir M; beo þe balder L; be þe bolder NH; be þe baldore
     V.
     beten]   bete TH₂ChDUT₂WNDi; mysdo H.
     hynen]   hynden Ch; hyne DW; hynes T₂M; hewys A; hyen I;
     buxume L; henene N; hewyn Di; puple H; V *om.*

95   reste]   reste hym TH₂D; LH *om.*
     shal reste]   resteþ WT₂AMIWV.
     the]   H₂URW *om.*; my AMIN.

97   Thanne summe]   Summe men TH₂ChDRT₂; þanne U; Summe
     MAILWDi.
     Thanne summe redde Resoun]   þanne was resoun redde N.

103 childris cherisshing]   children chersynges Ch; Children chiresshenge
     D; childrenes cherischyng U; childres chersyng RMW; chesysyng
     of chylder T₂; childeris chastisyng A; childerys cherissyng I;
     children chere cheryschest L; children cherissyng N; childern
     cherischyng Di; children Chereschinge V; childrens chiding H.
     chastid]   chastisid TH₂ChAMILWDiH; castyd T₂; chastet V.

104 holden]   holde TH₂W; preised H; (N *om. line*).

106 And haten to here harlotrie]   And haten here harlotrie TH₂ChD;
     & hate to here harlotrye URIDi; And hate all harlottre T₂; And
     alle harlotrie haten M; And haten to heren L; And haten to don
     heor harlotrie V; & haten to do harletries H; (AWN *om. line*).
     or mouthe it]   oþer mouþe it with tungis TH₂ (H₂ *has* or); to
     mowþen hit with tong Ch; oþer hit mouþen D; or mouthe it hem
     selue UR; to here or to mouthe T₂M; or mowthin it for euere I;
     of any harlotries ȝelpyng L; or mowthen it Di; and vsun hit no
     more V; & no more it vsen H.

109 be sought]   besouȝt T; be Isouȝt ChURLV; (H *om. line*).

110 yif]   ChUAMLWV *om.*; (H *om. line*).

111 Rome]   þe rome TH₂ChDR.

112 signe of king shewith]   signe of king shewide TH₂Ch (Ch *has* þe
     king); coyn of kyng schewith U; sygne of þe kyng schewt A;
     kyngis signe schewit M; signe of coyn haþ W; signe of kyng beris
     N; bereþ signe of þe kyng VH.

[198]

113 kynges] þe kyngys AWDiVH; (L *om. line*).
coroune] coyn TH₂ChDUR.

114 Upon] Upe T; Vp H₂ChURIN; D *om.*; Vppe þat M; I W; (L
om. line).
who so fynt hym at Dovere] who fynt hym do euere TH₂ChD; who
fynt hym diuerse U; who fynt hym dygnere R; wha sa fynd it may
T₂; ho so fynte hem at douyr AMI; who fynt hem at douorre W;
who so fynde hem at vouorre N; who so fynde it at dover DiH;
hose hit fynde at douere V.

115 or(1)] oþer TDiVH.
or(2)] oþer T.
messanger] messangeris T; messager H₂DURWV.

116 Or(1)] Oþer TH₂ChUH.
Or provisour or prest] Or Prouisours or Preestes V; Oþer prestis
oþer prouisours H.
that the pope avauncith] or penant for his synnes W; þat Popes a
vaunset V; þat popis doþ auaunce H.

118 mote] mo T; moo D; many Ch.
-ote in this h-] H *om. because of hole in MS.*

119 VH *om. line.*
ensaumplis] ensaumple ChRT₂MDi; example A; examplis I; an
ensample W; in example N.
as I se other] as I se forsoþe TH₂Ch; as I se I say it for my selue
D; y seie be my selue U; as I se oþer I sey hit for my selue R;
as ȝe sen othere A.

120 I seighe it for my self] DUR *om.*; (*see preceding line*; DUR *have
and it so were at beginning of line 121*).
I] For I TH₂VH; For ȝef I Ch.
for] be TH₂UDi; ChH *om.*

123 be(2)] at TH₂ChH; in T₂AINDi; for W.

124 my] T₂WNV *om.*; no MI.
giftes] gyft T₂AMILNV.

125 no] MIWDiV *om.*
made] make H₂T₂WDiV; (H *changes line*).

126 the man mette with *impunitum*] he may mete with Inpunitum
TH₂ChD (impunitum ChD); inpunitum þe may mete with U; þe
may mete wyþ Inpunitum R (Inpunitum *begins next line*); Erit to
man inpunitum T₂; met with infinitum A; þat man made with
Inpunitum M; ye man met with inpunitum IWNDi (impunitum
WDi); þe mon mette with irremuneratum L; þe Mon mette with
outen inpunitum V; inpunitum H (*has Latin only*).

127 *bonum*] malum TA.
be] TH₂ChDURT₂ *om.*; shold be W.
For this line L has:
Nec multum malum lawe wolde þat schulde beo Inpunitum.
H *has*:
nec vllum bonum irremuneratum (*with preceding line*).

128 the this] it þe TH₂DUR; þe hit ChLDi; yis T₂AMVH; it WN.
in] on TH₂ChDAIWN.

[199]

129   it in]   þis T (*seems to have been tampered with; possibly an original* it); this H₂; þes Ch; yis in T₂; (*for* it in werk H *has* þer after).
     myne]   boþe myn ULWNVH; boþe his R; yer to myn I.

133   declynede faste]   declynand fast Ch; declyned it faste D; & declyne it aftir U; and declyned faste RL; yai declyned fast T₂AM; he declindeyn fast I; þai clined fast W; & distinkte hit after V; & wite what it mened H.

134   Ac]   Bot ChLDiH; And AM; T₂IWNV *om.*
     whanne]   TH₂ChDRAI *om.*; þo L.
     hadde]   TH₂ChMLNVH *om.*

135   man]   no man TH₂ChD; IDi *om.*; non V.
     man in the mothalle]   no muthall T₂.

136   That ne held]   þat he ne held TH₂DURANDi; yen held yai T₂.
     maister]   Mayster þo V.

140   cokewald ycald]   Cukkold called DT₂; mad cokewald A; cald cokewald M; kokewold of kynde L; a Cokwolde W; Cokewolde Iclepid Di; A Cokewold I kore V; cokewold ykyd H.
     my nose]   boþe myn Eres V; myne eeris H.

141   *The readings are as follows:*
     TH₂: Warne wisdom þo ne no wyt his fere.
     Ch: Wary wisdam þo and witte his fere.
     D: Warne wysdom þo & wyt his owne fere.
     U: Vnwar was wisdom & ynwit his fere.
     R: On warned wysdom þo on wittes fere.
     T₂: War ne wisdom wer yer & witte hys fere.
     A: Than boþe witte & wysdom in fere.
     M: Reyth her wysdam þo ne wit is fere.
     I: Waren wisdom yo ne witty his fere.
     L: Waryn wisdom þo ny witty his fere.
     W: Waryn wisdom þo ne witti his fere.
     N: Waryn wisdom ne witty his fere.
     Di: Waren wisdome tho & witty his fere.
     V: Was nouþer wisdam þo ne witti his feere.
     H: I warne þat wysdom ne witty his fere.

142   Couthe nought]   Yai couth noȝt T₂; Couþ W; þat couþe V; ne couþe H; (U *om. line*).
     warpen]   carpen ChT₂AL; werpyn MNDi; werchin I; seie H.

143   stareden for stodyenge]   staring & stodyenge T; staryng and stondyng H₂; staring and stoding ChD; starende & studiande U; stareden and stodiede RH; staryd forth stridyng T₂; staryd for stodyeng AMLNDiV; staredyn for stondyng I; stared forth studying W.
     and]   TH₂ChDU *om.*
     as bestis]   forþ as bestes U; al stonyed L; stille as bestes WN.

144   sawis]   Connynge VH.

145   hadde]   TH₂ChD *om.*; hath A.

146   wel]   ful DRA; wol U; MWNVH *om.*
     herto it to bringe]   her to to bringe it TH₂INDi; here to bring hit Ch; herto to brynge DR; it þer to to brynge U; to me to bryng

yaim to geder T₂M; to brynge to gederis A; to bryng þis abowte L; here to it brynge WVH.

147 leden] lede hem TH₂ChDH; leden hem UR.

148 raughte] deiȝede TH₂ChD; ryst T₂W; was rauth A; henge M; reste L; rest hym H.

149 yif] UT₂AMLWNVH *om.*

150 so] TH₂ChDAL *om.*
at] of DURMLWNDiH.

151 And] AMVH *om.*

152 of(2)] TH₂ChILNDi *om.*

153 shalt not riden henne] shalt not wende henne TH₂; schalt nouȝt raike hennes Ch; shalt wende henne D; Rydest not heonnes VH. henne] hennes ChRAMILWNDiVH; hyne T₂.

154 lete the I nille] loue þe I wile TH₂ChDUR; love we sall to geder T₂; leuyn þe I nylle A; thy lyfelode I þe thonke M; we nele not depart H.

156 oure] ȝour TH₂ChDRAILDi; T₂WN *om.*

157 graunte] graunte wel LH; graunt þat W; graunte gladly V. Godis forbode] god forbede DT₂AWN; god forbeode DiV. he faille] I faile ChD; he failed U; elles AM; he feile H. Godis forbode he faille] so me god helpe L.

158 lyve] leue ChDT₂W; leue may A; lyffe I; libbe schal L. libbe] abyde T₂; leue AIV; dwelle M; lyue L; be W; loue H.

PASSUS FIVE

Title:

TH₂ChDURT₂AWNH: Passus quintus de visione (D *in margin*; N *adds* vt prius).

M: Quintus passus (*occurs between 5.2 and 5.3; no break between 4.158 and 5.1*).

IL: *no title or break.*
Di: Passus sextus de visione.
V: *no title; one line left blank.*

1 his] T *om.*; the H₂.
-g and his k-] H *om. because of hole in MS.*
chirche] kirke T₂ILN.

3 wynkyng] slep T₂; wink V.
and wo was] & wa was me T₂LH (H *om.* &); me was wo V.

4 yslepe saddere] slepe sadder H₂DURT₂IL (sclepte R); sleped hard Ch; slepyn hardere A; rather Islepte M; saddere slepte WNDi (yslept N; sclept Di); sadloker I slept V.
hadde yslepe saddere] ha............nger H (*the hole*).

5 hente] hadde TH₂DR; kauȝt Ch; hynt T₂.

6 I ne mighte ferthere a fote] I ne miȝt o fote ferþer ChDM; I mygth no ferþere A; A fote ne myght I ferþer WN; I ne might

[201]

forth a fote Di; Forþer mihti not a fote V; ferþer ne miȝte y one fote H; (L *om. line*).
slepyng] slepe DT₂WVH.

7 a-doun] in my bedis T; on my bedis H₂; downe T₂L; (D *om. line*).

9 muche] meke T; mekel RT₂; meche A; mychel MILN; mochel Di; myche H.

10 TChNH *om. line.*
For] H₂URT₂IW *om.*
I saugh] H₂W *om.*
that I before of tolde] that I furst I tolde H₂; þat I before tolde DDi; þat y by fore nempnyd U; þat I by fore sayde R; as I a forn telde A; þat I be for nemede MI; þat I of tolde W; þat ich of bi fore schewede V.

12 He] And TH₂ChDAMILH.

13 the] þise T; these H₂D; þes Ch; þis UIV; MN *om.*
pestilence] pestilences TH₂ChDDiV.
was] wern TH₂ChDIDiV; fell T₂.

14 the] R *om.*; a T₂; the grete M; an Di; þis V.
southwest] southwestryne T; southwesterne H₂T₂LVH; sowþwestren Ch; southerne wynde A.
on] on þe A; on a MIVH; at L.

16 plumtrees] plantes TH₂ChD.
puffed] put TH₂ChDUR; possyd T₂MH; passchet V.
erthe] grounde erthe H₂ (grounde *expuncted*); erde A; grounde WNVH.

17 segges] sent god TH₂Ch; sayd god D; seith god UR; I say T₂A; to men MVH; IWN *om.*; segges L; that ye segges Di.
that] URAMN *om.*
ye] we H₂ChV (*inserted above line in* H₂); they MH.

18 the] T *om.*
grounde] erþe NVH.

21 mamele] manle D; mamle U; mervell T₂; mamelyn AI; mamble Di; Momele V; momelid H; (WN *om. lines 21-23*).
ful] wel TH₂DRIDi; Ch *om.*; wol U.
mamele ful longe] muche mamele & longe L.

25 craft] of craft TH₂Ch.

27 kepen] kepte T.

29 hom Felis] felis his wyf TH₂; felys hom RL; home his wyf H.

31 not] MWV *om.*
worth(2)] ChURT₂IDi *om.*

32 chasten] chastice TH₂DN; chastise ChUW; chaste RH; chasty T₂; chastisin MIL; (A *om. line*; H₃ *C-text*).

33 Let no wynnyng forwanye hem] Let hem wonte non eiȝe VH; *original reading of* I (= T) *crossed out, and* Lat hem want no wande *substituted above line*; (A *om. line*).
wynnyng] welthe U; wonnyng L.

[202]

forwanye] for weny R; for weyne T₂; forwane Di; MWN *om.* for-.
forwanye hem] hem weny N.
whiles thei] whiles þat þei UV (while V).

34 preyide] prechiþ T; prechide H₂ChDUR (preyde *in margin in
different hand and ink* H₂; prechet D).

36 love] leue TH₂ChMW; trast T₂; lowe N.

37 rewele] reweles TH₂ChDT₂.

38 apeire] apeiriþ T; apeired H.

39 stowid] stewid TI; stylet H₂; stiwed ChR; storyd T₂; cattelld W;
stow it N; stayed Di; stouwet V; (AL *om. line*).
til ye be stowid betere] so þat ȝe cheue þe betere U; & tillen ȝoure
stor bettere M; til þei were amendid H.

41 Sekith] Sekiþ at hom TH₂ChD.

42 faire] þat faire URNH.
mote yow] ȝow mote UR; might him T₂; ȝou A; mote ȝe MLW;
ȝe mot I.
mote yow befalle] ȝow- H (*hole in MS*).
befalle] hendyn M; falle LWDiV.

43 ran] TH₂ChDUR *om.*
and] TH₂ChDURT₂ *om.*; to WN.

44 Wil] wylkoc H₂; william VH.

46 lokide] lokide vp TH₂ChT₂; (WN *change line*).
and Lord mercy criede] and lord merci heo cryed H₂; and mercy
sho cryed T₂; and mercy gan crie AM; & oure lord mercy cried L;
& saide lord mercy WN; and to vr ladi criede V.

47 makede] made TH₂ChURT₂MWNVH; maked with his myght L;
(I *om. line*).

48 serke] syrke A; scherte MH; schorte L; smok DiV.

49 For to] To URW; Tho A; Fort N; Forte V.
affaiten] endaunten Ch; afauten R; frete T₂; afeyntyn AM; dawntyn
I; fayten V.
fers] fresch URLH; frele AV; fiers N; Fyrse Di.

53 envye] pride IWN.

54 on] to TH₂ChMV.

55 TH₂ChDUR: To make mercy for his mysdede betwyn god & hym
(*for* mercy U *has* amendes).
T₂: To make mercy for his misdede bitwix god & hys seaulle.
A: Tho makyn mercy for his sowle betwyn god & hym of mysdede.
M: To make amendis for him betwen god & his soule.
I: To makyn mercy mene for his misdedis (mene *added above line*).
L: To make mercy of his misdede bytweone god & his soule.
W: To gete mercy of god in help of his soule.
N: To gete mercy for his misdedis in mendyng of his soule.
Di: To make mercye for his mysdede betwen god & his sowle.
V: To maken him han Mercy for his misdede
Bitwene god almihti and his pore soule.
H: for his mysdedis bytwene god & hym siluen.

[203]

56 shulde] TH₂ChD *om.* (*see next line*).

57 Drinke] Shulde drinke TH₂Ch.

59 gilt] cope TH₂; synnes Ch; coupe DUT₂N; compte R; counte A; wilis M; coulpe W; Culpe Di; gultus VH.
begynneth] begynneþ he TH₂LWNDi; he gynneþ UR; he couettes T₂; com A.
to] for to ChAI.

60 pelet] palet TH₂Ch; polet D; pelat UM; piller T₂; erthe I; pobet L; pelled H (H *reads*: þe pelour was pelled).
in] & on TH₂Ch; on D; & UR; & in T₂Di.
the] DURMI *om.*; a WNDiV.

61 Clothid] He was cloþid TH₂ChDURIDi; He cled T₂; He was clad AW; Iclad M; And clothed L; Cladde N.
couthe] can TH₂ChDM; coude RAL.
descryve] discrie ChURT₂AMIL; deuise W; deserue Di.

65 louryng] lourande TH₂ChT₂; lourede he V.

66 bolnid] bolne A; ybolned L; forbolne W; forbolned N; Bolled VH.
wraththe] wroþ TH₂DUR; wreþþe ChT₂A; angre WN.
lippes] lippe TH₂ChDUR.

67 wrong] wroþ TH₂ChDUI.

68 or with] & TH₂ChI; or DLN; and with R.

69 Venym] Vermyn Ch; Wormes T₂AM; Venymour Di.
or] & TH₂; IN *om.*; than Di.
verjous] wynagre T₂ (*then for* vynegre T₂ *has* wenom); vermyn A; vemyn M; vernycchith I; vernysh WNDiV; verdegrese H.
(*For this line* L *has* Of leosardes or of lobbes venym hath me laghte).

70 Walewith] walkes T₂AM; And walweth L; Waldeþ W; Walleþ VH.
and] or MV; quoþ he or M.
waxith as I wene] worcheth me wrathe L; waxeþ as I trowe W; (A *om.* 70b, 71, 72a).
as] DRMVH *om.*

71 oughte] miȝte TH₂ChDURI; suld T₂; schulde MW.

74 fame] defaut LWH; disclaundre V; (AM *om. line*).

75 have] TH₂ChDURT₂IWNDiVH *om.*; (AM *om. line*).
pursuide] punissched V; preued H.
ful ofte] wel ofte TH₂RDi; ofte UIN; hym ofte T₂; hem oft W; feole sithes L; him ful ofte V.

78 grevide] greuyth AMV; greuyn IW; greue N; (LH *om. line*).
ful] wel TH₂ChRMNDi; UAI *om.*

80 lyme and his lif] lyme & lith T₂; lyfe & leme A; lyme & lyf MWNDi; lyf and his leome V. (ILH *om. line*)

81 mette] mete H₂IWN; mett T₂Di; met H.
market] a market TH₂Ch; þe markett T₂AVH.
hatide] hate IWNV.

82 halside] hailside TUIH; heylid AV; Grette M; hals W; hailse N.

84 I wolde murdre hym for evere] I wold a dystroyed hym for heuyr

A; I mordred hym for euere MV; y wolde him mayme foreuere L;
I wold hym al at fort morthere W; morthere him I wolde N; y
hadde maymed hym foreuere H.

85 and knele] & knelide TDADi; & suld knele T₂; I kneled M; to
knele WH.

86 To preye] I preyd A; I pray IL; And scholde preiȝe V.

87 Thanne] Aftir þanne TH₂RDi; After D; Aftir þat UW; & after I.
hem] hym TH₂ChDUMIDi; hom L.

88 bar] beryn M; bere Di; haþ I-bore V.

89 myn eighe I turne] I turne myn eiȝe UV; my ene I turned T₂AM;
I myn eien cast W; myn eyen down than I turne Di; I turne me
H; (L *om. line, except for* y byholde).
and beholde] and byhelde RT₂AM; y byholde L; (T₂AMLWDi *have*
and beholde *at beginning of next line*).

90-1. *These two lines form one line in* TH₂ChDUR, *the second half of
each line being omitted by this group.* UR *add a line:* And al þe
wele þat he haþ greueth me wel sore.

90 How Heyne hath a newe cote] how mony hed new coteȝ T₂; an hyne
þat hadde a newe Cote M; byhynde me on a neowe kote haue L;
How he haþ a newe cote H (heyne *is at end of preceding line in* H).
Heyne] herry Ch; hyne A; hoge I; hane W; hayne N; hyk Di.
hath] had AW.
and his wyf another] TH₂ChDURT₂AMLWDi *om.*

91 Thanne] TH₂ChDUR *om.*; Anon W.
wysshe] wissed ChT₂; wyschid AM.
it were] þat þai wer T₂.
myn] myn howne T; my owne H₂; myn owne ChU; myn owe R.
and al the web after] TH₂ChDUR *om.*; with all þe webbe after T₂;
& alle his wele after H.

92 it liketh] þerof in TH₂ChD; and þerof lawheþ UR; & light was
T₂; a lytil in A; ay lykend in M; hit lightenes L; it lyghteþ WN;
hit likeþ me in V.

93 for] of TH₂ChDURAMLNDi.

94 that thei] þere þei TH₂ChDR; þere y U; at mony T₂; þat IDiV;
þey LH; þat he W; (N *has* I deme þat men do yuel; M *om. first
half line*).
werse] wers TH₂T₂; wors ChWDiH; worse DLNV.

97 lyk] as TH₂Ch; liche AI.

98 That] And TH₂ChDA; Than W.
bolnith] Bolleþ VH.

99 aswage] swage TH₂ChDUT₂AMWN; swete R.
unnethe] an vnche TH₂ChDURT₂AMILWNDi.

101 Yif that shrift shulde] ȝif scrifte scholde me saue I; And þanne
ȝef any schryft scholde hit saue L; ȝif shrift sholde me þinke N;
ȝif schrit schulde hit þenne swopen out V; ȝif shrift shulde aswage
it H.
Yif] And ȝef ChT₂AWDi.
that] DRT₂AILNVH *om.*

it shop a gret wondir]   it stoppe it wer gret wonder T₂A; me thingith
  it were wondere I; semed hit a gret wondur L; nowe a wonder it
  were W; a gret wonder hit were V; wonder me þinkeþ H.
shop]   stoppe H₂T₂A; schope ChMNDi; schepe D; were URIWV;
  semed L; (H *om.; reads* me þinkeþ).

102   to goode]   þe best T₂AM; to þe best H.

103   synne]   his synne D; synnes T₂AMNDi; her synnys IVH (synneþ H).
  wel manye]   wol manye UM; full many T₂; many on A; men ful
  Monye V.

104   selden]   selde TH₂ChDRH; seldom UT₂AW; seilden L.

107   hungri]   hungirly TH₂ChDT₂LWN; angrey R.

108   He was bitel-browid and babirlippid]   He was bittirbrowid & babirlippid boþe T; He was baburlippud and biturbrowed bothe H₂;
  He was betilbrowed and babirlipped boþe Ch; He was betterbrowed
  & eke baberlypped D; He was babirlippid and eek biterbrowed U;
  He was byterbrowed and eke baberlypped R; He betyllbrowyd &
  alswa blaburlepyd T₂; He was bittilbrowid & eke babirlyppid AMH₃;
  Bitil browed and baberlipped WN; He was betilbrowed & blaber-
  lipped Di; He was bitelbrouwed V.
with two bleride eighen]   TH₂ChDURT₂AMH₃ *have this at the
  beginning of the next line* (109).
bleride]   brode H.
eighen]   eyn as a blynd hagge AMH₃T₂ (*with variations*).

109   And]   TH₂ChDUR *om.*
letherene]   liþerene T.
lollide his chekis]   likerd wer hys chekes T₂; so lokyd is chekys A;
  lokened hys chekes M; lokede hys chekys H₃; lolledyn bothe his
  chekes L; honged his chekes W; (U *om.*; R *has this at beginning
  of line* 110).

111   I may it nought leve]   I may not leue H₂; I may it not trowe DURDi;
  or flee as I trowe T₂; & schippe as I trowe A; I leue nouth I
  trowe H₃; I may it wele trowe I; leue þou for soþe W; I con hit
  not I leue V; (L *changes line, omitting this*).

112   He shulde]   He scholde nat H₂AH₃L; He ne schuld Ch; þat he ne
  schulde UR; Sho suld noght T₂W; Sche myght M; Heo scholde V;
  How heo shulde H.
wandre]   slideren U; slyde R; renne I; haue wandred L; walke H.
on that walsshe]   on þat walsshe scarlet TH₂ChD; þeron UR; on
  þat wede T₂H₃LH; on þat wolde A; þer upon M; þeron ʒerne I;
  on þat lugh W; or walk ther Di; on þat walk V.

113   I have ben coveitous]   I haue ylouid coueitise TH₂DUR; I haue
  loued conscience Ch; I haue ben coueityse T₂Di; I am caytif
  coueitous W; (*for* 113a L *has* I haue quod þat kaityf couetouse
  beo).
quath this caityf]   quaþ he al my lif tyme TH₂ChDUR (H₂U *om.*
  quaþ he; D *om.* tyme); quod þat katyf T₂AH₃LNH; quod þe
  Cayteue MI; quod he W.
I beknowe it here]   I knowe hire TH₂ChD (*at beginning of line* 114);
  I knowe it here UR (*for* I R *has* and; *in both MSS this is at*

beginning of line fol.); well I knaw it here T₂; I be knowe here A;
I knowe hit now here L; I am it wel a knowe W; I byknewe it
here N; (UR *add*: by fore crist & his clene modir; *for* clene R *has*
swete).

114 For sum tyme I servide] For somtyme served I UR; And qwen I
seruyd T₂; For sumtyme whan I serued W.
Symme at the noke] synne me thoght it semyd wele T₂; synne it
þouth me mery A; synne it semed me merthe M; symony it semyd
to me myrthe H₃; to symond atte nokke L; symoun at þe noke H.
noke] nok T; nokke IL.

115 prentis yplight] prentis aplight UAIW; prentise plight LNDi; pliht
prentys V; (T₂H *om. line*).
to loke] to wayten AMH₃.

116 lef] lesing ChM; leue H₃; lessun VH; (A *om. line*).

117 was my ferste lessoun] formest I lerned W; certis was þe þridde H.
ferste] next IN; oþer V.

118 To Wynchestre and to Wy] To wynchelsey and wynchester Ch; To
ware & to wynchestre T₂; To wy & to wynchestere M; Fro sleytforth
to wynchestyr H₃; To wynchestre & wyrcetre I; To wynchestre &
to woborne L; To wynchester & to wey Di; To winchestre and to
wych V; To wenchestre & to wellis H; (A *om. line*).
I wente] I was sent TH₂Ch; I sende D; went I T₂.

119 maner] maner of TH₂ChT₂; D *om.*; (A *om. line*).
me] T₂MH₃IWNDiV *om.*
me highte] myd medled L.
highte] tauȝte H₂ChU; het RDi; aght T₂; heghte M; hyth H₃;
hyte I; hyght WNV; bad H.

120 the] TH₂ChDAM *om.*

121 this seven yer] MH *om.*
seven] seue T; vij DURH₃.

122 drough I me] I drowe T₂; I was M; I drouȝ me VH.
lerne] lere TH₂ChDURT₂AILNDiV; (*missing in* H *because of hole*).

123 list] lysour URH₃IWN; listes L.

124 rendrit] lerned ChH₃VH.

125 a pakke-nedle] a nedel D; bat nedyls T₂; a bat nedil A; a betyng
nedyl H₃; a pak nelde LVH.
pleitide] pleit T; pleyȝt H₂; plite Ch; plyȝte D; ypleyted U; platte
A; plytyd MH₃W; platted L; pletede V.

128 My wyf was a wynstere] My self was a wenester (*or* weuester ?)
Ch; And my wyf at westmunstre VH.
wynstere] webbere H₂; wenester (*or* weuester ?) Ch; breustere U;
windster T₂; webstere AMH₃IW; vynnestre N; wevester Di.
and] þat VH.

129 And] And sho T₂; She AN; I H₃; VH *om.*; (L *om.* 129a).
spynsteres] spynstere TH₂ChDURDi.
softe] owt T₂AMH₃.

130 The] Two H.
　heo] I Ch; sche DUT₂AMH₃IWNDi; he R.
　payed by] weid by TH₂ChU; way to hym D; weyes by R; payd for
　　T₂W; payde hem A; way him by M; payid hem by H₃L; paysed
　　hem by Di; peysede VH.
　peiside] peisid TH₂ChDAI; was U; weyeþ R; passyd T₂H₃L; pysed
　　M; weied WH; paysed NDi.
　peiside a quarter more] a quartrum more peisede V.
　more] *This word comes at beginning of next line in* T₂AMH₃L.

131 myn aunsel dede] any aunsel dede T; þe aunsel dide H₂Ch; ony
　　aunser dede D; ony almesdede UR; my awne T₂; my poundur dede
　　A; myn hauncer M; it augthe H₃; myn awnselfe did I; myn owne
　　deode L; it is dede by myn ansere (*sic*; is *crossed out*) W; myn
　　auncere did N; aunsere ded Di.
　whanne] & TH₂Ch.
　whanne I weighede trewethe] þat was lytil trewþe A.
　weighede] wey ChDT₂MILN; waugh H₃.

133 pile whey] pele waye ChT₂; pele was (*sic*) D; pile whew U;
　　pigwhey R; pelaway A; spilawaye M; pylqwyt H₃; pilwyle ILN;
　　pewe W; piriwhit V; periwhit H.

134 lay] liþe Ch; lyuen URVH; lyth A; layne I; lyued L; layd W.

136 And] VH *om.*
　bummide] boused R; boght T₂; bubbith A; drange M; bybbyd H₃;
　　drong L; dronke H.

138 cuppe-mel—that craft my wyf uside] coppis medelid it ȝhe & þat
　　craft vsid A.
　that craft my wyf uside] such craftes me vsede V; siche craft heo
　　vsiþ H.

140 Heo] Sheo T; Sche H₂ChDURT₂AMH₃IWNDi.
　hath holde] haþ yholde T; hat Iholde H₂; haldeþ R; hade haldyn
　　T₂AINDi.
　huxterie] osterye URAMH₃; ostre T₂.
　ellevene wynter] þis elleuen winter ChURV; elleuen wynteres lang
　　T₂; long eleue wynter A; þis xv wynter M; wel elleoue wynter L;
　　al þis xxxti wynter H.

141 sothly] als mot I the T₂; so mote I the AMH₃; so I think I; to þe
　　L; so þike N; V *om.*
　that synne shal I lete] þat synne dyd she neuer T₂; þis synne schal
　　be lafte A; sum tyme shal I leuen M; þat synne to leue W.
　shal] wil IN; wol VH.
　lete] leue WMLH.

142 And] Ne TH₂ChDUR; I schal A; MH₃ *om.*
　wykkide] no UR; cursyd T₂; false AVH; W *om.*
　usen] make TH₂ChDURT₂MH₃ILNDi; myschaunge W.

145 go to] T *om.*

146 carieth] cariede TH₂DU; karyd T₂; carith A; koueryth H₃M;
　　kaireth LN; shope W; wendiþ H.
　chircheward] kirke ward ChN; þe kirke T₂; chirche AMH₃; shrift
　　warde W.
　his] hise T.

synne] synnes TH₂ChDMW; cowlpe T₂; countis A; culpe H₃Di; gilt I; schrift LVH; coupe N.
for] TH₂ChDRMH₃NDi *om.*
shewe] lete W; telle V.

147 And] Bot T₂M; Sone W; NH *om.*; þenne V.
bad him] þere bad he TDI; bad he H₂Di; þere bad him UR; bad here A; sche bad hym H₃; þen bade hym H.

152 ought in thi pors] TH₂ChDRT₂MH₃WDi *om.*; ought UAIL.

153 Glotoun gossib] glotoun DT₂; gossyp glotoun A; gossyb MN; good gossib W; god wot H.
God wot wel hote] god wote ful hote T₂MI; I am not al boute L; wel hote god wote Di; god wot ful goode V; ful hote I haue H.

154 pyanye] peynye T; pyonis H₂; pyeny D; pienye R; T₂ *om.*; pyanes A; pyouns M; pyan I; pionye W; piane V; (L *changes line*).

155 ferthing worth] pound T; (L *changes line*).
fenel] felkene T; fenkil URAH₃.
seed] sedis TH₂ChT₂.

156 Glotoun in] in glotoun TH₂ChD.

157 Cisse] Cesse DUNV; Sissot T₂; Sybbe A; kytte L; Symme H.
sewstere] soutere TMH; soustere U; sowestre RL; sewtere H₃; semstere W; sowter N; soweresse Di; souters wyf V.

158 warinar] waffrer TH₂ChDURDi; bewer T₂; bereward AMH₃; weuer IL; wollen webbe W; webster N.

159 Tom] Symme TH₂DRH₃; Tymkyn Ch; Thomme UAMWDi; Tynne I; Tome L; Tomkyn V; Tomlyn H.

160 and Hogge the nedelere] þat coude wel heue þe coppe L; his hors & hyne N.
Hogge] hobbe URH; hugh T₂MH₃IWDi; lawe A.
nedelere] myllere TH₂ChD; mylner URT₂; neldere VH.

162 TH₂ChDURILWDi *om. line.*

163 dykere] Drinker T₂A; dolfyn L; disschere VH.
doseyn] dusʒeyn T; dusseyn H₂.

164 A ribibour] A ribaud R; A rebauderere H₃; A bribure I; Harry bribour L; (A *om. line*).
A ribibour a ratoner] þe redylle maker of raton raw T₂; Alban þe retoner M; And Ribibor þe Ratoner V; Robyn þe ratonere H.
and] URT₂H₃IWNDiVH *om.*
rakiere] rakere H₂URMLWNDiV; rakar T₂I; baker Ch; ʒekere H₃.

166 TH₂ChDURILWDi *om. line.*
of Garlekithe] þe garlikmangar T₂.
Garlekithe] garlechythe A; garlek hethe MH₃; gloustre N; Garlesschire V.
Griffin] geffrey M; gruffiþ H.
the Walsche] of wales T₂H₃; of walsche A.

167 And] Of TH₂ChDT₂MLWNDi; And of H₃V.

168 gladchiere] gode wille ChVH; gude chere T₂A; (W *changes line*).

170   he]   TH₂ChDURT₂MH₃ILDi *om.*
nempnide]   ment D; nempneþ RW; must A; leyde VH.

171   hitte]   caste ChAMH₃H; hynt T₂; threwe I.

172   bad]   bed T; DURIN *om.*; (H₃ *om. line*).

173   that]   the ChURT₂AH₃WNVH.

174   of the cloke]   to þe cloke T₂; ILWNVH *om.*; L *adds line*: Of him
þat þe cloke had & þat heom thoghte skille.

175   Thei risen up in rape]   þo risen þei vp in a rape TH₂ChD (H₂ *om.*
þei; Ch *om. a*); Twa rase up in a rowte T₂; Two rysyn vp in rape
I; þo risen vp in rape L; Tho risen vp þo radde W; To rysen vp
in rape N; Twoo Rysen vp in a Rape Di; þei Risen vp Raply VH.
rouneden]   rombeden TH₂; rownys T₂; rownen N.

176   the peneworthis]   þe penworþes Ch; a penyworth DA; þo penyworþes
I; (LDiH *om. line*).
aperte]   apertly TH₂UR; pertely Ch; a perty D; inperty T₂; a party
I; & parteden V.

177   who so it herde]   TH₂ChDUR *om.*; ouer þe hude swornne T₂; for
þe hood & þe cloke A; overe þe hode & þe cloke MH₃; on aftre
oþer W; hose þat hit herde V; ouer þe ware H; (LDi *om. line*).

178   Thei couthe not]   (*In* TH₂ChDUR *this occupies second half of line*
177); þanne þei ne couþe TH₂; bot þen þei ne kouþe Ch; þen
cowde þey nouȝt D; þei couthe not ȝit iugge UR (cunne R); &
tweyn coude nought MH₃ (H₃ *om.* &); ȝit cowthen he nouht I;
(ALDi *om. line*).
be here consience]   Ne by here clene conscience U; Ne by here
conciens R; be consciens T₂WH; wele M.
acorden]   acceden T.

179   was]   were IV.
red]   H₂ *om.*; redy T₂; I rad IL; preyede Di.
to]   vp to UR; for to AMH₃W; forte V.
risen]   arisen TH₂ChDVH.

180   for]   hym for TChH₃LDi; him to H₂; DM *om.*; hym T₂H; hem for W.
were]   nere TChWNV; aros L.

181   Hikke]   Hichkok N; þenne Hikke VH.
hadde]   þanne hadde TChDURT₂MH₃LW (*margin* U); had than Di.

182   Clement]   clement þe coupere TH₂; clement þe cobbeler ChD.
shulde the cuppe fille]   shulde felle þe cuppe TH₂ChDL; þe cuppe
schulde fille URT₂AMH₃IWDi.

184   arise]   rise TH₂DURT₂A.

187   Bargaynes]   Bargoynes T; Barkeynes H₂.
to rise]   for to arise T; to aryse H₂ChMLDiV; for to rise DT₂H₃WN;
þo to rise H.

188   evensong]   euesong TChDRMH₃IL; mydnyȝt H.

189   ygluppid]   ygulpid TCh; gluppid H₂D; y golped UR; gobbed T₂A; I
bibbed M; I clobbyd H₃; gulpyd IDi; golped W; glowpyd N; I
gloupet V; y gloppid H; (*for* ygluppid L *has*: þorgh þe golet let
glide).

[210]

191 rewet] ryuet TU; ruet H₂WN; reuette ChDAH₃; rowet RT₂; rueite M; Revett Di; Ruwet V.

192 That] And TH₂ChD; Til A.

193 hadde be wexid] hadde waxid U; ben wipyd T₂; had ben waschid A; were wexyd IN; weore I-wipet V.
    hadde be wexid with a wysp of firsen] hadde wit a wisp ben on feere M.

195 lyk a glemans bicche] TH₂ChDRIDi *om.*; god wot þe sothe L; (W *om. line*).

196 *In* TH₂ChDRIDi *this line forms the 2nd half of* 195.

197 leith] leide TH₂ChDURT₂ALWNDi; leynd H₃; schuld ley I.
    to lacche with foules] to lacche wiþ larkes TH₂Ch; to lacche wilde foules DUR; to take with fowles T₂MH₃; to cacche with foulis AV; to lacche alle foules L; foules to cache W; to cacche wiþ briddis H.

199 stumblide] stumles Ch; stomelid AH₃; þrompelde V.
    thresshewold] throsfold H₂T₂; þreschfold ChH; þresshald D; throschfold U; þresfold RH₃N; threswald A; threschold MDi; threswold I; þrosschald L; þrexwolde V.
    threw] fel TH₂ChDRAMH₃H; stey U; þrogh W.
    erthe] erde H₃; grounde WNVH (*partly missing in* H; *hole in MS*).

In MSS UT₂AMH₃ *after line* 199 *occurs a six-line insertion. Compare Skeat's B-text, passus V, lines 358-63. The text of this insertion as found in MS* U *is given below, followed by variant readings from* T₂AMH₃.

a   Clement þe coblere cauȝte glotoun by þe mydle,
b   And for to lyfte hym aloft leide hym on his knees.
c   And glotoun was a gret cherl and grym in þe lyftynge,
d   And cowhede vp a cawdel in clementis lappe
e   þat þe hungriest hound of hertforde schire
f   Ne durst lape of þat laueyne so vnloueli it smakith.

a   coblere] coblere cast of his cloke U (*sic; all except* coblere *crossed out*).
    cauȝte] claght T₂ (*sic*).
    glotoun] hym AMH₃; T₂ *om.*
b   A *om. line.*
    And] T₂ *om.*
    aloft] on loft & T₂; vp M; on lofte H₃.
    hym] T₂ *om.*
    knees] knewes M; knowwys H₃.
c   And] Bot T₂; A *om.*
    cherl] carle T₂; charl H₃.
    grym] hevy T₂A.
    in þe lyftynge] to lifte T₂; for to lefte M.
d   And] He T₂M.
    cowhede] gave T₂; koughed M; cobbyd H₃.
    clementis] clement T₂.
e   þat þe hungriest] Is none so hungry a T₂; Is non so hungry AH₃; þer nis non so hungry M.
    hound] honde T₂; sowe H₃.
    of] in T₂AMH₃.

[211]

hertforde] herforth T₂H₃.

f   Ne durst] Might T₂; Durst AH₃; Wolde M.

of] on A.

laueyne] levyng T₂; laueney A; leuen M; lyuyng H₃.

vnloueli] vnlovesum T₂; loþely A; lothelych M.

smakith] smellyd T₂H₃; smakkid AM.

200   That] And Ch; UT₂AMH₃IWH *om.*

this] þe TH₂DRMWDiH.

201   hom] TH₂ChDURT₂AMH₃ILWDi *om.*

205   that he spak was] þat he spake DAMH₃V; þat he spak what URI, he sapke T₂; þat he warpe was W; was þat he spake H.

bolle] coppe NVH.

206   blamide] wytyd T₂A; wyssyd H₃; warnede V; blamy H (*sic*).

thanne] A *om.*; þo MH₃V; blyue (blyne ?) W.

207   was] T₂ *om.*; wax W.

the shrewe asshamide] þat shrewe asshamide TH₃; he asschamed þe schrewe DM; shamed þat schrew T₂; he a schamyd þat schrewe ALDiV; he shamed þe shrewe W; ashamed þat sherewe N.

shrapide] scharped Ch; gan sharpe T₂H₃N; gan to scharpyn I; gan schrapen L; robbed H.

shrapide hise eris] gan for to smert W.

208   doel] dele H₂Ch; dole DNDi; dool U; dol RAH₃; dule T₂; doole I; deol LVH; (M *om. line*).

to make] made TH₂DUR; make ChT₂AH₃Di.

210   VH *change line as follows:*

V: FOr hungur oþer for Furst I make myn A vow.

H: þo to fast he made a uow for hunger or for þurst.

for hungir or for thrist] for any hungir or þrist TH₂ChDDi; for thrist or for hungere I; for hunger or elles W; for eny first or hunger N.

211   mawe] wombe TH₂ChDT₂AMH₃LNDi (mawe wombe H₃).

214   fel] fil T; fylle M; feol L.

aswowen] a swowe TH; a swoune H₂DUM; In a swouȝe ChI; on sowen R; in swoune T₂; in sweye A; on swoune H₃; y swowe L; in swowe N; in a swowne Di; I swowene V.

215   the veil] þer while TH₂; þer wol Ch; DURM *om.*; þat wille T₂; had W; þe wakere H.

fette] fet TAH₃ILWN; wol fecche U; wile fecche R; fett T₂Di.

fette water at his eighen] warned hym þo H.

at] to TDURT₂; for from H₂ (for *crossed out*); of Ch; atte M; (H *changes* 215b; *see above*).

216   flatte] flattide it TH₂D; flatted ChI; flapte hit RN; platt it T₂H₃; plat A; plattyd M; flat hit LDi; flascht hym W.

217   war the for] be ware of I; Be wel war of N; þat H.

for] fro DUAH₃; from T₂MDi; (Ch *om. line*).

wile] he wil UDi; þat wald T₂MH₃; he wolde IN; he wol L; þat Wol V.

wile the] wolde hym H.

[212]

218 synnes] synne TH₂ChDRW; (U *om. line*).

219 hym] god H₃WNDiVH.

220 goodnesse] grace T₂; mercy NVH; (UR *om. line*).

221 seynide hym faste] sayned him self fast Ch; semed hym faste D;
shryued him faste R; schraffe hym full fast T₂; syhed ful faste
A; syhed faste MH₃; crowchid him fast I; signed him faste L;
sayned hem fast W; siked faste N; seynyd hym ofte Di; sikede
sore V; seide to hym siluen H.

223 be] ChT₂AMH₃WVH *om.*; be in Di.
seven] seue T; vij DURMH₃Di.

225 masse and matynes] matyns and messe H₂UT₂MNDiV.

227 evensong] euesong TChDRMIH; euesond H₃.
behote to] behote TURDi; hete to Ch; hett þe be T₂; hote þe be A;
hote be M; sey be H₃; hote to ILW; swere by H.

230 And] TH₂ChDA *om.*

231 iche] iche a T; ech Ch; eche DMH₃HDi; euery URA; ilke T₂; vche
LV; yche WN.

233 I wile] I wol ChUL; In wille M; Shal I W; I schal VH.
Treuthe] saynt trewth T₂LVH; trweth þer with M; þer wiþ trouþ
W; sir trewth Di.
er I se Rome] to fynde W.
se] seke TH₂Ch.

234 Roberd] Robert TChDT₂MNV; Robard ALDi; Robyn W; Robber H₃.
the robbour] of robberre T₂; MH₃ *om.*
on *Reddite*] on reddyte ful reufulli A; on reddite ful ruly M; on
reddere ful reufully H₃; rufulliche H.
lokide] he lokid AMLV.

235 Ac] Bot ChALDi; And URT₂MH₃WNV; H *om.*
swithe] ChH₃I *om.*; wel RLW; full T₂ANV.

236 Ac] And TH₂ChDURT₂AMH₃IWDi; Bote LNVH.

237 cros] rode TH₂ChD.

239 And thou] And H₃WV; ʒe I; þou N; As þou H.
memento] Memento is TH₂ChH₃H.

240 Thi wil worth upon me] þou haue mercye of me N.
worth] werche TChDURT₂A; werche not H₂ (not *inserted above line
in later hand*).
wel] DUAMIN *om.*

242 on this roberd] vpon Robyn W.
this] me NDiVH.
roberd] robert TChT₂MNV; robbere H₃I; Robart L; Rybawde Di.
no red] red non ne TH₂ChRN; reed non U; reddere ne T₂H₃; reddere
non A; rederd ne M; red non no L; no reed ne H.
have] hauiþ TH₂ChDURMH₃IL; haues T₂; hath AWDi.

243 wene] weniþ TH₂ChDURT₂ADi; we M (*sic*); wot H₃; W *om.*
I knowe] he knowiþ TH₂ChDUR; he knowe L; I owe N.

245 for] for þat TH₂ChURDi; (H *om. line*).

[213]

247 wepte] wep T; wepe ChD.

249 pik] body H₃; prest V; piked staf H.
     shulde] he shulde TH₂ChNDi; A *om.*; apertly schuld he I; myght W.
     pulisshe] pulsshe TH₂ChUR; polische it T₂; pollyschon A; pely-
     choun H₃; polysch him WV; be polischid H.

251 aunte] hyne TH₂Ch; lemman I; broþer V; (*in* R, aunte *is in original
     hand and ink over erasure of* douȝter).

252 A thousand] And þou sand T; And a thousande H₂ChD; A thowsyng
     I; And þoussand W (nd *in* And *crossed out*; ss *in* þoussand *is
     over an erasure*); A þousent V.
     tho] þe TH₂D; þan T₂; sagh I þo W; (A *om. line*).
     throngen] wrong TD; wronged H₂ (ed *added above in later hand*);
     wrongen Ch.

254 Criede] Cryand T₂; He cried A; Cryen Di; Criȝinge VH.
     clene] dere TH₂ChM; leoue L.

255 to seke Treuthe] to ga to trewth T₂AMH₃Di; to gon with agood
     wille/To seche seynt treouthe L; treuþ for to fynde W.
     so God leve] god leue TH₂ChDURAH₃ILNVH; godd graunte M;
     W *om.* 255b.
     that] H₂VH *om.*
     hy moten] they meten H₂; ȝe mote R; þei myght T₂; he mote AI;
     þei so mote H₃LVH.

PASSUS SIX

Title:
TH₂N: Passus sextus de visione vt prius.
ChURAH: Passus sextus de visione (H *adds* &c).
D: Passus Sextus (*margin*).
T₂W: Sextus Passus de visione.
M: Passus vj (*margin*).
H₃: Here endyth þe v part of þis book pers plowman.
IL: *no title or break.*
Di: Passus septimus de visione.
V: *no title; one line left blank.*

1 were] was TH₂DT₂AH₃; nas M; ne was Di.
   fewe men] nane T₂AMH₃; fewe N; wight none Di.
   that] UMIW *om.*
   the wey thider couthe] þei þider couþe TH₂R; walked on fote Ch;
   þeder coude D; þe way couthe LH; couþe þe wei þider V.

2 blustride] blustrid TH₂ChWDi; bluster DR; blustren UI; bloundered
   T₂; blusterid AH₃; blustreyng M; blostreþ N; bustelyng V;
   bolstride H.
   blustride forth] bleoseden forth blusteryng L.
   valeis and hilles] valeys or hilles U; bankes & hilles T₂A; dales &
   helles M; dalus & hylle H₃; hulles & dales L; baches & hilles W.

3 Til late and longe] So late & so lang T₂; Til late and to longe A;
   Till late & till longe MH₃; Til it was late and longe WDiH; Til
   late was & long N; Til was late & longe V.
   that] AH₃W *om.*

[214]

4   paynym] palmer T₂LDiVH.
pilgrimes] pilgrim T; palmeres W.
wyse] wede T₂AWDi; wedes V.

6   withwindes] way wendis T; wode bynde H₂; weyward Ch; wodbyndes
T₂; wyrnde wythys H₃; wrethewyndes L; wethewyndes N; withwynd
Di; weþe bondes V; wodebyndes H; (URA *om. line*; I *om.* 6a).
In a withwindes wyse] In þe way of a wode wynde D; All on
wrythen wyse M; In an ynyn wise W.
ywounden] he bond hym TH₂; bounden D; wonden T₂N; wounden
IW; I bounden M; I wriþen V; wriþen H.

8   hundred] hundrit T; hundreþ ChT₂N; vndred M; honderd H₃; C H.
ampollis] apples H₂; hanpolles Ch; ensaumples T₂; ampullos H₃;
saumples L; hampnels W; appolles N; hampolles Di.

10 a] TH₂T₂H₃NVH *om.*
crouch] cros URT₂V; croche Di; crosses H.
on] in TD.

13 faire] fast AMW; fryst H₃; (T₂ *om.* 13a).
fro] TH₂ChDRT₂MIN *om.*

15 At] ac R; Atte M; From V.
at] and RT₂V; & at H.
in] T₂ *om.*; at AH₃WDi.

16 Ermonye] armonye TH₂Ch; ermenye UH₃; hermony T₂MN; ynde V.

18 ful] wel TH₂ChL; wil D; URMIW *om.*; wol A.

20 quod thei] MNV *om.*; quod I WDi.
that] T₂AV *om.*

21 that wy] the wy H₂T₂; þat he DURIVH; þat wyte A; þat man M;
þat wyth H₃; þat wyghe L; as he W; truthe Di (*C-text*).

22 so me God helpe] so god mote me helpe TH₂Ch; so god me help
AWH; so god helpe me Di (*C-text*); so God glade me V.
gome] man TH₂ChDMH₃; grome T₂N; pilgrym H.

27 Clene consience and wyt] Clene consience and kynd wyt H₂ (kynd
crossed out and expuncted); klene concience & wygte M; Conscience
and clene witte W; Conscience & kynde witt NDi; Kynde conscience
H.

28 And dede me suren hym sithen] And dude enseure me seþþe V.
suren hym sithen] to sure hym TChDUR; to ensure him H₂; to
swere T₂; sweryn sythen A; sweren sothe M; swere sothenesse H₃;
asuryn him syþin I; ensuren him sithen L; syker hym sithe Di
(*C-text*); assure hym H (hym *erased*); (W *om. line*).

29 to sowen and to setten] sowe his seed TH₂; to sowe his sede Ch;
sowe & seden D; now and sithe UR; to sett & to sawe T₂; sowyn
& settyn IL.

30 fourty] foure I; seuenty N; fiftene VH.

33 Dyked] Dyken TH₂ChDUR; I diked T₂AMV.
dolven] deluen TChD; delued T₂W; I dalfe A; I doluen MV.

34 waytide] wayten D; to wayten URDi; I watyd T₂; I wayted MNVH;
weele I; & wayted L; a waited W.

35 his] þys MLWV; H *om.*
lordsshipe] lond W; leod V.

36 paye] pay TT₂AH₃DiH; plese UW.

37 I] And TH₂Ch.
hire] here TChW; hyre H₂AH₃; hure DNV; ere M; huyre LH;
hyere Di.
of hym wel] wele of hym T₂; at my wyl W.
wel] TH₂ChMLH *om.*

39 with-halt] ne halt TChDUR; ne with holdith A.

41 willeth wite] wilneþ to wyte TH₂LN; wol wete ChWH; willeþ to
weten DNDi; wille wite URT₂AMH₃; desyrin to wityn I; wolleþ
I wite V.
that wy] he H₂T₂W; þat he DURLVH; þat wyte A; þat man M;
þat wytt H₃; þe wyht I; þat treuthe Di (*C-text*).

42 I shal wisse yow] I wil ȝow wisse W; I wil wysch you Di; I wol
wissen ow V; I shal teche ȝou H.
wel the right way] wel the wey H₂D; þe wey right U; wel ryȝth
RINDi; full right T₂H₃; wel A; ryght M; wel riȝt hom L; W *om.*;
þe wey hom V; ful riȝt home H.
to his place] vnto hys awne place T₂; to his owyn place AMH₃;
to his house H.

46 Treuthe] For treuþe TH₂ChDUR; For he W.
wers] lasse LNDiV.
long tyme] long while ALW; grete wyle MVH.

47 wilneth to wende] wil wende RT₂A; þenkyn to wenden MH₃; ȝernyn
to wite I; wilneþ to wite W (to *added above line*); wendeþ to him
V; wole to hym wende H.

51 apeire] apeiriþ TH₂Ch; ȝe pare T₂; (M *om.* 51b; Di *C-text*; H
defective).

53 bougheth] bouȝ T; vowe H₂; bowes ChL; bowe D; at behofes yow
T₂; wende A; shal ȝe bowe W.
brok] bank TH₂ChUR.

54 For to] For D; Forþ til URA; Vnto T₂; For til M; Til WN.
forde] foorþe T; forthe H₂MH₃N; ferde R; furth T₂; I *om.*; for
W; (Di *C-text*; V *om. line*; H *defective*).

56 lightloker] liȝtliere TRT₂N; liȝtlere H₂; liȝter Ch; bettre M;
lytthere H₃; lithlichere I; (A *om. line*).

57 So shalt thou se] So schalt þow Ch; So schul ȝe se URM; And þen
sal ȝe T₂; So schal ȝe gon be I; So schal ȝe seo L; And than shal
ȝe se W; þanne shal ȝe se N; Sone schaltou þenne I seo V; (*for*
57a A *has* Thou schalt not swere).
yif] TH₂ChDUR *om.*
yif-it-be-for] ȝyf þou se H₃; if it be gret W; þou haue V.

58 And] A (*sic*) T.
on] an TH₂Ch; on þe U; in T₂AMH₃INV.
almighty] almiȝt TH₂; almyȝte DU; al mygth A; almyten M;
almyhtyn I.

[216]

59   shul ye]   shalt þou TH₂ChMH₃W; schal þou D; Thou schalt A.
ye(2)]   þou TH₂ChA; DURT₂MH₃ILWN *om.*

60   The]   þat TH₂ChR; *(for* The croft W *has* That).
hattith]   hatte H₂UL; hat Ch; hiȝte D; heght T₂; hite AI; hoteth
M; hight W; hatt N; hette V.

62   bow]   bowis TH₂ChDURW; braunche N.
yif]   TH₂ChDURAIW *om.*

64   hote]   hat ChI; hoten DU; hatte RH₃; heght T₂; hyten A; higten
M; hatte L; hight WN; hetten V.
strik]   but strik TH₂ChURW; stirte A.

66   heighe]   heiȝ TH₂R; heyliche D; holly A; fro morwe M; hay H₃;
hye IL; holi W; alwey forþ N; euere V; (U *om. line*).
even]   þe euen TH₂R; þe ende W; *(for* 66b T₂ *has* it is þe way to
euen).

67   blenche at a bergh]   see blenche abak U; blenchen abak R; blenche A.
bergh]   bourne TH₂Ch; berwe DN; brige T₂; broke MH₃V; bowhe I;
berwh L.

68   frithid]   frettid TH₂ChMH₃ILV; frethid U; fetterd T₂; federid A;
frayd W; feffyd N.
othere fees manye]   many oþer floures Ch; oþes wel monye V.
fees]   flouris TH₂ChD; federis A; feese I; foos W; foes N.

69   Loke]   And loke TH₂ChD.
plante]   plantis TH₂DUR.

70   Thanne]   And þanne TH₂ChDI; And L; (AN *om. line*).
se]   TH₂ChV *om.*

71   And]   TH₂ChDAMH₃ *om.*

72   as(1)]   TH₂ChT₂NV *om.*; is M.

73   mote]   mot TRH₃; moot H₂U; motte A.

76   Boterasid]   And boterasid TH₂DAH₃L; And boterace Ch; And
briteschid UT₂; And burased R; I botrasde M; & boteraseded I;
Botrace it W; þe botraces N; Brutaget V.
so]   TH₂ChUT₂MNV *om.*; wel W.
or-thou-best-not-savid]   longe to stonden M; wherþorow we be saued
N; wher þorw we moten beo sauet V.
or]   oþer T; elles D; or elles UA; I *om.*
best]   worst TD; worth þou best I; beo L.

77   hallis and chaumbris]   halle and chambres UR; bath halles &
chaumbres T₂; alle & chamberis with led A; with loue wete þou
þe sothe M; halle & chamberys with no led H₃; boþe alle and
chambre W.

78   With no led]   AMH₃ *om. (see preceding line)*: With 1 (no led bot
added above line); Wiþ no lord W; (M *om. line; see* 77 *above*).
but]   but with H₂ChRH₃LNV; but al wiþ U; With A.
Love and Loughnesse]   loue ULNV; love & lufsumness T₂; pure
loue I; lownes & loue W.
as bretheren of o wombe]   of herte H₂Ch; also T₂; echon oþer W.

[217]

79 is hym self] him selue is U; is inne hym selfe A; is Inne MV; is
IN; W *om.*
is up to] is vp on IN; is in sette by W; I set Is aboue V.

82 gateward] porter TH₂ChD.

83 men] man TH₂ChDUH₃IWN.
he] hym DURT₂V.

85 perfourmide] perfournide TUMN; performe W.
that] TH₂ChDILN *om.*

88 ones] TH₂ChDURILN *have this at beginning of next line*; W *om.*

89 To] Ones to TH₂ChDURILN (*see preceding line*); Prey hym to A;
And W.
wayve] weue TH₂D; wayue (*or* wayne) ChLWN; wynne URMIV;
put T₂; weyn A; weyen H₃.
up] out TChD.
the wy] he with TChDI; he with wylle H₂; þe wight UR; þe way
T₂; þe aungel A; þe wey MV; þe weyʒe H₃; þe whye L; he W;
þe wy N.
shette] scette H₂; schettet D; schetteþ UMH₃; stekett T₂; schet A;
schytte I; stoppet W; chette N; schutte V.

91 keighe] keiʒes TH₂ChDUR.
and] of T₂AMH₃LWV.

92 in in] in TChDMH₃W; on H₂T₂A; in on URI.

93 him self] þy self ChMI; your selfe T₂; þe selfe A; N *om.*
sitten] wel sitte TH₂ChL; wil sette D; sette T₂W; wil syttyn I;
wel syttyng N.

94 And lere the for to love hym] þenne loke þat þou loue him wel V.
lere] lerne ChUMH₃I.
hym] TH₂ChDURT₂MH₃ *om.*; (A *om. line*).

95 Ac] Bot ChT₂AMWV; And H₃LN.
be war] be þou wel ʒit war W; be wel ware N; beo wel I war V.
thanne] URT₂AMH₃IWNV *om.*
of] D *om.*; þat T₂H₃.
Wraththe-nought] wraþþe TH₂ChAMLWV; wreth noye yow noght
T₂; wratthe neyth ʒou nouth H₃; wrath he wrathe þe not I; wrathe
þe nouʒt N.
that wykkide shrewe] for he is a schrewe AV; þat schrewe I; þe
shrewe W.

97 pokith forth] pokiþ þe for TChDM; poke for H₂; lokith for U;
loke for no R; Put ye furth no T₂; poketh forth for H₃; prokerryth
forth I; wil prike þe wiþ W; put forþ N; puiteþ forþ V.

98 thi bien faites] þi bien fait TH₂N; þy benefait Ch; þy benfet D;
þat ben feet U; þat buffet R; þi lyffe fett T₂; þi benefeth A; thy
kyme M; þin benefetys H₃I; þy bienfaitʒ L; þi benfetes W; þi
benfes V.
makith the blynd thanne] mekenes & blynd hym T₂; blyndeth þe
þanne IN; make þe blynd sone W; blendeþ þin eiʒen V.

100 Ikeighid and ycliketed] With keyʒe & with cleket H₃; Boþe wiþ
cleket and keye W; (T₂ *changes line*).

[218]

ycliketed] ycliket T; cliked D; I hoked M; clekedyd I; yklyked N. kepe] holde URMIV.

103 yift] gift TH₂ChAH₃WN; gefte D; þing URM; gilt T₂; ʒiftys I.

104 ben] arn TH₂ChDURAMH₃IL; er T₂; beþ W; beoþ V.
serven Treuthe evere] treuþe louþ euere T (*louþ inserted above line in original ink*); treuth louen euere H₂; trewþe loueþ euer Ch; seruys trowth ellys T₂.

105 ben] bien H₂; beþ ChRW; arn A; bene I; beon L; N *om.; (for* And ben T₂ *has* To be, M *has* And kepen).
of] to TRL; at H₂UV; M *om.*

106 Humilite] meknesse TH₂ChD.

107 beth] bien H₂; ben ChUH₃N; er T₂; been M; boþin I; beon L; beoþ V; (A *om. line*).
hire] his T₂MH₃LN; þe W; tweyne ful V.

108 mekil] muche ChH₃NV; many D; þat þe W; (UR *om. line*).
peple] folk TH₂ChDIL.

109 Largesse] Largenesse TChDRAL; Largite U.
ful] wel TH₂ChDURAILN.

112 But] But ʒif TChUAH₃; & but MWNV; Ac bot if I; Bote þagh L.
ye] he H₂URAMH₃IW (*in* H₂ he *is expuncted, and* ʒe *written above in original hand and ink*).

113 ful] wel TH₂ChDURILWN.

115 have] ne haue TN.

117 Wyte God] Wate god T₂; I wys AV; I vow to god MH₃; God wote W; Wot god N.
this] þat TH₂ChDURL; T₂ *om.*; it M.

119 Piers] peris TH₂RI; pers UT₂AH₃V.
pokide] pukide TM; pullid H₂; pouked ChN; prechyd T₂V; pluckyd A; pookyde H₃; plocked L; poreth W.
hym] hem DH₃; here AMILNV.

120 is] haþ TH₂D; hadde UR.
ther] TH₂ChT₂AMH₃ *om.*
hem] TH₂ *om.*

122 two] TH₂ChD *om.*; bath twa T₂; to AMH₃; so I.

123 ther] TH₂ChUAW *om.*

PASSUS SEVEN

Title:

TH₂ChN:	Passus septimus de visione ut prius.
D:	Passus septimus (*margin*).
URA:	Passus septimus de visione.
T₂W:	Septimus Passus de visione.
M:	Passus vij (*margin, opposite line* 6.115)
H₃IL:	*no title or break.*
Di:	Passus octauus de visione.
V:	*no title; one line left blank.*

2 til] til þat TH₂; for to DLDi; forte V; (H *defective*).
we] H₂Ch *om.*; he M.
were] come H₃NV.

3 Peter] poule TH₂ChUT₂AMH₃ILWNDi; thomas R; (D *om. line*).

4 to eren] to ern T; of erþe Ch; to erie UDi; to ere RNH; T₂ *om.*;
to herie AV; to eryȝe H₃; of hered lond L; to here W; (D *om. line*).
weye] weiȝe TH₃.

5-6 *The readings for these two lines are*:
TH₂Ch: Hadde y herd þat half akir so me god helpe,
    I wolde wende wiþ ȝow til ȝe were þere.
    (*for* herd H₂ *has* erid, Ch *has* eried; *for* wolde wende H₂ *has* wende wolde).
D: *om. lines 3-6.*
U: Hadde eryed myn half akir I schal brynge ȝou þere.
R: Had I ered myn half akre I wil with ȝou til ȝe be þere.
T₂AMH₃: Had I eryd þe halue aker & sawyn it after,
    I suld ga with you tyl ȝe were þere.
    (*for* þe AMH₃ *have* þat; *for* sawyn it A *has also* sowyn, M *has* sowen it, H₃ *has* Isowe it; *for* suld ga A *has* schuld wende, M *has* wold wende, H₃ *has* xulde wende; *for* ȝe were A *has* we come).
I: Had I erid þat with ȝow wold I wende,
    And techyn ȝow riht forth til þat ȝe bene þer.
L: yshal hye me in haste til I haue hit done,
    And þanne wol I wandre til ȝe beon there.
W: I wend wiþ ȝow hadde I don til ȝe be ritht þer.
N: Were it don I wolde fayn wende forþ wiþ ȝow,
    And wysse ȝow riȝt wel til ȝe were þere.
Di: Had I it heryed I would wend with you til ȝe wer there.
V: Weore he wel I Eried þenne with ou wolde I wende,
    And wissen ou þe rihte weye til ȝe founden treuþe.
H: Hadde y erid þat þen wolde y wiþ ȝou wende,
    & teche ȝow þe riȝte wey til ȝe come þere.

10 ye] TH₂ChDURM *om.*; oþer W.
han] haþe ChD; haueþ UH; haue RMILWDi (*inserted above line in* W); nowe hase T₂; habbeþ V.
wolle] wollene TH₂ChAH₃I; lenen MDi.

12 yif] ChUT₂AH₃ *om.*
holy day] on halydays T₂; an halday A; ony haliday MH₃.
or elles] oþer TH₂DRDi; or Ch; or on T₂A; or ony MH₃W.

14 nymeth] takeþ ChT₂H; nym URINV; (*for* nymeth yeme W *has* loke).
yeme] hed TH₂ChDURT₂MH₃IDi; kep ANH.

15 Casteth] Caste TH₂ChUT₂AMH₃WNH; And cast on V.
wile] wol ChUH; willeth D; biddes T₂; byddyth A; comandeth MH₃; wilneth L; techiþ N; would Di; wolde V.

18 longe] louely TH₂ChDUR (H₂ *has* louelich *crossed out, and* longe *written above in later hand*).

19 sewith whanne tyme is] sewiþ it whanne tyme is TH₂ChDURLNDi;

to sew it in tyme T$_2$; to sewe wha it is tyme MH$_3$; wyrche it qwen tyme is I; seweþ it in tyme W; (A *om. line*).

20 chapeleyns] chapellis TH$_2$DURAW; churchis H (*for* chirchis H *has* chapels).

22 hem] him MV; wel W.
that wynne] þat wynneþ ChDUMLNDiVH; þat wynnys T$_2$; wynnyth A; to wynnyn I; and wynneþ W.

23 kennest] techist TH$_2$ChDWV (teches D; kennys T$_2$AI).

24 Ac on the tem trewely] And on þis teme truly R; On þat teme trewely A; But on þe plough treuly M; And or þis tyme trewly H$_3$; Bote abetter teme L; But on tyme treuly so WH; For on þe tem trwly N; Saue o tyme trewely þus V.

25 and I wile conne eren] sum thyng for to werche A; for cristes loue of heoue[n] L; (H *om. line*).
and] DR *om.*
I wile] I shal M; I wel H$_3$; Ichul V.
conne eren] lerne to eren TH$_2$Ch; lere to eryen DU; leye þer to ere R; be þine ayre T$_2$; gynne eryn M; gon eryen H$_3$; gynne to eryyne I; fayn lern W; comse to erye N; comsen eiren Di; conne erie V.

28 And] Ac T.

29 holychirche and my selven] wel þe right of holy cherche W.
and my selven] TH$_2$ChD *om.*; righte UR; (*see next line*); & me N.

30 Fro] And my self fro TH$_2$Ch; And fro D; And me fro UR; (*see preceding line*).
and wikkide men] TH$_2$Ch *om.*
that wolde us] þat me wolde R; þat it wil W.
us] me TH$_2$ChDURT$_2$AMH$_3$; hem I.

31 to hares and to foxes] þe hare & þe fox TH$_2$ChDUR (R *om. 2nd* þe); at hare & at foxe T$_2$; at haris & at foxis A; to hare & to fox M; for harys & for foxis H$_3$; two haris & two foxis I; to hares & to foxe L; to fox and to hare W; to harys & foxes Di.

32 To(1)] And þe TH$_2$Ch; And to DURDi; At T$_2$; And H$_3$I; Both W.
boris] bore ChW; brokkys U; beres RIVH; bare T$_2$; Roes L.
and] in T$_2$; AH *om.*
to(2)] þe TH$_2$ChT$_2$; RH$_3$ILDi *om.*
bukkes] bockis H$_2$LVH; bole Ch; buskeȝ T$_2$; bolis A; bukke W.

33 kille] kulle H$_2$L; fell T$_2$; quelle V; (A *defective here*).

34 thise] þei ChT$_2$WNDiVH; þis I.

35 the] þise T; this H$_2$D.
conseived] comsiþ T; comsede H$_2$NH; conseiueþ ChDi; conceyuct D; rehersede MH$_3$; þoo answeryd I; (L *changes line*).

36 treuthe] trouthe H$_2$RT$_2$LWNDiV.

37 this] þe TH$_2$ChV; þy DI; þat U; my R.
whiles] while ChH$_3$WDiH; whiles þat U; whil þat LMNV.
I may stande] my liff may stonde T$_2$H; my lyf may lest H$_3$; my lyf dureþ W.

38 Ya and yet] And U; And ȝut R; Ya ȝit T₂; And ȝet MN; But ȝit
    V; ȝe ȝit H.
    more] no more H₂V (no *changed to* of *in* H₂); of mare T₂; forþere
    W; sire more H.

39 assente] assent TChT₂H₃IWNH; accorde UR.

40 thei] ȝef ChDT₂MVH.
    the] ȝou LN; ou V.
    presauntis or] T₂MH₃H *om.*
    or] other H₂U; and RDILWN.

41 hem(1&2)] it DRT₂MH₃LWNDi (T₂ *om. 1*).

43 purgatorie] purcatorie TCh.

44 beter] bet TH₂DMLN.
    shalt thou] þou myght URH; may þou T₂; þou schalt LWV.

45 thi] TH₂DV *om.*; (T₂A *defective*).

48 atte] at TChDRIWNDi; at þe ULH; at þy M; att H₃.
    suche] for suche TH₂Ch (for *changed to* fro *in* H₂).

49 it ben] it arn TH₂ChDURL; þey ben MINV; Thei beþ W; thay
    ar Di; it beþ H. (*compare* 7.193)

52 pilgrymis] pilgrym TH₂Ch; palmers NH.

53 the wey] þe rihte wei V; on þe way H.
    we] I Ch; ȝe UMV.

56 at his hals] on his bak URV; on hys hals H₃MI; on his rugge H;
    (H₂T₂A *defective*).

57 bryng me] brouȝte he TChM; bryng I H₃; bryng me he bad L; he
    bringeþ V; he brouȝte H.

59 to(2)] TChDURW *om.*; (H₂T₂A *defective*; MH₃ *change line*).

60 hire] here TChMH₃W; mede UI; huyre V; hure H.

66 forther] forþ TChDH₃WNDi.

67 shulde] ne shulde TCh; schal DH₃; (VH *om. 2nd half line*).

68 tithe] tiþes TChDRMNDi; teche W; (MLW *change line*).
    asken] axen ChDUIN; taken RWV; craueth M; askith L.

69 ben] arn TCh; beþ RH; beon L; be WDi.

71 so] TChDT₂ *om.*
    dame] *stroke over the* a *in* T.

75 now] TChD *om.*

76 I wile] wile I TChDRT₂; I M.
    this] TChDURT₂W *om.*

77 do wryte] do wyte T; write VHMH₃; make W.
    bequest] queste DH₃; by questes UR; intest T₂; bequethe I; Testa-
    ment VH.

79 He] For he TH₂ChDURT₂.

81 me techith] techeþ ChT₂MLWH; me telleþ V.

[222]

83   careyn]   caroyn TM; body T_2; carayne H_3; caryon N.

84   he cravide]   I crauide TH_2; he craueþ DURINH; he cravys T_2; he cleymeth M; crawed L; þer gaf I W; heo Craueþ V.
tithe]   tiþes TH_2ChDUR; tendes T_2.

85   I]   And TW; And I ChD; It U.
hym]   hem DR; it UMIW; hit him LN (it *inserted above line in* N); (T_2 *reads*: I prayd þe prest *etc.*).

87   menge]   monewe T; mynne Ch; menewyn D; menewe U; monne R; mene T_2; monewen M; mengyt H_3; munge V; mynwe H; (H_2 *defective*; A *om. line*).

90   today]   þys day MH_3V.
quytte]   quyt TH; quyted D; yquytte UMV; yquytted RDi; aqwytyd H_3; paied L.

95   My...pyk-staf]   My staffe shal be pyked M; I xal now poyntyn my pekyd staf H_3; (H_2 *defective*; W *om. line*).
pyk-staf]   pyk TChV; pekedstaf D; potent A; pilgrime staffe NH.
pyche]   putte TChDDi; pyke RT_2AH_3; potten (?) M; rende N; posschen V; posse H.
at the]   atte DV; vp þe $URAH_3$N; owt T_2; aweye þe M; (*all after* pyche *in* L *is illegible*).

96   close]   clense AMINDi; clause L (clanse ?); (H_3 *changes line*).

98   eren]   erien TChDU; herye RALN; eyre T_2; eryien H_3; eere W; heren VH.

99   dyken]   dykeþ TCh; dyggen UT_2Di; dyggyng R; diggid AN; duluen M; deluyn H_3; doluyn IL; Dikeden V; diȝten H.

100   payed]   ypaied UA; apayde RMH_3VH (apayn *changed to* apayd H).

101   that]   & TChD; (H_3 *changes line*).

102   in]   on $TChDURT_2$AILWN.
hym]   hym self TChDMILDi; hem H_3.

106   He] $TChDURT_2$ILNDi *om.*; For he H_3; Thei WH.

108   eren]   ere T; to erie $ChURMH_3$INH; erye D; to eyre T_2; to herye AL; to eere W; earye Di; to herien V.
eren the half akir]   him to erye NIVH.

109   Now] $TChDURT_2AMH_3$ILDi *om.*

110   But]   But ȝif TH_2ChDMILWDi.

114   leggis]   leg $TH_2ChDURT_2$LW.
a-lery]   a lyry UI; of lery T_2; on lery A; alirrye M; on lyre H_3; on lyry L; a lirie W; a liri V.
losellis]   lorellis TH_2ChMW; locels I.

116   no lymes]   none hondis TH_2; no handes ChD; lemmes M.
Lord ygracid be ye]   lord ygraced be þe UN; lord gyff vs grace T_2; lord grace be ȝe A; lord gracied be þou M; lord þankyd be ye IL; lord þonked be thou W; lord Igraced be thou Di; vr lord we hit þonken VH.

120   nouther]   not TChDA; in no maner N; (*for* mowe nouther MW *have* ne may).

[223]

123   holde]   olde TChDURH₃WDi; awne T₂.

124   Whiche]   Suche TChDT₂LH; Sweche AMH₃; Qwyche I; Whuche V.

125   thei]   I TR; hij N.

127   tilthe]   telþe TChDH.

128   Cacche]   Chase TChDURT₂; To kepyn I; Kaire L; Caste W; Gaste VH.
      gees]   coos A; crowes MILNDiVH.
      his]   þe URT₂AIWNH.
      kepen]   and kepe ChURT₂MH₃IWDiVH; & also kepe N.

129   brok]   brod T (*a small k written above the* d *in original hand and ink*).

130   he]   ʒe T₂AMWNH; heo V.

131   Thei shuln ete]   ʒe schul eten URT₂Di (R *om.* eten); Schul þai ete A; Than shul ʒe ete W; þei schul haue V; þen shulle ʒe haue H.

132   gar]   gare T; ger Ch; gere R; make MH₃Di; graunte IL.
      hem]   hym TT₂; hom L; ʒow W; (H₂ *defective*; UNVH *om. line*).

135   er]   til on þe TCh; or DT₂Di; ar R; til A; or a M; tyl þe H₃H; til on I; er þe W; til a V.
      er morewe]   aftre N.

136   his flessh and the fend]   þe feend and his flesche U; heore flesch & þe feond L; þe fend & þe flesh W; þe Fend and heore flesch VH; H₂ *defective*; T₂AI *change line*).
      foulide his soule]   folowed to gidre U; fowele his sowele MH₃Di; fouled heore soules LV; greuen here soule W; folewen here soulis H.
      In T₂AI *the readings are as follows*:
      T₂: þai lat þe flesh & þe fend folow þe saule.
      A: In auenture þat bred flesche & þe fende schuld foulyn here soule.
      I: þat þe fende ne his fleche defowle nouht his sowle.

137   usith]   ne vsiþ TRNDiVH; vsyd H₃.

139   Thanne gan Wastour arise]   þanne gan þe wastour arise TCh; þan gan þe wastores aryse R; þan wald wastour ryse T₂; Tho be gan wastour AMH₃; þan gan a wastour a risyn I; þanne can wastour arise L; Thanne rose wastour N; þEnne wastours gunne arise V; þan by gan wastour to rise H.

141   a-bostide]   he bostide TH₂ChD; bostide URDi; bost T₂; he bost A; he bosteth L.

142   hym go pisse]   hym go pisse hym ChRT₂MH₃H; him I (*sic*); go pisse him V.
      pilide shrewe]   pelyd shrew T₂L; foule pyne wreche A; pyned schre M; pynyd swerwe H₃; pillede screwe V.

143-4   *For these two lines* TH₂ChDURT₂ *have* (*with minor differences*):
      Wilt þou nilt þou we wile haue oure wil of þis flour
      And þi flessh fecche awey whanne vs likeþ.
      VH *have*:

[224]

V :   For we wolen habbe of þi Flour wol þou so nulle þou
      And of þi Flesch fecche whon þat vs lykeþ.
H :   Woltou neltou we wole haue y now of þy floure
      & of þy flesch & þy fysch when þat vs like þ.

143   Wilt thou nilt thou]   Will þou or nyll þou T₂AMH₃L; For wiltow
      or nyltow W; For wiltow ne wiltow N; wol þou so nulle þou V.
      oure wille]   oure wil TRH₃; þe wil D; UV *om.*; y now H.

144   thi(1)]   þis TH₂ChD.
      of(2)]   TChDURW *om.* (H₂ *defective*; T₂ *om. line*).
      fecche]   fecche awey TH₂ChDUR; & þy fysch H.
      whanne]   whan þat DVH; whan so UR.

149   the knight thanne]   tho þe knyȝth RH; þe knyth be kende A; þan
      þe knygt MH₃W; þe knyht þoo I; þe kniht V.

150   Wastour]   þe wastour TChDi; wastores RVH; þan wastour M; þe
      wastours W.
      hym]   hem RWVH; L *om. (changes line).*

152   wont]   wonid TRH; wonne M.
      now wile I not]   ne now forsoþe wil I not D; ne now will I not T₂;
      I wol not now A; it wille I not M; & I nel not H₃; now I wol not
      L; And ȝit I wil not W; ȝit wol I not VH.

154   countide]   a conptede M; acontyd H₃; acountyt I; acounteth L;
      sette WN; coumpted Di; a countid H.
      countide Peris at a pese]   bad piers go pisse U.

155   thei]   he TH₃.

157   houpide]   hawnted Ch; hopyd RLDiV (Di *has* u *inserted above line*);
      wyschid A; clepid M; wepyd H₃; hoppyd IW; huntid H.
      that]   he AMH₃W; þo þat V.

158   thise wastours]   wastour TCh; wastours DILWNH.
      shendith]   apeiriþ TCh; schenden DH₃NDiH; schendis RT₂; schendt
      A; schendyt M; stroie W.

159   thanne]   þou D (*sic*); UT₂LWNVH *om.*; þoo I.

160   bothe his eighen watride]   al watride his eiȝen TChDUA; alle watered
      her eyen R; wateryd þair eyneȝ T₂; his eyun waterden MH₃IWDi;
      bo his eynen wattred L.

163   hem so bothe]   hym boþe U; þaim so sore both T₂; so bothe H₃;
      so hem bothin IN; hym so boþe W; so þe Boyes V.
      he(2)]   þat he TChDH₃NDi; and URT₂.
      he brast ner here mawis]   here mouþ brosten W.
      ner]   negh T₂MH₃NDiVH.
      mawis]   mawȝe Ch; wombis A; Ribbes V.

164   Ne hadde]   N hadde T (*sic*); Nadde D; No hadde L; Til W; Nedde
      V.
      with]   but TChD.
      preyede hym beleue]   þei preyede hym beleue TChD; help þaim
      in hast T₂; a preyed hem be leue A; preyde him stynte M; preyid
      hym to leue H₃WN; I preyed him to leue V; y preied hem to lyue H.

165 benen] bene TChDRT₂AMH₃ILNDi; beny U.
 yede] he hadde TChDUR; he wente A; he ȝede MH₃IWN; busked
 L; had hyhyd Di; I bot V.
 yede hem betwene] he had betwen his handes Ch; þai abade T₂.
 hem] TChDURT₂INDi *om.*

166 amydde] amyddes ChDT₂IDi; in myddis of A; þe meddys of H₃;
 right so by twyx W.
 hise] þe UAMH₃IWNDi; bothe L; boþe his VH.

167 And] þat he ChMH₃LWN; And he V.
 bledde] made hym blede DiH.

168 defendit] defendite T; defende UT₂; a defende A; fette W; fast
 fett Di.

170 al warme] al warm TVH; as warme I; ful depe W; in erthe Di.

171 Faitours for fer thanne] Faitours for fer TChDURLDi; Fatours
 ben ferd a T₂; For ferd þese wastouris A; For ferede this faitours
 M; For ferd þo faytouris H₃; Faytours for drede þoo I; Sone
 wastours for ferde W; Faitours for fere þo N; þEnne Faytors
 for fere V; Faitours for ferde þan H.

172 flappide] flatte TCh; flatted D; flappe URDi; flapten LV; flyp
 flapt W.
 eve] euen ChDUT₂AMH₃ILWNDiVH.

173 hardy] so hardy URT₂MH₃IWH.

174 potel] potful ILWNDiV.
 pesen] pecis T; pesoun Ch; pese T₂; pece A; pesys IL.
 hadde imakid] hadde mad TAIN; had I made ChV; hade gert make
 T₂; wif had made W; let make H.

175 An hep] In helpe TChD; þen þe hep T₂; And an hep AH; A grete
 epe MLN; And þan an hepe W.

176 ditte] driuen ChURT₂; holdyn AMH₃W; fil Di.
 out Hunger] hunger oute DURAMH₃WNV; away hungre T₂; hungers
 throte Di.

177 bedrede] blere bedderede D (blere *crossed out*); blere eyȝed UR;
 blered T₂ (H₂ *defective*; Di *om. line*).
 were botnid] weren aboute URT₂; were betyn A; weren boted MW;
 leyn aboutyn H₃; weryn þer I botyd I; were wotned N.

178 TChD *om. line* (H₂ *defective*).
 That layen] Lay T₂; Thei leyn A; And leyn H₃; That hadde laien
 W; þei had yleye N; Thay þat liggyd Di; þat lyȝen V.
 for blynde and for brokeleggide] longe W.
 for (1)] RAMH₃IDi *om.*
 for (2)] URT₂AMH₃Di *om.*
 brokeleggide] blered T₂; bedrede AH₃; brokyn leggys I.
 by the heighe waye] On softe segys on sonundayes be þe hye weye
 I; Vpon soft sondayes by þe hiegh wey NH; Vppon softe sonenday
 bi þe heiȝe weye V; (178 *is two lines in* INVH).

179 hem helide] þaim halsyd T₂; hem held M; þoo helid hem I; heled
 hem so W; heled hem alle N.
 hotel] hot TDRH₃V; ote ULN; oten H.

180 lithid] liþnid T; litid A; lissed M; lechyd H₃L; louses & liþes W.

182 pur] for URT₂AMWVH; per H₃IN; pro L.

183 Al] And DRT₂V; AW *om.*; And alle M.
cache] chase TChDUR; chache T₂; kayre L; kepe W; caste VH.

185 monie] T *has original* mone *with* i *inserted above between* n *and* e;
mone URAILN; money ChDDiVH; mony T₂MH₃; monoie W.
deserve] asserue TDUR; serue ChT₂; dysseruyn A.

187 erd] erþe TChDLDiH; ȝerde URT₂I; lond AH₃; lord M; hous WN;
hurde V; (H₂ *defective*).

188 And yet] Ac ȝet TD; Bot ȝit ChNDi; ȝit A; And þat L; But WH.

189 is best] best is TChDIN; best beo L.

190 went] ywent TDV.
hy] þei ChDURT₂MH₃ILWNDiVH; he A.
ful] TChDURT₂MIDi *om.*; wel L.

191 hy] hȳ T (*sic*); þei ChDURT₂AMH₃ILNDiVH; þe W.
meke] mek T.

193 it ben] hit be D; hit beþ R; þai ben T₂H₃LDi; alle ben A; it bene
þey I (þey *added above line*); we beþ W; heo beoþ V; þei beþ
H; (*compare* 7.49).
my blody bretheren] may bodely brether T₂; my breþeryn AM;
our bretheryn H₃; brethren of blood W; myne breþeren of one
blood H.

195 aftir that hem nedide] þat hem of nedide TCh; þat hem nedeþ D;
what þat hem nedith UR; qwat at þai nede T₂; Thei þat han nede
A; aftir þat þey nedit M; after þat hem nedyth H₃ILWNDiVH
(W *om.* þat).

196 Now wolde I] I wolde TH₂Ch; Wold I D; ȝit wolde I V.

199 beggeris and bigge] beggerys & bydderys T₂Di; beggeris þat beggyn
A; Bidders and Beggers VH.
that mowe here mete beswynken] þat may noght swete ne swynke T₂.
mete] breed TChRAMLNDi; (H₂D *defective*).
beswynken] swinken ChUAMH₃IWDi.

201 And bane] And batten Ch; Abane DAINDiH; And bayte U; And
bayne H₃; And abate L; And fede W; And Bamme V.
benes] bones TH₂ChDRDiVH.
wombes] wombe TChDT₂AI; belyes N; (H₂ *defective*).

202 swynke] & swynke TRMLDi; and work Ch; worche WN; (A *om.*
line).

203 he(1)] þei UNVH; T₂ *om.*; (A *om. line*).
swettere] þe betere UT₂; betere M; þe swettore VH.
he(2)] þei UMNVH.
it hath] it han UMN; haþ hit RLW; hase it T₂; hat H₃; hath I;
han hit V; haue H.

204 And] Ac TDUR; A *om.*; But MLWDi.

205 fonde] fond TUAH₃L.
to] TD *om.*; forto H.

207 and so the] for so þe UT₂; for so RMH₃DiH; for þe A; as WN;
      so þe V.
      wole] wolde TChDURMH₃ILN; T₂ *om.*; it wolle A; askeþ W;
      techith Di.

208-12 TChDURT₂ *misarrange these lines*; (H₂ *defective*).
      T: And alle maner of men þat þou miȝte aspien,
            þat nedy ben or nakid & nouȝt han to spende,
            Wiþ mete or mone let make hem at ese,
            And make þe Frendis þer miþ for so matheu vs techiþ.
      Ch: And alle maner of men þat þow myȝt a spien,
            þat nedy ben or naked and nauȝt han to spende,
            With mete or with money make hem at ese,
            And make þe frendes þer with for so mathew vs techeþ.
      D: And alle maner men þat þou myȝt aspyen þat nedy ben or
              naked
            And nouȝt haue to spende with mete or with mone
            Late make þe frendes þer with & so Matheu vs teches.
      U: And þo þou myght aspie þat nedy ben or nakyd
            And han noght to spenden wiþ mete ne wiþ mone
            Lat make þi frendes þer myde & so matheu vs techith.
      R: And alle men þat þou myȝthe aspye þat nedy beþ or naked
            And nouȝth haue to spende with mete ne with mone
            Lat make þe frendys þer with and so matheu vs techys.
      T₂: And if þou may aspye þat nedy be or nakyd
            And noght haue to spende in mete ne in mony
            Bot make þi frend þer mede & so mathew byddes.

210 with(2)] T *om.*; in T₂ (1&2); þi W.
      let hem be the betere] let make hem at ese T; make hem at ese
      Ch; DURT₂ *om.*; lete hem be releued N; mak hem fare þe betere
      VH.

211 TChDURT₂ *om. line*; (H₂ *defective*).
      werk or with word] werke or with dede A; word or with werk V;
      werk oþer wiþ wordis H.
      whiles] whil AW; þe while ML; qwyl H₃; qwylis I; wyl þat N;
      the whiles Di; while þat V; whils H.

212 Make] And make TCh; Late make DUR; Bot make T₂.
      with] miþ T; myde UN; mede T₂; mydde A.
      and] for TChVH; (*for* and so W *has* as).
      Matheu us techith] mathew byddes T₂; seiþ þe gospel H.
      us] T₂MH₃V *om.*; þe W.
      TChDURT₂A *combine Latin with part of following line*:
      Facite vobis Amicos I wolde not greue god (*so* T; *variants are*: I
        wold not god greue D; wolde noght greue god URT₂; I ne wold god
        greue A); (H₂ *defective*).
      de mammona iniquitatis] TChDURT₂AMLN *om.*

213 I wolde not greve God] TChDURT₂A *have in preceding line*; (U
      om. remainder of this line; T₂ *ends*).
      gold] gode ChLWNH; gold goode I (gold *expuncted*).
      on ground] on þis ground TH₃; þat groweth on þis ground ChR;
      þat groneth on grounde D; on þe grounde ADi; on eorthe LH; in
      erþe W.

[228]

215 I behote the] I hote þe TChAIN; y hote god U; hardyly R; be goode
     M; (W *changes line*).
     or] oþer T.

217 *In sudore* and swynke] In sudore &c & swynke TChD; In sudore
     uultus tui swynke UR; þer he seyth in sudore & labore H₃; In
     sudore & in swynke Di; In sweting & swinking H; (A *om. line*).
     tilien] TChDUR *om. here; see next line*; telle H₃; wynne W;
     tylthe Di.

218 And(1)] Tilen & T; Telien and ChD; Tylien and U; Tile and R;
     (A *om. line*).
     and(2)] for WDiVH; (*for* and so R *has* as).

220 *propter*] ppter T (*sic*).
     no feld wolde tilie] he nolde his lond tilie M; arare noluit H.
     feld] fold H₃L; mete I; fote W; lond MN.
     wolde] nolde DRMNV; wild I.
     tilie] it telle A; he tylye LWV; tylthe Di.

221 go] RINH *om.*; cone H₃.
     begge and bidde] bidde & begge TChV; bygge and begge RH.

222 with] UINVH *om.*
     mouthith thise wordis] mouthith vs þe same U; þes wordes þus
     mowtheþ R.
     mouthith] nempniþ T; nempned Ch; nemened D; mevith AH₃;
     mowuyt M; techeth L; he mouþed W; mowthed DiH; he Mommeþ
     V.

223 That] TChDWV *om.*; (*for 223a* H *has*: Serue nequam sciebas quia
     &c þe wicked seruaunt made a couenaunt).
     nam] name RL; man AH₃; besant M; naam I; ilman (?) W;
     Mnam NDi (M *crossed out in* N); npnam V (*glossed* .1. talentum).

224 maugre] a maugre TDAML; (WDi *om. line*).
     evere] for euere TDILN.

225 nam] namme R; man A; mam M; namp H₃; naam I; name L;
     Mnam NDi (M *crossed out in* N); npnam V (*glossed* besaunt);
     besaunt H; (W *om. line*).

226 it] TDR *om.*; (U *om. line*).
     there before] before ChMH₃IWVH; ȝeer before D; of his owen L;
     afore N.

227 sithen] sone after M; sithen sone L.
     sithen he seide] D *om.*
     he seide] hit seyde R; he saide hym also W; he þus seide V; he
     seide hym to H.
     that] TChUINV *om.*
     servauntis] seruaunt TH₂ChDLWH; mayster R.
     it] LW *om.*
     herde] hadde TH₂ChDR; harde AMDi.

228 there nede is] him at is nede M; ther is nede W; þere it nediþ NH.

229 shal nought] -uȝt schal H₂ (*torn*); nouȝt schal VHH₃ILWDi.

230 that he] he þat DH₃INVH.
     wel] AMDi *om.*; best W; for V.

[229]

I wile it be hym berevid] I wol hit hym bereuen ChAM; I wil þat
hit him be reued R; it xal hym be reuyd H₃; I wol þat hit fro
him beo reued L; shal hym be bereued W; it schal hym by breuyd
N; it schal from hym be reved Di; hit him beo bi reuet V.

231 wight] man ChUAMH₃DiVH.

232 Or(1)] Oþer TIH; Eyþer Ch; AMWV *om.*; (H₂ *defective*; U *om.*
line).
or(2)] oþer T; or with AH₃LDiV; oþer wiþ H.
tiling] telling TDRAMH₃LW; telieng Ch; tilying NI.
travaillyng of hondis] traveling of handes Ch; traualyng of hande
R; with handis or with trauelyng A; trauaile of handis M; trauaill
of honde W; trauel of hondis H.

233 or] oþer TH; & WN.

234 The Sauter seith] þe sauter seiþe hit ChUNDi; Oure lord seyth
A; And so seit þe sautir M; As in þe sautyr seyth H₃; The sautre
saiþ so W; For so seiþ þe Sauter V; As þe sauter hym self seiþ H.
in the salme of *Beati omnes*] in a psalme of Beati omnes UL; in
a psalmis hende M; of Beati omnes qui timent dominum qui
ambulant H₃; In Psalm of beati omnes V; in a psalme H.

236 hem] TCh *om.*; hym UAMWDiVH.
here(1)] his UVH.
here(2)] DUH₃ILNDiVH *om.*; (*for 236b* M *has*: þat him be hire
[liue ?] wynnyt; W *has*: þat so wiþ treuþ geten).

237 conne] kenne TChDRW; Canne Di; canst H; (AMH₃ *change line*).

238 lef] lif TChRAMH₃V; lyft D; lessoun H.

240 hy] TChDRW *om.*; þei UAMH₃ILNDiH; heo V.

243 wilnest] woldest Ch; willest DM; desirest UI; weldest R; woldis
hauyn AH₃; wylne V.

244 er] or ChDAMLDi; til UNVH.
dyne sum-what] ete sum what R; dyen sum qwat I; somwhad dyne
L; haue dyned somwhat NWV; haue ydyned H.

245 Ete nought] And ete nouʒt TCh; And nouʒt DU; And not ete R;
And not ʒet AH₃; And ʒit nout MI; Ete no thyn L; Ne ete not W.
er] or ChAIDi; til DVH; ar MN.

246 thi lippes] wiþ þi lippes UMH₃I (with þin mawe lippis I; mawe
expuncted); þe þe betere V.

247 til] for TMLDi; to ChIW.

248 Appetit] aptid T.
have] haþ TAW; hat H₃; habbe V.

251 maner] maner of TM; VH *om.*; (A *om. line*).

252 eres] armes TDRAMH₃INDi; hede ChL; eie W; lyf H.

254 ek] AH₃W *om.*
of(1)] wiþ TChDRDi; and his W.
and the] & his AMH₃H; with IWV; & N.

255 fisik] fesik TChDA; (UH₃N *om. line*).

257 ben] arn TH₂DAMH₃ILDi; be Ch; are R; beþ WH; beoþ V.

259 Poul] pernel TH₂DAMH₃H.
ben] arn TH₂UMH₃ILDi; beþ DH; are RN; be W; beoþ V.

261 thi wille is] þi wille is T (*is expuncted*); þou wilt D.
that] for R; AH₃VH *om.*; & M; þere N.
be thou] be þe UM; þe INVH.

262 the] god TDRAMWDi.
I wende] I not wende T (*not inserted above line*); I nauȝt wende
Ch; (*for 262b* W *has* ȝit wil I not wende).

265 gees] gos ChAWNDiH.

266 an haver] non oþer TChD; an hote WN; a þerf V; two hauere H.

268 yet] TChDAVH *om.*

270 persile and poret] percely and porettis ChMINH; porettes & persely
H₃V; percell and plantes W.

272 a-feld] on feld TChDUAMLWDi; to felde H₃.

275 And] RMH₃ILWNVH *om.*; (UA *om. line*).

277 Benes and baken applis] Benes & blake applis TD; Bedes and bake
apples Ch; Benys & appillis A; Benys bakon aplys H₃; Benes &
bacoun & apples N; Bake Benes in Bred V; Benys & bacoun H.
lappes] lappe TChD; (*for 277b* H *has* wiþ hem þei brouȝten).

278 chirivellis] chiriuellis (chirinellis ?) T; cheruelles ChUMH₃IWNDi;
Chiryfellys D; skalonys R; cheruel A; chiryuels L; Cheef mete V;
chefteyns (chesteyns ?) H.
ripe] riche T.

279 this] a TCh; to N; (W *om. line*).
with] þere wiþ TChURILDi.

280 Hungir] And hungir TChDRMDi; (W *om. line*).
eet] hente TChAMH₃.

282 TChD *om. line*; H₂ *defective*; (*this line given twice in* A).
Grene] Grete H₃; Of grene L; VH *om.*
porettis] porret URAA; portes I; garly W.
pesen] percely M; poysyn H₃; peoses L; gresse W; peris H.
to poysen hym hy wolde] for þei him plese wolden V; applis &
plowmes H.
to] for MW; IN *om.*
poysen] a poysened A; a poysyn AN; plesen LV; ple W.
wolde] þouȝte URMH₃; wode I.

283 Be that it neighide ner hervest] By þat heruest neghed W; By þat
was comyn heruest N; Til hit to heruest hiȝede V.
Be that] By þenne URI; Whan A; Til V.
it] LWN *om.*
neighide] neschid A; was M; was comyn N; hiȝede V.
ner] nyȝe ChDMDi; RH₃WNH *om.*; to V.
that] TCh *om.*; and RAMWN; for Di.
newe] A *om.*; ne newe W (ne *expuncted*; newe *inset above line*).
com to chepyng] cam to towne UR; kam to sellyn M; come to
markete W; to chepyng N; to cheping come Di; riped H.

[231]

284 with the beste] of þe best N; ȝeorne V; fast H.

285 and(2)] he TD; þei ChURMLWNDi; þen H₃; (*for this line A has*: With good ale bad gloton go slepe).

286 wolde Wastour not] nolde wastour not TD; wolde no wastours U; ne wolde no wastour M; no wold not wastour I; nolde wastour L; wold not wastour W; nolde þe wastor V.
wandrite] wandre H₂RMLNV.

288 or(1)] and RMIWNVH.
or of] of þe M; oþir of I; mad of L; & of NH; orels Di; an of V.

289 non] no TDAH₃W.

290 brouneste] brunneste TI; brinest M; (*for 290a* N *has*: But of alderbest).

291 to lyve on but] but lyue on TH₂M; but leue be ChWH; to lyue by but UR; but leuyd be A.
here handis] here honde W; heore honden V; hem silue H.

292 Deyneth] Deyned ChDUAMIL; Loue H₃; Deynen WVH; Dyneþ N.

294 yif it be] it be H₂ChURAH₃H; W *om.*; hit weore V.
fressh flessh] rostid flesche U.
fissh yfried] fische fryed or rostid AM; fryid fysch or rostyd H₃; fresch fysch yfryed LH; fysh fried or rost W; fysche þat is fried N; fisch wel Ifryed Di.

295 plus chaud] pluys chaud TH₂MH; pluis chawt Ch; plus chaut D; plus chaufed R; pluchaud A; purchaud H₃.
here] his TH₂IN.
mawe] mawis AH₃WDiH; chekys U; nailes LM.

298 his] þe TH₂ChDAMILN; that Di.

299 chaste] chastise T; chastice ChH₃; chastesyn A; chastyn MIL; chastien Di.

301 the] his ChH₃LWDi; her I.
statute] statut T; state Ch; statutes UH₃INH; statuet M; statues V.

303 hiderward hastith] is hedirward & hastet DAM (*for & A has* he); hiderward hyeth UR; rit hidirword hithid I; hieþ hym a ȝen and hast W; hiderward aȝeyn hiȝeþ V.

304 thurh] þis TH₂ChD; ȝour UAI; ȝow thorw H₃N; wiþ W.
water] weþer Ch; wele U; wateris AH.

305 Er] Or TChDAH₃LDiH; And er þe W.
fyve yer] fyue DWNDi; fyue wynter R; syn L; fewe ȝere H.

306 floodis] flood TH₂DRAMH₃IWDi; tempestes U.
and] oþer T; or H₂ChD.
thorugh(2)] ChURAMH₃IWNVH *om.*
fayle] falle TH₂ChDUL; be dystroyid H₃.

307 T *has, in right hand margin opposite this line, the following note in a sixteenth century hand*:

here is lefte oute
v. versis which is in

the olde coppi/& ar
set be nethe

and at foot of the page in the same hand:

and when you se the sune a misse, & to mvnks heades
and a mayde have the masteri, And mvltiply by/eight/hight/
than shall deathe with drave, and derth be Justice
and davi the diker, shall die for hunger
But if god of his goodnes graunte vs a treue

PASSUS EIGHT

Title:

TH₂ChN: Passus octauus de visione vt prius.
D: Passus Octauus (*margin*).
URAIWH: Passus octauus de visione (I *has this in margin*).
ML: *no title or break.*
H₃: Here endyth þe sexte part of þis book pers plowman.
Di: Passus nonus de visione.
V: *no title; one line left blank.*

2 tilien the erthe] his erþe tilien TH₂ChDR.

3 purchacede] purchace TH₂ChDURMH.

4 evere] for euere TH₂DMLNDi.

5 eren] erien TH₂ChDURMH₃ILNH; eiren Di; heren V.

6 al that] þo þat TH₂ChA; þat D; alle þo þat N; al þat euere V.
al that holpen hym] þat ȝe shul helpe R.
holpen hym] hym holpyn AI; holpen hendely L; hym helpen H.
holpen] helpen H₂ChDRH₃DiH.
hym] TChDH₃LN *om.*
eren] erien TH₂ChDURAH₃; heryen L; eere W; earen Di; heren V.
or] or ellys D; and RALNH; er I.
to sowen] sowe or sette W; sowen N.

7 myster] of mester TH₂Ch.
helpen] availe L.

8 that] þe TH₂Ch; þu H₃ (*sic*).
pope] people D; Piers W.
ygrauntid] hem grauntid TH₂DUMIWNDi; hym graunted Ch.

10 rightfulliche] rewfulliche TH₂M; (A *om. line*).
in reaum] in this reme H₂; in here rewme U; þe rewme R; in Revmes MN; in þe rewme I.
in reaum rewlith] þe rewme rewlyþ and R; Rulen þe Reame and VH.

11 purgatorie] purcatorie TCh.
ful] wel TH₂ChDUMILWDi.

13 lawes] þe lawes ChVH.
conne] kenne TH₂ChUI; kene D; kunne R; conyn A; cunnen V; knowen H.

16 peril] periles TH₂DLNDi.

17 that] þat þe RDi; fro M; þe LW; þat a N; heore V; þat here H.
scabbide] shabbide TChRAMIVH; scallide H₂.
shul] shulde TH₂DADiH; þey may M.

[233]

19 And] URAH₃ILH *om.*
    at here deis] at þe des A; on hey deis MH; on hys dees H₃; on
    des W; on her deys N; at the hye desse Di; with hem on deis V.
    to] for to A; schal M; IWNV *om.*

21 et a] & a T (*expuncted*); & of D; & UN; A *om.*; ne a M.
    nolde] wolde TH₂ChDUAMIDi; wyl H₃.
    hem] hym TH₂; UR *om.*; non A; hem non H₃.

22 holde] helde TH₂ChI.
    haly dayes] haly day UAMV.

25 hem] hym TH₂ChRA; UIVH *om.*

26 hem(1)] hym TH₂ChRAM.
    bigge] begge TR; bye ChH₃; bugge LWV.
    hem best likide] þat hym likeþ TH₂; þat him liked Ch; þat hem
    lykeþ D; hem best likith UH₃L; him best lykede RAM.

28 *meson deu*] mesonis deux TH₂; mesondeux ChWNH; mensoun de
    dieu D; maisouns dieus M; mesendews H₃; mesendew I; maisen
    dieux L; meysondieux Di.
    myseise] myseises TH₂; meseles ChWH; þe myseyse UN; myssede
    men A; mischefs M; meysyn H₃; þe meseyse I; meseise men L;
    mysselles Di; Meseyse V.

29 Wykkide weyes] And wickede weyes H₂ChMIDi; wikked ways also
    W; Also wikke weies N; And wikkede wones V; & also wicked
    weies H.
    Wykkide weyes wightly] Wightliche wikkide weyes U.
    wightly] wytlyche DRAH₃; þer with M; wyttylyche I; wide wher
    nedful weore L; witterly W.
    to amende] for to amende TH₂Ch (for *inserted above line in* T);
    for to don amende U; amende AIN; to mende W.

30 bete] bynde TH₂Ch; byende D; þinke on R; a mendyn M; makyn
    I; Feble L; broken W; boten Di; Beete V; bigge H; (UA *om.*
    line).

31 or] also & TH₂Ch; also or DRDi; & AH₃W; þer with or M; elles
    N; or ellis H.

32 Pore] TH₂ChMH₃ *om.*; warde W; (A *defective*).
    that wiln be] þat wiln not be TH₂Ch; þat wil nede be D; þat wolde
    beo VH.
    non wyves aftir] wyues helpe hem þere aftir TH₂Ch; wyfes after D;
    wyues non ofter R; no more wyfes after H; (I *has* Aftur *at*
    beginning of next line).
    UMH₃LDi *change line as follows*:
    U: þat pore wydewes wol ben and none wyues aftir.
    M: As wydewys þat wyues willen none ben after.
    H₃: And wedewys þat wyuys wyl be non oftere.
    L: And pore wydewes þat wilnen no wyues to beon after.
    Di: Pore widowis that willen not to be wifes after.

34 or] other H₂Ch.
    to(2)] TH₂ChRN *om.*
    other] skynes TH₂DH₃; kynnes ChRILN; kynne UDi; maner M;
    kynde W.

36 And] TH₂ChD *om.*
   yow] TDRL *om.*; hem H₂Ch.

37 dighe whan ye dighe] when ȝe to deth go L; die whan ȝe shull W; whan þat ȝe ben dede N; die whan yow done Di; whon ȝe dye schulle V; when ȝe beþ dede H.

38 youre soules] his soule TH₂DRLDi; ȝowre soule W; (A *defective*; M *om. line*).

39 fourme youre setis] forme ȝow settys D; for me ȝow sette R; þat formyd ȝowr setys (ȝowr setys *over original* ȝow alle) I; forme his sete L; fourme ȝow to sitte W; frely ȝow sette H.

41 graith treuthe] grete treuthe URH; heye weye M; hey trewthe H₃; hard truthe I; grace of treuþe V.

42 and] many TH₂H₃N; and many ChD; and some R; svme M; þei IWV.

43 yaven] ȝaf TH₂ChRWH; ȝeue D; ȝeuyn UMDi; ȝouyn H₃I; gaf N; ȝeeuen V.

44 For] And for TH₂W.
   he copiede] he coupide TH₂; he coped DRMLNDi; þat copy W; to copie H.
   clause] a b c M; cause H₃V.
   couden] ȝeue TH₂DW; ȝaf Ch; cowde U; konne R; kennyt M; comandyn H₃; cowthin I; konned L; cowþe NH; could Di.
   mede] þonk VH.

45 lettride thei ben alle] lewid þei ben alle TH₂Ch; lered þey ben alle DR; þai beþ lerned all W; þe ben alle lettred N; heo beoþ lettred alle V; þey beþ loþ H; (H *adds line*: To mote for mene men but ȝif þei hadde money).

46 And(1)] For TH₂ChD; IVH *om.*
   And so seith the Sauter] To loke vpon he sawter N; As þe sauter seiþ H.
   innocentem] innocentes VH.
   accipies] accipiens ChL; acceperunt M; accepit H₃.
   &c] TH₂Ch *om.*; erit UR; erit merces eorum MH₃IWNDi; erit merces eius &c L.

48 worth] TH₂Ch *om.*; (*for* no peny worth to W *has* þai shold not).

53 derie] deren UMH₃ILWNDiVH.

54 sykirly sauf] sauf sykirly TH₂ChDRDi; sone sauid M; syker sauf NVH; (MH₃ *add quotation from Ps. 15:1*; WH *add quotation from Ps. 15:5*).

57 throwe] trowen H₂; proued R; sowen H₃; þriuen V; y ȝeuen H.

58 and wanyen] and wayn U; & to wanien M; and wayten L; and to wane W; or to wanen N; or to wonien V; or to wanye H.
   where that] þe while R; wheyþer þat WH; wheþer NV.

59 purgatorie] purcatorie TCh.
   wel litel is] ful litel is ChH; wel petit is RLDi; is peti M; is ful petyful H₃; petit W; ful petit is N; is petit V.

61 lawyers] lawisteris TD.
ye(2)] TH₂Ch *om.*
yif] wher VH; (A *defective*; M *changes line*; H₃ *om. line*).

62 it is so] it is þus TH₂ChDURMH₃ILN; þis is soþ W; it is this
Di; þat hit is so VH.
sewith] sheweþ RH₃IL; serueþ VH.

65 lyven] louen *changed to* lyuen T; leuen ChDH₃; ledyn M.
in(2)] TH₂ChIW *om.*
lowe hertis] louȝ herte TH₂ChDUR; (Di *om.* 65b).

67 ben] be H₂DWN; beþ ChRMH; weryn I; beoth LV.

68 shapith hem to begge] þei fore begge TH₂ChH; him nede to begge R;
makith hom to begge L; þei for asken W; schapith them bigge Di.

69 biddith] bit TH₂DUI; bidit M; byd L; borweþ W.

70 defraudith] kiliþ T; gyleth H₂ChD; frawdeþ R.
defraudith the nedy] nedys dysseiuyt M; defouleþ trouþ W.

71 ek] TH₂ChDWN *om.*

72 nought in love] nouȝt in no loue MN; in no loue W; in no lawe V.

73 wedde] ne wedde TH₂Ch.

74 with wehe] with wouh Ch; þat wiþ wo U; with whe he R; wehe
MW; H₃ *om.*; þat with wehe I; when heo L; wiþ vche N; þat wo
V; wiþ woo H.
worthen up] & worþvp TH₂RM; worþe vp ChN; & wurchup D;
werchyn vp H₃; worche vp W; worcheþ V; worþen H.

75 bastardis] bois TChDi; boies *changed to* bastardes H₂; þey D;
barnes RL; barons W.

76 thei breken] bien broke H₂; he brekith UILWNDi; heo brekeþ V.
his(3)] þe Ch; M *om.*; heore VH.

78 mysshapen] myschapmen H₂; mischape ChRW; mischefes Di; mis
happes V; myshappis H.

79 of alle] U *om.*; with al H₃; alle I; amonges al W.
other] H₂ChMH₃NH *om.*
maner] maner of H₂ChUMI; WV *om.*
this] WVH *om.*; the Di.

81 hennis] henne TH₂DV.

85 meschief] his meschief TH₂D; her myschef ChRAMDi; þis myschef
H₃L; meschefs H.

87 lowe hertis] louȝ herte TH₂ChDURILWN; lewtie Di.

88 purgatorie] purcatorie TCh.
upon this pur erthe] vpon þore erþe D; vpon þis pleyn erthe R;
here vp on erde A; here in þis erthe M; ryth vp on þis erthe H₃;
here apon eorthe LWH; is her vppon eorþe V.

89 tho] TH₂ChR *om.*; þanne A.

90 For I shal] For y wol UIV; I shal RAN; & H.
iche] it iche TD; it the iche H₂; euerich a Ch; it euery UH; euery
R; eche a H₃LV; þe vche N.

kenne] ken ChUL; telle RA; teche H₃; knowen V; vndo H.
it] AH₃IW *om.*
the] heom L; VH *om.*
on] in UH₃VH.

91 unfoldith] onfolded ChAINDi; vnfeldith M; vnlapped W; vnfeld H

92 bulle] bille TChM.

93 nought a lettre] nouȝt o lettre T; nouȝt on letter D; a lettre M;
a litel L; no letter H.

94 *Et*] ChUMWDiH *om.*

97 and(3)] URH₃V *om.*

98 to helle shalt thou wende] þou shalt wende to helle R; þe deuyl
schal haue þi soule AMH₃.
shalt thou] ne shalt þou TH₂; s ne schalt þow Ch (*sic*); þou
schalt UI; for to W.

99 pure] TH₂ChDR *om.*; (pure *inserted above line in* H₂; W *om.* for
pure tene).
pullide] pulde T; plukked W; pollede VH.
assondir] assondir & seide TH₂ChDURILDiV; on tweyne and seyde
AM; on tweyne H₃; a two and to þe prest sayde W.
And seide] TH₂ChDURAMILWDiV *have at end of preceding line;*
N *om.;* H *expands:* & siþþe he seide to hem þese semely sawis.

100 quath Peris] UAMH₃IWNH *om.*

103 beloure] lowren U; be loue M.
belough] louȝ TChILN; lawehede MH₃; love Di.
er] er (*expuncted*) T; DNDi *om.;* or H.
theigh] MVH *om.;* þat H₃; þe N.
liflode] my lyflode H₃I; my lyf V.
me] IV *om.*

104 The prophet his payne eet] þe prophet his peyned T (d *of* peyned
added, possibly by original scribe); The profet hadde his peynes H₂;
And perfit In praiers Ch; The profete is fayn D; þe prophete his
peyne haþ R (peyne haþ *over erasure*); The prophetis were pyned
A; Oculus xal be ocupyid H₃; The profete hym peyned Di; þe
prophetes peyneden hem V; þer is profyt in peyne H; (MW *om.*
line).

106 well muche] þe more TH₂ChDRMI; ful mete A; ful mechyl H₃;
leche W; myche H; (N *om. line*).

107 a-nother] be folis A; to ben foles M; þat ben folys H₃; anoþer by
þe foules L; by birdes W; by fowlys N; non oþer H.

108 That] We folys þat D; By fowles he vs techith þat U; By foules
þat RIDi; AH₃ *om.*; And bitd vs M; He biddeþ vs H; (*see pre-*
ceding line).
we shuln nought] we ne shuln nouȝt T; we schuld nat ChADi; we
schulde U; are not R; be nout M; we ne schuldyn INV; we no
scholde not L; we be nowght W; we shuld not here H.
be to besy] besyen D.
to] TH₂URAH₃ *om.*; so M.
aboute the bely joye] about bely Ioye ChDMH₃; aboute bodyly ioyes

A; aboute þe lif ioye L; aboute wombe ioye W; to make þe bely
Ioye N; (*for UIVH see below*).
four MSS expand 108 into two lines:
U: By fowles he vs techith þat we schulde besy ben
    For to make wombe ioye in þis wonynge here.
I: Be fowlys þat we ne schuldyn to besy bene a boute
    Ne trauellyn to myche to makyn þe wombe Ioye.
V: þat to bisi we ne schulde beo her vppon eorþe
    While we woneþ in þis world to make vs wombe Ioye.
H: He biddeþ vs we shuld not here be to besy
    In no maner wise aboute oure wombe ioiȝe.

109 *Ne soliciti sitis*] DRW *have Latin in separate line*; W *adds*: dicentes
     quid manducemus; *after Latin* H *adds line 111 complete, omitting
     109b;* (*in* H *110 precedes 109*).
     seith] seiþ it TChWDi.
     gospel] gospel & schewith it ous D; gospel and sheweþ hit vs
     fayre R; gospel & sheweþ is an ensample W (*sic*).

110 And shewith it us be ensaumple] By ensample D; By on exaumple
     R; W *om.;* (*see preceding line*).
     it] UAH₃INH *om.*
     us] to vs Ch; AV *om.*
     be] By on RH; in L; WN *om.*
     ensaumple] ensamples U; ensaumples (?) L (*final s faded*).
     oure selue to wisse] ous selue to wisse DUAMI; vs seurly to wisse
     L; To done on þe selue wise & wisdom it kenneþ W; owre sowlys
     to wisse NVH.

111 who fynt] he fynt Ch; ho fynt DAH₃I; heo feedeþ V.
     in] a TH₂ChD; (R *om. line*).

113 to go to] þer to TH₂ChD (*go added above line in* H₂); greiþ H.

115 lettrid] lernid TH₂ChDR.
     lernide] lered RLWV; taugthe MI.

117 aftir] aftirward UAMILN; (Ch *om.* com aftir and).
     betere] moche more UR; michell better Di.

118 whan the likide] where þe likiþ TH₂Ch; þe soþe A; whon þe luste
     V; (H₃ *defective*; Di *om. line*).

119 that] RAIWNVH *om.*

121 seldom] litel TH₂ChRAIVH.
     beholdist] beholdis TCh.

122 The] And þe TH₂ChD; þus þe UMDi.
     prest] prest þanne N.
     aposide either other] aposid eiþer oþer TH₂ChD; eiþer apposid oþer
     UAM; aposed here eyþer oþer R; þus oythir aposyd oþer I; þo
     apposed eyþer oþer WV.

123 wok] awook URMWNDiVH.

125 Meteles and moneyless] Metelis on merueilles TH₂; Mynnyng on þe
     mervailles Ch.

127 hath] han TH₂ChAV; had M; RW *om.;* (H₃ *defective*).

128 ful] wel TH₂ChDRLWNDi; UI *om.*

130 nay] TH₂Ch *om.*; nouȝt D.

131 And seggen be hem selve] TH₂ChDNH *om.*; And by hem selue U;
  And Iugyn hem seluen R; And he hem selfe boþe A; And hem
  seluen siggyn M; And seyn be hem selfe I; Caton saiþ him self W;
  And saith hym self Di; And siggen bi hem seluen V; H₃ *defective
  here*; L *illegible, but has something before the Latin.*

133 Daniel] Dauid TDR; Daniel þe prophete UI.
  devynide] demide TH₂RM; dremyd D.
  drem] dremys URIWNDi; dremeyd M; Dremels V; dremyng H.

136 uncouthe knightes shuln] an vnkynde kniȝt shal TH₂; an onkynde
  king schal Ch; an vncouþe kyng schal D; vncouthe kynges schul
  U; vn kyd knyȝt shal R; vnconyng knytis schul A; vnkouth men
  schal M; vnkowþe kyngis schal I; an vnkouthe knyght schal L;
  (L *extremely faded and rubbed here*).

137 lowere] lewide TH₂ChD; hyere A; lether M.

138 devynide] demide TH₂ChDRA; dymde M; deuysed H.

141 halsiden] hailsed ChDUINDi; hayled RAV; gretyn M; worshipt W.

147 men] I UMILWNV.

148 hadde] hauiþ TH₂ChDR; hath Di; hedde V.

149 be pure] before TH₂ChD; to pure A; be poure M.

150 demide] he leuide TH₂Ch; he leueth D; dyuyned UAIV.
  passide] passiþ TH₂ChDR.

153 of] at TChD.

155 to passe to joye] a pena & a culpa TH₂Ch; D *om.*

156 a lef] þe lif TH₂Ch.
  techith] shewiþ TH₂Ch.

158 do save] do salue TH₂; doþe saue Ch; to gidres UI; ben salue R;
  may saven M; shal saue W; doun salue N.

160 Ac] And TH₂ChD; For A; But WMNDiV.

161 Is] It is TH₂ChRMDi.

164 Be ye] Be þou TH₂DUR; Beth M; (A *om. line*).

166 welthe of this world] world at wille TH₂Ch; world D; wele of þis
  world W; (A *om. line*).

167 TH₂ChD *om. line.*

168 dom day] domes day H₂ChD; day of dome URIV; dom AMWNDi.
  dede] þe dede TH₂D; men A; dedes W; deth Di.

169 alle] TH₂ChDA *om.*; forþ N.

171 be day] T *om.* (*line is marked for correction*).

172 ne] ne þe TH₂ChD; no A; and N; UH₃ *defective.*

175 thi patent] þe patent of þy pardoun DR; þi patentis of pardon
  A; ȝoure patentis M; ȝoure pardoun IN; the patentes of thy
  pardone Di; þi pardoun V.

176 For-thi] For þi (þi *inserted above line after* For *in original hand and ink*) T.
　　　to] TH₂Ch *om.*

178 grace] grace here DRAINDi; such grace W.

PASSUS NINE

Colophon:

T:　Explicit hic visio willelmi de Petro de Plouȝman Eciam/
　　　Incipit vita de do wel do bet & do best secundum wyt & resoun.

H₂:　Explicit hic visio willelmi de petro the plouȝman Eciam/
　　　incipit uita de dowel do bet and dobest secundum wit & reson.

Ch:　Explicit visio willelmi de petro le plouȝman Eciam incipit
　　　vita/de dowel dobet et dobest secundum witte and Resoun.

D:　Vita de dowel dobet and dobest secundum wyt and resoun.

U:　Explicit hic visio willelmi de petro plowman/Et hic
　　　incipit dowel dobet & dobest secundum/wit & resoun.

R:　Explicit hic visio willelmi de petro &c Et hic incipit/
　　　vita de dowel dobet & dobest secundum wit & resoun.

A:　Hic incipit vita de dowel dobet & dobest.

M:　Explicit visio de petro plouthman/
　　　hic incipit prologus de dowel dobet & dobest.

H₃:　*defective.*

I:　Explicit visio willelmi de Petro Plowhman/Hic incipit
　　　vita de dowele dobet & dobest secundum wit & resoun.

W:　Sequitur prologus de dowel dobett & dobest.

N:　Passus nonus de visione & vltimus & hic desinit/
　　　Et decetero tangit auctor de inquisicionibus de Dowel/
　　　Do bettre & Dobest sicut patebit speculantibus
　　　Inquisicio prima.

Di　　　　　　　　　　　　　　　　Explicit visio/
　　　Hic Incipit vita de dowell dobett & dobest secundum/
　　　Witte & Resoun.

V:　Incipit hic Dowel Dobet and Dobest.

1　romide] rombide T; rome H₂; Rowmed N.

6　wente] wene TH₂ChDUR.

7　lede] ladde DV; dowel M.
　　lengide] logged DAWV; lengith U; longeþ R; duellit M.
　　lesse ne more] þe lesse ne þe more TH₂; þe lesse and þe more Ch.

13　dwellith] dwellide TH₂ChA.

14　menours] maistris TH₂ChDUR; menour WV.

15　as] TH₂ChD *om.*

17　on the day] TH₂ChD *om.*; a day DiV.
　　seith the bok] AMI *om.*
　　synneth] fallïþ TH₂ChDUR.

[240]

18 And] Ac TH₂; Bot Ch; M *om.*
I seide] I seiȝe TH₂ChDMI; he seiþ U; he sayde R; as I say A.
as] TH₂ChDURAI *om.*

19 That] TH₂ChI *om.*

20 nis] is URAIWDi.

30 raughte to the stere] ariȝt sterede TH₂; riȝt stired Ch; ariȝt stere
D; raughte þe stere UI; rauȝthe þe sterne RMWDi; ȝede to þe
sterne A; rauhte to þe steorne V.

33 it] TH₂ *om.*

35 lik to the] lik þe TH₂Di; like to Ch; lyk þis V; lykened to þe A;
liknyd to M; lyknyth to þes I.
grete] DURAI *om.*

36 walwen] wawen TH₂ChD; wawes UR; walkyn A.

37 liknid] lik TDURMWDi; liken H₂; leked Ch.

39 sithes] tymes TH₂.

41 That] And þat TH₂ChDWDi.

47 thi self hast] þou hast UR; þe selfe to haue A; þinseluyn is M;
þou art V; thy self hath Di.

52 grounde] erþe TH₂ChDURMIW; erde A.

54 And] TChD *om.*; (A *om. line*).

56 I] I me TH₂ChURM; (I *om. line*).

57 lythen] lerne TH₂ChDV; lystyn ADi; lestnyn M; leren W.
foulis] briddis TH₂ChDUR.

58 the] þise TW.

65 Wot ich quath I] Wot quod ych quod I D (*sic*); wost icche A;
I schuld wetyn M.
who art thou] hoo þou art DM; what þou art quot I A; artow I;
what art þou W.
seide] T *has* ·I· *above line just before* seide.

66 this] TH₂ChMI *om.*; al þis A.

67 tho quath I] quod I ChRAW; quod I þo MIV; þo quod he U.

70 fer] for TH₂; A *om.*

75 is] TH₂ChD *om.*

76 doth thus] þus doþ TH₂ChDR; (UA *om. line*).

79 bygirdles] breigerdlis TH₂; begger doles D; (A *om. line*).

83 *sufferte*] suffertis RAWDi; (UI *om. Lat.*).

84 Ye] The TH₂ChDRAW.
for] TH₂ChD *om.*

85 so God hym self highte] so god bit hym TH₂; so god biddiþ hym
Ch; so god hem hiȝte D; so our lord highte U; so god him hyȝte
R; so god hym selfe hite AM; so hem god hyhte I; god so hym
self hyght W; god hym self hete Di; so god him self hiȝte V.

86 bothe] hem bothe TH₂ChDURA.

88 the] þat TH₂ChI; (H₃ *defective*; A *om. line*).

90 hem] hym ChDURAMIW.

94 Thanne] þat þanne TH₂ChDWDi.

96 yif] TH₂ChDAM *om.*

98 here] his TH₂ChURH₃.

103 lere] lerne DURH₃IWDi; here V; (A *om. line*).

107 thus] þese A; wente H₃; also V; MI *om.*
    thre dayes] þroly V.
    we yeden] ȝedyn disputyng on dowele I; ȝedyn dysputyng on dowel
        day be day A; day be othir M; disputyng with dowel day after
        oþer H₃; (*see line 108*); ȝeden W; we eodem V (*sic*).

109 And] Ac TH₂; Bot Ch; A *om.*; (H₃ *om. line*).

111 in] on TH₂D; (URV *om. line*).

112 of] of a TH₂DUR; (A *om. line*).

113 durste] ne durste TH₂Ch.

115 to(2)] and TDMH₃I.

118 Here is Wil] Her his wille ChUR; His wil A; To heryn fawen M;
    Oure wille V.
    Here is Wil wolde wyte] To heryn hys wytt wold I H₃.
    hym] DRMH₃DiV *om.*; me A.

PASSUS TEN

Title:

TH₂: Passus primus de dowel &c.
ChUR: Passus primus de Dowelle.
D: Primus passus in secundo libro (*margin*).
AIW: Primus passus de dowel (I *has this in margin*).
MH₃: *no title or break.*
Di: Secundus passus de dowell.
V: *no title; one line left blank.*

2 kynnes] skenis T; skynnes H₂M; maner D; kynne UWDiV; kynde
    A; kene H₃; I *om.*

4 wittyliche] wiȝtliche TH₂; witlich Ch; wyttyrly H₃; ful wittiliche V.

7 *Anima* heo hatte] Anima he haþ TH₂; þat hiȝt anima Ch; Anima
    hit hatteþ R; Anima M; Anima he hythe H₃; Annima sche hate Di.
    to hire hath envye] to hire enuye T; to hem enuye H₂; he haþe to
    her enuy Ch.

10 this] hire TH₂AH₃; him Ch; his wille I; it WDiV.

12 doughter] sistir TH₂Ch.

17 Inwyt] þouȝt TH₂Ch; þe wyt D; Iewet A.

20 a] & TUR; AW *om.*

24 to] & DURMH₃IV.

[242]

26 TChD *om. line.*

30 light] liþ TH₂Ch; lyt R; lyth AMH₃; litthe I; lyst W.
lisse] blisse URMH₃IWV; blyssis A.

34 thing] TH₂ChDUR *om.*

39 as(2)] þat TH₂.

40 werk] werkis TH₂ChD; word A; (UR *om. line*).
word] wordis TH₂ChD; werke A.

47 help] halle TH₂Ch.

48 the grettest is Inwyt] Inwyt is þe grettest TH₂ChDUR; (M *om. line*).

53 connyng] goynge URIDi; good dede AWMH₃.

64 fend] deuil TH₂ChD; (W *om. line*).

66 faderis] fadir TH₂ChDURH₃Di.

67 yonge] ȝouþe T; I *om.*; (RW *om. line*).

69 owyng] holde ChMWDi; be holdyn A; a signet V.

70 Fro folies and fynde hem] And for to fynde hem forþ U; Fro falsed
& folyes and fyndyn A; Fro falsnesse and fro folys and to fynde
hem W; Fro falsnesse and folie and techyn hem M; From falsnesse
from folyis and fende hem H₃; and fyndyn hem fro folyys I.
wisere] wise TH₂ChWM.

71 Ac] And TH₂UMH₃; ChA *om.*; For W; But IDiV.

73 chevisshen] cheuisshiþ TU; cheuysscytȝ H₂; cheuiseþ Ch; cheuese
DW; chefneschyn R; clense AM; to cheuyn H₃; To kepyn I;
chevessen Di.
fro] for TH₂ChDURDi.

78 roten] roren TH₂Ch.

80 douten] dredyn AWMH₃V.

81 *timor*] est timor TH₂.

84 kynne] kynde TH₂ChD; skynnys RMH₃; A *om.*

86 thi self] þe salme TH₂DUR; In a Salme Ch.
might it rede] þou miȝt rede TH₂ChDUR; þou might it rede WM;
þou mayt rede I; þou miht reden V.

88 for] why for T (why *expuncted*); whi for H₂ChUR; I *om.*

89 with] TChD *om.*; of H₂; wil W; to I.

92 TD *om. English, but have Latin.*

93 for] TH₂ChRMI *om.*

95 so] TCh *om.*; a H₂ (*expuncted*); to D; þe to U; þe so WH₃.

100 lernide] herd TH₂ChDURDi.
han leride] han lernid TH₂ChDi; lerne AM; lerne ȝe W; leryn H₃I.

101 mosith] men seþ TH₂ChDUR; men seyn þat M.
marbil] marbel þryuen D; marbil mose UR; Marbelston V.

treden] dreden T; mouen U; on wenedyn I.
two MSS have an additional line:
Ch: Be ouer molded with mosse men to beholde.
M: Is wol seldyn I sein wit mos be growyn.

102 romeris] romberis TH₂; renneres URAM; walkers V.

104 clergie it tellith] clergie techiþ euere TD; and clergie boþe U; as
  clerkes and oþer R; as clergie tellit M; clergyȝe tellyth H₃I;
  clergie it techith Di; (H₂ *defective*; Ch *om. line*).

105 Thrift other thedom] That thrifte of or thedom A; wit sweche
  þrift and þedam M; þat thryf or thedom H₃; That þrift oþer
  þedam WI.
  with tho] MI *om.*; with þat H₃; wiþ hym W; with hem V.

107 of suche] of which D; þat siche URMIDi; How such W.

111 ye beggere theigh thou were] þe biggere þeiȝ þou were TCh; begger
  þouȝt þou were D; ȝif þou a beggere were U; a beggere þow þou
  were A; beggere þey þou were MI; beggere ȝyf þou were H₃; ȝe
  beggere þogh þow wel W; yea a begger though thou were Di.

113 thi] þe TDR; that Di.

114 and] TCh *om.*

115 soveraynes] souereyn DMV; souereynte AH₃; sufference I; souer-
  aignce W; soferaunce Di.

117 and his dede] and here dede T; and of dede D; and of our dede UR;
  of dede A; and of doubte M; and dede H₃; (W *om. line*).

119 that red is and] TChD *om.*; (H₂ *defective*).

120 *All MSS except* IV *have first half of this line with* 119, *and second
  half with* 121.

122 of the] out of þe TChURH₃; out of D; of I; on þe W; vppon V.

126 werkis] werch T; werk ChDR; worche W.
  that] as TCh.

127 Formest] And formest TCh.
  ferst] fest T (r *inserted above between* e *and* s *in original hand and
  ink*).

128 lawe wile] lawis wiln TR; lawes whil D.

129 For] þat TChDR; And U; A *om.*

132 martires] nonnes TUR; Mynchons Ch; nonne D; maystris A.

135 as] DRMH₃IWDiV *om.*

137 Eve] she TChDMH₃Di.

139 angir] haste URDiV; a while M.
  hem] hym TM.
  highte hem to wende] made hem to wende A; þennes hem tornde V.

141 in(2)] TDH₃I *om.*; (V *om. line*).

145 *dolore*] dolorem ChRAWH₃IDi; in dolore MV; (H₂ *defective*; U
  has Latin for 11.23).

[244]

146 hatid] hatide hem URA; hem hated DiV.

148 That] And TUR; Ther A.

149 with curside men] wiþ þe curside men U; with cursed to men R; with cursid hed with men A; with men MW; vnmesourly to men I; to cursyd blode to men Di; to corsed Men þat comen V.

151 with] D *om.*; to AH₃IWV; (UR *om. line*).
dedliche] euere TD; after ChAM.

152 sente to Sem] sente hym to seyn TCh; sente hem to seye UR; sente him to sende M.

153 that] TChAMI *om.*
couplide] couple DURH₃W.

154 suster sed] suster TChDURAM; susterys sed H₃I; sustre seþ WDi.

156 suche wordis seide] seide suche wordis TChD; seide þese wordis URM.

160 ship] sship T.

162 Busken] Buskide TChURM; Buskym (*sic*) A; Bring WV.
hem] TChDR *om.*

163 that] þe UH₃IV; that the Di.

168 with] miþ T; myd DM.

170 That in the shynglid ship] Put þat in þe same ship þat TH₂Ch (Ch *om. first* þat).
the] þat M; ȝoure I; þis W.
shynglid] sengle DURA; sollyd H₃.
shuln] shal TH₂ChDUIW; shul RA; schulde MDi; xal H₃; schullen V.

172 Thus thorough curside Caym] þoruȝ curside caym þus TH₂Ch.

174 leighen] ley hem TH₂Ch; loyn A; lyȝen V; (M *om. line*).

175 were] TH₂ChD *om.*

179 that I] as TH₂; as I ChDR; þat M; (U *om. line*).

180 me thinketh] I wene TH₂ChDUR.

182 any(2)] MIWV *om.*
wele] welþe ChAWIV; lykyg (*sic*) M.
of] of here WMIV.

183 barn bere] bere child TH₂ChU; bere barn D; baron bere A; bern barn M; barun beryn H₃; beryn barne I; child bere V; (R *om. line*).

184 on] of TH₂; a DUR; in ADiV; (W *changes second half line*).

185 the] þis TH₂ChW; þese D; I *om.*
plight] piȝt TH₂; put D.

187 cheste] chiding TH₂ChH₃; chost R; chestes V; (A *om. line*).
hem betwene] togidere TH₂Ch; betwene DUMI; be twythen R; togyders hem betwen Di (togyders *crossed out; all in original hand and ink*).

[245]

192 or of] or for UR; and of A; no of non M; ne for H₃; ne of IWDiV.
kynrede riche] kyn Riche ChWIV; riche ken M.

193 macche yow togideres] macche ȝow ysamme T; marie ȝou to gyderis
H₂; mache ȝou þe same D; ȝou to same take UR; meke ȝou to
gederis A; makkyth ȝow same I; clene ow saue V.

194 werchith right also] werchith the same H₂M; wircheþ Riȝt so
ChDi; wurche ȝe also UR; werche ȝe þe same AW; werchyth ryth
ryth þe same H₃ (*second* ryth *expuncted*); worschupeþ also V.

195 thanne] TH₂D *om.*; (A *om. line*).

196 untyme] my tyme TH₂ChDUR (D *om.* my); no tyme WMH₃.
man and womman] men & wommen TH₂ChD; (A *om. line*).

199 shulde] ne shulde TH₂R; no scholde I; (A *om. line*).

201 mariage] maner TH₂Ch.

202 werche that werk] do þat werk TH₂Ch; þe werle D; wurche UR;
werche þou þat werke A; worche þat V; (M *om. half line*).

204 alse] as ChH₃; also DURDi; I *om.*; and W; ben V; (M *om. half
line*; A *om. line*).
leigheris] folis TH₂Ch.

206 wandrith and wastith] wandres & walwes D; wandryn as wolues
RMH₃IDiV; wandren aboute as wolues W; (U *defective*; A *om.
line*).
what that thei mowe] and waste if þey mowe DRIDiV; and wastit
þat þey mowe MH₃; and wast what þei mowe W.

208 the] þat H₂ChI.
same] schrewe IDiV.

209 hem] hym TH₂; (AWMH₃ *om. line*).

212 werk] werkes RW; mannis werkis M; wight Di; men V.

PASSUS ELEVEN

Title:

TH₂: Passus secundus de dowel &c.
ChRAW: Passus secundus de Dowelle (U *defective*).
DMI: *no title or break.*
H₃: Here endyth þe seueth part of þis book.
Di: Passus tercius de dowell.
V: *no title; one line left blank.*

1 was hoten] þat hatte TH₂; þat hiȝt Ch; þai clepid A; and heithe
M; hyr name was H₃; þat hyte I; that hote Di.

2 lough] loþly TH₂Ch.

3 me thus] so TChD; so me H₂; þus me RAW.

4 al staringe dame Studie sterneliche] sterneliche staringe dame studie
TH₂ChD; al sternely starynge dam stodie R; alle schornely dam
stodie sternely A; al scornynge dam stodie sterneliche M; skorn-
fullych dame stody to vs bothe H₃; al scornyng sternly she W.

5 quath she to Wyt] wyt quaþ she TH₂ChDR; quot she AWIV.
 any] my R; MIV *om.*
 wisdomis] wisdam RAWMDiV.

7 and bannide hym] bitterly TH₂Ch; for his Beere V; I *om.*

9 *Nolite*] noli RWDiV.
 man] ChAWMV *om.*; þese H₃.

13 it] TH₂ChDRMI *om.*

19 conterfeten] construe þe TH₂Ch; construe DR; contryven Di;
 (AWMH₃ *omit first half line*; U *defective*).

21 to counseil ben yclepid] ben yclepid to counseil TH₂ChDA; is cleped
 to counseyl R.
 yclepid] callid MH₃W.

23 it] AWMH₃ *om.*; it for a sawe Di; (R *om. line*).
 prosperatur] preparatur TH₂ChDRDi; preparabitur AWM; pro-
 babitur H₃.
 bene] ve TH₂ChWDi; ve ve (*sic*) D.
 et inique agunt] agunt & inique TH₂ChD.

26 Pilatus] pilatis TH₂; pilat MH₃I.

30 daunselid] dauntid TH₂Di; daunteþ Ch; damseld R; honourid A;
 ho so can daunce H₃; daunsels W.

32 almighty] almiȝt TW; al myȝte D; IV *om.*

35 Ac] TH₂ChDA *om.*; but MH₃DiV; For I.

39 At] At þe TH₂; Atte MV.
 in here] & at TH₂ChDA; (U *defective*).

41 tak] tok T; R *om.* (*for* resoun R *has* tokne); (H₂ *defective*).

44 gorge] þrote TH₂D; þrotes Ch.

46 quake] quakiþ TH₂ChD.

47 his noye] ne his anguyssh TH₂ChD; ne angwys R; þat is noye A;
 and his disease M; and hys anyr H₃; ne his noyce I; ne his anoye
 Di.
 to(2)] TH₂DRMH₃WDi *om.*; wil A.

48 honesshen hym] hunsen hym TH₂Ch; Hold hym out AW; comaundin
 him out MH₃; hoynyn on him I; huschen hym Di.
 thennes] þenne TH₂; hennys Di.

52 Manye mendynauntz meteles] Wiþ Mony defauti Meeles V.
 mendynauntz] men TH₂ChHH₃; pore men DM; (A *om. line*).

53 gorge] þrote TD; mouth M.

54 mene] TH₂ *om.*; (meene *inserted above line in* H₂ *in a late hand*);
 (U *om. line*).

55 seke] se TH₂Ch.

56 kete] kid TH₂Ch; ked DUR; courte AI; grete MH₃.

57 hym] TURDi *om.*

[247]

60 feith] false TH₂ (*in* H₂ *original* false *has been altered to* fase *or* ?
   fae); face D; Fey V.
   festis] þe feste TH₂D.

64 ek] TChDDi *om.*; to U; (H₂ *defective*).

65 carpen] carpide T; Craken V.

67 begilide] he gilide TD; to be gile A; þat deceyuyd I; begile W; (V
   changes line).
   wy] why Ch; wey DR; man UAMH₃IDi; worm W.

68 whiche a werk and wille] swyche a werk and wille UW; wheche and
   while A; who is wilis and his werkys M; qweche werk and wyl H₃;
   wykkyd werkys and wylle I; such worke and wile Di; (V *changes
   line*).

71 in] to TChR; (H₂ *defective*); DUV *om.*

76 on the] of TH₂Ch; on þat RV; þe M; in þe I; (A *om. line*).

77 in] be TH₂ChDUR; (A *om. line*).

79 weyis] werkes TH₂Ch; wordes D; priuytes M; whyys Di; (I *om.
   half line*).
   almighty] almiȝt TH₂D; almyȝte U; M *om.*

80 eighe were] eiȝen wern TH₂Ch.

81 that(2)] TH₂Ch *om.*

82 Suffren Sathan] suffrede satan R; To suffre satan A; suffryn þat
   schrewe satan M; Suffur satan þe vnsaut H₃; suffryn sory sathan
   I; suffre Satan vnsaght W; Suffre so sathan Di.

83 Or] Er TH₂; Eythyr H₃; Oþer W.
   betraye] betrayede TH₂DRI.

84 Lord yworsshipid be thou] lord worschiped beþe D; lord I wyrchepid
   þou be UR; now worchepid be he A; þat lord be heried M; lord
   worcheped be to the H₃; lord thankyd be þou I; lord yworshipt be
   he W; lord I heried be þou V.

90 I dar] For I dar UMIWDi.

93 become] becomiþ T.

94 And alse] Also TD; als so H₂; As ChA; And also URH; And as
   IWDiV; (M *om. line*).
   aside] asid T; on syde AH₃; be syde I.

95 that] TH₂ChDAI *om.*

96 greyn] gayn TH₂; graunte Ch.

98 of] of his T; of here D.

101 the while] þer whiles TH₂; while ChDRWV; wil U; qwyl H₃I.

102 Kenne] To kenne DURAWIDi; To techyn MH₃; Teche V.

107 as] TH₂ChDUR *om.*

109 as(1)] TH₂Ch *om.*; a D.

111 dwellide] wonide TH₂ChDURDi.

114 wilt] wile TH₂; wit M.

120   Fro]   For T; from For H₂ (from *in left-hand margin in late hand*).
lither]   liȝeris TH₂ChDURV.

121   simplite]   sympel ChV; symplesse UIDi; symplenesse RAMH₃; sym-
plece W.

123   thinges]   wyttes TH₂ChD.

125   I(1)]   þou TH₂; Ch *om.*; (U *om. line*).
the bible]   þe bille WMH₃; a Bulle V.

126   hire(2)]   þe URAWMDi.

128   to knowe]   knowe alse TH₂; knowe also Ch; knowe after D.

133   Of]   And TH₂ChDUR; For A.
tolis]   *begins next line in* TH₂DUR; Ch *om.*; ferst to lere U; to
lerne R.

134   Of]   Tolis of TH₂DUR; ChI *om.*; as H₃.

135   hem]   hym TH₂; MI *om.*

141   lat]   last URH₃; lateþ W; letteth Di; let I; set V; (A *om. line*).

142   lakkith]   lakkede H₂ChMIDiV.

144   lovis scole]   louis skile TH₂ChD; loue scole UI; lowest lore A;
louis lore MH₃W; lore In scole V.

145   *simulat*]   similat TH₂DAMH₃I; DRMIWDi *have additional line*:
Tu quoque fac simile sic ars deluditur arte.

146   techith]   techiþ vs TUR; techit it H₂Ch; techeþ ous D; telleþ
WMH₃; teneth Di.
so(2)]   TH₂ *om.*

148   biddith]   TD *om.*

152   Ac]   TH₂ChDAI *om.*

154   werche]   werche werche T (*sic*); dele H₂; Ch *om.*

156   menis]   manis TH₂ChDRAH₃Di; (U *om. half line*).

158   perimansie]   permansie TChDRAMH₃I; peramancie WDi.

160   my self]   my self foundit TH₂ChDUR; me selue formest AWMH₃;
my self made Di; (*see following line*).

161   Foundit]   TH₂R *om.* (*see preceding line*); And founden hem Ch;
And made hem D; þurw U; Haue I founded V.
Foundit hem formest]   Hem foundyd in feth A; He fondeth in feith
M; Hem foundyd in feyth H₃; In fayþ W.
to]   for to TH₂.

170   gome]   grom TH₂DUDi; man MH₃.

172   as heo]   heo it TH₂; he it Ch; as sche DDi; as sche it UR; as þey
M; þei me H₃; so sche I; so þai W; (A *om. line*).

174   clergie]   clergise T; clerkys M; (clergie *inserted above line in* Di
in original hand and ink).
collide]   callide TUAMH₃Di; Clupte V; (DRW *om. line*).

176   seide]   seiȝe T.

[249]

177 lerne] lere TH₂DUR.

179 lelle] lelly TH₂DUR; trewe MH₃; feir V.
she] scheo H₂; he ChAWMH₃; heo V; (I *om.* quath she).

180 husbondis] lewide men TH₂Ch; husbondryȝe H₃.

181 on] of þe MH₃Di; of I.

183 toille] tilie URWMH₃I; (A *om. line*).

186 castel] castels WIDi.

188 and sustren to othere] and sustren to alle othir H₂; and susteryn I;
AWMH₃ *om.*

189 Thus bed the Do-bet] þus bad dobette ChD; þese ben þat dobet U;
þis beþ þo þat dobet RH₃IDi; þus ben dobet A; þys is þat dowel
vsit M; þese ben þo þat dobet askeþ W.

191 God wot this is Do-bet] Sekyrly þis is dobet dobest wot þe soþe A;
Dredles þis is dobet dobest wote þe sothe W; Dredles it is dobest
dobet wot þe sothe M; Dredles is dobet dobest wot þe sothe H₈;
God wote this is dobest and therfor I sayen Di.
Do-bet] dobest UMDi.

192 TH₂ChDUR *have the first half of this line with 191, and the second
half with 193*; (U *om. second half of 192 and all of 193 and Latin*).

194 a] TH₂WDi *om.*

196 dewid] dowel DURW; endued A; doutid M; dowed Di.

198 tho] þe TH₂; þes Ch; þat D.

202 he reherside] he rehersit U; he reherseþ RWDi; rehersyth AI;
rehercid MH₃.

205 liggen] lengen T; leggen H₂; long ChUR.

208 romere be stretis] rennere aboute TH₂Ch; rennere be strete D;
rennere be stretis URH₃.

209 love-daies] ladies TDAWMH₃Di.

210 fro toune to toune] to toune and to toune T; fro parkes to townes
Ch.

213 the] DURH₃IDi *om.*

215 wolde] shulde TH₂ChU; wele M.

216 knighthed] knyghthode quod I WADi.

217 of alle] of hem alle TH₂DUR; (A *om. line*).

223 ward] TH₂ChD *om.*
one heris ende] at one ȝeris ende TH₂ChDURA; atte ȝerys ende I.

225 it] it is TH₂; URAM *om.*

228 that can I with-seye] þat can I þe wisse TH₂ChD (D *om.* þe); and
þat I dar wel say A.

230 among] as TH₂ChD; with I.

231 Thei] TH₂ChDUR *om.*; (A *om. line*).

[250]

232 an uncristene] arn vncristene TH₂I; buþ vncristene D; oon cristen
UR; vn cristene AWH₃; iche cristene M.

234 as an heigh cristene] as a man þat is cristene AH₃; as he þat is
cristene M; as a man þat is cristened W; as ony cristene I.
heigh] her R (*sic*).

236 here] þe TH₂D; on Ch; our UR; he W (*sic*).

237 dele] dele oure enemys TH₂ChDUR (*see following line*).

238 Oure enemys] TH₂ChDUR *have with preceding line.*
and pore] and pore men and suche T; as pore men and such
H₂ChUR; pore men and suche D; and pore and seyth I; pore nedy
and syke Di.
four MSS have an additional line:
And schewit þis sermoun þat sone sueth aftir AWMH₃ (schewit vs
M; *for* sueth H₃ *has* schewt).
fidei] fidi (?) T (*rubbed*); H₂ *om.*; &c A.

239 ben lyche] beleuiþ TH₂Ch; longen D.

240 be holde] beholde T.

243 creature] man TH₂ChDUR.

244 hethene] hem TH₂DUR; hym Ch; trauaylyn H₃; (A *om. line*).

247 *Non mecaberis*] Ne mecaberis TH₂; Non mechaberis U; Non occides
H₃; þat is to seyn I; (M *om. line*).

250 nevere the ner] never the nere quod I DiW; quod I neuere ner M.

252 wrong] TH₂Ch *om.*; amys I.

253 withoute] with ChU; to I.

255 unwriten] vndir writen TH₂D; writen Ch.

256 it be] on TH₂ChUR; it wel be AWMH₃ (H₃ *om.* be).
no] on no TH₂ChDUM.

258 hym] hem TH₂.

260 writ] chirche TH₂DURA.

263 holden] hold D; holdiþ URMH₃; helt I.

266 ensaumple] ensaumples TD.

269 wende to pyne] þei went to helle Ch; wynde to pyne D; wende to
payne R; wynne me pyne AWM; wonyn in peyne H₃; þei wentyn
to pyne I; wenten to pyne Di.

283 arn none] arn now TH₂ChDi; buþ nou D; Arne þer non AWH₃.
so sovereyne] souereynes TH₂Ch; more souereyn D; so fer UR;
so souereyne liche AW; so sikirly M; souereynlych H₃; so
souereynglich Di.

285 am I] any I TH₂; haue I ChH₃Di; I A; arn þei W.
forget ferthere] forget for TH₂; for gete ChD; for ȝote for soþe R;
aferd of þe M; forgyd ferther IDi; forked forþere W; (U *om. line*).

286 was it evere] what is neuere TH₂R; hit neuere D; was A; was it
neuere M; was neuer H₃I; (UW *om. line*).

287 *steteritis*] steteris TD.

289 Whanne] Wheþer TH₂Ch; Whar D.

292 alle] at wille TH₂Ch.

294 was] TH₂ChDA *om.*

295 thus] þis TH₂ChDW.

303 in-to the heighe blisse] in to heiȝe blisse TD; in to þe blisse of
     heuyn A; to comyn to blys H₃; passyn into hye blisse amen Di
     (passyn *inserted above line in original hand and ink*; amen *crossed
     out in original ink*).

PASSUS TWELVE

After line 303 the MSS have:

TH₂Ch: Passus tercius de dowel Breuis oracio penetrat celum.
        (*then follows the C-addition, beginning with C 12.297*).
D: Now of þis litel book y haue makyd an ende.
        Goddis blessyng mote he haue þat drinke wil me sende.
        Explicit liber petri plowman.
UR: Passus tercius de dowel &c (R *om.* &c).
A: *lacks colophon.*
M: Explicit prologus de dowel dobet & dobest.
H₃: Explicit tractus de perys plowman. q. herun (?).
        Qui cum patre et spiritu sancto viuit et regnat per omnia
        secula seculorum Amen.
I: Passus tercius de dowele (*in right hand margin*).
W: passus iiij de dowel (*sic*); (*then follows C 13.1*).
Di: *no break in text; continues with C 12.297.*

9   That] þat it U.
    me] men R.

12 tho Scripture] þe scripture R; scripture þo I.
    set] sherte R; schet I.
    here] his R.

13 crieth] criyd I; cryede U.

14 but yif stryf were] but if it stryf were U; but I schriuen were I.

16 seyde] seide it U.

19 *prevaricantes*] preuaricationes R; (*last line in U*).

22 *archana verba*] archane R.

24 wrecches] schrewys I.

30 red] rede I.

31 wolde] ȝernyth to I.
    wis] wysse I.

33 me carpeth] men Iangelyth I.

34 wyt] scole I; *Skeat emends to* skile.

41 That Kynde Wit the confessour] Kynde wt hure confessour R.
    cosyn] kynnysman I.

42 low] lowhe on me I.

45 a-byde] dwelle I.

46 wisse] wyssyn wynlyche I.

47 her wel] here fete I.

48 And thanked hure a thousand sythes] A thowsyng tymes I thankyd
      hire I.
    throbbant] throbbyng I.

49 called me] callyd I; called to ken me *Skeat.*

49-50 *All one line in* R.

50 That hyght] *with preceding line in* I.

52 burgh] bowhe I.

55 I *om. line.*

57 court] cuntreyys I.

59 a-fyngrid] an hunger it I.

60 youthe] ȝou·þe R.

62 answered] seyd I.

64 in] and I.

65 R *om. line.*
    theigh] þei I.

67 quod I] R *om.*
    feyntise] fentesye R; fayntys I.
    henteth] hendeþ R.

68 feyntise] fentyse R; fayntyse I.
    no ferther] not forth I.

70 At my bak] Of battys and I.

72 him] R *om.*
    to] at R.

73 the] I *om.*

74-76 R *om. lines.*

78 R *om. line.*

79 he halsed me] I haysyd haylsyd me hym I (*sic;* haysyd *crossed out;*
      me *crossed out and* hym *written above it*).
    I] I *om.*

80 whennes] when R; qwennys I.

82 a-threst] a-first *Skeat.*

83 masager] mensenger I; messager *Skeat.*

86 tyne] tyme R.

88 Myghth I so] Myht I se quod he I; (*last line in* I).

91 The] Thou *Skeat.*

92 wroughth] *Skeat suggests* worþ.

99 Wille] Wille wiste *Skeat.*

[253]

GLOSSARY

Note

No attempt has been made to record every occurrence of every word in the text. In a number of cases, however, several citations are given, especially where the student may find it useful to compare different contexts in which a word is used. The order is alphabetical, except that vocalic *y* appears with *i*, thus reducing the number of cross references. The standard dictionary abbreviations (*n.*, noun, *adj.*, adjective, AF, Anglo-French, OE, Old English, etc.) are used throughout and require no explanation. Etymologies are given (enclosed in brackets) except where the word is of imitative or unknown origin. In doubtful cases the etymology is preceded by a question mark.

A

A, *adj.*, one. 10. 34, 11. 236. [OE ān]

ABATEN, *v.*, soften, alleviate. 7.169. [OF abatre]

ABIGGEN, *v.*, ABIEN, pay for. 2.92, 7. 73. [OE abycgan]

ABIT, *n.*, habit, costume. pr. 3. [OF habit]

ABOSTEN, *v.*, address arrogantly. 7.141.

ABOUTE, BE ABOUTE, *v.*, be busy, be on the move, astir. 4. 68. [OE abūtan]

AC, *conj.*, but. pr. 13. [OE ac]

ACORDEN, *v.*, agree. 5. 178, 10.87. [OF acorder]

ACUMBREN, *v.*, encumber, oppress. 1. 170. [OF combrer]

A-DOUN, *adv.*, down. 5. 7. [OE a-dūn]

AFERD, *adj.*, afraid. 1. 10. [OE afǣran]

A-FYNGRID, *adj.*, oppressed with hunger. 12. 59. [OE ofhyngrod]

AFTIR, *adv.*, afterwards. pr. 97. [OE æfter]

AFTIR THAT, *conj.*, according to what. 7. 195.

AGAST, *adj.*, afraid. 2. 173. [OE gǣstan]

AGEYNS, *prep.*, against. 8. 71. [OE ongēanes]

AKEN, *v.*, ache. 7. 240. [OE acan]

AKIR, *n.*, acre, field. 7. 4. [OE æcer]

ALE, *n.*, ale-house. pr. 42. [OE ealu]

A-LEGGED, *pp.*, alleged, declared. 12. 107. [OE alecgan, ONF alegier]

A-LERY, *adj.*, ? out of joint; ? concealed in the grass, behind a ridge or furrow. 7. 114. [? OE on lǣghrycge *fr.* lēah, hrycg]

[254]

ALIEN, *n.*, foreigner. 3.196. [OF alien]

ALKENEMYE, *n.*, alchemy. 11.157. [OF alquimie, -kemie]

ALONGID, *pp.*, greedy. 7.251. [OE oflangod]

ALS, ALSE, *adv.*, also. 2.122, 3. 209. [OE eal swā]

AMAISTRIEN, *v.*, master, overcome. 2.112. [OF maistrier]

AMENDEN, *v.*, mend, make better. 1.142; cure. 4.83; repair. 8. 29; reform. 3.82; alleviate. 11.47. [OF amender]

AMOUNTEN, *v.*, amount to, signify. 3.84. [OF amonter]

AMPOLLE, *n.*, small vial, filled with holy water or oil. 6.8. [L ampulla]

ANCRE, ANKERE, *n.*, recluse, hermit; nun. pr. 28, 7.133, 10.132. [OE āncra]

AND, *conj.*, if. 2.154, 4.75, 120, 11.61, 215.

ANOYED, *pp.*, annoyed, harmed. 2.131, 3.174. *See* NOIEN. [OF anuire]

APARAILEN, APPARAILEN, *v.*, dress, deck out. pr. 23, 6.4. [OF aparailler]

APEIREN, *v.*, impair, render worse, injure. 3.115, 11.63. [OF apeier] *god, empeirer, am-*

APENDEN, *v.*, belong to. 1.43, 98. [OF apendre]

APEREN, *v.*, appear. 3.101. [OF aperer, aparir]

APERTE, *adv.*, openly, manifestly. 5.176. [OF apert]

APERTLY, *adv.*, openly, plainly,

evidently, clearly. 1.98. [OF apertement]

APEWARD, *n.*, keeper of an ape. 6.116. [OE apa, weard]

APOISENEN, *v.*, poison; deceive, seduce. 3.115. [OF poison]

APOSEN, *v.*, examine, question; debate. 1.45, 3.5, 8.122, 11.289, 12.8, 26. [OF aposer]

APOSTATA, *n.*, one who abandons an order of knights or monks. 1.102. [L apostata]

ARCHIDEKEN, *n.*, archdeacon. pr. 92. (*See Introduction*).

ARERAN, *v.*, raise, prepare, bring forth. 2.48. [OE arǣran]

ARST, *adv.*, first. 4.5, 29. [OE ǣrest]

AS, *conj.*, as if. pr. 2. [OE eal swā]

AS SWITHE, *adv.*, at once, as quickly as possible. 3.89. [OE eal swā swīþe]

ASKAPEN, *v.*, escape, avoid. 2.167, 7.69. [OF escaper]

ASKEN, *v.*, demand, require. pr. 19. [OE āscian, āxian]

ASPIEN, *v.*, investigate, examine, observe. 2.187, 7.121, 208, 12. 103. [OF espier]

ASSAIEN, *v.*, try, have a try at. 3.5, 5.151. [OF essaier]

ASSELEN, *v.*, seal, attach a seal to. 2.35, 77. [OF seel]

ASSIGNEN, *v.*, direct. 4.109. [OF assigner]

ASSOILEN, *v.*, absolve. pr. 67; explain, answer. 12.11. [OF assolir, *pres. subj.* assoille]

ASWOWEN, *adj.*, a-swoon. 5. 214. [OE geswōgen]

ATACHEN, *v.*, attach, arrest. 2. 161, 198. [OF atachier]

A-THREST, *adj.*, a-thirst, very thirsty. 12. 82. [OE ofþyrst]

AUGHTEST, *v.*, oughtst, shouldst. 1. 73. [OE āhte]

AUNGEL, *n.*, angel. 10. 31, 139, 152. [OF angele]

AUNSEL, *n.*, steel-yard. 5. 131. [AF aunselle]

AUNTE, *n.*, sweetheart, lover. 5. 251. [OF ante]

AUNTER, *n.*, chance. AN AUNTER, lest perchance. 3. 62. [OF aventure]

AUTER, *n.*, altar. 3. 50. [OF auter]

AVAUNCEN, *v.*, advance. 1. 165. [OF avancer]

AVOWE, *n.*, vow. 5. 222. [OF vou, vo]

AVOWEN, *v.*, vow. 3. 233.

AWREKEN, *v.*, avenge. 7. 158. *See* WREKEN.

AXEN, *v.*, ask. 4. 90. *See* ASKEN. [OE āxian, āscian]

AXESSE, *n.*, fever. 5. 202. [OF accez]

AYEN, AYENS, *prep.*, against. 3. 80. [OE ongēan]

AYEN, *adv.*, back. 4. 40. [OE ongēan]

B

BABELEN, *v.*, talk indistinctly or inarticulately. 5. 8.

BABIRLIPPID, *adj.*, with large, hanging lips. 5. 108.

BACHELER OF DEVYN, Bachelor of Divinity. pr. 90. (*See Introduction*). [OF bacheler]

BAD, *v. pret.* BEDEN, bade, commanded. 10. 159.

BAD, *v. pret.* BIDDEN, asked, prayed. 1. 108.

BAYARD, *n.*, a common name for a horse. 4. 40. [OF baiard]

BAILLIF, *n.*, official on a manor; summoner in a shire or hundred court. 3. 2. [OF baillif]

BAKKEN, *v.*, provide with clothes for the back; clothe. 11. 185.

BALDERE, *adj.*, bolder. 4. 94. [OE bald]

BALE, *n.*, harm, injury. 4. 76. [OE bealu]

BALEIS, *n.*, rod, stick. 11. 132. [OF baleis]

BALKE, *n.*, ridge of earth left unplowed between two strips of land to mark the boundary between two holdings. 7. 99. [OE balca]

BALLID, *adj.*, bald; trite, hackneyed. 11. 41.

BANE, *n.*, injury. 6. 90. [OE bana]

BANEN, *v.*, injure, hurt. 7. 201. [OE bana]

BANK, *n.*, bank of a stream. pr. 8.

BANNEN, *v.*, curse. 1. 60. [OE bannan, "command, summon," ON banna, "prohibit, curse"]

BAR, *v. pret.* BEREN, bore. 2. 3.

BARGAYNES, *n.*, agreements to exchange, or to purchase or sell. 5. 187. [OF bargaigne]

BARN, *n.*, child. 2.3. [OE barn]

BAROUNS, *n.*, the great nobles, large and wealthy land-holders. pr. 96. [OF baron]

BASELARD, *n.*, a dagger. 11.211. [AF baselarde]

BATEREN, *v.*, strike, clap. 3.184. [OF batre]

BAUDE, *n.*, bawd, procurer. 3.45. [OF baud]

BAUDEKYN, *n.*, *colloquial*, little bawd. 3.40.

BAXTER, *n.*, baker, either male or female. pr. 98. [OE bæcestre]

BE, *prep.*, (1) by, beside. pr. 8. (2) in accordance with. 1.92. (3) according to. 1.22. (4) through, by permission of. pr. 77. (5) by means of. 2.4. (6) with reference to. 9.33, 11. 206. [OE be, bi]

BEAU FITZ, fair son. 8.142. [AF beau fitz]

BECH, *n.*, beech-tree. 5.18. [OE bēce]

BED, *v. pret.*, BEDEN, bade, ordered. 11.189.

BED-BOURD, *n.*, bed-play. 10.197. [OE bedd, OF bourde]

BEDDREDE, *adj.*, bedridden. 7.130. [OE bedreda, bedrida]

BEDE, *v. pret. subj.* BIDDEN, should ask, entreat. 9.96.

BEDEL, *n.*, crier, herald (in court of justice, assembly, etc.). 2.74, 3.2. [OF bedel, OE bydel]

BEDEMAN, *n.*, beadsman, one who offers prayer for another. 3.45.

BEDEN, *pp.*, invited. 2.34. [OE biddan, *pp.* beden]

BEDEN, *v. pret. pl.* BIDDEN, bade, invited. 3.26. [OE bædon]

BEDIS, *n.*, beads; prayers, then the beads on which prayers were counted. 5.8. [OE bed, " prayer "]

BEFALLEN, *v.*, befall; belong to, be due to. 1.50. [OE befeallan]

BEFORN, *adv.*, before. 6.11. [OE beforan]

BEGON, *pp.*, persuaded. 2.24. [OE begān]

BEGRUCCHEN, *v.*, begrudge. 7.61. [OF grouchier]

BEHESTE, *n.*, promise. 3.114. [OE behǣs]

BEHIGHTE, *v. pret.*, BEHOTEN, promised. 3.28. [OE heht]

BEHOTEN, *v.*, promise. 5.227. [OE behātan]

BEHOVEN, *v.*, behoove, befit. 8.112, 9.29. [OE behōfian]

BEKENNEN, *v.*, commend, commit. 2.31. [OE be, cennan]

BEKNOWE, *pp.*, acknowledged; well-known. 3.32.

BEKNOWEN, *v.*, acknowledge; confess. 5.113. [OE becnāwan]

BELEVE, *adv.*, belive, quickly. 7. 164.

BELEVE, *n.*, creed. 5.7, 8.156. [OE gelēafa]

BELY, *n.*, belly, stomach. pr. 41. [OE belg]

BELOUGH, *v. pret.* BELAUGHEN, laughed at, looked on favorably. 8.103. [OE be, hlōh]

BELOUREN, *v.*, frown at, scowl at. 8. 103. [? OE *lūrian]

BELOWEN, *v. pp.*, lied about. 5. 76. [OE belēogan, *pp.* belogen]

BEN, *v. pres. pl.*, are. pr. 94.

BENE, *n.*, bean. 7. 165, 169, 201. [OE bēan]

BENEFICES, *n.*, possessions. 11. 192. [OF benefice, L beneficium]

BENIMAN, *v.*, take away. 7. 225. [OE beniman]

BENOM, *v. pret.* BENIMAN, took away. 7. 225.

BEQUEST, *n.*, will, testament. 7. 77.

BERE, *v. pret. pl.* BEREN, bore. 5. 201. [OE bæron]

BEREVEN, *v.*, bereave, take away. 7. 230. [OE berēafian]

BERGH, *n.*, hill. 6. 67. [OE berg, beorh]

BERYNG, *n.*, bearing, conduct. 10. 111.

BERITH, *v. imperat. pl.* BEREN, bear. 8. 132.

BERNE, *n.*, barn. 4. 44. [OE bere-ærn, bern]

BESEKEN, BESECHEN, *v.*, beseech, pray. 5. 52, 244. [OE sēcan]

BESY, *adj.*, busy. 1. 6. [OE KENT besig]

BESITTEN, *v.*, encompass, assail. 2. 105. [OE besittan]

BESSHETTEN, *v.*, shut up, imprison. 2. 175. [OE scyttan]

BESWYNKEN, *v.*, earn by labor. 7. 199. [OE beswincan]

BET, *v. pp.* BETEN, beaten. 4. 80.

BET, *adv.*, better. pr. 63. [OE bet]

BETEN, *v.*, beat. 4. 94, 7. 71, 11. 132. [OE· bēatan]

BETEN, *v.*, remedy, cure. 7. 221, 8. 30. [OE bētan]

BEVERECHIS, *n.*, drinks. 5. 187. [OF bevrage]

BICCHE, *n.*, female dog. 5. 195. [OE bicce]

BIDDEN, *v.*, pray, ask, beg. 1. 138. [OE biddan]

BIDDERE, *n.*, beggar. pr. 40. [OE biddere]

BIDDYNG, *n.*, command. 1. 75; begging. 3. 204. [OE bēodung, biddung]

BIDOWE, *n.*, a curved dagger. 11. 211.

BIEN FAITES, *n.*, good deeds. 6. 98. *See* FAIT. [OF bien faites]

BIENALIS, *n.*, masses said for a period of two years. 8. 151. [L biennalis]

BIGGEN, *v.*, buy. 3. 69. [OE bycgan]

BYGGERE, *n.*, buyer. 2. 44, 11. 209.

BYGIRDLES, *n.*, purses. 9. 79. [OE bīgyrdel]

BILLE, *n.*, a legal statement of particulars by the plaintiff. 4. 34. [AF bille, L billa]

BYMENEN, *v.*, mean, signify. 1. 1. [OE mǣnan]

BYRDE, *n.*, lady. 3. 14. [OE brȳd]

BISECHEN, BYSEKEN, *v.*, beseech, ask, pray. 1. 58; intercede. 12. 116. [OE sēcan]

BISSHOP, *n.*, bishop. pr. 66. [OE biscop]

BITEL-BROWID, *adj.*, with shaggy, overhanging eyebrows. 5. 108.

BITTIR, *n.*, bitterness. 5. 98. [OE bitter]

BLAMEN, *v.*, blame, accuse. 3. 260, 5. 74, 206, 10. 66. [OF blamer]

BLEDEN, *v.*, cause to bleed. 7. 167. [OE blēdan]

BLENCHEN, *v.*, blench; shrink from, turn aside. 6. 67. [OE blencean]

BLEREN, *v.*, blear (a person's eye); deceive, fool. pr. 71.

BLEUGH, *v. pret.* BLOWEN, blew. 5. 191. [OE blēow]

BLISSEN, *v.*, bless, confirm. pr. 75, 3. 136, 8. 13. [OE bledsian, bletsian, blessian, *confused with* blis, blissian]

BLISSING, *n.*, blessing. 7. 236.

BLODY, *adj.*, by blood, kindred. 7. 193. [OE blōdig]

BLUSTREN, *v.*, rush wildly, hastily. 6. 2.

BOCHER, *n.*, butcher. pr. 98. [OF bocher]

BODE, *n.*, command, message. 2. 51, 3. 248. *See* FORBODE. [OE bod]

BOY, *n.*, rude fellow. pr. 77, 11. 61.

BOYSTE, *n.*, box. 12. 69. [OF boiste]

BOLLE, *n.*, bowl. 5. 88. [OE bolla]

BOLLNYNG, *n.*, swelling. 7. 201.

BOLNEN, *v.*, swell. 5. 98. [ON bólgna]

BOLNID, *pp.*, swollen; enraged. 5. 66.

BONDEMAN, *n.*, villein, serf. pr. 96. [OE bonda]

BOORD, *n.*, table. 2. 52. BORD, 7. 249. [OE bord]

BOOT, BOT, *n.*, boat. 9. 25, 26, 31, 37, 43, 10. 162. [OE bāt]

BOR, *n.*, boar. 7. 32. [OE bār]

BOREWE, *n.*, pledge. 1. 75. [OE borg]

BORUGH, *n.*, 4. 76, 11. 90. *See* BOREWE.

BOST, *n.*, boast; arrogance. 1. 111.

BOT, *v. pret.* BITEN, bit. 5. 66. [OE bāt]

BOTE, *n.*, remedy, cure, medicine; amends, compensation. 4. 76. [OE bōt]

BOTERASID, *pp.*, buttressed. 6. 76. [OF bouterets]

BOTHE, *adv.*, also. 7. 154, 11. 168. [ON báðir]

BOTNID, *pp.*, improved, cured, bettered. 7. 177. [OE bōt]

BOUGHEN, *v.*, bend, bow; turn one's way. 6. 53. [OE būgan]

BOUGHTE, *v. pret.* BIGGEN, redeemed. 2. 3. [OE bohte]

BOUN, *adj.*, ready, prepared. 2. 124, 3. 242. [ON búinn]

BOUR, *n.*, private room. 3. 14. [OE būr]

BOURNE, *n.*, burn, brook. pr. 8. [OE burna]

BRAYNWOOD, *adj.*, brain-mad, mad. 10. 61. [OE brægen, wōd]

BRAK, *v. pret.* BREKEN, broke. 1. 111. [OE bræc]

BRAS, *n.*, brass; ? brazen armor. 3. 181. [OE bræs]

BRAST, *v. pret.* BERSTEN, burst. 7. 163. [OE bærst, bræst]

BREDE, *n.*, breadth. 2. 61. [OE brǣdu]

BREKEN, *v.*, break; divide, distribute. 11. 185. [OE brecan]

BREKEN UP, *v.*, break in, through. 4. 44.

BREMERE, *adj.*, stronger. 10. 56. [OE brēmra]

BREMEST, *adj.*, strongest. 10.55.

BREN, *n.*, bran. 7. 267. [OF bren]

BRENNEN, *v.*, burn. 3. 247. [OE brennan]

BRERE, *n.*, briar. 10. 120. [OE brēr]

BRETFUL, *adj.*, brimful, completely stuffed. pr. 41. [OE brerd]

BRETONER, *n.*, braggart. 7. 141, 161.

BREUGH, *v. pret.* BREWEN, brewed. 5. 132.

BREUSTER, *n.*, brewer, male or female. pr. 98. [OE brēowan]

BREVET, *n.*, letter of indulgence. pr. 71. [OF brevet]

BRIDDIS, *n.*, birds. 9. 55, 58. [OE bridd]

BRITEL, *adj.*, frail, brittle. 9. 37. [OE *brytel]

BROCHE, *n.*, brooch. pr. 72. [OF broche]

BROCHEN, *v.*, stitch together. 5. 125.

BROK, *n.*, brook. 6. 53. [OE brōc]

BROKEN, *pp.*, torn. 5. 88. [OE brocen]

BROL, *n.*, wretched child. 3. 190.

BROOD, *adj.*, broad. pr. 8. [OE brād]

BRUGG, *n.*, bridge. 8. 30. [OE brycg]

BUFFETEN, *v.*, slap, strike. 7. 161. [OF bufet]

BUKKE, *n.*, buck. 7. 32. [OE bucca]

BULLE, *n.*, a papal edict, document. pr. 66. [L bulla]

BUMMEN, *v.*, drink deeply, become intoxicated. 5. 136, 7. 138.

BUNCHEN, *v.*, strike. pr. 71.

BURDOUN, *n.*, pilgrim's staff. 6. 5. [OF bourdon]

BURGAGE, *n.*, property, building, especially in a town. 3. 74. [OF bourgage]

BURGEIS, *n.*, citizens, townspeople. pr. 96. [OF burgeis]

BUSKEN, *v.*, prepare to go, go; hasten. 3. 14, 10. 162. [ON búask]

BUT, *conj.*, unless. pr. 63. [OE būtan]

BUT YIF, *conj.*, unless. 1. 155. [OE būtan gif]

BUXUM, *adj.*, pliant; obedient. 1. 108. [OE būhsum]

BUXUMNESSE, *n.*, obedience, humility. 1. 111.

C

CABAN, *n.*, hut. 3. 176. [OF cabane]

CACCHEN, *v.*, catch. 2. 154, 7. 128; chase. 7. 183. [ONF cachier, OF chacier]

CAIREN, *v.*, go, proceed. pr. 29, 4. 22. *See* CARIEN. [ON keyra]

CAITYF, *n.*, wretch. 5. 113. [OF caitif]

CALABRE, *n.*, a gray fur, with black belly. 7. 254.

CAN, *v.*, know. 3. 3. [OE cunnan, can]

CANONISTRIS, *n.*, canonists, pro-

GLOSSARY

fessors of canon law. 8.130. [OF canoniste]

CAPEL, *n.*, horse. 2.126. [ON kapall]

CARDINAL, *adj.*, chief, supreme. 12. 15. [L cardinalis]

CARDIT, *v. pp.*, carded, combed. 11.18. [OF carder]

CAREYN, *n.*, body. 7.83. [OF careigne]

CAREN, *v.*, care for, want. 2.126. [OE caru]

CARFUL, *adj.*, burdened with care. 1.177. [OE caru]

CARFULLICHE, *adv.*, anxiously. 5. 59.

CARIEN, *v.*, carry; betake oneself, go. 2.126, 5.146. [OF carier]

CARPEN, *v.*, tell, say. 2.153. [ON karpa]

CARPING, *n.*, speech, talking. 11. 95.

CARTESADILEN, *v.*, saddle with a small saddle which is part of a harness; harness. 2.141. [OE cræt, sadol]

CARTEWEY, *n.*, cartroad. 3.119.

CAS, *n.*, condition, fortune; misfortune. 8.51. [OF cas]

CASTEN, *v.*, cast, throw. 9.94; contrive, devise. 3.18; give. 7.15; put on (clothes). 7.54. [ON kasta]

CATEL, *n.*, movable property, goods; cattle. 3.249. [ONF catel]

CATELES, *adj.*, without property, destitute. 10.68.

CAURY-MAURY, *n.*, ? rough cloth; ? large cloak. 5.61.

CERTIS, *adv.*, certainly. 2.116. [OF cert]

CESEN, CESSEN, *v.*, cease. 2.116, 8.100. [OF cesser]

CHAFFARE, *n.*, merchandise, wares; trade, buying and selling. pr. 31, 5.142, 173. [OE cēap, faru]

CHANOUN, *n.*, canon. 10.109. [OF chanone]

CHAPELLEN, *n.*, chaplain. 1.164, 7.20. [OF chapelein]

CHAPMAN, *n.*, peddler, buyer or seller. pr. 61. [OE cēapman]

CHARGE, *n.*, blame. 10.73. [OF charge]

CHARTRES, *n.*, documents showing ownership of real property. 2. 35. [OF chartre]

CHASTEN, *v.*, punish. 4.103, 11. 195. [OF chastier]

CHAUD, *adj.*, hot. 7.295. [OF chaud]

CHAUMBRE, *n.*, chamber, private room. 3.10. [OF chambre]

CHAUNCERIE, *n.*, chancery court. 4.26. [OF chancellerie]

CHEKER, *n.*, exchequer. 4.26. [OF eschequier]

CHEKIS, *n.*, cheeks. 4.37, 7.145. [OE cēace]

CHELE, *n.*, chill, cold. 1.23. [OE cēle]

CHEPYNG, *n.*, market. 4.43, 7.283. [OE cēapung]

CHERE, *n.*, face; appearance. 11.2. [OF chiere, AF chere]

CHERL, *n.*, serf, peasant. 3.244. [OE ceorl]

CHERUBYN, *n.*, cherubim. 1.104.

CHESIBLE, *n.*, chasuble, priest's

robe. 7. 20. (*See Introduction*).
[OF chasuble]

CHESTE, *n.*, strife, quarrelling. 10.
187. [OE cēast]

CHEVEN, *v.*, achieve, accomplish.
pr. 31. [OF achever]

CHEVISSHEN, *v.*, keep clear, save.
10. 73. [OF chevir, cheviss-]

CHEWEN, *v.*, chew; consume. 1.
167. [OE cēowan]

CHIBOLLE, *n.*, a vegetable intermediate between an onion and a
leek. 7. 278. [OF cibole]

CHIDEN, *v.*, chide, quarrel; strive.
1. 167. [OE cīdan]

CHIEF, *n.*, principal person. pr.
61. [OF chief]

CHIEF, *adj.*, principal. 6. 107.

CHIRIVELLE, *n.*, chervil. 7. 278.
[OE cerfille]

CHOPPIS, *n.*, blows, disputes. 10.
187.

CYVYLE, *n.*, civil law. 2. 54. [L
civilis]

CLAUSE, *n.*, clause, phrase; an
entry in a document. 4. 133,
8. 44, 8. 90. [OF clause]

CLEYMEN, *v.*, proclaim, publish,
cry aloud. 1. 91. [OF clamer,
claime (*subj.*)]

CLENE, *adj.*, pure. 1. 169, 3. 21,
etc. [OE clǣne]

CLEPEN, *v.*, call. *pp.* YCLEPID,
called. 11. 21. [OE cleopian]

CLERGIE, *n.*, clergy; learning. 3. 15,
150, 11. 65, 286. [OF clergie]

CLERJOUN, *n.*, young scholar,
school-boy. 12. 49. [OF clerjon]

CLERK, *n.*, clerk, *i. e.*, an educated

man, an ecclesiastic. 3. 3. [OE
clerc]

CLERMATYN, *n.*, fine wheat bread.
7. 288.

CLIKET, *n.*, key. 6. 91. [OF cliquet]

CLIKETEN, *v.*, lock. 6. 100.

CLOKKEN, *v.*, limp, halt. 3. 33.
[OF cloquer]

CLOSEN, *v.*, enclose. 10. 5, 12. 105.
[AF clos]

CLOUT, *n.*, clothing. 2. 182. [OE
clūt]

CLOUTEN, *v.*, patch. 7. 54.

COKENAY, *n.*, small egg. 7. 269.

COKERE, *n.*, boot; stocking. 7. 55.
[OE cocer]

COKET, *n.*, fine white bread. 7. 288.

COKEWALD, *n.*, cuckold. 4. 140.
[OF cucuault]

COKKISLANE, *n.*, one of the streets
within which women of ill repute
were supposed to be restrained.
5. 161.

COLE PLANT, *n.*, cabbage, colewort,
turnip. 7. 270. [OE caul]

COLLEN, *v.*, embrace. 11. 174. [OF
col]

COLOP, *n.*, an egg fried on bacon;
fried ham and eggs. 7. 269.

COMBREN, *v.*, encumber, injure.
10. 91. [OF combrer]

COMERE, *n.*, random or chance
comer. 2. 43, 192. [OE cuma]

COMISSARIE, *n.*, an officer of the
bishop, who exercises spiritual
jurisdiction in parts of the diocese far distant from the cathedral, where the principal consistory court was held. 2. 141,
3. 130. [OF comissier]

COMPSEN, COMSEN, *v.*, commence, begin. 1. 128, 10. 98. [OF commencer]

COMUNES, *n.*, common property. 5. 38. [OF comun]

COMUNES, *n.*, common people. 3. 65.

CONFORTEN, COUNFORTEN, *v.*, comfort. 1. 177. [OF conforter]

CONYON, *n.*, wretch, stupid fellow. 11. 86.

CONNEN, *v.*, know, know how, understand. pr. 33. [OE cunnan]

CONNYNG, *n.*, knowledge, wit. 10. 50.

CONSEIVEN, *v.*, conceive, think; utter. 7. 35; understand. 9. 48. [OF concever]

CONSTABLE, *n.*, officer who makes arrests. 4. 72. [OF conestable]

CONSTORIE, *n.*, ecclesiastical court; church council; assembly of prelates. 2. 139. [OF consistorie]

CONSTRUEN, *v.*, interpret, translate. pr. 58, 4. 128, 4. 133, 8. 90, 130. [OF construire]

CONTERFETEN, *v.*, contrive. 11. 19. [OF contrefet]

CONTRA, *adv.*, on the contrary. 9. 16. [L]

COPE, *n.*, cloak (of friar, monk, hermit). pr. 53.

COPEN, *v.*, clothe in copes. 2. 192.

CORN, *n.*, grain, wheat. 6. 32. [OE corn]

COROUNE, *n.*, crown. 2. 10. [OF corone]

COROUNEN, *v.*, crown. 2. 10.

CORS, *n.*, living body. 1. 128. [OF cors]

CORSEINT, *n.*, holy body, body of a saint. 6. 20.

COSYN, *n.*, cousin, relation; kin. 2. 97, 11. 104.

COSTIS, *n.*, coasts, regions. 9. 12. [OF coste]

COTEN, *v.*, clothe. 3. 130. [OF cote]

COTIDIAN, *n.*, quotidian, daily fever. 12. 84. [OF cotidian]

COUDEN, *v. pret.* CONNEN, made known. 8. 44.

COUNFORTEN, *v.*, comfort. 1. 177. [OF conforter]

COUNSEIL, *n.*, counsel. 9. 98; council. 3. 88, 102. [OF concile, conseil]

COUNSEILEN, *v.*, counsel, advise. 1. 64.

COUNTEN, *v.*, count; esteem. 7. 154. [OF conter]

COUP, *n.*, cup, bowl. 3. 21.

COUPLEN, *v.*, couple, join. 3. 150. [OF cople]

COURT, *n.*, enclosure; building. 6. 72. [OF cort, court]

COURTEPY, *n.*, short coat. 5. 62.

COUTHE, *v. pret.* CONNEN, could; knew, knew how. 4. 41, 142, 5. 24, 111, 178, 6. 1, 9. 67, 118, 11. 93. [OE cūþe]

COVEITEN, *v.*, desire. pr. 29. [OF coveiter]

COVEITISE, *n.*, covetousness. pr. 58.

COVENAUNT, *n.*, agreement. 7. 29. [OF covenant]

COVENT, *n.*, convent. 11. 207. [OF covent, convent]

CRABBIDE, *adj.*, cross, angry. 11. 65.

CRAFT, *n.*, skill, art; knowledge; trade. pr. 101; a plot. 3. 18; dishonesty. 5. 138. [OE cræft]

CRAFTY, *adj.*, belonging to the crafts, trades. 3. 210, 11. 182.

CRAVEN, *v.*, ask, demand. 3. 207. [OE crafian]

CREDE, *n.*, creed. 7. 81.

CREM, *n.*, cream. 7. 266. [OF creme]

CROCE, *n.*, crosier, bishop's staff. 9. 86. [OF croce]

CROFT, *n.*, a small enclosed field. 6. 59. [OE croft]

CROPE, *v. pret.* CREPEN, crept. 3. 176. [OE crēopan, crupon]

CROPPEN, *v.*, devour. 7. 34. [ON kroppa]

CROUCH, *n.*, cross. 6. 10.

CRUDDIS, *n.*, curds. 7. 266.

CUFF, *n.*, glove, mitten. 7. 55.

CULORUM, *n.*, end; logical outcome. 3. 255. [L]

CULTIR, *n.*, colter. 7. 96.

CUMSEN, *v.*, *See* COMPSEN.

CUNGEN, *v.*, dismiss, give leave to depart. 3. 159, 4. 4. [OF congier]

CUNNEN, *v.*, *See* CONNEN.

CUNNYNG, *adj.*, learned, intelligent. 3. 33.

CUNTENAUNCE, *n.*, appearance, mien, looks; show. pr. 24. [OF contenance]

CUNTRE, *n.*, country. pr. 95. [OF contree]

CUPPE, *n.*, cup. 5. 182, 186. [OE cuppe]

CUPPE-MEL, *adv.*, a cupful at a time. 5. 138.

CURATOUR, *n.*, curate, priest, clergyman with care of souls. 1. 169. [OF curatier]

CURTEIS, *adj.*, courteous. 4. 17. [OF corteis]

CURTEISIE, *n.*, courtesy. 1. 20.

CUTTEPURS, *n.*, cut-purse. 6. 115.

D

DAFFE, *n.*, fool. 1. 129.

DAY-STERRE, *n.*, day-star, sun. 6. 80.

DAMYSELE, *n.*, damsel, maid. 10. 12. [OF damoisele]

DAMPNEN, *v.*, condemn. 5. 245. [OF damner]

DAUNSELID, *v. pp.*, cherished, honored. 11. 30.

DAUNTEN, *v.*, subdue, vanquish. 3. 261. [OF danter]

DEBATE, *n.*, contention; quarrel. 5. 180. [OF debat]

DECLYNEN, *v.*, decline; parse (Latin). 4. 133. [OF decliner]

DEDE, *v. pret.* DON, did. 1. 28; made, caused. 9. 90; should act (*subj.*). 9. 92. [OE dēdun]

DEDIS, *n.*, legal documents. 12. 87. [OE dǣd]

DEFAUTE, *n.*, default. 2. 104; need, famine. 8. 142. [OF defaute]

DEFENDEN, *v.*, forbid. 3. 53. [OF defendre]

DEFIEN, *v.*, digest. pr. 108, 5. 211. [OF defier]

DEFOULEN, *v.*, trample on, profane. 11. 60. [OF defouler]

DEIEN, DEIGHEN, DIGHEN, *v.*, die. 1. 141.

DEYNEN, *v.*, deign. 7. 292. [OF deigner]

DEYNOUS, *adj.*, disdainful, proud. 9. 75.

DEIS, *n.*, daïs, high table. 8. 19, 11. 43. [OF deis]

DELEN, *v.*, deal out, distribute; give alms. 1. 173; have to do with. 7. 67, 8. 73. [OE dǣlan]

DELITABLE, *adj.*, delightful, pleasant. 1. 32. [OF delit]

DELVEN, *v.*, dig. 6. 33, 11. 184. [OE delfan]

DELVERE, *n.*, farm laborer. pr. 102.

DEMEN, *v.*, judge, condemn; give an opinion; suppose, think; say. 1. 84, 3. 173, 5. 94, 7. 73, 8. 150. [OE dēman]

DEN, *n.*, dean. pr. 92. [OF dean, deien] *doien*

DENT, *n.*, blow, stroke. 12. 104. [OE dynt]

DEPARTID, *v. pp.*, divided. 8. 137. [OF departir]

DEPRAVEN, *v.*, defame, slander. 3. 164. [OF depraver]

DERE, *adj.*, dear, beloved. 1. 85. [OE dēore]

DEREN, DERIEN, *v.*, harm, injure. 8. 37, 53. [OE derian]

DERK, *adj.*, dark. pr. 16. [OE deorc]

DERNE, *adj.*, secret. 10. 199. [OE derne]

DERWORTH, *adj.*, precious. 1. 85. [OE dēorwurþe]

DESCRYVEN, *v.*, describe. 5. 61. [OF descrivre]

DESTRER, *n.*, horse; war-horse. 2. 137. [OF destrier]

DESTROIEN, *v.*, destroy, waste. pr. 22. [OF destruire]

DETTE, *n.*, debt. 5. 144. [OF dette]

DEVER, *n.*, duty. 12. 2. [OF devoir]

DEVYNEN, *v.*, interpret. 8. 133, 138.

DEWID, *v. pp.*, endowed. 11. 196, 198. [OF douer]

DYAPENDYON, *n.*, an expectorant made of sugared thread. 5. 100.

DID, *v. pret.* DON, caused, made. 1. 97. [OE dyde]

DIGHTEN, *v.*, prepare, make ready. 2. 137. [OE dihtan]

DIGNELICHE, *adv.*, worthily. 8. 152.

DIGNITE, *n.*, worthiness; high office. pr. 92. [OF dignite]

DIKE, *n.*, ditch, dike; ditch with a ridge of earth. pr. 16. [OE dīc]

DYKEN, *v.*, dig ditches and throw up a ridge of earth. 6. 33, 11. 184. [OE dīcian]

DIKERE, *n.*, ditcher, laborer. pr. 102.

DISGISEN, *v.*, dress, attire, clothe in ostentatious or fantastic fashion. pr. 24. [OF desguiser]

DISOUR, *n.*, professional storyteller, jester. 7. 49, 11. 30. [OF disour]

DISSEYVEN, *v.*, deceive. pr. 76. [OF deceveir]

DISSHERE, *n.*, dish-seller, dish-maker. 5.165. [OE disc]

DITTEN, *v.*, close, shut; put out, drive away. 7.176. [OE dyttan]

DYVYNOUR, *n.*, interpreter, commentator. 11.293.

DOCTOR, *n.*, learned scholar, doctor (of divinity, laws, etc.). 2.73. [L doctor]

DOEL, *n.*, grief, sorrow. 7.112. [OF duel, AF doel, dol]

DOKE, *n.*, duck. 5.57.

DOLES, *n.*, alms. 3.61. [OE dal]

DOLVEN, *v. pp.* DELVEN, dug. 7.170; *pret. pl.*, dug. 7.176.

DOMISDAY, *n.*, judgment day. 5.20. [OE dōmes dæg]

DON, *v.*, do, make, cause; cite. 2.157, 173, 3.123, 5.76, 77, 7.49, 77, 258, 8.158, 9.13, 68, 93; betake oneself. 5.224, 10.188; give, entrust. 10.11. Do IT ON, call to witness. 1.84, 3.173. Do HYM LAWE, execute law on him. 3.266. [OE dōn]

DONET, *n.*, primer, reading book. 5.122.

DONGE, *n.*, dung, manure. 4.130.

DOOM, *n.*, judgment. 2.169. [OE dōm]

DORENAIL, *n.*, doornail. 1.161.

DOTIDE, *adj.*, foolish. 1.129.

DOUGHTIEST, *adj.*, mightiest, greatest. 11.293. [OE dyhtigost]

DOUNES, *n.*, downs, hills. 10.167. [OE dūn]

DOUTE, *n.*, fear. 9.60, 10.82, 11.290. [OF doute]

DOUTEN, *v.*, fear. 10.80.

DRAF, *n.*, hogwash, refuse. 11.11. [OE *dræf]

DRAPERE, *n.*, dealer in cloth. 5.122. [OF draper]

DRAVELEN, *v.*, slobber, drool. 11.11; chatter, talk foolishly. 11.43. [OE *draflian]

DRAWEN, *v.*, draw, pull, stretch. 5.123; DRAWE FORTH, advanced, praised. 11.30. [OE dragan]

DRENCHEN, *v.*, drown. 9.46, 10.60. [OE drencan]

DREURY, *n.*, treasure. 1.85. [OF drut, druerie]

DRIEN, DRIGHEN, *v.*, become dry. 1.25. [OE drygan]

DRIGHT, *n.*, man. 9.60. [OE dryht]

DRIT, *n.*, dung, manure. 7.176. [ON drítr]

DRYVELEN, *v.*, *See* DRAVELEN.

DROUGH, *v. pret.* DRAWEN, drew. 5.122, 198, 11.94. [OE drōg]

DRUNKELEWE, *adj.*, drunken, addicted to drink. 9.75. [ME drunke, -lewe]

DUBBEN, *v.*, strike; dub; knight. 1.96. [OE dubbian]

DUNGEOUN, *n.*, dungeon. pr. 15. [OF dongeon]

DUREN, *v.*, endure, last. 1.76. [OF durer]

DURSTE, *v. pret.* DURREN, DAR, dared. 2.196, 3.187, 9.113.

E

EFT, *adv.*, again; back. 4.94, 6.101, 11.81. [OE eft]

EFT-SONES, *adv.*, soon after. 5. 248. [OE eft, sōna]

EGGEN, *v.*, urge on, incite. 1. 63, 10. 52. [ON eggja]

EIGHE, EIE, *n.*, eye. pr. 71. [OE ēage]

EILEN, *v.*, ail. 7. 120. [OE eglan]

EIR, *n.*, air. 1. 114. [OF air]

EIRES, *n.*, heirs. 2. 67, 10. 204. [OF heir]

EK, *conj.*, eke, also. 1. 1. [OE ēac]

ELDE, *n.*, age. 3. 87. [OE eldu]

ELDREN, *n.*, ancestors. 3. 239.

ELLES, *adv.*, else. 1. 51. [OE elles]

ELLIR, *n.*, elder tree. 1. 66. [OE ellen]

ENGENDREN, *v.*, engender, beget. 2. 83. [OF engendrer]

ENGENDROUR, *n.*, begetter, originator. 7. 216.

ENY, *adj.*, any. 7. 238. [OE ǣnig]

ENJOYNEN, *v.*, join, put together. 10. 4. [OF enjoindre]

ENLEVENE, *num. adj.*, eleven. 8. 141. [OE endleofan]

ENSAUMPLE, *n.*, example; illustrative story. 1. 146, 4. 119, 8. 110; warning. 5. 17. [OF ensample]

ENVYE, *n.*, hatred, despite. 5. 53, 6. 96. [OF envye]

ER, *adv.*, before, formerly. 1. 123. [OE ǣr]

ERANDE, *n.*, message. 3. 40. [OE ǣrende]

ERD, *n.*, home, dwelling. 7. 187. [OE eard]

ERE, *n.*, ear. pr. 75. [OE ēare]

EREN, ERIEN, *v.*, plow. 7. 4. [OE erian]

ERGO, *adv., conj.*, therefore. 9. 20. [L]

ERITAGE, *n.*, heritage. 11. 227, 234. [OF heritage]

ERL, *n.*, earl, one of the greatest nobles. 3. 198. [OE eorl]

ERLICHE, *adv.*, early. 5. 167.

ERMYTE, *n.*, hermit, recluse. pr. 3. (*See Introduction*). [OF ermite]

ERTHE, *n.*, earth; land, country. 1. 7. [OE eorþe]

ESE, *n.*, ease. pr. 54. [OF aise]

EST, *n.*, east. pr. 13. [OE ēast]

EVAUNGELIE, *n.*, evangel, gospel. 1. 174.

EVEN, EVE, *n.*, evening. 5. 14. [OE ǣfen]

EVENE, *adv.*, equally, justly. 4. 147. [OE efen]

EVENSONG, *n.*, the last church service of the day. 5. 188. (*See Introduction*).

EVIL, *adj.*, difficult. 11. 152. [OE yfel]

EXCUSEN, *v.*, excuse; prove innocent. 3. 158. [OF excuser]

F

FADER, *n.*, father. 1. 14. [OE fæder]

FAILEN, *v.*, lack, be deprived of. 11. 204. [OF faillir]

FAIR, *adj.*, beautiful. pr. 17. [OE fæger]

FAIRE, *adv.*, beautifully, well. 1. 2.

FAIRIE, *n.*, enchantment. pr. 6. [OF faerie]

FAIT, *n.*, deed. 1. 160. *See* BIEN
FAITES. [OF fait]

FAYTEN, *v.*, deceive; beg under
false pretences. pr. 42, 8. 77.
[OF fait]

FAITOUR, *n.*, deceiver, pretender,
liar. 2. 94. [OF faitour]

FALLEN, *v.*, happen, befall. pr.
62, 2. 159, 10. 179; fall to, belong to. 1. 140. [OE feallan]

FALSHED, *n.*, falsehood. 1. 62, 2.
50.

FALSNESSE, *n.*, falseness. pr. 68.

FAME, *n.*, ill repute. 5. 74. [OF
fame]

FAMEN, *v.*, defame, calumniate.
3. 171. [OF famer]

FAND, *v. pret.* FINDEN, found. pr.
17. [OE fand]

FANTASIES, *n.*, fantastic imagin-
ings, confusions of meanings.
pr. 36, 11. 63. [OF fantasie]

FAREN, *v.*, go. 2. 145; happen.
9. 33. [OE faran]

FASTE, *adv.*, tightly, firmly, closely.
1. 42, 94, 2. 162, 3. 127; swiftly.
1. 113, 4. 22, 68. [OE fæste]

FAUCON, *n.*, falcon. 7. 33. [OF
faucon]

FAUNT, *n.*, child, infant. 8. 77, 10.
58. [OF fant]

FAVEL, *n.*, flattery; deceit; hypo-
crisy. 2. 6, 23. [OF fauvel]

FE, *n.*, property; money; bribe.
4. 114, 6. 68. [OE feoh]

FEBICCHIS, *n.*, ? hobgoblins; ? con-
trivances. 11. 156.

FECCHEN, *v.*, fetch. 3. 89. [OE
feccan, fetian]

FEFFEN, *v.*, endow, give to; put in
possession of. 2. 37, 47, 58, 111.
[OF fieffer, AF feffer]

FEFFEMENT, *n.*, deed of endowment. 2. 55. [AF feoffement]

FEYNTISE, *n.*, faintness, weakness.
5. 5, 12. 67, 68. [OF feintise]

FEIR, *n.*, fair, market. 4. 43, 5.
118. [OF feire]

FEL, *n.*, skin. 1. 15. [OE fell]

FEL, *v. pret.* FALLEN, happened.
8. 138.

FELASSHIPE, *n.*, companionship.
3. 106.

FELAWE, *n.*, companion. 1. 112.
[OE fēolaga]

FELD, *n.*, field. pr. 17. [OE feld]

FELLEN, *v.*, strike down. 3. 41.
[OE fellen]

FELOUN, *n.*, felon, criminal. 5. 246,
11. 271. [OF felon]

FEND, *n.*, fiend, foe; the devil.
1. 38, 112, 7. 80, 9. 38, 45, 10. 64.
[OE fēond]

FENEL, *n.*, fennel. 5. 155. [OF
fenoil, OE finugl, fenol]

FER, FEER, *n.*, fear. 2. 171. [OE
fǣr]

FER, *adv., adj.*, far. 9. 70. [OE
feorr]

FERE, *n.*, companion, partner. 2. 6.
[OE gefēra]

FERLY, *n.*, strange thing, wonder.
pr. 6, 62, 12. 58. [OE fǣrlic]

FERS, *adj.*, frail, inclined to sin.
5. 49.

FERST, *adj., adv.*, first. 1. 74. [OE
fyrst]

FERTHERE, *adv.*, further. 2. 163.

FERTHING, *n.*, farthing, one-fourth

of a penny. 4. 41. [OE fēorþing, -ung]

FERTHING-WORTH, *n.*, farthing-worth; a very small amount. 5. 155.

FEST, *n.*, fist. 5. 67. [OE fyst]

FESTIS, *n.*, feasts. 11. 60. [OF feste]

FETEREN, *v.*, fetter, enchain, lock up. 2. 162. [OE gefeterian]

FETISLICHE, *adv.*, suitably, handsomely, elegantly. 2. 130. [OF faitis, faitissement]

FETTEN, *v.*, fetch, bring. 2. 49. [OE fetian, WS feccean]

FIKEL, *adj.*, changeable, false. 3. 109. [OE ficol]

FIL, *v. pret.* FALLEN, fell. 1. 112. [OE KENT fīoll]

FYN, *n.*, legally paid sum of money to king or lord upon transfer or inheritance of property. 2. 36. [OF fin, L finis]

FYNDEN, *v.*, find. pr. 17; provide, provide for, support. 2. 50, 10. 70. [OE findan]

FYNT, *v. 3d sg. pres.* FYNDEN, finds. 4. 114.

FIRSEN, *n.*, furze. 5. 193.

FISICIAN, *n.*, physician. 7. 168.

FISIK, *n.*, physic, medicine. 7. 253. [OF fisique]

FLAPPEN, *v.*, beat, flap. 7. 172.

FLATTEN, *v.*, dash, slap. 5. 216. [OF flatir]

FLEIGH, *v. pret.* FLEWEN, fled. 2. 172. [OE flēah]

FLESSH, *n.*, meat. 7. 144. [OE flǣsc]

FLICCHE, *n.*, flitch, side of bacon. 10. 189. [OE flicce]

FLOREYN, *n.*, florin, gold coin of value of (*approx.*) 6s. 8d. 2. 108. [OF florin]

FLOWEN, *v. pret.* FLEWEN, fled. 2. 195.

FOLEWEN, *v.*, follow. 3. 7. [OE folgian]

FOLIES, *n.*, follies. 10. 70. [OF folie]

FOLIS, *n.*, foals. 2. 127. [OE fola]

FOLIS, *n.*, fools. 2. 144. [OF fol]

FON, *n.*, foes. 5. 77. [OE fāh]

FOND, *v. pret.* FYNDEN, found. pr. 55. [OE fond, fand]

FONDEN, *v.*, try; prove; endeavor. 7. 205. [OE fandian]

FONGEN, *v.*, receive, take. 6. 45. [OE fōn, *pp.* fongen]

FOR, *prep.*, (1) for the sake of. 1. 56; for the benefit of. 1. 91.

(2) as an object of. 3. 204, 10. 108.

(3) because of, on account of. 1. 27, 116, 3. 176, 178, 8. 129, 142, 143, 11. 78, 11. 269.

(4) in spite of. 2. 32, 59, 139, 161, 162, 168, 3. 246.

(5) against. 1. 24, 2. 192, 5. 217, 222, 7. 9, 15, 55, 295, 11. 72, 73.

(6) as for, with respect to. 8. 132.

FOR, *conj.*, (1) because (*correlative*). pr. 60.

(2) because (*subordinating*). pr. 83, 3. 248, 5. 105, 10. 173, 11. 273, 12. 109.

(3) in order that. 1. 40, 4. 27, 6. 11.

(4) in spite of the fact that. 3. 18.

FOR THAT, *conj.*, because. 4. 54.

FOR TO, *conj.*, (1) to, in order to. pr. 27, 47, 1. 16, 131, 2. 186. (2) until. 6. 54.

FORBODE, *n.*, prohibition. 4. 157. [OE forbod]

FORBODEN, *pp.*, forbidden. 3. 139.

FORBRENNEN, *v.*, burn completely. 3. 85. [OE for-brennan]

FORDON, *v.*, destroy utterly. 5. 20. [OE for-dōn]

FOREBISENE, *n.*, example. 9. 24. [OE fōrebȳsn]

FORELLIS, *n.*, containers; boxes, chests. 11. 156. [OF forel]

FORE-SLEVYS, *n.*, that part of the sleeves on the fore-arm. 5. 63.

FOREWARD, *n.*, agreement. 2. 50, 4. 13, 7. 37. [OE foreweard]

FOREWE, *n.*, furrow. 7. 96. [OE furh]

FORGOERE, *n.*, an officer who went in advance and provided food and lodgings for his lord and retinue. 2. 149.

FORMEST, *adj.*, *adv.*, foremost, first. 10. 127, 11. 161. [OE formest]

FORNICATOUR, *n.*, adulterer. 2. 142. [OF fornicatour]

FORSOTHE, *excl.*, forsooth. 4. 2, 6. 117.

FORSTALLEN, *v.*, forestall; buy up the whole supply of a commodity in advance of the market, so as to raise the price. 4. 43.

FORTH, *n.*, way, journey. 3. 145.

FOR-THI, *conj.*, therefore; because. 1. 123, 149, 180, 3. 59, 8. 162. [OE for þī]

FORTHER, *adv.*, further. 7. 66.

FORTHINKEN, *v.*, repent. 10. 158. [OE for-þencan]

FOR-WANDRED, *pp.*, spent with wandering. pr. 7. [OE wandrian]

FOR-WANYEN, *v.*, spoil by indulgence. 5. 33. [OE for-wenian]

FORWARD, *n.*, agreement. *See* FOREWARD.

FORYELDEN, *v.*, repay amply. 7. 260. [OE forgieldan]

FOULEN, *v.*, befoul, besmirch. 3. 141, 7. 136. [OE fūl]

FOUNDEN, *v.*, found; create; establish. pr. 36, 1. 62. [OF fonder]

FOURMEN, *v.*, form; create. 1. 14, 140, 8. 39. [OF former]

FOURMOUR, *n.*, former, creator. 10. 28.

FRAYNEN, *v.*, ask, question. 1. 56, 6. 13, 9. 3. [OE fregnan, frignan]

FREEL, *adj.*, frail. 3. 109. [OF fraile]

FREKE, *n.*, man. 4. 13, 7. 204, 12. 66. [OE freca]

FRENTYK, *adj.*, insane. 11. 6. [OF frenetique]

FRERE, *n.*, friar. pr. 55. (*See Introduction*). [OF frere]

FRETTEN, *v.*, adorn, decorate. 2. 11. [OE frætwian]

FRITHEN, *v.*, enclose in hedge or row of trees. 6. 68. [OE friþ]

FRO, *prep.*, from. 1. 4. [ON frá]

FROKKE, *n.*, frock. 5. 63. [OF froc]

FUYR, *n.*, fire. 3. 85. [OE fȳr]

FUL, *adv.*, very, extremely. pr. 21. [OE full]

FULLEN, *v.*, become full. 11. 44. [OE fyllan]

FURST, *adj., adv.*, first. 2. 72. [OE fyrst]

G

GADELYNG, *n.*, follower, retainer (frequently disreputable). 4. 38, 10. 203. [OE gædeling]

GAILERE, *n.*, jailer. 3. 125. [OF gaiolier]

GAN, *v. pret. with inf.*, did. pr. 11. [OE gan]

GANGEN, *v.*, walk, go. 2. 132. [OE gangan]

GAREN, *v.*, make; cause. 7. 132, 285, 11. 131. [ON göra]

GAT, *v. pret.* GETEN, got. 4. 65.

GATE, *n.*, way, road. 1. 179, 6. 114, 12. 88. OTHERE GATIS, otherwise. 10. 203. [ON gata]

GATEWARD, *n.*, gate-keeper. 6. 82. [OE geat, ON gat]

GEAUNT, *n.*, giant. 7. 216. [OF geant]

GEOMESIE, *n.*, geomancy, divination made first by figures made on the ground, and later, by dots made on paper. 11. 153. [OF geomancie]

GERTHE, *n.*, girth. 4. 19. [ON gjorþ]

GESTIS, *n.*, stories, history. 11. 23. [OF geste]

GET, *v. 3d sg. pres.* GETEN, gets. 7. 235.

GETEN, *v. pret. pl.* GETEN, begat. 10. 155. [OE gēaton]

GIDE, *n.*, guide. 7. 1. [OF gide]

GYEN, *v.*, guide. 2. 149. [OF guier]

GILE, *n.*, guile. 2. 109. [OF guile]

GILEN, *v.*, beguile, deceive. 8. 71. [OF guiler]

GILOUR, *n.*, deceiver, liar. 2. 85. [OF guileor]

GILT, *n.*, guilt; sin, crime. 3. 8, 95, 4. 65, 88. [OE gylt]

GYNFUL, *adj.*, deceitful. 11. 153. [OF (en)gin, OE -full] *L. ingenium auch: fr. ruse*

GYNNEN, *v.*, begin. 10. 123. [OE -ginnan]

GYNNYNG, *n.*, beginning. 10. 29.

GIRLIS, *n.*, children (of either sex). 10. 155, 11. 131.

GLADCHIERE, *n.*, loud mirth (*probably colloquial*). 5. 168. [OE glæd, OF chiere]

GLADEN, *v.*, please, gratify. 10. 195. [OE gladian]

GLASEN, *v.*, glaze, furnish glass. 3. 48. [OE glæs]

GLE, *n.*, glee; singing, music; entertainment. pr. 34. [OE glēo]

GLEMAN, *n.*, minstrel, probably of the poorer sort; here, a blind minstrel. 5. 195. [OE glēoman]

GLOSEN, *v.*, gloss; interpret, comment upon. pr. 57. [OF gloser]

GLOTONY, *n.*, gluttony. pr. 43. [OF gloutonie]

GLUPPEN, *v.*, swallow or drink greedily till gorged. 5. 189. [OF gloupyon, " a draught "]

GOME, *n.*, man. 2. 56, 6. 22, 12. 69. [OE guma]

GOMMES, *n.*, gums, aromatic gums. 2. 188. [OF gomme]

GONNE, *v. pret. with inf.*, did. 9. 109. [OE -gunnon]

GOODLYCHE, *adv.*, generously. 1. 156.

GORGE, *n.*, throat. 11. 44, 53. [OF gorge]

GOSSIB, *n.*, friend, crony. 5. 151. [OE god, sibb]

GOST, *n.*, spirit, soul. 1. 34. [OE gāst]

GOWE, *v.*, let us go. pr. 105. [OE gā wē]

GRACE, *n.*, grace, favor; permission; success; luck; power. 3. 157, 95, 217, 4. 59, 124, 5. 78, 120, 238, 255, 7. 118, 132. [OF grace]

GRACEN, *v.*, favor, reward; bless. 7. 116.

GRAITH, *adj.*, ready, prepared; direct. 1. 179, 8. 41. [ON greiðr]

GRAUNTEN, *v.*, grant. 1. 147. [OF granter]

GRAVEN, *v.*, engrave, inscribe. 3. 48. [OE grafan]

GRAVYNG, *n.*, engraving, carving, inscription. 3. 53.

GREDEN, *v.*, cry loudly, call. 2. 56, 3. 61. [OE grǣdan]

GREYN, *n.*, grain, particle. 11. 96. [OF grein]

GRETEN, *v.*, weep; cry out. 5. 208. [OE grǣtan]

GRIPEN, *v.*, grip, seize; take. 3. 167, 226. [OE grīpan]

GRIS, *n.*, pigs, little pigs. pr. 105, 4. 38, 7. 265. [ON gríss]

GROME, *n.*, man. 7. 202.

GROTE, *n.*, a coin (silver) equal in weight to four pennies. 3. 125, 11. 34. [MDu groot]

GROWEL, *n.*, gruel, porridge. 7. 167. [OF gruel]

GRUCCHEN, *v.*, complain, grumble. 7. 202, 10. 112. [OF groucher]

GURDEN, *v.*, strike, strike off. 2. 163.

GUT, *n.*, stomach, belly. 1. 34. [OE gutt]

H

HAILSEN, *v.*, salute. 9. 10. [ON heilsa]

HAKENEYMAN, *n.*, hostler, stableman. 5. 160. [OF haquenee, OE man]

HALDEN, *v.*, hold. 2. 36. [OE haldan]

HALF, *n.*, side. 2. 5. [OE half]

HALIDAY, *n.*, holy day. 6. 66. [OE hālig, dæg]

HALLE, *n.*, the great main room in a castle or large building. 2. 38. [OE hall]

HALP, *v. pret.* HELPEN, helped. 11. 31.

HALPENY, *adj.*, half penny; cheap. 7. 289. *See* PENYALE.

HALS, *n.*, neck. 2. 157. [OE hals]

HALSEN, *v.*, embrace; beseech, inquire. 1. 71; salute. 8. 141. [OE halsian]

HAN, *v. pres. pl.* HAVEN, have. pr. 62; *pres. inf.* 3. 177.

HANDY-DANDY, *n.*, a secret bribe. 4. 61.

HANSELE, *n.*, greeting; a toast; something to bring luck. 5. 168. [OE handselen, ON handsal]

HAP, *n.*, a happening; luck; good luck, fortune. 5. 78, 12. 111. [OE gehæp]

HAPPILY, *adv.*, perhaps. 6. 101.

HARD, *adj.*, hard-hearted. 1. 165. [OE hard, heard]

HARDE, *adv.*, diligently. pr. 21.

HARDY, *adj.*, bold. 4. 47, 7. 173, 12. 23.

HARDILY, *adv.*, boldly. 7. 31.

HARLOT, *n.*, buffoon, scurrilous fellow. 4. 104. [OF herlot, harlot, " rascal," " rogue "]

HARLOTRIE, *n.*, loose, scurrilous gossip, buffoonery. 4. 106, 11. 31.

HASPEN, *v.*, hasp, lock; enclose. 1. 171. [OE hæps, hæpsian]

HATTE, HATTETH, *v.*, be named, be called. 2. 140. [OE hātte]

HATTREDE, *n.*, hatred. 3. 128.

HAUNTEN, *v.*, haunt; frequent; indulge in. pr. 74. [OF hanter]

HAVER, *adj.*, oaten. 7. 266.

HAWE, *n.*, (*pl.* HAWEN) haw, hawthorn berry. 11. 10. [OE haga]

HED, *n.*, head. 2. 163. [OE hēafod]

HEGG, *n.*, hedge. 3. 120. [OE hegg]

HEIGH, *adj.*, high. pr. 13. [OE MERC hēh]

HEIGHE, *adv.*, highly; solemnly. 6. 66; loudly. 2. 56.

HEIGHLICHE, *adv.*, highly, at high wages. 7. 296.

HEIRE, *n.*, hair-shirt, sack-cloth. 5. 48. [OE hǣre, OF haire]

HELDEN, *v.*, incline; pour, drink. 10. 60. [OE heldan, hyldan]

HELE, *n.*, health; salvation. 6. 19, 7. 243. [OE hǣl, hǣlu]

HELEN, *v.*, cover; roof. 6. 77. [OE helan]

HELEN, *v.*, heal. 7. 179. [OE hǣlan]

HEM, *pron. 3d. pl. dat. acc.*, them, themselves. pr. 20. [OE hem]

HENDE, *adj.*, courteous, gentle. 2. 52, 10. 19. [OE gehende]

HENDELY, *adv.*, courteously. 3. 28, 9. 10.

HENG, *v. pret.* HONGEN, hung. 7. 56.

HENNES, HENIS, HENNE, *adv.*, hence. 1. 152, 3. 96, 4. 153. [OE heonan]

HENTEN, *v.*, seize. 5. 5. [OE hentan]

HEO, *pron. 3d. sg. fem. nom.*, she. 1. 10. [OE hēo]

HEO, *pron. 3d. pl.*, they. 1. 165, 11. 172. [OE hēo, hīo]

HEP, *n.*, heap; crowd, large number. pr. 50, 5. 167, 177, 7. 175. [OE hēap]

HERBERWEN, *v.*, shelter. 2. 38. [OE herebeorgian]

HERE, *n.*, hair. 11. 223. [OE hǣr]

HERE, *pron. 3d. pl. gen.*, their. pr. 30. [OE heora]

HEREMYTE, *n.*, hermit. 7. 175. (*See Introduction*). [OF ermite]

HEREN, *v.*, hear. pr. 4. [OE KENT hēran]

HERIEN, *v.*, praise. 11. 240. [OE herian]

HERNE, *n.*, corner. 2. 195. [OE hyrne]

HERRE, *adj., adv.*, higher. 10. 98. [OE hīerra]

HERTE, *n.*, heart. 1. 139. [OE heorte]

HERVIST, *n.*, harvest. 7. 60. [OE hærfest]

HESTE, *n.*, command. 3. 100, 10. 138, 11. 246. [OE hǣs]

HEVENE, *n.*, heaven. 1. 9. [OE heofon]

HEVENE-RICHE, *n.*, kingdom of heaven. pr. 27. [OE heofon, rīce]

HEVID, *n.*, head. 10. 49. [OE hēafod]

HY, *pron. 3d. pl. nom.*, they. pr. 63. [OE hī]

HIGHTE, *v. pret.*, commanded. 1. 17. [OE hātan, heht]

HYNE, *n.*, peasant; servant. pr. 39; *pl.* HYNEN. 4. 42. [OE hīna]

HIRE, *n.*, pay, reward. 6. 37. [OE hȳr]

HIRE, *pron. 3d sg. fem. poss.*, her. 1. 56. [OE hire]

HIRE, *pron. 3d. pl. poss.*, their. pr. 94. [OE hyra]

HISE, *pron. 3d. sg. poss.*, modifying pl. n., his. pr. 75.

HITTEN, *v.*, throw, cast. 5. 171; strike. 7. 166. [ON hitta]

HOBELEN, *v.*, hobble, limp, stumble; fall. 1. 113. [? OE hoppian]

HOD, *n.*, hood, hat. 5. 31. [OE hōd]

HOKID, *adj.*, curved, hook-shaped. 9. 87.

HOLDE, *adj.*, faithful. 7. 123. [OE hold]

HOLDEN, *v.*, (1) hold. 5. 50.

(2) restrain. 5. 226.

(3) hold, keep. pr. 28, 7. 133, 9. 87.

(4) hold, maintain. 7. 200, 3. 138.

(5) require, oblige. 7. 68, 86, 11. 240.

(6) keep, observe. 5. 37, 6. 66, 94, 8. 22, 72.

(7) practice, employ oneself in. 5. 140.

(8) hold, count, regard. 1. 9, 82, 3. 197, 4. 104, 5. 183, 7. 198, 8. 75, 8. 166, 11. 62. [OE MERC haldan, WS healdan]

HOLDEN WITH, consort with. 1. 100, 7. 47.

HOLDEN TOGIDERE, accord, agree. pr. 63, 1. 55.

HOLE, *adj.*, whole. 7. 54. [OE hāl]

HOLY, *adv.*, wholly. 3. 100.

HOLPEN, *v. pret.* HELPEN, helped. 7. 108, 8. 6.

HOND, *n.*, hand. 3. 54. [OE hand, hond]

HONESSHEN, *v.*, revile, drive out. 11. 48. [OF honir, honiss-]

HONGEN, *v.*, hang. 1. 66. [OE hangian]

HOPEN, *v.*, expect; think. 6. 122, 9. 15, 11. 107. [OE hopian]

HOPER, *n.*, seed-basket. 7. 56.

HOSTILER, *n.*, stableman. 5. 171. [OF hostel]

HOTE, *v. pp.* HOTEN, called, named. 6. 64, 11. 1, 180; YHOTEN, 1. 61. [OE gehāten]

HOTEN, *v.*, call; command. 2. 161, 168, 3. 241, 4. 3, 7. 243, 245, 11. 48, 104, 150. [OE hātan]

HOUPEN, *v.*, call, whoop. 7. 157. [OF houper]

HOUVE, *n.*, coif, hood. pr. 84, 3. 267. [OE hūfe]

HOVEN, *v.*, hover, hang above; stand, appear in view. pr. 84.

HUCCHE, *n.*, coffer, chest. 4. 102. [OF huche, OE hwicce]

HUSBONDIS, *n.*, husbandmen, farmers. 11. 180. [OE hūs-bonda]

HUSBONDRIE, *n.*, economy, care for wealth. 1. 55.

HUXTERIE, *n.*, retail trade. 5. 140.

I

I-, *verbal prefix. See the simple forms of the verbs.*

ICH, *pron. 1st. sg. nom.*, I. 9. 65. [OE ic]

ICHE, *pron.*, each, each one. 3. 52. [OE ilc]

ICHONE, *pron.*, each one. 1. 17.

YDEL, *adj.*, idle. ON YDEL, in vain. 6. 58. [OE īdel]

ILE, *n.*, isle, island. 2. 63. [OF isle]

ILKE, *pron.*, *adj.*, same, very same. 1. 81. [OE ilca]

INGANG, *n.*, entrance. 6. 114.

INNE, *n.*, inn, lodging. 9. 4. [OE inn]

INNE, *adv.*, within. 1. 163. [OE innan]

INOUGH, *adj.*, enough. 7. 135. [OE genōh]

YNOWE, *adj.*, enough. 2. 108.

INPUGNEN, *v.*, impugn, oppose. 8. 149. [OF inpugner]

INWYT, *n.*, conscience. 10. 17, 12. 99.

IRENS, *n.*, irons, chains, fetters. 4. 72. [OE īren]

IT, *pron. expletive.* pr. 85.

YWAR, *adj.*, aware. 9. 109. [OE gewær]

J

JANGLEN, *v.*, talk freely, argue. 9. 113. [OF jangler]

JANGLER, *n.*, chatterer, wrangler, jester, slanderer. pr. 35.

JANGLYNG, *n.*, quarrelling. 10. 184.

JAPEN, *v.*, jest; mock; deceive. 1. 65. [OF japer]

JAPER, *n.*, jester, buffoon; trickster; impostor. pr. 35.

JENTIL, *adj.*, gentle. 1. 159. [OF gentil]

JENTILY, *adv.*, gently, courteously. 3. 13.

JEWENE, *n. gen. pl.*, Jews'. 1. 65.

JOYNTLY, *adv.*, together, at the same time. 2. 121. [OF joint]

JOTTIS, *n.*, lowly or ignorant people, peasants. 11. 301.

JUELX, *n.*, jewels. 3. 143. [OF jouel]

JUGGEN, *v.*, judge; pronounce opinion; say. 1. 159, 2. 101, 2. 121. [OF juger]

K

KAYM, *n.*, Cain. 1. 64.

KEIEN, KEIGHEN, *v.*, key, *i. e.*, lock. 6. 100. [OE cæg]

KENNEN, *v.*, teach, inform, direct,

teach how. 1. 79, 90, 127, 11. 102, 104, 147, 219. [ON kenna]

KEP, *n.*, care, heed. 10. 95.

KEPEN, *v.*, (1) keep, maintain. 1. 169, 4. 156, 5. 27, 8. 170.
    (2) keep, restrain. 2. 29, 6. 100.
    (3) guard, protect. 1. 53, 92, 7. 29, 83, 147, 8. 9.
    (4) guard, care for. 1. 8, 6. 32, 7. 128, 181.
    (5) guard, take care, be cautious. 3. 255.
    (6) guard, govern. 3. 194, 262, 4. 121, 8. 145, 9. 91.
    (7) guard; enforce. 3. 65, 82. [OE cēpan]

KERTIL, *n.*, jacket. 5. 62. [OE cyrtel]

KERVEN, *v.*, carve. 7. 96. [OE ceorfan]

KERVERIS, *n.*, carvers, sculptors. 11. 134.

KETE, *adj.*, intelligent, keen-witted. 11. 56.

KILN, *v.*, kill. 1. 64.

KYN, *n.*, kin, lineage, race. 1. 166; kind, sort. 2. 162. [OE cynn]

KYNDE, *n.*, nature. 7. 149, 9. 37; kind; people. 11. 282. [OE gecynd]

KYNDE, *adj.*, natural; right, proper. 9. 62, 11. 247. KYNDE WYT, natural knowledge, common sense. 1. 53. KYNDE KNOW-YNG, natural knowledge, understanding. 1. 127, 9. 48, 103.

KYNDELY, *adv.*, naturally, properly. 1. 79.

KYNNE, KYNNES, KENNE, KENIS, *See* KYN.

KYNREDE, *n.*, kindred. 10. 153, 192.

KIRNEL, *n.*, battlement. 6. 75. [OF cernel]

KITH, *n.*, country. 3. 189. [OE cȳþ]

KITTEN, *v.*, cut. 4. 140.

KNAVE, *n.*, boy; servant boy; rascally fellow. pr. 44, 104, 4. 17, 5. 159, 3. 119, 5. 95, 7. 181. [OE cnafa]

KNEUGH, *v. pret.* KNOWEN, knew. 2. 188; acknowledged. 11. 273.

KNIGHT, *n.*, knight. 3. 41. [OE cniht]

KNOP, *n.*, knob, button. 7. 254. [OE cnæp]

KNOWELECHEN, *v.*, acknowledge. 5. 248.

KONNEN, *v.*, *See* CONNEN.

L

LACCHEN, *v.*, seize, take. 2. 167, 5. 197. [OE læccean]

LACCHESSE, *n.*, negligence. 9. 32.

LACCHING, *n.*, taking, seizing. 1. 101.

LAIES, *n.*, lays, songs. 9. 57. [OF lai]

LAIGHES, *n.*, untilled lands. 8. 5. [OE lēah]

LAKKEN, *v.*, lack. 5. 230.

LAKKEN, *v.*, find fault with, blame. 2. 17.

LAMMASSE, *n.*, Lammas; August first. 7. 273. [OE hlāfmæsse]

LANG, *adj.*, long. 2. 143. [OE lang]

LAPPE, *n.*, fold in a garment; pocket. 7. 277. [OE læppa]

LARGESSE, *n.*, generosity. 6. 109.

LASSE, *adj.*, lesser, less. 2. 28, 5. 137. [OE læssa]

LAT, *v. See* LETEN, (6). 11. 141.

LATRO, *n.*, robber. 5. 251. [L]

LATTERE, *adv.*, later; more slowly; more grudgingly. 1. 173. [OE læt]

LAUGHTE, *v. pret.* LACCHEN, caught, seized. 1. 30, 3. 24, 12. 42, 55. [OE læhte]

LAUMPE, *n.*, lamp. 1. 163. [OF lampe]

LAUNDE, *n.*, lawn, meadow. 9. 56, 11. 117. [OF launde]

LEAUTE, *n.*, loyalty. 2. 100. [OF lealte, leaute]

LECCHERIE, *n.*, lechery. pr. 74. [OF lecherie]

LECHE, *n.*, physician. 2. 185. [OE læce]

LECHECRAFT, *n.*, knowledge, skill, in medicine. 7. 238.

LED, *n.*, lead. 6. 78. [OE lēad]

LEDE, *n.*, person. 3. 31. [OE lēod]

LEDEN, *v.*, lead. 2. 99. LEDEN LAWE, practice law. 3. 146. LEDEN LAND, cultivate land. 4. 131. [OE lǣdan]

LEF, *adj.*, lief; dear. 1. 35. [OE lēof]

LEF, *n.*, leaf, page. 5. 116, 8. 156. [OE lēaf]

LEGENDE, *n.*, writing; book. 11. 254. [OF legende]

LEGISTRE, *n.*, lawyer, barrister. 8. 61. [OF legistre]

LEYEN, *v.*, wager. 7. 252. [OE lecgan]

LEIEN, LEIGHEN, *v.*, tell lies. pr. 49; deceive. 1. 67. LIGHEN ON, lie against. 11. 149. [OE lēogan]

LEK, *n.*, leek. 5. 64. [OE lēac]

LELLE, *adj.*, loyal, true, honest. 11. 179, 233. [OF leel]

LELLY, *adv.*, loyally, truly. 1. 76.

LEMMAN, *n.*, a person beloved; a concubine. 3. 138, 10. 6. [OE lēof, man]

LENEN, *v.*, lend. 1. 155, 3. 221. [OE lǣnan]

LENEN, *v.*, recline, lean; rest. pr. 9. [OE hlǣnan]

LENGEN, *v.*, delay, wait. 1. 183; tarry, dwell. 9. 7. [OE lengan]

LENGERE, *adv.*, longer. 1. 183. [OE lengra]

LEPEN, *v.*, run, run off. pr. 94. [OE hlēapan]

LERE, *n.*, face. 1. 3. [OE hlēor]

LEREN, *v.*, teach; learn. 1. 109, 125, 9. 103, 11. 270. [OE lǣran]

LERID, *adj.*, the educated, learned. 2. 45.

LERNEN, *v.*, learn; teach. 5. 122, 8. 115, 9. 10, 49. [OE leornian]

LERNING, *n.*, instruction. 1. 173. [OE leornung]

LES, *v. pret.* LESEN, lost. 8. 139.

LESEN, *v.*, lose. 3. 123, 10. 99. [OE lēosan]

LESING, *n.*, loss. 5. 92.

LESING, *n.*, lie, falsehood. 2. 89. [OE lēasung]

LESSE, *adj.*, lesser, less. 8. 139, 9. 7. [OE læssa]

LESTEN, *v.*, last, hold out. 12. 93. [OE lǣstan]

LET, *v. 3d. sg. pres.*, letteth or leadeth. 6. 109.

LETEN, *v.*, (1) let, allow, permit. 2. 167, 3. 124, 5. 186.
(2) leave off. 3. 183; cease. 5. 230.
(3) abandon. 4. 154, 5. 141, 7. 255, 12. 21.
(4) release. 1. 176.
(5) cause (*with inf.*). 1. 141, 2. 123, 135, 141, 159, 3. 100, 4. 19, 7. 210, 9. 25.
(6) think; esteem (*usually with adv.*). 4. 137, 6. 102, 7. 153, 11. 29, 141. [OE lǣtan]

LETTEN, *v.*, hinder, delay, stay. 2. 31, 3. 31, 10. 159, 11. 20. [OE lettan]

LETTERE, *n.*, one who hinders. 1. 67.

LETTYNG, *n.*, delay. 7. 7, 11. 164.

LETTRID, *adj.*, lettered; educated; wise. 1. 125. [OF lettre]

LETTRURE, *n.*, literature, scripture; learning. 11. 256.

LEVE, *n.*, leave, permission, license. pr. 49, 82. [OE lēaf]

LEVE, *adj.*, *See* LEF.

LEVEN, *v.*, leave; abandon; make a gift of. pr. 74; abandon, part from. 1. 101. [OE lǣfan]

LEVEN, *v.*, believe. pr. 69, 8. 157, 11. 256. [OE gelēfan]

LEVERE, *adj.*, dearer. 11. 11, 14; *adv.*, more dearly. 1. 131. [OE lēofra]

LEVEST, *adj.*, most beloved; most precious. 1. 136.

LEWID, *adj.*, common, ignorant, uneducated. pr. 69. [OE lǣwed]

LEWIDNESSE, *n.*, ignorance. 3. 31.

LIBBEN, *v.*, live. 2. 148. [OE libban]

LICENCE, *n.*, license; permission. pr. 82. [OF licence]

LICH, *n.*, body. 11. 2. [OE līc]

LYCHE, *adj.*, like. 11. 239. [OE gelīc]

LIFLODE, *n.*, livelihood, means of living. pr. 30. [OE līflāde]

LIGE, *adj.*, subject, vassal. 4. 147. [OF lige]

LIGGEN, *v.*, lie, recline. 2. 100. [OE licgan]

LIGHTE, *adv.*, lightly; scornfully. 4. 137. [OE liht]

LIGHTLOKER, *adv.*, more lightly. 6. 56.

LIKAM, LYKHAME, *n.*, living body. pr. 30, 1. 35, 12. 93. [OE līchama]

LIKE, *adv.*, likewise. 1. 48. [OE gelīce]

LIKEN, *v.*, please (*with indir. obj.*). pr. 57; like. pr. 69. [OE līcian]

LIKEROUS, *adj.*, pleasurable dainty; luxurious; lecherous. pr. 30, 7. 250, 11. 120. [AF likerous]

LYKING, *n.*, liking; wish, desire, pleasure, will. pr. 59.

LIKNEN, *v.*, compare, liken. 9. 34, 37.

LYME, *n.*, limb. 5. 80. [OE lim]

LYNDE, *n.*, linden, lime-tree. 9. 56. [OE lind]

LISSE, *n.*, joy, bliss. 10. 30. [OE liss]

LIST, *n.*, edge; edge of cloth; strip of cloth. 5. 123, 6. 5. [OE liste]

LISTEN, *v.*, please. pr. 37. [OE lystan]

LITEL, *adj.*, little. 2. 150. [OE lytel]

LITH, *v. 3d. sg. pres.* LIGGEN, lies. 1. 115, 4. 46, 10. 114, 11. 140.

LITHEN, *v.*, ease, make comfortable. 7. 180. [OE līþian]

LYTHEN, *v.*, hear, listen to. 9. 57. [ON hlýða]

LYTHER, *adj.*, evil; wicked, base. 5. 97. [OE lyþre]

LOBIES, *n.*, lubbers, stout, lazy fellows. pr. 52.

LOF, *n.*, loaf; bread. 7. 267. [OE hlāf]

LOGGYNG, *n.*, lodging. 12. 44. [OF loge]

LOK, *n.*, lock. 1. 176. [OE loca]

LOKEN, *v.*, (1) look, turn the eyes in a certain direction. pr. 9, 1. 141, 2. 5, 7, 5. 234, 6. 65, 7. 173, 8. 14.

 (2) look, look up, raise the eyes. 4. 47, 5. 46.

 (3) look at, examine. 2. 186, 7. 13.

 (4) look after, protect. 1. 183.

 (5) look out for, be on the watch for. 5. 115.

 (6) see that. 1. 134, 3. 245, 6. 62, 71, 7. 39.

 (7) appear. 5. 65, 107, 7. 162, 301.

 (8) find out. 2. 120.

 (9) provide. 2. 159, 7. 299.

 (10) permit. 2. 100. [OE lōcian]

LOKING, *n.*, glance, twinkling. 12. 96.

LOLLEN, *v.*, hang tremblingly. 5. 109.

LOMB, *n.*, lamb. 6. 40. [OE lamb, lomb]

LOND, *n.*, land. 3. 188. [OE land, lond]

LONG, *adj.*, long; tall. pr. 52. [OE lang, long]

LONGE, *adv.*, late. 6. 3.

LONGEN, *v.*, belong. 2. 28. [OE gelang]

LOPEN, *v. pp.* LEPEN, leapt, gone. pr. 94.

LORE, *n.*, lore; teaching, learning. 2. 17. [OE lār]

LOREL, *n.*, wretch, abandoned creature. 8. 120. [OE lēosan, *pp.* loren]

LOSEL, *n.*, wretch, profligate, vagabond. pr. 74.

LOSENGERIE, *n.*, flattery; lying. 11. 36.

LOTEBY, *n.*, paramour, concubine. 3. 138.

LOTH, *n.*, Lot. 1. 27.

LOTH, *adj.*, loath, disinclined. 3. 148. [OE lāþ]

LOTHEN, *v.*, loathe, hate. 8. 80.

LOUGH, *v. pret.* LAUGHEN, laughed. 4. 137. [OE hlōh]

LOUGH, *adj.*, low, humble, meek. 3. 231. [ON lágr]

LOUGHNESSE, *n.*, lowness; humility, meekness. 3. 264, 10. 99, 125.

LOUREN, *v.*, lower, frown, scowl; look on with disfavor. 2. 185, 5. 65, 186. [OE *lūrian]

LOUTEN, *v.*, lout; bow, bend low. 3. 35, 103, 11. 97. [OE lūtan]

LOVEDAY, *n.*, day set apart for settling disputes out of court, amicably and equitably, but

which had fallen into serious
abuses. 3. 146, 11. 20, 209. [OE
lufu, dæg]

LOVELICHE, *adj.*, lovable, loving.
6. 40.

LOVELOKEST, *adj.*, loveliest. 1. 110.

LOW, *v. pret.* LAUGHEN, laughed.
12. 42. [OE hlōh]

LOWTYNG, *v. pres. part.* LOUTEN,
bowing. 12. 55.

LURKEN, *v.*, lurk; run crouchingly
and fearfully. 2. 178.

LUST, *n.*, pleasure; sensuality
(gluttony). 2. 65. [OE lust]

M

MAD, *v. pp.* MAKEN, made. 8. 127,
9. 81, 10. 3, 11. 171.

MAGESTE, *n.*, majesty; power. 1.
105. [OF majesté]

MAY, *n.*, maid, virgin. 12. 116.
[OE mǣg]

MAY, *v.*, can; may. 1. 58, 2. 112.
[OE mæg]

MAIDENHOD, *n.*, virginity. 1. 158.
[OE mægdenhād]

MAIDENIS, *n.*, virgins (either sex).
10.193. [OE mægden]

MAYNE, *n.*, *See* MEYNE.

MAYNPRISE, *n.*, security, bail. 4.
75. [OF mainprise]

MAYNTENEN, *v.*, support; aid; be
sponsor for a band of retainers
who robbed and assaulted. 2.
157, 3. 78, 137, 152, 170, 201,
224, 4. 42. [OF maintenir]

MAIR, *n.*, *See* MEIR.

MAISTER, *n.*, master. 3. 203; most
powerful person. 3. 154; title of

respect, perhaps the MA degree.
pr. 59, 9. 9.

MAISTER, *n.*, magistrate. 3. 64, 223,
8. 165.

MAISTRIE, *n.*, power, predominat-
ing power. 4. 118, 5. 84; favor-
able decision (of a court). 3.
214.

MAKE, *n.*, spouse, wife, husband.
3. 106. [OE gemace, gemaca]

MAKEN, *v.*, make; bring to; bring
about. 2. 112, 5. 223, 8. 146, 11.
71; amend, repair. 4. 58, 96;
cause to be otherwise. 10. 51,
11. 249; beget. 10. 164; write,
compose. 11. 257. [OE macian]

MAKYNG, *n.*, composing, writing
poetry. 11. 32, 12. 109.

MAMELEN, *v.*, mumble; say in a
low voice. 5. 21.

MANACEN, *v.*, menace; threaten.
7. 155. [OF menacer]

MANER, *n.*, kind, sort. pr. 18. [OF
maniere]

MANER, *n.*, manor. 6. 73, 10. 15.
[OF manoir]

MANGEN, *v.*, eat. 7. 242, 12. 72.
[OF manger]

MARBIL, *n.*, marble; stone. 10. 101.
[OF marbre]

MARCHAL, *n.*, marshal; leader;
general. 3. 186. [OF mareschal]

MARCHAUNDISE, *n.*, merchandise.
pr. 60. [OF marchandise]

MARCHAUNT, *n.*, merchant. 2. 174.
[OF marchant]

MARCHIS, *n.*, borders, districts. 10.
11. [OF marche]

MARGERIE-PERLIS, *n.*, pearls. 11. 9.
[OF margerie, perle]

MARK, *n.*, a coin, value (approximately) 13s. 4d. 5. 31. [OE marc]

MARK, *n.*, feature, appearance. 10. 32. [OE mearc]

MASAGER, *n.*, messenger. 12. 83. [OF message]

MASE, *n.*, maze; confusion. 1. 6, 3. 147. [OE āmasian]

MASON, *n.*, mason. pr. 101. [OF macon]

MASSE, *n.*, mass (church service). 1. 157. [OE mæsse]

MATYNES, *n.*, matins. 5. 2. (*See Introduction*).

MAUGRE, *n.*, ill will. 7. 224. [OF maugre]

MAUGRE, *prep.*, in spite of. 2. 164.

MAUNGED, *v.*, *See* MANGEN.

MAWE, *n.*, maw; stomach. 5. 211. [OE maga]

MECHEL, *adj.*, many. 12. 102. [OE mycel]

MEDE, *n.*, pay, reward (legitimate). 3. 195, 8. 60. [OE mēd]

MEDE, *n.*, bribery, graft. 2. 16.

MEDEN, *v.*, meed, pay. 3. 201.

MEDLEN, *v.*, mix, mingle. 10. 3. [ONF medler]

MEEL, *n.*, meal. 1. 24. [OE mǣl]

MEYNE, *n.*, household; retinue, train. 1. 106. [OF maisnee]

MEYNPERNOUR, *n.*, one who goes surety, bondsman. 4. 99. [OF mainprenour]

MEYNPRISEN, *v.*, go bail or surety. 2. 158. [OF main, prendre]

MEYNTENEN, *v.*, *See* MAYNTENEN.

MEIR, *n.*, mayor. 3. 64. [OF maire]

MEKEN, *v.*, be meek; make humble. 5. 52, 6. 88. [ON mjúkr]

MEKIL, *adj.*, much, many. 6. 108. [OE mycel]

MELEN, *v.*, speak, say. 3. 92, 11. 93. [OE mǣlan]

MEMBRE, *n.*, member; limb. 8. 84. [OF membre]

MEMENTO, *v. imperat.*, remember. 5. 239. [L]

MEN, *pron.*, Mod. Eng. *colloquial*, they. 1. 138, 6. 52.

MENDEN, *v.*, repair. 3. 51. [OF amender]

MENDES, *n.*, amends, rightful exchange. 2. 83. [OF amende]

MENDYNAUNTZ, *n.*, beggars, mendicants. 11. 52, 198. [AF mendinant]

MENE, *adj.*, poor, mean, of low estate. pr. 18. [OE gemæne]

MENE, *adj.*, intermediate. 3. 64. [OF meen, OE gemǣne]

MENE, *n.*, mediator, intercessor. 8. 177, 9. 114.

MENEN, *v.*, moan, complain. 3. 155. [OE mǣnan]

MENEN, *v.*, mean, signify. 1. 11. [OE mǣnan]

MENGEN, *v.*, keep in mind. 7. 87. [OE myngean]

MENOURS, *n.*, minorite (Franciscan) friars. 9. 9. (*See Introduction*).

MENSKEN, *v.*, honor. 3. 169. [ON mennska]

MENSTRALSIE, *n.*, minstrelsy. 11. 35. [AF mynstralcye]

MERCY, *n.*, thanks. 1. 41. [OF merci]

MERCIEN, *v.*, thank. 3. 19.

MERY, *adj.*, merry; glad, happy; delightful; pleasant, agreeable. pr. 10. [OE myrig]

MERTHE, *n.*, mirth; merriment; pleasure. pr. 33. [OE myrhþ]

MERVEILLESTE, *adj.*, most marvelous. 9. 59.

MERVEILLOUS, *adj.*, marvelous. pr. 11. [OF merveille]

MERVEILLOUSLY, *adv.*, marvelously. 8. 140.

MESCHAUNCE, *n.*, mischance; bad luck. 3. 152. [OF meschance]

MESCHIEF, MESCHEF, *n.*, mischief; hardship. pr. 64, 3. 253. AT MESCHIEF, with ill results. 10. 175; in trouble. 11. 198. [OF meschief]

MESON DEU, *n.*, hospital. 8. 28. [OF maison dieu]

MESOUR, *n.*, measure. 1. 151; moderation. 12. 73. [OF mesure]

MESSANGER, *n.*, messenger. 2. 189. [OF message]

MESSE, *n.*, mass (religious service). 3. 209. [OE messe, mæsse, OF messe]

MESURABLE, *adj.*, moderate. 1. 19. [OF mesure]

METE, *n.*, food; meal. 3. 209. [OE mete]

METELIS, *n.*, dream. 8. 127, 146. [OE mætan]

METEN, *v.*, dream. pr. 11. [OE mǣtan]

METEN, *v.*, measure. pr. 88. [OE metan]

METEN, *v.*, meet, encounter. 9. 109. [OE mētan]

METYNG, *n.*, dream, dreaming. 9. 59.

METTE, *v. pret.* METEN, dreamed. 8. 140, 9. 59.

METTE, *v. pret.* METEN, met, encountered. 9. 3, 8.

MEVEN, *v.*, propose, bring forward. 9. 113, 11. 70. [OF movoir, muev-]

MYDDEL, *n.*, waist. 3. 10. [OE middel]

MYDDES, *n.*, midst. IN THE MYDDES, midst. 2. 40. [OE middes]

MIGHT, *n.*, might, power. 1. 105. [OE myht]

MIGHTE, *v. pret.* MAY, could, might. pr. 67. [OE mihte]

MIGHTFUL, *adj.*, mighty, powerful. 1. 147.

MILDELICHE, *adv.*, mildly, gently. 3. 19. [OE milde]

MYLE WEY, *n.*, a mile. 8. 126. [OE mīl, weg]

MYLNERE, *n.*, miller. 2. 76. [OE myln]

MYN ONE, *adv. phr.*, alone. 9. 54.

MYNOUR, *n.*, miner. pr. 101. [OF miner]

MYNSTRAL, *n.*, minstrel. pr. 33. [OF menestrel]

MYSBEDEN, *v.*, misgovern. 7. 44. [OE bēodan]

MYSBELEVE, *n.*, misbelief, false faith. 11. 71. [OE mis-, gelēafa]

MYSDEDE, *v. pret.* MYSDON, injured. 4. 86.

MYSEISE, *n.*, illness. 1. 24. [OF aise]

MYSEL, *n.*, leper. 3. 120. [AF mesel]

MYSTER, *n.*, trade, craft, occupation. 8. 7. [OF mestier]

MISTLOKERE, *adj.*, more mysterious. 11. 137.

MYTE, *n.*, mite, bit, particle. 8. 53.

MO, *adj.*, more. 2. 76. [OE mā]

MODY, *n.*, proud, obstinate (person). 10. 211. [OE mōdig]

MOYLERE, *n.*, a legitimately born person. 2. 83, 96. [OF mulier]

MOYSES, *n.*, Moses. 3. 240.

MOLDE, *n.*, earth. pr. 64. [OE molde]

MOM, *n.*, mum, mumble, unintelligible sound. pr. 89.

MONE, *n.*, moon. 8. 140. [OE mōna]

MONETH, *n.*, month. 3. 132. [OE mōnaþ]

MONY, MONE, MONIE, MONEY, MANYE, *n.*, money. pr. 60. [OF moneie]

MOREWE, *n.*, morrow; morning. 5. 147. [OE morgen]

MORWENYNG, *n.*, morning. pr. 5.

MOSEN, *v.*, moss; become mossy. 10. 101. [OE mos]

MOT, *v.*, may; must. 1. 127, 3. 211, 5. 42, 6. 48. [OE mōt]

MOTE, *n.*, moat. 6. 73. [OF mote]

MOTEN, *v.*, issue orders; command. 1. 150. [OE mōtan]

MOTEN, *v.*, talk; plead. 3. 147, 4. 118, 8. 60. [OE mōtian]

MOTHALLE, *n.*, law court, hall for pleading. 4. 135.

MOTIFS, *n.*, arguments. 11. 70. [OF motif]

MOTYNG, *n.*, pleading in law court. 8. 60.

MOTOUN, *n.*, French coin (gold) of value of 5s., so-called because it carried the image of a sheep or lamb on one side. 3. 23.

MOUTHEN, *v.*, mouthe, speak. 4. 106, 7. 222. [OE mūþ]

MOWE, *v. pret.*, may, can. 1. 121, *etc.* [LWS muge]

MUCHE, *adj.*, great, large. 4. 136.

MUCHEL, *adj.*, much. 5. 228; great, large. 9. 61. [OE mycel]

MURDREN, MURTHREN, *v.*, put to a violent death, assault violently. 3. 246, 4. 42, 5. 84. [OE morþer]

MUSONS, *n.*, measures. 11. 128. [OF moison]

N

NA, *adv.*, no. *See* NAMORE.

NALE, *n.*, ale; ale-house. 10. 59. [OE ealu]

NAM, *n.*, mina, talent (money). 7. 223.

NAMELICHE, *adv.*, especially. 2. 110.

NAMORE, *adv.*, no more. 7. 88.

NAS, *v. pret. neg.* NE WAS, was not. 2. 38.

NE, *neg.*, not. pr. 79.

NE, *conj.*, nor. 4. 141. [OE ne]

NEDELERE, *n.*, needle seller. 5. 160. [OE nǣdl]

NEIGH, *adv.*, nigh, nearly. 3. 132; *adj.*, 5. 73. [OE nēh]

NEMPNEN, *v.*, name. 1. 21. [OE nemnan]

NER, *prep.*, near. 7. 283; *comp.*, nearer. 11. 250; *adv.*, nearly. 7. 163.

Nere, *v. pret. subj.* Ne Were, were not. 5. 241, 11. 51.

Newe Feire, *n.*, the " new fair," a game. 5. 170. (*See note*).

Nigromancie, *n.*, necromancy. 11. 158. [OF nigromance]

Nille, *v. pres.· neg.* Ne Wille, will not. 4. 154. Nilt. 7. 143.

Nymen, *v.*, take. 4. 63, 7. 14, 41, 11. 47. [OE niman]

Nis, *v. pres. neg.* Ne Is, is not. 3. 50.

Noble, *n.*, coin (gold) of value of 6s. 8d. 3. 44.

Noye, *n.*, suffering; discomfort. 11. 47. [OF anoi]

Noien, Noighen, *v.*, harm, injure. 2. 16. [OF nuire] *See* Anoyed.

Noke, *n.*, At The Noke, at the oak (tree). 5. 114. [OE āc]

Nolde, *v. pret. neg.* Ne Wolde, would not. 6. 45.

Nomen, *v. pret. pl.* Niman, took. 4. 63. [OE nāmon, nōmon]

Non, *n.*, nones. 7. 135. (*See Introduction*).

Nones, *phrase* For The Nones, very, exceedingly. 2. 41.

Nother, *conj.*, neither. 7. 265.

Notories, *n.*, clerks who drew up legal documents. 2. 78. [OF notaire]

Nought, *adv.*, not. 1. 25.

Nought, *pron.*, naught. 1. 108.

Noumpere, *n.*, umpire. 5. 180. [OF nompere]

Nouthe, *adv.*, now. 7. 191, 11. 35. [OE nū þā]

Nouther, *conj.*, neither. 7. 120.

O

O, *adj.*, one. 2. 69. [OE ān]

O, *prep.*, on, a-. 2. 14.

Of, *prep.*, from. pr. 68; with. .1. 18. [OE of]

Of-Senden, *v.*, send for, send after. 2. 35, 3. 89. [OE sendan]

Ok, *n.*, oak. 5. 18. [OE āc]

On, *prep.*, on, in. pr. 50.

On, *adj.*, one. 3. 262; *pron.*, 1. 23, 9. 98, 12. 84. [OE ān]

Ones, *adv.*, once. pr. 87.

Or, *conj.*, either. 7. 232.

Ordre, *n.*, organization, order of monks, friars, or knights. pr. 55, 1. 102, 7. 151. [OF ordre]

Ost, *n.*, host; army. 3. 243. [OF hoste]

Other, *conj.*, or. 1. 151.

Other, *pron., adj.*, second. 1. 24.

Other-While, *adv.*, sometimes. 6. 37, 9. 21.

Ought, *pron.*, aught. 6. 20.

Oure, *n.*, hour (canonical). 1. 157. [OF (h)ure, (h)ore] (*See Introduction*).

Out Of, *prep.*, beyond. 1. 25.

Out-Take, *prep.*, except. 10. 169.

Overal, *adv.*, everywhere. 2. 180.

Over-Hoven, *v.*, hang over. 3. 193.

P

Paye, *n.*, pleasure; satisfaction. 6. 36. [OF paye]

Payen, *v.*, please. 7. 100, 293, 10. 113. With Paied, pleased with. 10. 126. [OF payer]

Payne, *n.*, bread. 8. 104. [OF pain]

PAYNYM, *n.*, a pagan. 6. 4. [OF paien, paiennisme]

PAKKE-NEDLE, *n.*, a strong, coarse needle, used to sew heavy cloth. 5. 125.

PALESIE, *n.*, palsy. 5. 60. [OF paralysie]

PALFREY, *n.*, saddle-horse, ambler. 2. 135. [OF palefrei]

PALMER, *n.*, "professional" pilgrim. pr. 46, 6. 23. [AF palmer]

PANES, PANIS, *n.*, pennies, pence. 2. 184. [OE penning]

PANNE, *n.*, pan; head. 4. 64. [OE (hēafod) -panne]

PARAVENTURE, *adv.*, perchance, perhaps. 12. 8. [OF paraventure]

PARCEL, *n.*, share, portion. 11. 50. [OF parcele]

PARCEL-MEL, *adv.*, bit by bit, a little at a time. 3. 69. [OF parcele, OE mǣl]

PARDONER, *n.*, pardoner. pr. 65. (*See Introduction*).

PARLEMENT, *n.*, here used of a meeting of the king with his chief counsellors, to administer justice. 4. 34. [OF parlement]

PARTEN, *v.*, divide, give (alms). pr. 78, 1. 156, 3. 56, 11. 50. [OF partir]

PARTIE, *n.*, part. 1. 7. [OF partie]

PASSEN, *v.*, pass; escape. 3. 124; surpass. 8. 150, 153, 12. 4. [OF passer]

PATENT, *n.*, indulgence, pardon. 8. 175. [OF patente]

PATER NOSTER, *n.*, the Lord's prayer. 5. 190. [L]

PAVYLOUN, *n.*, pavilion, large and gorgeous tent. 2. 41. [OF pavillon]

PECE, *n.*, cup, bowl. 3. 21, 77. [OF piece]

PEYNE, *n.*, pain. 1. 116. [OF peine]

PEISEN, *v.*, weigh. 5. 130. [OF peiser]

PELET, *n.*, stone cannon ball. 5. 60. [OF pelote]

PELURE, *n.*, fur. 2. 9, 3.268. [OF peleure]

PENCIOUN, *n.*, pension; payment for services. 8. 47. [OF pension]

PENY, *n.*, penny, silver coin weighing 18 grains. 1. 45. [OE penning]

PENYALE, *n.*, thin, poor ale. 5. 133, 7. 293. [OE ealu]

PENIS, *n.*, pence. pr. 86.

PENY-WORTH, *n.*, a penny's worth; goods, merchandise. 3. 234, 5. 176.

PENSIF, *adj.*, thoughtful, pensive. 8. 128. [OF pensif]

PERE, *n.*, equal. 3. 190. [OF per, peer]

PERFOURMEN, *v.*, perform. 6. 85. [OF parfournir]

PERIMANSIE, *n.*, pyromancy, divination by fire. 11. 158. [OF pyromancie]

PERMUTACIOUN, *n.*, exchange. 3. 234. [OF permutacion]

PERNEL, *n.*, name used for women of the streets. 4. 102, 5. 26, 45, 162.

PERREIGHE, *n.*, gems, jewelry. 2. 12, 11. 12. [OF perree]

PERSILE, *n.*, parsley. 7. 270. [OF percil]

PES, *n.*, peace. 1. 137. [OF pais]

PESE, *n.*, pea. 7. 154. [OE pise]

PESE-COD, *n.*, pea-pod. 7. 276.

PESE-LOF, *n.*, bread made of ground peas. 7. 164.

PESTILENCE, *n.*, pestilence; the " Black Death." pr. 81, 5. 13, 10. 185. [OF pestilence]

PETIR, *exclam.*, by St. Peter! 6. 25.

PYANYE, *n.*, peony seeds, used as spice. 5. 154. [OF pione]

PYE HELE, *n.*, pie heel; crust. 8. 175.

PIGHT, *v. pp.* PICCHEN, pitched, erected (tent, pavilion). 2. 41. [OE *piccean]

PIK, *n.*, pike, staff. 5. 249; point, spike. 9. 88. [OE pīc]

PILE-WHEY, *n.*, some kind of weak drink. 5. 133.

PILIDE, *adj.*, a term of angry insult. 7. 142. [OF peler]

PILLORIE, *n.*, pillory. 2. 168. [OF pilori]

PILOUR, *n.*, robber, plunderer. 3. 180. [OF pelour]

PYNE, *n.*, torture. 1. 143; torment; hell. 11. 269. [OE pīn]

PYNEN, *v.*, torture. 1. 145. [OE pīnian]

PYNYNG-STOL, *n.*, stool of punishment. 3. 66.

PYNNEN, *v.*, fasten. 5. 126. [OE pinn]

PIRIES, *n.*, pear-trees. 5. 16. [OE pirige]

PISTIL, *n.*, epistle. 10. 106, 11. 229. [OF epistle]

PLAY, *n.*, pleasure. 12. 95. [OE plega]

PLATTEN, *v.*, throw flat. 5. 45. [OE plættan]

PLEDEN, *v.*, plead (a case in court). pr. 86. [OF plaidier]

PLEIEN, *v.*, play, amuse oneself. pr. 20. [OE plegian]

PLEYN, *adj.*, full. 8. 86. [OF plein]

PLEYNEN, *v.*, complain. pr. 80. [OF plaindre]

PLEITEN, *v.*, plait, fold, fasten together. 5. 125. [OF pleit]

PLESEN, *v.*, please, gratify. pr. 30. [OF plaisir]

PLIGHTEN, *v.*, plight, pledge. pr. 46, 7. 36, 10. 185; bind. 5. 115. [OE plihtan]

PLOUGH-POTE, *n.*, plow-share. 7. 95.

PLURALITES, *n.*, endowments. 11. 197.

PLUS, *adv.*, very. 7. 295. [OF plus]

POYNT, *n.*, point; thing; consideration. 5. 15. [OF point]

POKEFUL, *n.*, bagful. 8. 172.

POKEN, *v.*, poke; push; urge, incite. 6. 97, 119.

POPERITH, *v.*, trots, ambles. 11. 210.

PORE, *adj.*, poor. pr. 79. [OF povre]

PORET, *n.*, leek, or garlic. 7. 270, 282. [OF poret]

PORS, *n.*, purse. 5. 152.

POSTERNE, *n.*, small gate or door, frequently cut in a large gate. 6. 105. [OF posterne]

POTEL, *n.*, a measure of two quarts. 5. 190, 7. 174. [OF potel]

POTENT, *n.*, staff. 9. 88.

POUK, *n.*, puck; demon, devil. 10. 62, 11. 158.

POUNDMEL, *adv.*, by the pound. 2. 184.

POVERE, *adj.*, poor. 3. 153. [OF povre]

POVERT, *n.*, poverty; meanness. 9. 111.

PRECHEN, *v.*, preach. pr. 93. [OF precher]

PREYOUR, *n.*, prayer. pr. 25. [OF preiere]

PREISEN, *v.*, appraise, value. 5. 173, 176. [OF preiser]

PRELATE, *n.*, a great church dignitary, bishop or abbot. 3. 200, 5. 34. [OF prelat]

PRENTIS, *n.*, apprentice. 2. 176, 3. 210. [OF aprentis]

PRESSOUR, *n.*, a press for cloth. 5. 126. [OF pressour]

PREST, *adj.*, prompt, quick. 12. 98. [OF prest]

PRESTEST, *adj.*, promptest, swiftest. 6. 38.

PRESTLY, *adv.*, promptly. 7. 85.

PREVEN, *v.*, prove. 4. 107, 5. 35. [OF prover, preuve (*subj.*)]

PREVY, *adj.*, private, intimate. 2. 18, 3. 134. [OF privet]

PREVYLICHE, *adv.*, privately, secretly. 3. 56, 70.

PRIKEN, *v.*, prick; spur; ride hard. 2. 151. [OE prician]

PRIKERE, *n.*, rider. 10. 8. [OE prician]

PRIME, *n.*, prime (6 a.m.). 7. 104. [OF prime]

PRIME, *adj.*, vigorous. 12. 60.

PROVENDREN, *v.*, furnish with a prebend or benefice. 3. 137. [OF provender]

PROVINCIALES, *adj.*, provincial. 8. 172. [OF *pl. adj.* provinciales]

PROVISOUR, *n.*, provisor, person nominated by the pope to an ecclesiastical office not yet vacant. 2. 135, 3. 134, 4. 116.

PUFFEN, *v.*, blow; blow violently. 5. 16.

PULDEN, *v. pret. pl.* PULLEN, pulled. 2. 181. [OE pullian]

PULET, *n.*, pullet. 7. 264. [OF polete]

PULISSHEN, *v.*, polish. 5. 249. [OF polir, poliss-]

PUNGEN, *v.*, push, drive. 9. 88. [OE pyngan]

PUR, *prep.*, for. 7. 182, 237, 9. 11. [OF pour]

PURCHACEN, *v.*, purchase; convey or acquire by some other means than inheritance; give. 8. 3. [OF pourchacier]

PURE, *adj.*, pure; very; absolute. 5. 13, 8. 88, 99. [OF pur]

PURESTE, *adj.*, unique. 2. 9, 12.

PURFILE, *n.*, fringe, trimming. 4. 102, 5. 26. [OF pourfiler]

PURFILEN, *v.*, edge, trim. 2. 9.

PURID, *adj.*, refined, purified. 4. 82.

PURPOS, *n.*, proposition, matter. 9. 115. [OF purpos]

PURSUEN, *v.*, pursue; persecute; prosecute unjustly. 5. 75. [OF poursuir]

PURTENAUNCE, *n.*, appurtenance. 2. 68. [OF apurtenance]

PUT, *n.*, pit. 11. 248. [OE pytt]

PUT OUT, *v. 3d. sg. pret.*, exhibited. 1. 116.

PUT UP, *v. 3d. sg. pret.*, submitted. 4. 34.

PUTTE FORTH, *v.*, set forward, propose. 9. 115.

Q

QUARTER, *n.*, eight bushels of grain. 4. 45. [OF quarter]

QUATH, *v., pret. sg.*, said. 1. 12. [OE cwæþ]

QUEYNTERE, *adj.*, more elegant, more magnificently dressed. 2. 14. [OF cointe]

QUYK, *adj.*, alive. 2. 14. [OE cwic]

QUYTTEN, *v.*, pay, discharge (debt). 7. 90. [OF quiter]

QUOD, *v. pret. sg.*, said. 3. 160.

R

RAGEMAN, *n.*, list of names or signatures; here, a bull with seals. pr. 72.

RAY, *n.*, striped cloth. 3. 268, 5. 124. [OF raie]

RAKIERE, *n.*, streetsweeper, scavenger. 5. 164.

RAPE, *n.*, haste. 5. 175.

RAPEN, RAPPEN, *v.*, hasten. 1. 93, 4. 7, 23, 7. 110. [ON hrapa]

RATHE, *adv.*, soon, early. 3. 54. [OE hraþe]

RATHERE, *adv.*, sooner. 4. 4, 7. 110, 9. 30, 66, 11. 277, 297.

RATHEST, *adv.*, soonest. 5. 184.

RATONER, *n.*, rat-catcher. 5. 164. [OF raton, OE -ere]

RAUGHTE, *v. pret.* RECHEN, reached, stretched. pr. 72, 4. 148, 9. 30. [OE rǣcean, *pret.* rǣhte]

RAVISSHEN, *v.*, ravish, violate. 4. 36; draw, lead away. 11. 297. [OF ravir, raviss-]

REALTE, *n.*, pomp, royal state. 11. 224. [OF realte]

REAUME, *n.*, realm. 1. 93. [OF reaume]

RECCHELES, *n.*, recklessness. 10. 51. [OE recceléas]

RECCHELES, *adj.*, reckless; careless, neglectful of duty. 10. 103.

RECCHEN, *v.*, reck, reckon. 4. 51, 7. 112. [OE reccean]

RECHEN, *v.*, reach. pr. 72. [OE rǣcean]

RECREIEDE, *adj.*, recreant, false, unfaithful. 3. 235. [OF recreire]

RED, *n.*, reed, advice; help, assistance; means of help. 5. 242. [OE rǣd]

REDDE, *v. pret.* REDEN, advised. 4. 97.

REDDITE, *v. imperat.*, make restitution. 5. 234. [L]

REDEN, *v.*, read. 3. 235. [OE rǣdan]

REDEN, *v.*, advise. 1. 149. [OE rǣdan]

REDYNG-KING, *n.*, lackey. 5. 165.

REGNEN, *v.*, reign. 3. 258. [OF regner]

REGRATERIE, *n.*, retail selling; dishonesty in trade. 3. 71. [OF regratterie]

REGRATOUR, *n.*, retailer, huckster. 3. 78, 5. 139.

REGUM, *n.*, the biblical book of Kings. 3. 235. [L]

REHERSEN, *v.*, repeat; say; deliver (a speech). 1. 22, 4. 134, 145, 5. 43, 8. 171, 180, 11. 202. [OF rehercer]

REYN, *n.*, rain. 3. 193. [OE regn]

REISEN, *v.*, raise. 11. 158. [ON reisa]

REKNEN, *v.*, recount, tell of. 1. 22. [OE gerecenian]

RELES, *n.*, release. 7. 82. [OF reles]

RELIGIOUN, *n.*, religion; the religious orders. 5. 37, 8. 35, 11. 199. [OF religion]

RENDREN, *v.*, interpret, translate, construe. 5. 124, 9. 82. [OF rendre]

RENK, *n.*, man. 4. 134. [OE rinc]

RENNEN, *v.*, run. 2. 144, 3. 199. [OE rinnan, iornan, eornan]

RENNER, *n.*, runner. 4. 111.

RENTAL, *n.*, schedule of rents of manor. 7. 82.

RENTE, *n.*, rent, revenue from rents. 3. 71. [OF rente]

RENTEN, *v.*, rent; provide with an income from rents. 8. 35.

RESCEYVEN, *v.*, receive. 8. 60. [OF receveir]

RETENAUNCE, *n.*, retinue, following. 2. 33. [OF retenaunce]

REUTHE, *n.*, pity, ruth. 1. 149. [OE hrēow]

REVE, *n.*, reeve, steward; farm bailiff; agent. 2. 75. [OE gerēfa]

REWELE, *n.*, rule; set of rules of government, especially of a religious order. 5. 37. [OF reule]

REWELEN, REULEN, *v.*, rule, govern. 1. 52.

REWEN, *v.*, have pity. 5. 242. [OE hrēowan]

REWET, *n.*, trumpet. 5. 191.

REWLYCHE, *adj.*, pitiable, miserable. 12. 78. [OE hrēowlīce]

REWME, *n.*, *See* REAUME.

RIBAND, *adj.*, beribboned, adorned. 2. 13. [OF riban]

RIBAUDIE, *n.*, ribaldry; lewd sayings. pr. 44. [OF ribaudie]

RIBAUDOUR, *n.*, a ribald. 7. 65.

RIBIBOUR, *n.*, fiddler. 5. 164. [OF rebebe]

RICHEN, *v.*, become rich. 3. 71. [OE rīce, OF riche]

RICHESSE, RICCHESSE, *n.*, treasure, riches. 3. 22, 78, 11. 15, 224, 258. [OF richesse]

RIGGE, *n.*, back. 5. 191. [OE hrycg]

RIGHT, *adv.*, rightly; exactly. 2. 159, 10. 119; straight, directly. 4. 14. [OE riht]

RISSHE, *n.*, rush. 3. 129, 11. 17. [OE risce]

RIT, *v. 3d. sg. pres.*, rideth. 4. 14.

ROBERD, *n.*, robber. pr. 44, 5. 242.

RODE, *n.*, rood, cross. 2. 3. [OE rōd]

ROILEN, *v.*, roam, gad about. 11. 206. [? OF rouler, roiller]

ROMEN, *v.*, roam; go. 4. 30, 9. 1.

ROMERE, *n.*, roamer. 11. 208.

RONNE, *v. pp.* RENNEN, run. 9 82.

ROPERE, *n.*, rope-maker. 5.165. [OE rāp, -ere]

ROSSET, *n.*, russet; a reddish-brown cloth. 9.1. [OF rousset]

ROTE, *n.*, root. 7.95, 10.120, 130. [ON rót]

ROTEN, *v.*, take root. 10.78.

ROUNEN, *v.*, whisper; consult. 4. 14, 5.175. [OE rūnian]

ROUTEN, *v.*, slumber, settle down. 10.78. [OE hrūtan]

RUSTY, *adj.*, rusty; foul, lewd. 7. 65. [OE rustig]

S

SADDE, *adj.*, sober, righteous. 9.23, 39. [OE sæd]

SADDERE, *adv.*, more heavily, sounder. 5.4.

SAGE, *adj.*, wise. 3.81. [OF sage]

SAIGH, *v. pret.* SEN, saw. pr. 14. [OE seh]

SALM, *n.*, psalm. 3.225. [OE salm]

SAPIENCE, *n.*, the apocryphal book of Wisdom. 7.219, 8.46, 11. 126, 257.

SARISINES, *n.*, Saracens, heathens. 11.230.

SARMON, *n.*, sermon. 3.81. [OF sermon]

SAUF, *adj.*, safe. 8.38, 54, 9.29, 44. [OF sauf]

SAUGH, *v. pret.* SEN, saw. pr. 90. [OE sah]

SAUGHTEN, *v.*, make peace; become reconciled. 4.2. [OE saht, sahtlian]

SAUS, *n.*, sauce, appetizer. 7.246. [OF sause]

SAUTER, *n.*, psalter. 3.219. [OF sautier]

SAVE, *v. pres. subj.*, may (God) save. 9.51.

SAWIS, *n.*, sayings. 4.144, 8.121, 11.266. [OE sagu]

SCABBIDE, *adj.*, scabbed; diseased; mangy. 8.17.

SCLEIRE, *n.*, veil. 7.7.

SCRIPPE, *n.*, bag, wallet. 6.23, 7. 56. [ON skreppa]

SCRYVEYNS, *n.*, scriveners, scribes. 11.221. [OF escrivein]

SECRE, *adj.*, secret; private. 8.25. [OF secre]

SED, *n.*, seed; offspring, descendants. 3.252, 10.154, 11.69, 75, 82. [OE sǣd]

SEGG, *n.*, man. 2.123, 3.52, 12.54. [OE secg]

SEGGEN, *v.*, say. 2.53. [OE secgan]

SEGGING, *n.*, saying. 9.102.

SEIEN, *v.*, say. 1.123, 2.150; tell, show. 9.22.

SEIGH, *v. pret.* SEN, saw. 2.150.

SEIGNOURIE, *n.*, landed estate, manor. 2.66. [OF seigneurie]

SEYNEN, *v.*, sign; make the sign of the cross. 5.221. [OF seignier]

SEINT, *adj.*, holy, sacred. 1.82. [OF saint]

SEKE, *adj.*, sick. 7.239. [OE sēoc]

SEKNESSE, *n.*, sickness. 7.120.

SEL, *n.*, seal. pr. 66. [OF seel]

SELDE, SELDEN, *adv.*, seldom. pr. 20. [OE seldum, -an, -on]

SELLE, *n.*, cell, hut of hermit. pr. 28. [OF celle]

SEM, *n.*, 8 bushels (of grain). 3. 39. [OE sēam]

SEMBLAUNT, *n.*, appearance. 9. 112. [OF semblaunt]

SEMBLE, *n.*, assembly, assemblage. pr. 97. [OF semble]

SEN, *v.*, see. 1. 146. [OE sēon]

SENDEL, *n.*, thin fabric of silk or linen. 7. 19. [OF cendal]

SENNE, *n.*, sin. 1. 78. [OE KENT senne]

SENT, *v. 3d. sg. pres.* SENDEN, sendeth. 1. 156.

SERAPHYN, *n.*, seraphim. 1. 104.

SERJAUNT, *n.*, sergeant of the law; a leading lawyer; one chosen by the king to represent the royal side of causes. pr. 85, 3. 267. [OF serjant]

SERKE, *n.*, shirt; chemise. 5. 48. [OE serce, ON serkr]

SERTIS, *adv.*, certainly. 9. 18.

SERVEN, *v.*, serve. pr. 85. [OF servir]

SESEN, *v.*, seize; endow; put in physical possession of. 2. 66. [OF saisir, seisir]

SESOUN, *n.*, season. pr. 1. [OF saison]

SESSEN, *v.*, cease. 4. 1. [OF cesser] *See* CESSEN.

SETEN, *v. pret. pl.* SITTEN, sat. 5. 188. [OE sǣton]

SETTEN, *v.*, set; plant. 6. 29. [OE settan]

SETTYNG, *n.*, planting. pr. 21.

SEWEN, *v.*, pursue, follow. pr. 45, 9. 66, 11. 242. [OF suir]

SEWEN, *v.*, sow. 7. 19. [OE seowian]

SEWERIS, *n.*, sewers, cobblers. 11. 301.

SEWSTERE, *n.*, seamstress. 5. 157.

SHAL, *v.*, ought, have as a duty; must. 1. 26, *etc.* [OE sceal]

SHAPEN, *v.*, shape, create, make; cause; dispose, arrange. 3. 17, 8. 68, 10. 160. [OE sceapan]

SHENDEN, *v.*, harm; destroy, ruin; shame. pr. 95, 10. 212. [OE scendan]

SHENDFULLY, *adv.*, shamefully. 3. 252.

SHENT, *v. 3d. sg. pres.* SHENDEN, ruins. 1. 39.

SHEP, *n.*, sheep; shepherd. pr. 2. [OE scēap]

SHETTEN, *v.*, shut. 6. 89. [OE scyttan]

SHEWEN, *v.*, show. pr. 89. [OE scēawian]

SHIDIS, *n.*, planks, boards. 10. 160. [OE scīde]

SHILL, *n.*, shell. 6. 9. [OE scyll, sciell, scell]

SHYNGLID, *adj.*, shingled. 10. 170.

SHIRREVE, *n.*, sheriff; the lord who represented the king in the county. 2. 128. [OE scīrgerēfa]

SHOPEN, SHOP, *v. pret.* SHAPEN, made. 5. 101. [OE scēop, scōp]

SHRAPEN, *v.*, scrape. 5. 207.

SHREF, *v. pret.* SHRYVEN, confessed. 11. 273.

SHREWE, *n.*, shrew, cursed person. 1. 118.

SHREWIDNESSE, *n.*, wickedness. 3. 43.

SHRIFTE, *n.*, shrift, confession. 3. 36. [OE scrift]

SHROUD, *n.*, clothing, garment. pr. 2. [OE scrūd]

SHRYVEN, *v.*, shrive, hear confession and absolve. pr. 61. [OE scrīfan]

SHULDE, *v. pret.* SHAL, should. 1. 40.

SHULN, *v.*, *See* SHAL. pr. 97, *etc.*

SIB, *adj.*, akin. 6. 110, 11. 106. [OE sib, gesib]

SIGNE, *n.*, sign; signature; " souvenir." 2. 78, 107, 4. 112, 6. 9. [OF signe]

SIKEN, *v.*, sigh, grieve. 11. 190. [OE sīcan]

SIKIR, SIKUR, *adj.*, *adv.*, sure, certain. 1. 121, 3. 49, 11. 160. [OE sicor]

SYKIRLY, *adv.*, surely. 8. 54.

SYMONYE, *n.*, money paid for ecclesiastical advancement. pr. 83, 2. 35, 53. [OF simonie]

SISOUR, *n.*, sizor, juryman. 2. 44, 129, 3. 121. [OF assise]

SITH, *conj.*, since; after; because. pr. 61. [OE siþþan]

SITHEN, SITHTHE, *adv.*, afterwards. 1. 66, 134, 4. 15. [OE siþþan]

SITHES, *n.*, times. pr. 109. [OE sīþ]

SKATHE, *n.*, harm, injury. 4. 65, 12. 17. [OE sceaþa, ON skaði]

SKLAUNDRE, *n.*, shame, scandal. 12. 17. [OF esclaundre]

SLEN, *v.*, strike, slay. 3. 260, 6. 64, 11. 245, 247. [OE slēan]

SLEUTHE, *n.*, sloth. pr. 45. [OE slǣwþ]

SLOMEREN, *v.*, fall asleep. pr. 10. [OE slumerian]

SLOUTHE, *n.*, sloth. 2. 66, 5. 222.

SLOWE, *v. pret.* SLEN, slew. 11. 40.

SMERTEN, *v.*, hurt. 3. 153. [OE smeortan]

So, *conj.*, so; as. 5. 8, 6. 70. [OE swā]

SOFTE, *adj.*, soft; mild, warm. pr. 1. [OE sōfte]

SOFTE, *adv.*, gently. 5. 129.

SOKNE, *n.*, soke, jurisdiction, territory. 2. 75. [OE sōcn]

SOMENOUR, *n.*, officer who summoned to an ecclesiastical court. 2. 44. [OF somoner]

SOMME, *adj.*, some. pr. 31. [OE sum]

SOMME, *adv.*, together. 3. 13. [OE (æt-, tō-)somne]

SOMOUNEN, *v.*, summon. 2. 123. [OF somoner]

SONE, *n.*, 1. 5. [OE sunu]

SONE, *adv.*, immediately; soon. 3. 46, 7. 121. [OE sōna]

SONNE, *n.*, sun. pr. 1. [OE sunne]

SONGE, *v. pret.* SINGEN, sang. 5. 188.

SORE, *adv.*, sorely. 2. 105. [OE sār]

SOREWE, *n.*, sorrow. 2. 80. [OE sorh]

SOTH, *adj.*, true. 7. 121.

SOTHE, *n.*, truth. 1. 84. [OE sōþ]

SOTHLY, *adv.*, truly. 3. 5.

SOTHNESSE, *n.*, truthfulness. 2. 150.

SOTILEN, *v.*, argue subtly. 11. 139. [OF sotil]

SOTTIS, *n.*, fools, sots. 10. 59. [OF sot]

SOUNEST, *adv.*, soonest. 1. 68.

SOUPEN, *v.*, sup; eat. 7. 203. [OF souper]

SOUTERIS, *n.*, cobblers, shoemakers. 11. 181, 301. [OE sūtere]

SOVERAYN, *adj.*, chief, supreme. 11. 155. [OF soverain]

SOVEREYNLICHE, *adv.*, especially. 11. 242.

SPECHE, *n.*, speech, discourse. pr. 69. [OE spǣce]

SPEDELICH, *adj.*, profitable. 12. 100. [OE spēdiglīce]

SPEDEN, *v.*, succeed. 3. 156. [OE spēdan]

SPEKE, *v. pret. pl.* SPEKEN, spoke. 2. 187. [OE spǣcon]

SPICERE, *n.*, dealer in food-stuffs. 2. 187, 10. 121. [OF espice]

STANT, *v. 3d. sg. pres.*, stands, exists. 10. 129.

STAVES, *n. pl.* STAFF, staves. pr. 50. [OE stæf]

STEDE, *n.*, place; property. 5. 39. [OE stede]

STERE, *n.*, helm. 9. 30. [ON stýri]

STERRIS, *n.*, stars. 8. 141. [OE steorra]

STERVEN, *v.*, die, perish. 11. 206. [OE steorfan]

STEWARD, *n.*, custodian. 5. 39. [OE stigweard]

STEWES, *n.*, district given over to brothels. 7. 64.

STIF, *adv.*, stiffly, steadily. 9. 28. [OE stif]

STYNTEN, *v.*, pause, stop. 6. 63, 11. 166. [OE styntan]

STODIEN, *v.*, study. 8. 127. [OF estudier]

STODYENGE, *n.*, studying. 4. 143. [OF estudie]

STOKKIS, *n.*, stems; trunks (tree). 6. 63; stocks (punishment). 4. 95. [OE stoc]

STONDEN, *v.*, stand. 2. 54. [OE stondan]

STOWED, *v. pp.*, held back, restrained. 5. 39. [OE stōw]

STREITE, *adv.*, strictly. pr. 26. [OF estreit]

STRENGTHETH, *v.*, strengthens. 9. 42. [OE strengþu]

STRIKEN, *v.*, strike; go straight on. 6. 64. [OE strīcan]

SUDEN, *n.*, subdean. 2. 137.

SUDORE, *n.*, sweat. 7. 217. [L]

SUFFRAUNCE, *n.*, patience. 10. 115. [OF suffraunce]

SUFFREN, *v.*, suffer; permit. 1. 134, 3. 80. [OF soffrir]

SUM-DEL, *adv.*, somewhat. 3. 80. [OE sum, dǣl]

SUMME, *adj.*, some. pr. 20. [OE sum]

SUREN, *v.*, assure. 6. 28. [OF assurer]

SURFET, *n.*, surfeit, over-eating, over-drinking. 5. 202. [OF surfait]

SWERD, *n.*, sword. 1. 97. [OE sweord]

SWEREN, *v.*, swear. 1. 97. [OE swerian]

SWETTERE, *adv.*, more sweetly, with more appetite. 7. 203. [OE swēt]

SWEVENE, *n.*, dream. pr. 11. [OE swefn, swefen]

SWIEN, SWIGHEN, *v.*, sound. pr. 10. [OE swēgan]

SWINKE, *n.*, labor. 7. 217.

SWYNKEN, *v.*, toil, labor. pr. 52. [OE swincan]

SWITHE, *adv.*, very; quickly. 4. 23, 5. 235, 10. 160. [OE swīþe]

SWONKE, *v. pret.* SWYNKEN, labored. pr. 21.

T

TABBARD, *n.*, short coat. 5. 110. [OF tabard]

TAIL, *n.*, tail; train; root. 2. 147, 3. 118, 5. 19. [OE tægl]

TAILE, *n.*, tally, stick on which accounts were kept by cutting notches. 4. 45. [OF taille]

TAILENDE, *n.*, reckoning, accounting. 9. 74.

TAKEN, *v.*, take; give. 3. 231, 1. 54; seize, arrest. 1. 94. [ON taka]

TALE, *n.*, number; account. 1. 9. [OE talu]

TALE, *n.*, story. pr. 48, 2. 179, 7. 45, 47, 10. 81, 11. 36.

TALEWYS, *adj.*, talkative; lying. 3. 118.

TECHEN, *v.*, teach; direct. 1. 81, 7. 126. [OE tǣcean]

TEIEN, TEIGHEN, *v.*, tie, bind. 1. 94. [OE *tēgan, tīgan]

TELDEN, *v.*, erect, put up. 2. 42. [OE teldian]

TEM, *n.*, team. 7. 126. [OE tēam]

TEM, TEME, TEEME, *n.*, theme. 3. 83. [OF theme]

TENE, *n.*, vexation. 8. 99, 10. 141. [OE tēona]

TENEN, *v.*, vex, make angry. 2. 79; injure, aggravate. 3. 111, 7. 39, 9. 89, 11. 136. [OE tēona, tȳnan]

TERCIAN, *n.*, tertian (fever). 12. 85.

TERMINEN, *v.*, end; fix; decide, determine. 1. 95. [OF terminer]

TEXT, *n.*, text; quotation from an authority. 1. 123, 180, 2. 86. [OF texte]

THANNE, *adv.*, then. pr. 11. [OE þanne]

THAT, *conj.*, so that. 2. 119, 9. 38, 43, 10. 77, 156. [OE þæt]

THAT, *pron.*, (1) that which, what. pr. 38, 8. 129, 11. 187.
  (2) who. 9. 41, 50.
  (3) whom. 8. 134.
  (4) those who, he who, *etc.* 11. 19, 21, 154.

THEDOM, *n.*, prosperity, thrift. 10. 105. [OE þēon, -dōm]

THEIGH, *conj.*, though. 1. 10. [OE þēh]

THENKEN, *v.*, think; intend. 1. 21. [OE þencean]

THENNIS, *adv.*, thence. 1. 71.

THER, THERE, *conj.*, where. 1. 122. [OE þǣr]

THERE, *adv.*, then; at that point. 9. 32.

THERE THAT, *conj.*, where. 3. 162.

THER-TO, *adv.*, also, in addition. 4. 46.

THIDER, *adv.*, thither. 2. 126. [OE þider]

THINGES, *n.*, affairs, business. 4. 26. [OE þing]

THINKEN, *v.*, seem (*with indir. obj.*). 3. 168. [OE þyncean]

THIRLEN, *v.*, pierce. 1. 148. [OE þyrlian]

THISE, *dem. pron.*, these. pr. 22.

THO, *dem. pron.*, those. 1. 21.

THO, *adv.*, then. 4. 141, 9. 63, 67, 101. [OE þā]

THO, *conj.*, when. 1. 45, 2. 113. [OE þā]

THOLEN, *v.*, endure; experience. 4. 71. [OE þolian]

THONKING, *n.*, thanking, thanks. 2. 113.

THORUGH, *prep.*, through. 3. 71. [OE þurh]

THOUGHTE, *v. pret.* THINKEN, seemed. pr. 6. [OE þūhte]

THRALL, *n.*, thrall, slave; servant. 8. 57. [OE þræl]

THRESSHEWOLD, *n.*, threshold. 5. 199. [OE þerscwold]

THREW, *v. pret.* THROWEN, threw; fell. 5. 199. [OE þrāwan]

THRIDDE, *adj.*, third. 8. 55, 9. 69, 11. 40. [OE þridda]

THRINGEN, *v.*, throng, crowd. 5. 252. [OE þringan]

THRIST, THREST, *n.*, thirst. 5. 210, 11. 46. [OE þyrst]

THRITTENE, *adj.*, thirteen. 5. 127. [OE þrytene]

THRIVEN, *v.*, thrive, prosper. pr. 32. [ON þrífa]

THROBBANT, *v. pres. part.*, throbbing. 12. 48.

THRONGEN, *v. pret.* THRINGEN, thronged. 5. 252.

THROP, *n.*, thorp, small village. 2. 45. [OE þorp]

THROWE, *v. pp.*, thrown; put, placed. 8. 57.

TIDE, *n.*, tide, time, season. 2. 40. [OE tīd]

TYKIL, *adj.*, wanton. 3. 118.

TILIEN, *v.*, till, cultivate. 7. 217. [OE tilian]

TILING, *n.*, plowing, labor. 7. 232.

TILTHE, *n.*, culture; produce, crops. 7. 127. [OE tilþ]

TYMBREN, *v.*, build (of timber). 3. 73. [OE tymbrian]

TYNEN, *v.*, lose, fail to win. 10. 190, 11. 233, 12. 86. [ON tȳna]

TIRAUNT, *n.*, tyrant, oppressor. 2. 161. [OF tirant]

TIXTE, *n.*, See TEXT.

TO-BROKE, *v. pp.*, badly broken, fallen into decay. 8. 30.

TO-DROWE, *v. pret. pl.* TO-DRAWEN, tortured. 11. 27.

TOFORE, *prep.*, before. 5. 222.

TOFT, *n.*, hill. pr. 14, 1. 12. [OE toft, ON topt, toft]

TOGIDERE, *adv.*, together. pr. 46. [OE tōgædere]

TOK, *v. pret.* TAKEN, took, acted. 3. 73.

TOKKERE, *n.*, fuller. pr. 100. [OE tucian]

TOKNE, *n.*, sign, pass-word. 6. 84. [OE tācn]

TOKNYNG, *n.*, sign, portent. 5. 19.

TOLLEN, *v.*, count, reckon. 5. 127. [ON tolla]

TOLLERE, *n.*, toll-taker. pr. 100. [OE tollere]

TO-LUGGID, *adj.*, pushed, kicked. 2. 178.

Tom, *n.*, leisure, space. 2. 147. [ON tom, OE tom]

Tomblest, *v.*, tumble. 12. 91. [OE tumbian]

Top, *n.*, top of the head. 3. 127. [OE topp]

Toune, *n.*, farm, settlement. 10. 134. [OE tūn]

Tour, *n.*, tower, castle. pr. 14. [OF tur, tour]

Tras, *n.*, trace, path. 12. 91. [OF trace]

Travaile, *n.*, labor. 7. 235. [OF travail]

Treden, *v.*, walk on, tread. 10. 101. [OE tredan]

Trepget, *n.*, trap. 12. 91.

Tresour, *n.*, treasure. 1. 43. [OF tresor]

Treuthe, *n.*, truth; honor; pledge. 1. 83, 7. 36. [OE treowþe]

Treweliche, *adv.*, truly, honestly. 1. 153.

Triely, Trighely, *adv.*, excellently. pr. 14. [OF trier]

Trien, *v.*, try; test. 1. 83. [OF trier]

Trienalis, *n.*, masses said for a period of three years. 8. 151.

Triest, Trighest, *adj.*, most excellent. 1. 126. [OF trier]

Trist, *n.*, trust. 8. 163.

Tristen, *v.*, trust. 8. 160.

Tronen, *v.*, throne, enthrone. 1. 122. [OF trone]

Trowen, *v.*, believe. pr. 34. [OE trēowian]

Trussen, *v.*, pack; go; begone. 2. 180. [OF trusser]

Tunge, *n.*, tongue. 1. 86. [OE tunge]

Tutour, *n.*, guard. 1. 54. [OF tuteur]

Tweie, *adj.*, twain, two. 5. 116. [OE twēgen]

Tweyne, *adj.*, twain, two. 5. 159.

U

Unbuxum, *adj.*, disobedient. 9. 93.

Uncouthe, *adj.*, unknown, strange. 8. 136. [OE uncūþ]

Underfangen, *v.*, receive. 1. 74, 3. 200, 6. 111, 8. 152, 11. 171. [OE underfōn, -fangen]

Ungracious, *adj.*, without grace. 10. 205.

Unkynde, *adj.*, unnatural. 1. 166.

Unkyndely, *adv.*, unnaturally. 10. 177.

Unlosen, *v.*, open. pr. 87. [OE losian]

Unnethe, *adv.*, scarcely, with difficulty; hardly. 4. 47, 5. 99. [OE unēaþe]

Unsewen, *v.*, unsew; doff. 5. 48.

Untyme, *n.*, an unfit season. 10. 196.

Unwittily, *adv.*, unwisely. 3. 93.

Upholder, *n.*, upholsterer; secondhand dealer. 5. 167.

Usen, *v.*, use; employ, engage in. 5. 138, 142, 7. 137, 11. 180. [OF user]

V

Veil, *n.*, veil; nun. 5. 215. [OF veile]

Vengen, *v.*, avenge. 5. 105. [OF venger]

VERJOUS, *n.*, an acid juice. 5. 69. [OF verjus]

VERNICLE, *n.*, vernicle; handkerchief bearing image of Christ, a souvenir of a pilgrimage to Rome. 6. 11.

VIGILATE, *v. imperat.*, be watchful. 5. 215. [L]

VITAILES, *n.*, food. 2. 142. [OF vitaille]

W

WAFFRER, *n.*, confectioner. 6. 117. [OF waufre, gaufre]

WAGEN, *v.*, engage; pledge; guarantee. 4. 84. [ONF wage]

WAGGYNG, *v. pres. part.*, rocking, shaking. 9. 26. [OE wagian]

WAYTEN, *v.*, watch; look. 6. 34, 7. 148, 8. 123, 9. 89. [OF waitier, guaitier]

WAYVEN, *v.*, move, push. 6. 89. [ON veifa]

WALEWEN, *v.*, roll. 5. 70, 9. 36. [OE wealwian]

WALSSHE, *adj.*, Welsh; here applied to a fabric. 5. 112. [OE weallisc]

WAN, *v. pret.* WINNEN, won. 7.88.

WANHOPE, *n.*, despair. 5. 217. [OE wan-, hopa]

WANYEN, *v.*, wane, diminish. 8. 58. [OE wanian]

WANTONNESSE, *n.*, wantonness; looseness (moral). 3. 112. [OE wan-, togen]

WAR, *adj.*, wary, watchful. 1. 40; aware. 3. 55. [OE wær]

WARDEYN, *n.*, warden, guard, keeper. 1. 53. [OF wardein]

WARE, *n.*, wares, goods. 2. 175. [OE waru]

WARIEN, *v.*, curse. 7. 297. [OE werian]

WARINAR, *n.*, game-keeper. 5. 158. [OF warene]

WARPEN, *v.*, cast; utter. 4. 142, 10. 33. [OE weorpan]

WARROKEN, *v.*, gird, fasten on a girth. 4. 19.

WASSHEN, *v.*, wash, bathe. 6. 55. [OE wæscan]

WASTOUR, *n.*, waster; idler, loafer. pr. 22. [OF waster]

WAWES, *n.*, waves. 9. 35. [OE wǣg, ON vágr]

WAXEN, *v.*, grow, increase. 5. 70; become. 3. 270. [OE weaxan]

WEB, *n.*, texture; piece of cloth. 5. 91. [OE webb]

WEBSTERE, *n.*, weaver. pr. 99.

WED, *n.*, pledge, surety. 3. 187. [OE wed]

WEDDEN, *v.*, pledge. 4. 129. [OE weddian]

WEDER, *n.*, weather; season. 7. 306. [OE weder]

WEHE, *n.*, cry of a beast; neigh of a horse. 4. 21, 8. 74.

WEY, *n.*, way; road. pr. 48. [OE weg]

WEL-A-WEY, *exclam.*, far and away, very much. 11. 215.

WELE, *n.*, wealth, prosperity. 10. 182. [OE wela]

WENCH, *n.*, young woman; maidservant; prostitute. pr. 51, 5. 200, 10. 181. [OE wencel]

WENDEN, *v.*, turn; go, wend. pr. 4. [OE wendan]

WENEN, *v.*, ween; expect; suppose; think. 3. 177, 5. 243, 11. 216, 220. [OE wēnan]

WEP, *v. pret.* WEPEN, wept. 2. 198.

WERCHEN, WERKEN, *v.*, work. 1. 26, 7. 240. [OE wyrcean]

WEREN, *v.*, wear. 2. 12. [OE werian]

WERY, *adj.*, weary. pr. 7. [OE wērig]

WERK, *n.*, work. pr. 3. [OE weorc]

WERNARD, *n.*, deceiver, liar. 2. 93. [OF wernart, guernart]

WERS, WERSE, *adv.*, worse. 1. 26. [OE wyrse]

WEXE, *v. pret.* WAXEN, grew. 10. 33.

WEXEN, *v.*, wax, grow. 5. 72. [OE weaxan]

WEXID, *v. pp.*, waxed, wiped. 5. 193.

WHANNE, *conj.*, when. pr. 1. [OE hwanne]

WHAT, *pron.*, what sort of. 1. 69, 72, 2. 15, 9. 5; who. 9. 63. [OE hwæt]

WHEDER, *adv.*, whither. 12. 80. [OE hwider]

WHENIS, *adv.*, whence. 6. 13.

WHETHER, which of the two. 12. 37. [OE hwæþer]

WHICHE, *pron.*, which, of which sort. 2. 27. [OE hwilc]

WHILES, *conj.*, whilst. 1. 16. [OE hwīl]

WY, *n.*, man, person. 6. 21, 89, 11. 67. [OE wīga]

WYCKE, *adv.*, wickedly. 12. 37.

WYDEWE, *n.*, widow. 8. 32. [OE widuwe]

WYDE-WHERE, *adv.*, here and there. 9. 53.

WYF, *n.*, wife; woman. 6. 48, 7. 10, 10. 18. [OE wīf]

WIGHT, *n.*, being, creature. 1. 61. [OE wiht]

WIGHT, *adj.*, active, strong. 10. 20.

WIGHTLICHE, *adv.*, quickly, swiftly. 2. 170.

WYKE, *n.*, week. 7. 240, 11. 105. [OE wicu, wucu]

WYKET, *n.*, wicket, small gate in a large door. 6. 89. [OF wiket]

WYKKIDE WEY, *n.*, bad road. 7. 1, 8. 29.

WIL, WILLE, *n.*, will; wish, desire; wrongful desire, unrestrained ambition. pr. 37, 4. 56, 6. 74. [OE willa]

WYLES, *n.*, wiles; tricks. 10. 9.

WILLEN, *v.*, will; wish, desire; determine; be willing. pr. 58, 6. 41, 7. 230. [OE willan]

WILNEN, *v.*, wish, desire. 1. 87, 2. 30, 3. 98, 4. 139, 10. 88, 11. 74, 79, 81, 88.

WYNKYNG, *n.*, sleep. 5. 3, 204. [OE wincian]

WYNNEN, *v.*, win; gain; earn; acquire. 1. 153. [OE winnan]

WYNNERE, *n.*, winner; worker, earner; laborer. 7. 148.

WYNNYNG, *n.*, gain, profit. 5. 33, 93, 8. 27.

WYNSTERE, *n.*, one who gains; profit maker. 5. 128.

WYNTER, *n.*, winter; year. 1. 99. [OE winter]

WIRCHEN, *v.*, work. pr. 37. [OE wyrcean]

WISDOM, *n.*, piece of wisdom, wise thing. 7. 198, 11. 5. [OE wisdom]

WYSE, *n.*, manner. 6. 4. [OE wīsa]

WISE, *adj.*, wise; knowing; cunning. pr. 48, 4. 55. [OE wīs]

WYSP, *n.*, tuft. 5. 193.

WISSEN, *v.*, teach, direct, advise; point out. 1. 40, 9. 13, 68, 10. 90, 11. 267. [OE wissian]

WISTE, *v. pret.* WYTEN, knew. pr. 12.

WYT, *n.*, knowledge; wisdom resulting from experience. pr. 37, 3. 7, 5. 229, 9. 9; mind. 1. 69; cunning. 2. 117. [OE wit]

WYT, *n.*, blame, fault. 10. 75. [OE wītan]

WYTEN, *v.*, know. 2. 27. [OE witan]

WITEN, *v.*, guard, defend. 10. 67; WYTE GOD, God protect (me). 6. 117.

WITEN, *v.*, blame. 1. 31. [OE wītan]

WITFUL, *adj.*, wise, prudent. 4. 19.

WITH, *prep.*, against, contrary to. 2. 81. [OE wiþ]

WITH-HALT, *v. 3d. sg. pres.* WITH-HALDEN, with-holds. 6. 39.

WITH-SIGGEN, *v.*, withsay, oppose. 4. 142, 11. 228.

WITHWYND, *n.*, climbing plant, which twists around its support. 6. 6. [OE wiþwinde]

WYTNESSEN, *v.*, act as a legal witness. 2. 125. [OE gewitnes]

WITTERLY, *adv.*, assuredly. 1. 72, 3. 161, 11. 251, 12. 10.

WYTTES, *n.*, senses. 1. 15. [OE witt, gewitt]

WITTY, *adj.*, wise, intelligent. 2. 102.

WITTYLICHE, *adv.*, skillfully. 10. 4. [OE wittig-līce]

WYVENE, *n. gen. pl.*, wives'. 5. 29.

WOLDE, *v. pret.* WILLEN, would, wished. pr. 58.

WOLE, *v.*, *See* WILLEN.

WOMBE, *n.*, stomach, belly; womb. pr. 56, 6. 78. [OE wamb]

WONDER, *n.*, wonder, strange thing. pr. 4. [OE wundor]

WONDIRLICHE, *adv.*, wonderfully; magnificently; strangely. 2. 8.

WONEN, *v.*, dwell. 1. 61. [OE wunian]

WONT, *adj.*, wont, accustomed. 7. 152.

WORCHEN, *v.*, work. pr. 19.

WORDEN, *v.*, speak. 4. 33, 10. 94.

WORSSHIPE, *n.*, esteem, honor. 1. 8. [OE weorþscipe]

WORT, *n.*, root (edible); vegetable. 7. 292. [OE wurt, wyrt]

WORTHEN, *v.*, become; be (*frequently used as the passive auxiliary*). 1. 26. [OE weorþan]

WORTHI, *adj.*, deserving. 3. 214.

WORTHILY, *adv.*, worthily; in such a manner as to secure respect, awe, admiration. 2. 15.

WOSSHEN, *v. pret. pl.* WASSHEN, washed. 2. 182.

WOST, *v. 2d. sg.* WITEN, know. 3. 165, 9. 64. [OE wāst]

Wot, *v. 1st., 3d. sg.* Witen, know. pr. 43. [OE wāt]

Wough, *n.,* wall. 5. 135. [OE wāg, wāh]

Wouke, *n.,* week. 11. 105. *See* Wyke.

Wox, *v. pret.* Waxen, grew, sprang. 2. 20.

Wrang, *v. pret.* Wringen, wrung hands. 2. 198.

Wraththen, *v.,* enrage, anger; become angry. 2. 81, 10. 94. [OE wrāþian]

Wreken, *v.,* avenge, wreak vengeance. 5. 67. [OE wrecan]

Writ, *n.,* writ, document. 2. 46. [OE writ]

Wroken, *v. pp.* Wreken, avenged. 2. 156.

Wrong, *v. pret.* Wringen, twisted, wrung. 7. 160.

Wrotherhele, *in phrase,* To Wrotherhele, evil fortune. 2. 20. [OE tō wrāþre hǣle]

Wrothliche, *adv.,* wrathfully. 5. 67.

Wroughte, *v. pret.* Werchen, fashioned, made. 1. 80.

Y

Y-, *verbal prefix. See the simple forms of the verbs.*

Ya, yea, yes. 3. 99, 5. 153, 6. 43, 7. 38. [OE gēa]

Yaf, Yaven, *v. pret.* Yiven, gave. 1. 105.

Yarde, *n., See* Yerd.

Yate, *n.,* gate. 11. 45. [OE geat]

Ye, yea, yes. 7. 215, 10. 111.

Yedden, *v.,* sing, recite. 1. 138. [OE giddian]

Yede, *v. pret.,* went. pr. 40. [OE ge-ēode]

Yef, *conj.,* if. 7. 121.

Yefte, Yifte, *n.,* gift. 1. 101. To Yifte, as a gift 11. 110. [OE giefu]

Yelden, *v.,* yield, give up; pay. 2. 69, 7. 119, 8. 169. [OE gieldan]

Yelden Ayen, *v.,* repay. 5. 228.

Yeme, *n.,* care, heed. 7. 14. [OE gȳme]

Yemen, *v.,* care for, rule, govern. 10. 72. [OE gȳman, gēman]

Yerd, *n.,* stick; switch. 4. 103. [OE gyrd]

Yeris Yive, *n.,* annual gift. 11. 34.

Yerne, *adv.,* eagerly, gladly. 7. 100. [OE georne]

Yernen, *v.,* yearn, desire. 1. 33. [OE geornian]

Yet, *adv.,* furthermore, besides. 3. 169, 4. 46. [OE get]

Yeven, *v., See* Yiven.

Yif, *conj.,* if; whether. pr. 37. [OE gif]

Yif, *v.,* give. 3. 151.

Yifte, *n., See* Yefte.

Yis, yes. 5. 102. [OE gyse]

Yiven, *v.,* give. 2. 85. [OE giefan]

Yonge, *adj.,* young. 3. 199, 10. 181. [OE geong]

INDEX